The Book of Revelation

FOR

DUMMIES®

by Larry R. Helyer, PhD, and Richard Wagner

WILEY

Wiley Publishing, Inc.

Book of Revelation For Dummies®
Published by
Wiley Publishing, Inc.
111 River St.
Hoboken, NJ 07030-5774
www.wiley.com

WILEY

About the Authors

Dr. Larry R. Helyer: Larry is Professor of Biblical Studies at Taylor University in Upland, Indiana. He received his doctorate in New Testament from Fuller Theological Seminary, Pasadena, California. He pastored Baptist churches in Portland, Oregon, and Sun Valley, California, before moving to the Midwest and teaching biblical studies at Taylor University for 28 years. He has taught a wide range of Bible courses covering both the Old and New Testaments and Jewish literature of the Second Temple. Larry has traveled extensively in the land of the Bible and lived in Israel for a year during his student days at Jerusalem University College.

Larry is author of two books, *Yesterday, Today, and Forever: The Continuing Relevance of the Old Testament* and *Exploring Jewish Literature of the Second Temple Period: A Guide for New Testament Students.* Larry has authored numerous journal and dictionary articles on biblical and theological subjects and has just finished a book on New Testament theology. He was the initial translator of 2 Samuel for the *Holman Christian Standard Bible.*

Richard Wagner: Rich is author of *The Expeditionary Man, The Myth of Happiness, The Gospel Unplugged,* and several *For Dummies* books, including *C. S. Lewis & Narnia For Dummies, Christianity For Dummies,* and *Christian Prayer For Dummies.* He has been a guest on Christian radio programs across the country discussing Christian discipleship issues as well as C.S. Lewis. Richard has served in church leadership and teaching roles for more than a dozen years.

Rich graduated with a bachelor of arts degree from Taylor University and pursued graduate studies at The American University in Washington, DC. Rich lives in New England with his wife and three sons. You can find him online at richwagnerwords.com.

Dedication

Larry dedicates this book in memory of his mother, Hazel M. Helyer (1916–2000). Her love for the Bible, large portions of which she knew from memory, left a legacy far beyond what she could have imagined.

Rich also dedicates the book to his mother, Carolyn, for her lifelong testimony of Jesus Christ as well as her tireless, selfless example of living as a disciple.

Authors' Acknowledgments

We would like to thank the helpful people at Wiley Publishing who shepherded us through this entire process. Their expertise and encouragement made this book possible. Special thanks go to our indefatigable project editor, Stephen Clark, and our most congenial and efficient acquisitions editor, Lindsay Lefevere. Stephen's many, helpful suggestions and comments — and timely encouragement — greatly improved this book. Danielle Voirol, our sharp-eyed and savvy copy editor, and our two technical editors, Dr. Robert Berg and Rev. Ken Cavanagh, saved us from more mistakes than we'd like to admit. In short, we're better writers because of this collaboration.

We're grateful to our literary agent, Matt Wagner, for his efficient handling of contract, schedule, and financial matters.

Finally, we acknowledge our indebtedness to former teachers, biblical scholars, colleagues, friends, and fellow travelers on the way to the New Jerusalem. Their contributions are too numerous to list. May they all join in for the final chorus: "Salvation belongs to our God who is seated on the throne, and to the Lamb!" (Revelation 7:10).

Publisher's Acknowledgments

We're proud of this book; please send us your comments through our Dummies online registration form located at www.dummies.com/register/.

Some of the people who helped bring this book to market include the following:

Acquisitions, Editorial, and Media Development

Project Editor: Stephen R. Clark

Acquisitions Editor: Lindsay Sandman Lefevere

Copy Editor: Danielle Voirol

Editorial Program Coordinator: Erin Calligan Mooney

Technical Editors: Dr. Robert A. Berg, Rev. Ken Cavanagh, M.Div.

Editorial Manager: Christine Meloy Beck

Editorial Assistants: Joe Niesen, David Lutton

Special Help: Alicia South, Kristin DeMint

Cover Photos: © SuperStock, Inc.

Cartoons: Rich Tennant (www.the5thwave.com)

Composition Services

Project Coordinator: Katie Key

Layout and Graphics: Reuben W. Davis, Alissa D. Ellet, Melissa K. Jester, Stephanie D. Jumper, Christine Williams

Proofreader: C.M. Jones

Indexer: Potomac Indexing. LLC

Publishing and Editorial for Consumer Dummies

    Diane Graves Steele, Vice President and Publisher, Consumer Dummies

    Joyce Pepple, Acquisitions Director, Consumer Dummies

    Kristin A. Cocks, Product Development Director, Consumer Dummies

    Michael Spring, Vice President and Publisher, Travel

    Kelly Regan, Editorial Director, Travel

Publishing for Technology Dummies

    Andy Cummings, Vice President and Publisher, Dummies Technology/General User

Composition Services

    Gerry Fahey, Vice President of Production Services

    Debbie Stailey, Director of Composition Services

Contents at a Glance

Table of Contents

Introduction

· ·

A common cartoon theme involves a person wearing a sandwich sign or carrying a poster that proclaims, "Repent! The end is near!" What's implied is that some sudden, violent event is just around the corner and that people need to brace themselves for whatever's coming. And usually, the end that's near involves something nasty, if not totally devastating.

The idea of a dramatic and destructive end to the earth has been around for ages. It's the stuff of some really great sci-fi movies, and a lot of the elements that go into these stories come right out of the Bible. In fact, terms such as *repent* and *Antichrist* and *Armageddon* are direct references to messages, characters, and events that make up the book of Revelation. When you examine these themes and images in the context of religion, faith, and biblical history, things get even more interesting.

But the book of Revelation is no easy read. Some people, after slogging through Revelation, seem to suffer from what we call PTRRD: Post-Traumatic Revelation Reading Disorder. Maybe you've had this experience. You start reading with a rush of enthusiasm, and all goes well through the first three chapters and their letters to the seven churches. Then things start to get hairy: visions from heaven, creatures with eyes covering their bodies, plagues, horses of different colors, angels everywhere. Seven seals are opened, seven trumpets are sounded, seven bowls are poured out, and things get really confusing. Throw in grapes of wrath, red dragons, giant hail, and something called the rapture, and, well, you get the idea. *Lost* becomes more than just the name of a television series — it's the perfect descriptor of your mental state.

Our intent is to help you avoid PTRRD. We act as your tour guides to help you navigate the amazing book of Revelation. Even if you can't figure out every single detail, clues that open up large chunks of the text abound. We promise you'll come away with a better understanding of what Revelation is about, as well as a ton of cool information that you can sprinkle into conversations and impress your friends!

About This Book

The first thing you may discover is that there's no one dominant or right way to interpret the book of Revelation. About the only thing all serious students of Revelation can agree on is that in the end, good wins over evil. Theological views about what happens, when it happens, and to whom it happens vary widely. In *The Book of Revelation For Dummies,* we introduce the leading views and point you to some of the most likely meanings.

Revelation is arguably the most perplexing book in all the Bible, so our goal is to be clear and concise. Therefore, we aim for an easy-to-understand, approachable discussion, without trying to bombard you with a lot of theological gobbledygook.

The topics in the book are logically ordered, so you can read from start to finish if you want to. But this is a reference book, so don't feel you have to read it from cover to cover. You may prefer to browse the Table of Contents, flip through the pages, or thumb through the index to locate a topic that you find particularly engaging.

Conventions Used in This Book

To make sure you get the most out of this book, keep the following conventions and definitions in mind.

Apocalypse

The word *apocalypse* has become associated with a devastating event, including the end of the world. But the term actually means "to unveil" or "to reveal." And so, Revelation is a revealing (apocalypse) of the biblical view of how all things come to an end. People often refer to any literature that addresses the end of the world as *apocalyptic.*

Bible references

The Bible verses we quote are from the New Revised Standard Version translation, unless otherwise noted. We cite passages using the standard convention, *Book chapter:verse.* For example, John 3:16 refers to *John* as the book of the Bible, 3 as the chapter of the book, and 16 as the verse of the chapter. If you don't see a colon in a Bible reference, the number refers to an entire chapter; in other words, Rev. 4–5 means chapters 4 through 5 of the book of Revelation.

When we refer to the *Old Testament*, we're talking about those sacred scriptures that Christianity shares with Judaism. Jews refer to these scriptures as the *Tanak,* or Hebrew Bible. For Protestants and Jews, these scriptures consist of the same 39 books; Catholics include several additional books, collectively called the *Apocrypha.*

We occasionally refer to Jewish works that aren't part of the Bible, such as *1 Enoch.* If you're really interested in reading the book of *1 Enoch*, check out the English translation with introduction and notes by E. Isaac in James H. Charlesworth, ed., *Volume 1. The Old Testament Pseudepigrapha: Apocalyptic Literature & Testaments* (Doubleday).

Christianity

For the purposes of this book, *historical Christianity, biblical Christianity*, and *orthodox Christianity* are interchangeable terms. Each speaks of beliefs that the church has historically upheld for some 2,000 years. Simply, Christianity is monotheistic (believing in one God), is based on the teachings of Jesus, and embraces the entire Bible as truth.

Dates

When we refer to dates, we use the newer designations BCE (before common era) and CE (common era) rather than the more traditional BC (before Christ) and AD (*Anno Domini,* in the year of the Lord). If you're unfamiliar with the newer terms, no sweat. The year 34 BCE is the same as 34 BC, and 1050 CE is equivalent to AD 1050.

Names of God

Although God has many names, we generally use *God* and *Lord* in this book. Also, in accordance with historical usage, we use the traditional masculine pronoun *he* to refer to God.

Prophecy and prophesying

People often think of prophecy as being limited to future events. But from a biblical perspective, *prophecy* is a noun that refers to something more general: the act of speaking the mind and counsel of God. Biblical prophets were, in a sense, the mouthpiece of God, delivering important information to God's people. Biblical prophecy, among other things, addressed current events, offered guidance on behavior, revealed elements of the character of God, reassured God's people, and often predicted future events. Sometimes, prophecy about the future was conditional: If bad behavior continued, bad things would happen; if behavior was brought back in line with God's will, bad things would be averted. The point is that biblically speaking, all prophesy isn't just about foretelling the future.

Note that *prophesy* is the verb usage of the word: Prophets prophesy prophecy!

Formatting

In order to draw your attention to particular words and phrases, we use the following formatting conventions:

- *Italics* highlight terms that we define.
- **Boldface** indicates keywords in explanatory bulleted lists.
- When we provide a cross-reference to another chapter within this book, we capitalize the word *Chapter* before the chapter number; however, when we're referring to a book of the Bible, the word *chapter* is lowercased.

What You're Not to Read

Although we focus on what you need to know about the book of Revelation, we also include some additional topics that, although informative, you can skip during your first read-through of the book. These include sidebars, the shaded boxes that show up every so often throughout the book. Sidebars deal with subjects related to the chapter, but they aren't necessary reading.

You can also bypass text with a Technical Stuff icon beside it — this icon indicates technical, theological, or historical bits of info that's helpful but more advanced. If your eyes start to glaze over in reading them, you can pass over them without missing the basics.

Foolish Assumptions

In writing this book, we didn't assume any particular religious faith leanings for the reader. You may be a Christian, Muslim, Jew, or atheist. But regardless of your faith background, we believe you're generally curious about biblical prophecy and the book of Revelation.

Although we don't assume you have previous knowledge of the Christian Bible, we figure you have access to one — either in print or online — so you can check out our references to specific Bible passages.

How This Book Is Organized

The Book of Revelation For Dummies is divided into four parts. Here's a glimpse of each one.

Part 1: Revealing the End of the Biblical Story

Part I begins with an overview of Revelation and its major themes, side detours, and often-confusing symbolism. You then explore who the book's author is and when he likely wrote it. Rounding out the discussion, Part I helps you better understand the prophecy of Revelation by diving into the Old Testament prophetic writings and exploring the characteristics of *apocalyptic literature,* a genre of Jewish and Christian literature that claims to foretell catastrophic events that'll transpire during the last days of the world.

Part 11: Interpreting the Book of Revelation

In Part II, we introduce you to the sticky topic of interpreting Revelation. Within the Christian church, four views on how to understand Revelation have been long dominant. We explain each of these perspectives and compare and contrast them, noting their strengths and weaknesses. After that, we begin to show you how to make sense of all the symbolism that runs throughout the book's 22 chapters.

Part III: Taking a Grand Tour of the Book of Revelation

Part III is, in many ways, the heart of this book. In it, we take you on a guided expedition through each and every chapter of Revelation. We identify the key themes and explain the likely meaning of the underlying symbolism along the way.

Part IV: The Part of Tens

In the final part, we explain ten confusing terms that often stymie people when they read Revelation. We then give you ten practical tips to think about when you're reading and studying Revelation and the Bible as a whole. A glossary of terms follows the Tens chapters for easy reference.

Icons Used in This Book

The icons in this book help you quickly identify specific kinds of information that may be of use to you:

The Remember icon highlights important ideas for you to keep in mind to deepen your understanding of Revelation.

This icon draws attention to important points that help you make sense of Revelation's prophecy.

Steer clear of the pitfalls we flag in the Warning paragraphs.

The Technical Stuff icon indicates more-advanced or scholarly information about the topic being discussed. It's useful but not essential for an overall understanding of the discussion.

Where to Go from Here

Now that you're at the end of the introduction, you have your boarding pass and are ready to begin your travel into the apocalyptical world of Revelation. You have several routes to choose from as you begin your trip:

- ✔ If you're interested in reading the book from cover to cover, turn the page and proceed to Chapter 1.

- ✔ If you'd like to know who this guy called John is (who wrote the book), go to Chapter 2.

- ✔ To get a perspective on the major ways people interpret Revelation, check out Chapter 4.

- ✔ If you'd like to use this book as a companion guide as you're simultaneously reading your Bible, turn directly to Part III.

- ✔ If you like to read the last page of a novel first, then read Chapters 14 and 15. They tell you how it all turns out in the end!

Part I

Revealing the End of the Biblical Story

THE APOCALYPSE of JOHN

@RICHTENNANT

Okay, no one's going to believe this without a snappy title. Let's see, "The Awesome Moment of John," naah. "The Mindblowing Story," nah, that's no good. "The Eye Opener," or maybe, "John's Tell-All Book," or something like, "Look Out Below!", or "Don't Look Now!"...

In this part . . .

The book of Revelation may be about the "end of all things," but we have to start somewhere. This part gets your apocalyptic feel wet, so to speak, by introducing you to the book's author, the original recipients of the book, and the world in which it was written.

After you've immersed your feet in the waters around Patmos (where the author wrote the book), you're ready to dive into biblical prophecy, which is essential to a solid understanding of the symbolism in Revelation. We introduce you to biblical prophecy, taking it step-by-step so you don't get the bends. After that, we provide a first look at Revelation, giving an overview of the book's structure and timeline. So come on in, the water's fine . . . though we do seem to recall a certain beast that may be lurking in the sea! (But you have to wait for Revelation 13 for that.)

Chapter 1

One Man's Visions, All Humans' Fate

● ●

In This Chapter

▶ Understanding why Revelation is important

▶ Getting a big-picture look at Revelation

▶ Discovering the five natural divisions of the book

▶ Looking for clues to the chronology

● ●

Many people love fantasy stories populated with strange apparitions. Others love a good mystery. And still others love an adventure story full of action and battle scenes. If you fall into one of those camps, you're in luck. The book of Revelation is all these and more.

But Revelation is a challenging book. Those fantastic beasts and creatures are symbols for individuals, nations, governments, and the like. The storyline of the book twists and turns in on itself, not following a straight, chronological narrative. And the whole package is a prophetic vision that's related to what's actually supposed to happen when the world comes to an end, at least from a biblical perspective.

This chapter doesn't try to explore the symbolism behind the events that are chronicled throughout Revelation (we save that for Chapter 5). It also doesn't pore over the details of these events, personalities, and issues (that's what's Part III is all about). In this chapter, we get you started in the right direction. We begin by painting broad strokes of the structure and content of the final book of the Bible. As we do so, we point you to parts of this book where you can find more details on each specific subject.

Why Read Revelation, Anyway?

Humans have always had an insatiable curiosity to know their future and what's going to happen in the "last days." That's at least part of the reason the *Left Behind* series was popular and why new Nostradamus documentaries show up almost every year. For many, the appeal in reading and understanding Revelation is, quite frankly, not altogether different from the desire to peek into a fortuneteller's crystal ball. Understanding how it all ends can give you a sense of what your purpose is now.

Revelation can be tough going because of its structure and symbolism and the many ways in which scholars interpret the book. You can easily become discouraged and wonder why you should read Revelation, anyway. Here are several reasons many people consider Revelation to be essential reading:

- ✔ **It helps explain the biblical view of God and his relationship with humans.** Many people turn to Revelation in search of definitive answers about what will happen. But Revelation is far more about grasping the nature of God and the close relationship that exists between God and people who believe in him.

- ✔ **It gives readers a glimpse of heaven.** The Bible offers few specifics on what heaven will be like. The Old Testament says very little. Jesus and Paul offer more in the New Testament. As if saving the best for last, the final chapters of Revelation offer a rare glimpse into the new heaven and new earth (see Chapter 14).

- ✔ **It offers a message of hope.** It's easy to be a little freaked out by the gloom and doom warnings of the book. But in spite of all of the battles and judgments depicted, Revelation is really all about hope. It portrays, in vivid detail, the biblical view of good triumphing over evil and suffering.

Taking a Whirlwind Tour through Revelation

A major challenge in reading Revelation is sorting out and identifying the overall themes and messages while images — seals, trumpets, bowls, beasts, witnesses, and so on — are ever coming at you. But if you take a step back and get a solid understanding of the big picture, you can begin to dive into the details and make sense of how they all fit together.

Although Revelation contains a lot of confusing symbolism and has many interpretations (see Chapter 4 for a discussion of these interpretations), the book actually divides up rather nicely. At the most basic level, you can split Revelation into five major parts, as illustrated in Figure 1-1. We discuss each of these parts in this section, so read on.

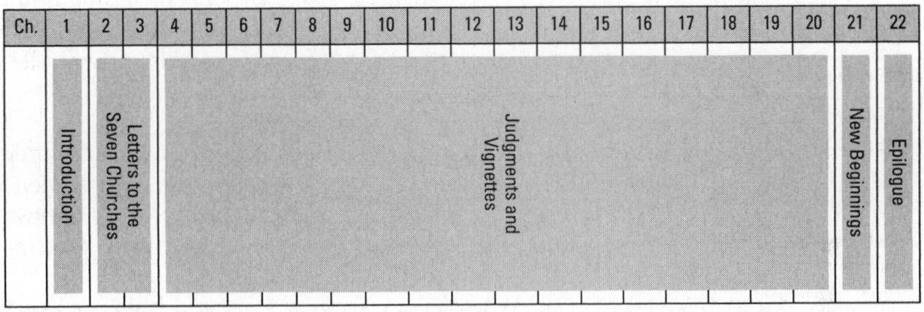

Figure 1-1:
The basic
structure of
Revelation.

| Ch. | 1 | 2 | 3 | 4 | 5 | 6 | 7 | 8 | 9 | 10 | 11 | 12 | 13 | 14 | 15 | 16 | 17 | 18 | 19 | 20 | 21 | 22 |

Introduction | Letters to the Seven Churches | Judgments and Vignettes | New Beginnings | Epilogue

Introduction (Rev. 1)

The first chapter of Revelation serves as a prologue or introduction to the entire book. Its purpose is to provide a context to help you make sense of the rest of the chapters (also see Chapter 6). Within the first several verses, you discover that

- ✔ This is an unveiling of the plans of Jesus (from God) (1:1).
- ✔ The author is John (1:4).
- ✔ The audience is the seven churches of Asia (1:4).
- ✔ It was written on the island of Patmos, a Mediterranean island belonging to modern-day Greece (1:9).
- ✔ Its purpose is to give readers a sneak peek of what'll take place (1:1).

As Revelation 1:1 underscores, this book is Jesus's revealing of God's plans for the world. In this opening section, John provides explicit details about how his words came to appear in print: God gave the revelation to Jesus, who communicated the message to John through an angel, who was sent for this specific purpose. John wrote these series of visions as an extended letter, which he then sent to the seven churches in Asia (Rev. 2–3).

Today's readers are a secondary audience for this book because the original readers passed John's letter both to other churches and to their descendents. Figure 1-2 shows the chain of communication.

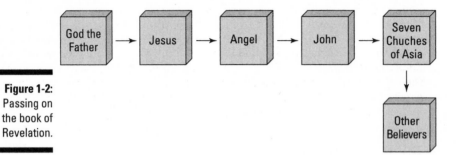

Figure 1-2:
Passing on
the book of
Revelation.

One of the keys to understanding Revelation is in 1:19. In this passage, Jesus instructs John, "Write, therefore, what you have seen, what is now, and what will take place later." Scholars offer various assessments on how to interpret this verse. However, the interpretation that seems to best fit the original grammar of the passage as well as the structure of the book itself is a three-fold timing of events: past tense, present tense, and future tense. In other words, Jesus tells John to write about

✔ The vision he has already seen (Rev. 1)

✔ The current state of the seven churches (Rev. 2–3)

✔ The events that will take place in the future (Rev. 1–22)

Figure 1-3 shows how Revelation 1:19 provides a broad chronology for looking at the entire book.

Figure 1-3:
Revelation
1:19 hints at
what John
wrote about
the past,
present, and
future (in
relation to
his day).

Ch.	1	2	3	4	5	6	7	8	9	10	11	12	13	14	15	16	17	18	19	20	21	22

What you have seen | What is now | What will take place later

Letters to the seven churches of Asia (Rev. 2–3)

Revelation 2–3 details the individual letters that Jesus dictates for the seven churches in Asia (see Chapter 8). Each of these churches is in a different spiritual state. For the faithful churches in Smyrna and Philadelphia, Jesus offers only encouragement for their steadfast faith. For the churches in Sardis, Ephesus, Pergamum, and Thyatira, he commends them for some aspects of their faith but also rebukes them for specific areas of failure. Finally, for the church in Laodicea, he offers no encouragement at all and simply calls for their repentance from a lukewarm, middle-of-the-road faith.

Judgments and vignettes (Rev. 4–20)

The primary plot of Revelation 4–20 is a series of progressively severe judgments that are unveiled through seven seals, seven trumpets, and seven bowls. These judgments climax with the return of Jesus, the ensuing battle of Armageddon, the Millennium, and the Last Judgment (see Chapters 9–14).

As you read Revelation 4–20, don't expect a single, linear storyline. The narrative includes a series of vignettes that make up a secondary plotline. These scenes help fill in the details of the main story, but they're not necessarily tied to the judgments that surround them. As such, commentators sometimes refer to these vignettes as *parentheses, interludes,* or *insets.*

Read on for an overview of the main plot and these interludes.

The primary storyline: Judgments and the last battle

The judgments in Revelation consist of three sets of seven judgments each, symbolized by the opening of seven seals, the sounding of seven trumpets, and the pouring of seven bowls. The three sets are tiered: The seals provide a partial judgment, the trumpets grow more severe, and the bowls show no restraint at all:

- ✔ **Seals:** Judgments begin in Revelation 6 when the Lamb (Jesus) opens seven seals on a heavenly scroll. As each seal is opened, a judgment occurs (see Chapter 9).

- ✔ **Trumpets:** As soon as Lamb opens the seventh seal, seven angels begin to play seven trumpets in succession. As each is played, a more severe judgment occurs (Chapter 10).

- ✔ **Bowls:** More judgments take place when seven angels pour out seven bowls of wrath on the earth (Chapter 12).

As Figure 1-4 shows, the seals, trumpets, and bowls seem to be interrelated. Some scholars hold that the seventh seal triggers the sounding of the trumpets (8:1), and then the seventh trumpet seems to kick off the pouring of the bowls (16:1). As Chapter 9 explores, others suggest that the judgments happen at the same time. *Note:* Figure 1-4 is not a timeline; it merely maps where Revelation mentions specific events. The events, in some instances, may occur simultaneously or in very rapid succession.

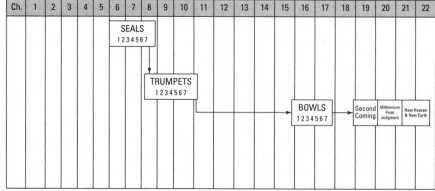

Figure 1-4:
The primary
storyline
from
Revelation
1–20.

The pouring of the final bowl sets the stage for the Second Coming of Jesus (the first coming was his earthly life) and the battle of Armageddon, in which Jesus leads his angelic army to victory over Satan's forces (see Chapter 12). Satan is bound for 1,000 years, commonly known as the *Millennium* (see Chapter 13). During this time, Jesus and his faithful reign on earth. At the end of this period, Satan is let loose one final time to deceive the world. However, Jesus defeats Satan again and permanently throws him into the lake of fire (Rev. 20:10).

Finally, Jesus judges each person. Believers in Jesus — those whose names are found in the book of life — are welcomed into heaven (see Chapter 13). Those whose names don't make the guest list get thrown into the lake of fire (Rev. 20:15).

The secondary storylines: Vignettes

Interrupting the primary narrative of Revelation is a series of vignettes that help form a secondary storyline. Some of these interludes may be related to the events that immediately surround them, though others seem not to have any chronological relationship at all to the main story. These vignettes include the following:

- ✔ Seals are placed on the foreheads of 144,000 believers from the 12 tribes of Israel (Rev. 7:1–8).

- ✔ A "great multitude" is delivered from the Great Tribulation (Rev. 7:9–17).

- John encounters an angel and eats a little scroll (Rev. 10).
- Two witnesses prophesy for 3.5 years and are then martyred (Rev. 11:3–12).
- A woman and a dragon (Satan) appear, and a war in heaven occurs (Rev. 12).
- A beast out of the sea and a beast out of the earth arrive (Rev. 13).
- Jesus appears with 144,000 believers on Mount Zion (Rev. 14:1–5).
- Three angels proclaim messages of repentance and warning (Rev. 14:6–13).
- The harvest of the earth separates the believers from nonbelievers (Rev. 14:11–20).
- The saga of the great prostitute on the beast (Babylon) and her eventual fall unfolds (Rev. 17:1–19:3).

Figure 1-5 shows how these vignettes fit into the flow of the judgments.

New beginnings (Rev. 21–22:6)

The last you hear of Satan and nonbelievers is at the end of Revelation 20, when they're thrown into the lake of fire. Revelation 21, however, tells the flip side: the future that reportedly awaits those who believe in Jesus. It tells of the "new heaven and new earth" that God will create as the permanent home for his children. But this new world is more than an improved version of their current surroundings. It's a perfect world in which God will live alongside humans (Rev. 21:3–5). See Chapter 14 for details.

Epilogue (Rev. 22:7–21)

John closes out Revelation with an epilogue that marks the end of the prophecy (see Chapter 15). The major refrain in this final section of the book is Jesus's reiterating three times, "Behold, I am coming soon!" (Rev. 22:7, 22:12, 22:20). Each of these alerts precedes a call:

- **Obedience:** A call to "keep the words contained in this book" (22:7)
- **Action:** A call to act because he will "give to everyone according to what he has done" (22:12)
- **Faith:** A call to believe Jesus when he says he is coming and to be able to testify to that claim to the rest of the world (22:20)

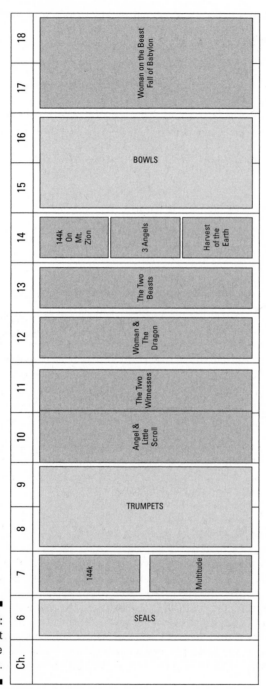

Figure 1-5:
The context
of the
vignettes.

Getting in the Spirit

As you read through Revelation, the curious phrase "in the Spirit" may jump out at you. John uses *in the Spirit* to mark the specific visions he has when writing Revelation. The Apostle Paul actually uses that same phrase in his epistles (Romans 8:9), but the way in which John uses the term is altogether different. John is referring to the mysterious state that he's in as he experiences these visions. In John's view, God somehow frees him from his normal human limitations and enables him to tangibly experience these visions in his mind and spirit.

In the Spirit appears four times in Revelation: 1:10, 4:2, 17:3, and 21:10. Every time John uses this phrase, he is documenting the details of one of these four visions (see the table). Each of these visions "transports" John to a new geographical location — the island of Patmos, heaven, a desert, and a mountaintop. John never clarifies whether these locations are part of the vision he has on the island of Patmos or whether he is somehow supernaturally beamed to these locales.

You can think of John's in-the-Spirit experiences as something like a four-part miniseries. Each experience is a separate installment, but together, they form a cohesive storyline.

Verse	John's Location	Vision	Theme
1:10	Patmos	Hears a loud voice	Messages to the churches
4:2	Heaven	Sees a throne with someone sitting in it	Judgments on a sinful world
17:3	Desert wilderness	Sees a woman on a beast	Final victory over evil
21:10	Mountain	Sees the new Jerusalem in heaven	A new world order

Monitoring the Book's Timeline

One of the biggest problems most people have with the book of Revelation is that they expect a traditional, linear model of storytelling. A *linear story* begins at a particular point in time and then uses progressive scenes to move the characters to some sort of destination. Other stories start out with the characters looking back at something, tell what happened in the form of a flashback, and return to the present. For the vast majority of films out of Hollywood, these two tried-and-true formulas are almost always used, primarily because they're a natural way to tell a story and are easy for audiences to understand.

However, once in while, a story comes along that — like the book of Revelation — doesn't fit into this storytelling model. *Snow Falling on Cedars* and *The English Patient* are two prime examples. Both have multiple story-lines with flashback sequences involving different characters. If you don't want a mental workout, stories like these can be quite frustrating. But if you persevere and stick with them, you can find the increased texture worth-while, adding to the overall experience.

As you read through Revelation, prepare yourself: The book of Revelation may start out linear for several chapters, but various vignettes or interludes interrupt the main story. When you equip yourself for that reality, you'll be in a much better position to deal with the timing of events.

As you consider the how the various pieces of the book fit together, keep in mind the following two topics: transition phrases and parallel events.

And then some: Interpreting transition phrases

Revelation is littered with scores of transition phrases that imply timing. The primary examples include "then I saw," "and I saw," "after this," and "after these things." Strictly speaking, these transitions may not always translate to the order of prophetic events. For example, you can find 53 instances of the word *then* in the book. Although some of them imply a connection between one event and the next, others reflect the author's technique of relaying his story, interweaving the content of his visions with his own experiences. In other words, the narrative has two layers:

- ✔ John's experience of having a vision while on Patmos
- ✔ The content of the visions — horsemen ride, beasts arise, angels fight, and so on

With this kind of setup, a transition may apply to the outer layer (the order of John's visions) or to the order of prophetic events themselves. For example, suppose I were to tell you, "I saw the season finale of *24*. Then I saw reruns of the rest of the episodes over the summer." In this example, the *then* relates wholly to the timing in which I saw the episodes. It says nothing about the logical order of episodes for the series.

Although some transitions may be open to interpretation, you shouldn't just dismiss all transitions, either. In particular, the phrases "after this" and "after these things" are noteworthy. Combined, these two phrases appear just six times and don't always seem to relate to the order in which John received the visions. For example, its usage in Revelation 4:1, 15:5, 18:1, and 19:1 seems to easily imply a logical sequence of events. However, its usage in 7:1 (which introduces the 144,000 believers of Israel) seems more of a writing device posed to answer the question raised at the end of chapter 6: Who can withstand the wrath of God? (6:17). John uses the term again in 7:9; in this context, the phrase seems to imply the order in which he received the visions rather than a sequential flow of events.

The four major interpretations of Revelation and the different perspectives on the Millennium all weigh in on the timing of events in the book. See Chapters 4 and 13 for details.

Parallelism: Watching things go down at the same time

Revelation has a flow of events, but how each section fits into the timeline isn't always apparent. Although commentators disagree on the particulars, most agree that at least a few of the portions of the book parallel each other. Perhaps the most obvious example is Revelation 12's story of the woman in the desert, which is told in two ways in different places in the chapter (12:6 and 12:13–17). A second example, though more contested, is the 3.5-year period mentioned several times throughout the book (11:3, 12:6, 12:14, and 13:5). Some hold that these references indicate that the associated sections parallel each other.

Many futurists (who believe Revelation describes real events that are going to occur — see Chapter 4) downplay parallelism. They think that, by and large, the book progresses in a linear fashion from beginning to end, except for the vignettes (see the earlier "Judgments and vignettes" section). Other futurists view Revelation 1–11 and 12–19 as parallel accounts of the Great Tribulation. Offering a different take, people who embrace a symbolic interpretation of the prophecy (once again, see Chapter 4) see up to seven parallel sections in the book.

The issue of parallelism is also key factor in the interpretation of the Millennium, which appears in Revelation 20:

- ✔ Premillennialists hold that all the events from Revelation 1–19 will happen before the Millennium.
- ✔ Amillennialists see the discussion of the Millennium as a parallel section that describes the entire church age; this church age goes from before Revelation 1:1 even starts up until the Second Coming of Jesus in Revelation 19.

Chapter 13 dives into the interpretations of the Millennium.

Chapter 2

Setting the Stage: The Apostle John and the World in Which He Lived

. . . .

In This Chapter

▶ Discovering who the author of Revelation really is

▶ Understanding how the first-century Roman Empire impacted the book

▶ Knowing why John wrote the book

▶ Looking at the when the book was written

▶ Discovering Revelation's textured style

. . . .

*B*ooks — perhaps with the exceptions of dictionaries and instructional manuals for gas grills — often reflect the personality of the author. What's inside a book has a lot to do with who the author is, the times in which he lives, the place where he lives, and the experiences that have shaped his life. So usually, the more you know of the author's story, the greater the understanding and appreciation you have for the book itself.

The books of the Bible are no exception. Although Christians believe the Bible to be the word of God, most still recognize that each book of the Bible retains the personality, writing style, and experiences of the individual author. Take the Gospel of Luke as an example. You don't have to know anything about the author to get something out of reading Luke's account of Jesus. However, when you discover Luke was a *gentile* (non-Jew) and was educated as a physician, you get a new appreciation for his Greek-oriented perspective and his keen attention to detail.

In this chapter, you get to know John, *the* John most scholars believe is the author of Revelation, as well as explore the world in which he lived. You gain insight into the man himself, as well as understand his reasons for writing the book. You also discover his unique textured style of writing for this final book of the New Testament.

ID-ing John Doe, Author of Revelation

When you walk into your local bookstore and scan the bestsellers display, you see the author's name spread out in large letters on each book. The more successful the author is, the larger the font. In fact, for super-selling authors like John Grisham and Tom Clancy, their names appear so large that you often have to search for the title. But regardless of whether you're dealing with a bestselling author or a first-time writer, you can usually pick up a book and find a biography telling you at least a snippet of the author's credentials. Even if the author is using a pseudonym (writing under an assumed name), someone somewhere knows the author's true identity — after all, the publisher needs to know where to send the royalty checks!

Unfortunately, the books of the Bible were written before there were even printing presses, let alone large publishing companies. Frankly, we wish the biblical authors would've been as outspoken about biographical details as they were in spreading their messages. It'd make our lives far easier by eliminating any debate about who exactly wrote a particular book.

In many instances, at the time of the writing, everyone knew who the author of a book was, whether the author's name was attached to it or not. In fact, a lot of the books in the New Testament part of the Bible were written as letters; when you write a letter to a friend, do you add a detailed biographical note at the end? Of course not! The recipient knows who the letter is from even if you merely sign off with your initials.

The authors of the books of the Bible had more important things on their minds than identifying themselves — namely, accurately communicating what was believed to be the word of God. Downplaying their role out of genuine humility, the biblical authors sometimes included their names and sometimes did not. The author of Revelation identifies himself four times (Rev. 1:1, 1:4, 1:9, and 22:8) by simply referring to himself as *John*. No last name. No title. No biographical data. Because John was a popular name of the day, he could be any old John.

The general consensus of the church since the second century has been that the author is the Apostle John. Yes, this is *the* John. He and his brother James were two of the original 12 disciples of Jesus, and John was viewed as Jesus's "best friend." He's the author of the Gospel of John and the three letters bearing his name (referred to as the *Johannine epistles*). In fact, the list of church fathers who credit the Apostle John as the author of Revelation reads as a virtual who's who of the early church, including Justin Martyr, Irenaeus, Hippolytus, Clement of Alexandria, Tertullian, and Origen.

As you consider the question of authorship today, be careful not to commit what a logician would call *chronological snobbery*, believing that modern people are more knowledgeable and sophisticated than people were in the past.

Doubting the Apostle John's authorship

Not everyone through the centuries has agreed that the Apostle John is the author. Dionysius, who was the pope of the influential Alexandrian church in the mid-third century, argued that the author was actually an obscure first-century church leader named John the Presbyter. He based his argument on *internal evidence,* or evidence found in the text itself, that he believed pointed to a different author. Dionysius claimed that the vocabulary and style of the book were so different from the Gospel of John and the Johannine epistles that it couldn't have been written by the same author. According to Dionysius, there are several discrepancies, including the following:

- ✔ **The author of Revelation identifies himself by name.** Although the author of Revelation names himself four times (Rev. 1:1, 1:4, 1:9, 22:8), the Apostle John generally avoids doing so in his other writings. In the Gospel of John, he identifies himself only as the "disciple whom Jesus loved" (John 13:23, 21:7, 21:20), and in two of his three epistles, he calls himself the "elder" (2 John 1:1; 3 John 1:1).

- ✔ **Revelation is written in a sloppier style of Greek than the other works of the Apostle John.** Clearly, the author of Revelation is highly knowledgeable in the Old Testament books, probably knowing both the original Hebrew texts and the Greek-translated *Septuagint* (an ancient Greek version of the Hebrew Scriptures). But his writing skills aren't always as sharp as his explanation of Scripture. Although John's Gospel and epistles are written in refined, polished Greek, Revelation is scribed in a Semitic Greek style that some scholars argue is slipshod in comparison. In other words, if you were to say the Apostle John's other writings were composed like a John Grisham novel, then Revelation seems more in the style of a hastily cobbled together term paper.

- ✔ **The vocabulary and writing style (the author's *voice*) of the acknowledged Johannine writings contrast with Revelation.** Most authors fall into similar writing patterns. If you have favorite authors, you can often discern their tone and voice, even if the topics they're writing about vary. The sentence structure, vocabulary, rhythm of the paragraphs, and so on tend to be similar from article to article and book to book. The Apostle John's Gospel and epistles have this common feel to them. For example, the Gospel of John begins with, "In the beginning was the Word" (John 1:1), and 1 John starts with a similar tone: "We declare to you what was from the beginning" (1 John 1:1). This type of similarity doesn't carry over to Revelation.

Dionysius's position gained a few followers over the centuries, including Martin Luther. However, not until recent times did his opinions gain momentum. Modern scholars in some circles have jumped on the Dionysius bandwagon and worked to expand on the issues originally raised by the third-century church leader.

Defending the Apostle John as author

As some modern scholars have rejected the Apostle John as author of Revelation (see the preceding section), other contemporary scholars have vigorously defended the traditional view of apostolic authorship. As we explain in this section, proponents of Johannine authorship raise several internal and *external issues* (evidence outside of the book itself) to back their claim.

The text: Addressing Dionysius's challenges

Here's how scholars have responded to Dionysius's claims that the Johannine epistles and Gospel differ too much from Revelation to have the same author:

- **John may have had a purpose in specifically naming himself in Revelation.** Though the Apostle John never identifies himself by name in his other books, the fact that he does so in Revelation doesn't necessarily eliminate him as its author. In fact, there are reasonable explanations for his doing so. In particular, keep in mind that Revelation is a completely different type of book from the other New Testament books. Authority is particularly important for prophetic writing, so he may have felt obligated to name himself to eliminate any question about the book's credibility.

- **John doesn't feel compelled to qualify himself.** When the author does give his name, he doesn't attempt to give himself a title. He's simply *John.* Given the Apostle John's preeminent role in the early church, he would've been able to simply drop his name and provide no further explanation.

- **John consistently stresses eyewitness testimony.** In his Gospel and epistles, the Apostle John stresses his eyewitness testimony. Revelation carries over this theme, such as in Revelation 1:1–2 ("He made it known by sending his angel to his servant John, who testified to the word of God and to the testimony of Jesus Christ, even to all that he saw") and in Revelation 22:8 ("I, John, am the one who heard and saw these things [. . .]"). Compare this to a similar emphasis in the Gospel of John (John 19:35, 21:24).

- **Details are consistent with what scholars know of the Apostle John's ministry.** The writer speaks of the churches in western Asia Minor in a way that clearly demonstrates that he had a relationship with them before the writing and was knowledgeable of its geography. Credible second-century historical records state that the Apostle John lived in Ephesus from 70–100 CE. While there, he had a thriving ministry that spread throughout the region. Scholars generally believe that he wrote his three epistles while he lived there, sometime between 80 and 100 CE.

✔ **The texts share some common words and phrases.** In spite of some stylistic differences between Revelation and the Gospel of John and John's epistles, many common words and phrases are actually scattered among all these books. The Gospel of John refers to Jesus as *Logos* ("Word") in John 1:1. The only other reference to Jesus as *Logos* in all the Bible is in Revelation 19:13. In addition, only John 1:29 and Revelation 5:6 refer to Jesus as a "Lamb." Moreover, both the Gospel of John (19:37) and Revelation (1:7) refer to the same Old Testament verse, Zechariah 12:10.

✔ **Teaching sections of Revelation are quite similar to the Gospel of John and Johannine epistles.** Although much of Revelation is obviously focused on the prophetic visions of John, the book contains some *expository* sections (text that presents information or explanations) as well (Rev. 1:1–8, 1:17–3:22, 22:18–21). Careful analysis of these sections reveals a similar style to Johannine books. The major differences, therefore, lie in the other, apocalyptic portions of the book.

✔ **Revelation's sloppier style has an explanation.** Although proponents of the Apostle John's authorship of Revelation fully agree that the book isn't as well-written as his other works, they suggest three possible explanations:

• The Book of Acts describes John as an "uneducated," "ordinary" man (Acts 4:13). He may have, therefore, used a well-educated secretary (called an *amanuensis*) when he wrote his Gospel and epistles. However, because he was exiled on the island of Patmos (Rev. 1:9) when he wrote Revelation, a secretary wouldn't have been available for him.

• Because of the way in which John received the prophetic visions of Revelation (see the later "Revelation as extraordinarily inspired" section), he may have hurriedly scribbled what he saw in what literary critics call a stream-of-consciousness manner. If so, then to ensure the contents of the original vision stayed intact, he may not have wanted to edit his writings afterward.

• Some suggest that John wrote Revelation around 65 CE. If the early date is correct (see the upcoming section "Playing the Dating Game"), it would've been the first book he wrote — years before he wrote his Gospel and epistles. Therefore, his rough writing skills may have improved over time.

Siding with the early church leaders

People may never be certain whether the Apostle John wrote Revelation. Getting a conclusive answer based on in-text clues is difficult because both sides can supply plenty of supporting evidence. So if the debate over internal evidence ends as a draw, then perhaps the view of the early church leaders can sway the balance.

Except for Dionysius, all the other respected church fathers in the second and third centuries claimed the Apostle John as author. In fact, adding even more weight to their claims, some of the original readers of Revelation (members of the churches to whom the book was addressed) were still alive during the lifetimes of Justin Martyr and Irenaeus.

Understanding the Troubled Times in Which John Lived

As the longest living Apostle, John saw a rapidly changing world and experienced major spiritual transformation (see Figure 2-1). After all, John went from a lowly, spiritually immature Average Joe to perhaps the disciple closest to Jesus — and ultimately, he became a major torchbearer for the Christian church. Throughout his long life, he saw extraordinary political, economic, social, and religious changes. This section explains some of what John witnessed back in the day.

Increasing Roman domination: Rise of the emperor-gods

Rome was at the peak of its military and political power during John's lifetime, expanding in territory like never before. Complete domination of the known world seemed like only a matter of time. The empire was also growing increasingly rich. And for the first time, wealth was flowing to more than just the emperor and the aristocratic patrician class. An upwardly mobile middle class, comprised of former slaves and skilled craftsmen, was developing. What's more, the stability created by the powerful empire enabled trade to flourish throughout the region. As a result, people of all socioeconomic levels became more and more focused on money and material goods.

Rome also had an increasing spiritual influence over the region, especially during the reign of the emperor Domitian (81–96 CE). Many people were beginning to view the former Greek and Roman gods as passé, replacing them with the tangible deity of the emperor himself. Table 2-1 lists some early Roman emperors.

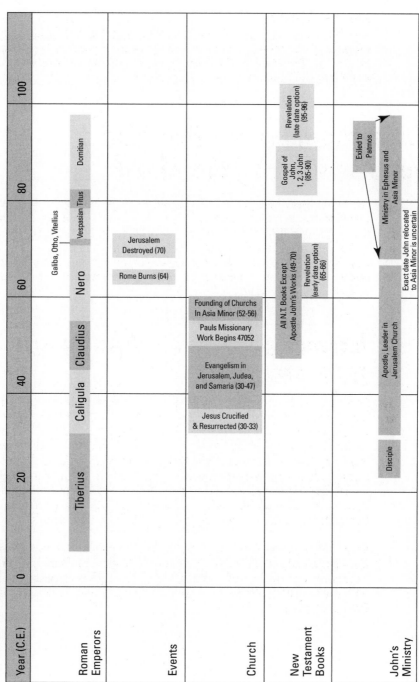

Figure 2-1:
Historical
events
during the
Apostle
John's
lifetime.

Table 2-1	First-Century Roman Emperors
Emperor	*Years of Reign*
Augustus	27 BCE – 14 CE
Tiberius	14–37
Caligula	37–41
Claudius	41–54
Nero	54–68
Galba	68–69
Otho	69
Vitellius	69
Vespasian	69–79
Titus	79–81
Domitian	81–96
Nerva	96–98

Rome was the model of a modern nation-state, looking for answers horizontally rather than vertically. In other words, Rome sought human solutions to human problems instead of looking for divine answers from above. Revelation 13 reflects this attitude by portraying humanity at war with God. As time went on, the emperors increasingly named their predecessors (and themselves!) to be gods, demanding worship and persecuting the people who refused.

Deification — god-making — usually required approval from the Roman Senate following the death of an emperor. However, Gaius Caligula, Nero, and Domitian demanded that they be worshipped as gods before their deaths. Significantly, the Senate denied them that honor because of their arrogance in making the claim while still living. On the other hand, each of the seven cities in Asia Minor competed for the honor of building and maintaining temples dedicated to Roman emperors such as Julius Caesar, Augustus Caesar, and even Livia Drusilla (Augustus's wife). And in Asia, Domitian was indeed addressed as "master" and "god" during his lifetime.

Jewish population fleeing ancient Palestine

The Jewish population was undergoing a major transition during John's lifetime. Before 70 CE, Jews lived in a relatively self-governing state within the Roman Empire. As such, they enjoyed special privileges. For example, if you were a Jew by birth, you didn't have to participate in state-related worship or serve in the military.

However, after the Jewish rebellion and the fall of Jerusalem in 70 CE, everything changed. With their independent Jewish state in Palestine a relic of the past and Jerusalem utterly destroyed, staying put seemed like a really bad idea. The Jews were forced to scatter across the empire as refugees or slaves (this scattering is commonly known as the *Diaspora*). The special privileges they previously enjoyed gradually fell by the wayside.

A widening gap between Jews and Christians

The gap between Jews and Christians grew during the last part of the first century. The rapid growth that was occurring in the Christian church during this time was coming largely from the gentile population rather than from the original Jewish base that developed immediately after the death and reported resurrection of Jesus. As a result, the common heritage that the Jews and Christians enjoyed in the 40–50s CE was increasingly ignored or forgotten.

The book of Revelation expresses this new reality but also retains ties to Christianity's origins. The target readers for the letter were gentile, not Jewish, and the book (like all other New Testament books) was written in Greek, not Hebrew. At the same time, not all ties to Judaism were gone. The book of Revelation is rooted in Jewish symbolism from Old Testament books like Daniel, Ezekiel, and Zechariah. What's more, John mentions the Jewish nation many times in his book, clearly noting that the futures of the Christian church and Israel are intertwined (see Rev. 2:9, 2:14, 3:9, 5:5, 7:4–8, 11:1–2, 21:12).

Growing persecution of Christians

Jews scattered around the Roman Empire probably still enjoyed some of their former privileges even after the fall of Jerusalem in 70 CE. Old religions, after all, were still legal, but new ones couldn't be practiced. As the Christian church began to distance itself from Judaism and old Israel, it increasingly came to be viewed as a new religion, not enjoying its former more-favored status under the umbrella of Judaism. Persecution inevitably increased the more this separation became apparent.

Becoming a Roman target

Roman-sponsored persecution, imprisonment, and even death were becoming distinct possibilities. For example, John tells of a man named Antipas who was killed for his faith (Rev. 2:13). John, too, likely experienced this persecution firsthand. He wrote the book of Revelation when he was staying on Patmos (see Figure 2-2), an island in the Aegean Sea where the Romans may have maintained a penal mining colony — a Roman version of a chain gang. John says he was on Patmos "because of the word of God" (Rev. 1:9). Like Paul and Peter before him, John was probably on the island as punishment for speaking out for his faith (although others suggest that John's wording may leave room for his being there as an evangelist instead).

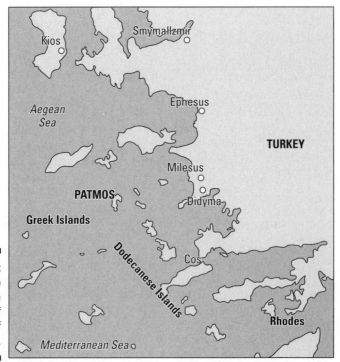

Figure 2-2:
Map
showing the
location of
the Island of
Patmos.

Refusal to worship the emperor resulted in harsh punishment (see the earlier section "Increasing Roman domination: Rise of the emperor-gods"). Initially within the city of Rome, Nero persecuted Christians who challenged his authority by refusing to worship him. But during the reign of Domitian — who demanded to be worshipped as "lord" and "god" — Christians were starting to experience persecution throughout the empire, which included all of the Mediterranean region and Asia Minor. In fact, some evidence suggests that Domitian may have tried to massively exterminate Christians during this period (though most scholars doubt this was the case; most of the persecution was local in nature).

When John wrote Revelation, he was addressing a church that was faltering under increasing persecution from Rome. In our view, especially in Asia Minor, *society's* popular response to promote emperor worship resulted in increasing persecution of dissenters such as the Christians. Heavy state-sponsored persecution came later — it's more of a second-century phenomenon.

Encouraging the suffering church through Revelation

John wrote the book of Revelation to a group of seven churches in western Asia Minor (see Figure 2-3), part of modern-day Turkey. The churches in this region had a rare and unique privilege: Over the last half of the first century, Apostles Paul and John visited them personally. (Paul wrote his epistles of Ephesians, Colossians, and 1 and 2 Timothy to churches in the same western part of Asia Minor.) This region also served as the home base for some of the best-known church leaders in the second century. Irenaeus and Ignatius, for example, grew up in Asia Minor area and eventually served as bishop in other parts of the region.

Figure 2-3:
Locations of the seven churches of Revelation.

John wrote the book of Revelation to churches that were on the verge of coming under full-scale assault by the state. Many of the believers in the early church were undoubtedly wondering whether the church could survive an all-out attack by the Roman Empire.

Revelation was designed to encourage Christians to persevere during these difficult times. The writing shows that the church was having major internal problems (Rev. 3), but John is clear that God's hand remains over the "Body of Christ" (the church) and will ensure its survival. John proclaims that justice will triumph in the end and the church will persist, no matter how difficult, until Jesus returns. Through Revelation, John presents a wake-up call to early Christian believers, underscoring that their faith is under an assault that, although carried out by the state and other religious and political entities, is actually fueled by forces under the control of Satan.

Even though John's primary audience is the seven churches in western Asia Minor, his letter communicates what he and his target audience believed to be God's word to future generations of readers — including people today!

Playing the Dating Game

If a murmur of debate surrounds the authorship of Revelation, there are outright grumblings regarding the timeframe in which John wrote the book. John sure would've saved a lot of hot-winded debate if he'd simply added a "Copyright © whatever-the-heck-year-he-wrote-it" line to the opening verse of Chapter 1. But he didn't.

Speakin' New Testament slang

John either read other books of the New Testament or perhaps picked up lingo from other Apostles. Revelation's writing reflects a vernacular that's consistent with the other New Testament books. For example, the first chapter of Revelation has some notable expressions that parallel Paul's epistle to the Colossians:

✔ Revelation 1:4 ("Grace and peace to you from him who is, and who was, and who is to come") closely mirrors Colossians 1:2 ("Grace and peace to you from God our Father").

✔ Revelation 1:5 ("Jesus Christ, who is the faithful witness, the firstborn from the dead") looks similar to Colossians 1:18 ("And he is the head of the body, the church; he is the beginning and the firstborn from among the dead").

Therefore, you need to look at both external and internal evidence for answers. Over the years, two major camps have developed, dating the book either sometime in the 60s CE or sometime in the 90s CE. We examine the arguments on both sides.

The rebel rousin' 60's

In the twentieth century, the 1960s were a time of social change, hippies, and disorder. But that recent decade is nothing in comparison with the centuries-ago rebel-rousing era of the emperor Nero's reign in the 60s CE. This decade was marked by widespread discontent among the Jews in Palestine, leading to an outright revolt. In response, the Roman army, led by General Titus, invaded and destroyed Jerusalem in 70 CE. Some scholars believe that John penned his book in the midst of this decade of strife, probably around 65 CE. The major arguments for an early date include the following:

- **A still-standing Temple in Jerusalem:** Revelation 11:1 refers to the Temple in Jerusalem: "Come and measure the temple of God and the altar and those who worship there." In this passage, the Temple clearly sounds like it's still standing. However, the Romans destroyed Jerusalem's Temple, along with everything else in the city, in 70 CE. Therefore, some early-date proponents argue that Revelation must've been written before the Temple was destroyed.

- **References to Nero:** Proponents of the early dating of Revelation see possible references to Nero in the text. First, Revelation 17:9–10 may be a reference to Nero as the sixth Roman emperor: "Also, they are seven kings, of whom five have fallen, one is living, and the other has not yet come; and when he comes, he must remain only a little while." And a myth during the years following Nero's death stated that he would return from the dead or be hidden in exile, leading some to believe Revelation 13:3–4 alludes to Nero himself.

  Some believe the reference to 666 in Revelation 13:18 is an allusion to Nero: "Let anyone with understanding calculate the number of the beast, for it is the number of a person. Its number is six hundred sixty-six." The reason is that Hebrew and Greek letters have a number value associated with them, enabling you to convert any word to a matching numeric value. Given this, many commentators hold that the letters of the beast's name equal 666. If you tweak the spelling of Nero's name, Neron Caesar in Hebrew comes out as 666.

- **Rough Greek, indicating Revelation is John's first writing:** Revelation is written in rough Greek, far less polished than the Apostle John's Gospel or epistles. This may very well indicate that it was his first attempt at writing a "book" and that his writing skills improved as time went on.

As Chapter 4 explains, the early-date theory is crucial for the preterist interpretation of Revelation because preterists contend that many of the prophecies John gives in the book were fulfilled in the first century.

Hip hoppin' in the 90's

Many Bible scholars believe Revelation was written sometime during the reign of Domitian (81–96 CE), likely around 95–96 CE. If so, then Revelation would be the appropriate end cap to the biblical canon — both in terms of subject matter and as the last book written by some 5 to 20 years. Arguments supporting a later date include the following:

✔ **Church tradition:** The consensus of early church leadership held that Revelation was written in the 90s. Irenaeus stated that Revelation was written during Domitian's reign. Other early church fathers — including Clement of Alexandria, Origen, Victorinus (who wrote perhaps the first-ever commentary on the book), Eusebius, and Jerome — agreed.

✔ **The state of the seven churches:** The depressing state of many of the seven churches in Revelation 3 sounds altogether different from what was going on during Paul's ministry to this same region in the 60s. During Paul's day, the churches did have their struggles with sin and other issues, but none were infected with all-out *apostasy* (defiant disbelief of God) to the extent that John talks of in Revelation 3.

✔ **The timing of John's ministry to Asia:** Scholars know John left Palestine before the fall of Jerusalem in 70 CE. However, they question the likelihood of his immediately assuming the major leadership position in the churches in Asia Minor. After all, during this timeframe, Paul's influence on the churches in the region would still have been strong.

✔ **Earthquake in Laodicea:** Historical evidence indicates that an earthquake destroyed the city of Laodicea in the early 60s. Therefore, the physical presence of the city, let alone an established church in Laodicea during the 60s, seems doubtful.

In addition, the judgment that Jesus has on the Laodicean church is that of lukewarmness (apathy or indifference): "So, because you are lukewarm, and neither cold nor hot, I am about to spit you out of my mouth" (Revelation 3:16). Indifference in the shadow of a major event such as an earthquake goes smack against human nature. After a person or group survives a catastrophe, they aren't usually lukewarm about their faith; rather, they may be angry at God or desperate for comfort.

However, if the earthquake occurred in the early 60s, a new generation would be of age in Laodicea by the 90s with no firsthand experience of the earthquake. Lukewarmness in this environment would be more likely.

Churches in start-up mode?

One of the most compelling arguments for the later date of Revelation is the deteriorating state of the seven churches in Revelation 3 — too little love, moral compromise with Rome, lukewarm faith, and so on. When you read the letters that John addressed to each, the churches don't sound like they're in "start-up mode" as they would've been back in the 60s. Instead, some time seems to have passed since the start of the church.

When you compare these churches to the Israelites in the Old Testament or even modern-day church, seeing faith deteriorate over a generation isn't unusual — but to have such problems within a few scant years is odd. The typical scenario occurs when a generation fails to pass its faith to the next generation, causing the up-and-comers to forget the faith of the earlier generation. If that's what happened to the Asian churches, then a later date seems more likely.

✔ **Emperor worship:** Some commentators believe that Revelation 13 alludes to the Roman practice of emperor worship. Worship of emperors while they were still living didn't gain prominence until the reign of Domitian (81–96 CE).

✔ **Christian persecution outside of Rome:** Although Nero is well-known for his persecution of Christians, his focus was limited to the city of Rome itself, not the entire Roman Empire. Some scholars argue that persecution was more widespread throughout the empire, including western Asia Minor, during Domitian's reign.

Later-date proponents also find two notable flaws in the early-date justifications:

✔ The Temple in Revelation 11 is discussed in a symbolic passage, so it may not be a reference to a physical Temple.

✔ The idea that 666 stands for *Nero* in Hebrew is a stretch. After all, the target audience for the book wasn't Jewish but gentile, so John's intention to convert a name in Hebrew to a number doesn't seem realistic. What's more, you have to change the common spelling of Caesar in Hebrew to get the 666, anyway. Finally, early church father Irenaeus denied it referred to Nero or any other Roman dictator.

Unraveling Revelation's Textured Style of Writing

The book of Revelation is one of the most unique books in the Bible, not only because of its subject matter but also because of the textured style in which it was written. It combines three distinctive types of writing:

- ✔ **Epistle:** In some ways, it's similar to other *epistles,* or letters, in the New Testament.

- ✔ **Prophecy:** It shares characteristics of books such as Isaiah, Jeremiah, Haggai, and others that focus on prophecy. *Prophecy* is a message from God, communicated through a prophet, that can speak the mind of God or foretell future events that God promises will happen.

- ✔ **Apocalyptic:** In other ways, Revelation is the natural follow-up to the Old Testament books of Daniel, Ezekiel, and Zechariah; they symbolically address the end of time when good overcomes evil. Apocalyptic books contain vivid, imaginative symbolism as a method of communication.

In this section, we take a close look at these three types of writing and how John wove them together to create his unique book. We also look at the role that Godly inspiration plays in biblical writing.

Revelation as epistle

When most people think of Revelation, the elements of prophecy and apocalyptic symbolism come to mind first. But in terms of overall structure, it shares the characteristics of an epistle superimposed on an apocalyptic writing (the next section explains more about that genre).

An *epistle* is the letter style of writing of all the New Testament books except the Gospels and Acts of the Apostles. These letters (which became books of the Bible) circulated among the various churches at the time and were read aloud. An epistle followed the Greek model of letter-writing, which normally included the following:

- ✔ An introduction that lists the writer and the recipients and provides a formal greeting and thanksgiving

- ✔ The body of the letter

- ✔ A conclusion that includes a farewell, which was typically written by the sender himself to show the credibility and authenticity of the letter

In some ways, Revelation follows this epistle model. Although the apocalyptic content that makes up the body of the letter isn't something you find elsewhere in the New Testament, the opening and closing of the letter are surprisingly common. At the start of the book, John writes in Revelation 1:4, "John to the seven churches that are in Asia," an opening line that's similar to other epistle openings, as is his identification of the recipients in Revelation 1:11. The closing benediction "The grace of the Lord Jesus be with all the saints. Amen" (Rev. 22:21) is similar to that of the Letter to the Hebrews and several epistles by the Apostle Paul.

John had a specific target audience for the book; therefore, as you read through Revelation (as well as the Old Testament prophetic works), ask yourself how the original readers would have understood John's words and how they would've applied the lessons. After that, you can consider how to best apply the teachings in your own context.

Revelation as apocalyptic literature

Revelation is popularly known for its apocalyptic style. *Apocalyptic literature* is a specific genre of writing that's characteristic of what Jews wrote between 300 BCE and 200 CE and of the early Christian church. The apocalyptic style had several unique characteristics, including the following:

- ✔ **It was written during times of hardship and persecution and longing.** Apocalyptic literature was popular in ancient Israel during some of its most difficult days. Biblical apocalyptic writing tells readers to prepare for suffering but to also have hope and confidence that God has ordained the events that are going to transpire. For example, Zechariah wrote his book to a defeated people of Israel who had just returned from exile and felt powerless to change their circumstances.

- ✔ **It uses vivid imagery and symbolism to represent real-world counterparts.** The most obvious quality of apocalyptic literature is its use of seemingly bizarre imagery. Although you tend to see fantastic imagery today only in sci-fi and horror films, the biblical apocalyptic style isn't considered fantasy fare or fiction. Instead, the symbolism adds drama and deepens the meaning of the message. Apocalyptic writing often represents people and countries as animals, such as a lamb, dragon, or strange beast. Take, for example, Daniel 8:21, which refers to a male goat as the king of Greece and a large horn between its eyes as the first king.

  Similarly, real cities and nations receive symbolic names, such as Babylon, Sodom, Egypt, and Jerusalem; these names are usually the great powers or cities of the era in which the book was written. What's more, political and social problems are often shown as natural disasters involving the sun, moon, or stars.

✔ **It often features angels as guides.** Angels are often the guides for the author during the visions. For example, as recorded in Daniel 7–12, Daniel has visions in the night, which an angel then explains to him.

✔ **It uses numbers to convey meaning.** In apocalyptic literature, numbers (such as seven) usually carry significance beyond their arithmetic purposes. Given that, be wary of assuming literal 24-hour, 7-days-a-week time periods when you come across a measurement of time. The "ten days" in Revelation 2:10 and "one hour" in Revelation 17:12 may simply refer to short periods of time. So, too, the 1,000 years in Revelation 20 may not necessarily mean 365,242 days but may instead refer to a more generic "very long time," much like Peter writes in 2 Peter 3:8: "But do not ignore this one fact, beloved, that with the Lord one day is like a thousand years, and a thousand years are like one day."

Besides Revelation, the only other apocalyptic book in the Bible is Daniel, although Ezekiel and Zechariah have similarities to this literary style. However, many apocalyptic works were written before and during the early church period but were not considered *Scripture* (coming directly from God). Nonetheless, the book of Revelation wasn't just the lucky one that made it to the big leagues of canon. It's altogether distinct from the "pretenders." Unlike the extra-biblical writings, in Revelation, John identifies himself as the writer, declares the book to be inspired by Jesus, and specifically states that the book is a prophecy.

Revelation as prophecy

The book of Revelation is not merely a book that contains prophecies; rather, as John states, the book as a whole is a prophecy (Rev. 1:3, 22:7, 22:10, 22:18–19). In the Bible, a *prophecy* is a special message from God to his people; it may concern future events that God promises will happen on earth and in heaven.

Most Old Testament prophecy is preaching designed to bring about repentance and recommitment to the *Old Covenant,* the promise between Moses and God on Mount Sinai (see Exodus 31–34 in the Bible). New Testament prophecy is similar, except believers are called to a renewed commitment to the New Covenant, the agreement between God and humanity made possible by the sacrificial death of Jesus.

Prediction, though not the predominant feature, is still an important part of prophecy in both the Old and New Testaments. Christians believe that in some cases, the predictions have already been completed in history. Most Christians, for instance, think that numerous Old Testament prophecies predicted the coming of Jesus as Messiah, as well as his death and resurrection. In other cases, the future events have yet to happen (such as passages in Daniel that deal with End Times).

In most cases, prophets who wrote down the message focused on the details of the event but avoided specifics concerning exactly when that event was going to occur in history. They did so because the point of the prophecy was to warn people to be faithful and expectant, not simply to provide a play-by-play guide to how history was going to play out.

Many people find biblical prophecy confusing and sometimes wonder whether it's God's way of teasing or confusing people for some reason. But that's not the case. The Bible is clear that prophecy is actually designed to

- Encourage and comfort believers (1 Corinthians 14:3)
- Give hope (Rev. 1:3)
- Refocus believers on God's character and promises (Rev. 1:3)

At its heart, Revelation is intended to accomplish each of these objectives as you read through it, even though getting to the meaning may take a little effort.

Revelation as extraordinarily inspired

Many Christians believe that all biblical Scripture originated from God but was written down by human authors. The terms that people often use to describe this process are *inspired* and *God-breathed*. However, how exactly the mechanics of this process work is an age-old mystery. We do know what didn't happen: God didn't just temporarily take over the minds of the Bible writers and turn them into zombie scribes, nor did he just rubberstamp the ideas of the human authors. Instead, Christians believe that the Holy Spirit guided and directed the writers without overriding their personality or personal expression during the process.

Not all the books of the Bible were written in exactly the same manner, even though they're all considered to be inspired. Matthew and John wrote personal accounts about the life and ministry of Jesus (John 14:26). Mark and Luke, both right-hand men of Apostles Peter and Paul respectively, relied on the Holy Spirit to guide them to provide an account through eyewitnesses. The New Testament epistles were personal letters written "in words not taught by human wisdom but taught by the Spirit" (1 Corinthians 2:13).

The way in which John received inspiration for the book of Revelation seems to be extraordinary, involving visions, dreams, and direct communication with the divine. According to Revelation 1:1, God the Father gave the revelation to his son Jesus. Jesus then shared the vision with John through an angel. While John was "in the spirit" (1:10), he received a series of visions, the details of which he faithfully wrote down (1:2), creating the book of Revelation.

Chapter 3

The Prequels: Prophecies throughout the Bible

Toss out the term *prophecy,* and your friends may start talking about Nostradamus or any number of other people who claim to have seen the future. But say *biblical prophecy,* and anyone familiar with the Bible is likely to turn the conversation to the book of Revelation and the End Times. However, prophetic (and apocalyptic) writings in the Bible run throughout both the Old and New Testaments, not just in Revelation. In fact, approximately one-third of the Bible is devoted to prophecy. According to Christians, some it has already been fulfilled, and some is still in the works.

In this chapter, you peek into some of the biblical prophecy outside the book of Revelation. You explore some of the prophetic works of the Old Testament that are often associated with End Times prophecies. You also explore the Olivet Discourse (a sermon delivered on the Mount of Olives), a key New Testament prophecy spoken by Jesus himself. As you examine these prophecies, you discover their interrelationships and the influence that these prophetic teachings have on the book of Revelation.

Understanding the Old Testament Backdrop to Revelation

Like most devout Jews of the time, John was familiar with the writings that now make up the Old Testament. These writings highly influenced the book of Revelation, more than they influenced any other New Testament book.

Revelation makes approximately 250 references and allusions to Old Testament books, including Isaiah, Daniel, Ezekiel, Psalms, Exodus, Jeremiah, Zechariah, Amos, and Joel. However, unlike many other books in the New Testament, Revelation contains no *direct* quotes from the Old Testament.

All the references Revelation makes to the Old Testament are more than just interesting factoids. These references add meaning and theological weight to John's text by showing that his experience and vision are not isolated from biblical history but rather are closely interwoven with the whole biblical story. This points to the essential unity of the Bible and its prophetic teaching. You can also use John's references as springboards to more meaning as you dive into the Old Testament Scriptures.

Here are just some of the more-significant allusions to the Old Testament. This first set is mostly in the first few books of the Bible:

- Revelation mentions the "tree of life" (from Genesis 3:22) four times — 2:7, 22:2, 22:14, and 22:19.

- The judgment on the enemies of God in Revelation 19:20 and 20:10 (their being thrown into the lake of fire burning with sulfur) resembles the burning of Sodom and Gomorrah in Genesis 19:24, where burning sulfur rains down.

- The symbol of the woman clothed with the sun, having the moon under her feet and wearing a crown of 12 stars on her head (Rev. 12:1) is similar to the imagery of Joseph's dream in Genesis 37:9.

Going meta with the story of stories

Scholars sometimes use the term *metanarrative* for a comprehensive story that explains many other stories. The Bible, considered as a whole, is a metanarrative, a story of redemption (saving from sin, delivering from evil). This framework is the context for the many stories within its pages.

In the book of Exodus, the Lord delivers the Hebrew people from Egypt (Exodus 8–12). A prominent feature of that deliverance is a series of devastating plagues, reducing Egypt to shambles. Yet in the midst of these plagues, the Hebrews are spared and, in the tenth and final plague, passed over. (The term *Passover* comes from this miraculous rescue.)

The historical books of the Old Testament (Judges, 1 and 2 Samuel, 1 and 2 Kings) also recount God's repeated interventions on behalf of his oppressed people. In every case, the Lord comes to their rescue. He wields his "strong right hand" (Exodus 15:6) — a biblical idiom denoting God's power and authority — in their defense.

The New Testament, at numerous points, employs the imagery of the Hebrew Passover to describe the salvation that Jesus, the "Passover Lamb," provides (John 1:19; 1 Corinthians 5:6–8; Colossians 1:13–14). Thus, the book of Revelation is the conclusion of the metanarrative unfolding in the pages of the Bible.

✔ Several times in Revelation, John loosely alludes to Exodus 3:14 ("I AM WHO I AM") when he refers to God as "he who is and who was and who is to come" (Rev. 1:4, 1:8, 11:17, 16:5).

✔ The plagues of hail (Rev. 8:7), locusts (Rev. 9:3), sores (Rev. 16:2), water changed to blood (Rev. 16:3–4), darkness (Rev. 16:10), and unclean spirits that look like frogs (Rev. 16:12–14) relate closely to six of the ten plague that befall Egypt in Exodus 8–11.

✔ Revelation 11:8 uses Egypt as a symbol of evil power. Egypt was an oppressor and enemy of Israel during the days of Moses.

✔ In Revelation 1:5, John says that believers gain freedom from sin at the cost of Jesus's blood, which symbolizes the Passover in Exodus 12.

✔ John says in Revelation 15:3 that the redeemed people sing the "song of Moses," which is similar to what Israel does after crossing the Red Sea (Exodus 15:1).

✔ The woman's protecting her child in the wilderness in Revelation 12:14 is reminiscent of Israel's being protected in the wilderness as they wander for 40 years with Moses.

✔ The symbolism of the Temple and the Ark of the Covenant in heaven in Revelation 11:19 bring to mind the many references of the Temple and Ark of the Covenant throughout the Old Testament.

✔ The use of trumpets in Revelation 8 resembles the way people use trumpets in the Old Testament — for worship, for battle, and as a symbol of the Lord's presence (for example, Numbers 10:9; Judges 7; 2 Samuel 6:15).

Many of Revelation's other references to the Old Testament borrow imagery from books named for the prophets:

✔ Jesus is described as being the "first and last" in Revelation 1:17 and 2:8 and the "alpha and omega" in Revelation 22:13. Isaiah depicts God in the same way in Isaiah 44:6 and 48:12.

✔ The winepress of the wrath of God in Revelation 14:9 echoes the winepresses in Joel 3:13 and Isaiah 63:3.

✔ The scroll that John eats in Revelation 10:8–11 resembles God's commissioning of Ezekiel as a prophet in Ezekiel 2–3.

✔ The beast depicted in Revelation 11–20 is similar to the imagery of Daniel 7. In Revelation, the beast is a single leopard-like being with bear-like feet and a lion's mouth. Daniel, however, refers to four different beasts; of the four, one looks like a lion, one like a bear, and one like a leopard.

✔ Revelation 12:14 uses the phrase "time, times, and half a time," which is the same phrase as in Daniel 7:25 and 12:7.

✔ The sealed scroll in Revelation 5 is similar to the sealed book in Daniel 12:4.

✔ The angel standing on the sea and on the land in Revelation 10:5 resembles the angel over the waters of the river in Daniel 12:7.

✔ The four horses from Revelation 6 parallel the chariots with horses in Zechariah 1:8–11 and 6:1–8.

✔ The olive trees in Revelation 11:4 are reminiscent of the olive trees in Zechariah 4.

✔ The seven lampstands in Revelation 1:12 are similar to the lampstands in Zechariah 4:2 and 4:10.

Clearly, John was well-versed in the Hebrew Scriptures; much of the symbolism and phrases he uses in Revelation have their roots in the Old Testament. One Bible scholar even referred to Revelation as a "rebirth of images," a term that emphasizes the extent to which the book borrows imagery.

In his classic *Commentary on the Apocalypse*, H.B. Swete says that 278 of the 404 verses in Revelation refer to the Old Testament.

Peeking into Old Testament Prophecy

In the Old Testament's opening scene of the history of the nation of Israel, God delivers his people from slavery in Egypt, using some motivational plagues and the parting of a sea. After only 40 years (they take the scenic route through the wilderness), God helps the Israelites establish a home in Canaan, which they call the *Promised Land.* However, during their time strolling in the desert — and as time goes on after they're settled — they continually forget about their agreement with God and fling themselves into idol worship, sinful lifestyles, civil war, and arrogance.

As a result, the Bible says, God raised up several men to be prophets to the nation of Israel to get them to return to their "first love," their God in heaven. These prophets — such as Isaiah, Jeremiah, Ezekiel, Daniel, Joel, and Zechariah — wrote down messages that readers believed were from God himself.

Here are a few reasons for writing down these messages:

✔ To document the sovereignty and power of God as demonstrated through events

✔ To reveal God's future plans for his people

✔ To provide advance warning to those rejecting God's commands

✔ To give comfort to God's faithful people

Prophecy in the Old Testament typically centers on the coming of the *Messiah* (the *Anointed One,* whom Christians identify as Jesus) as well as the future of the nation of Israel and of the earth as a whole. Many scholars hold that the Old Testament, particularly the book of Daniel, contains a considerable amount of End Times prophecy. Others maintain that these prophecies refer to historical events.

One of the great challenges of interpreting Old Testament prophecy is that the timing for fulfillment is usually absent from the text. For example, two prophecies may appear alongside each other, but the timetable of the two may be completely different. One helpful analogy is to think of the prophets as being able to see the mountaintops along a mountain range but unable to see into the valleys. In other words, what they recount in their prophecies are the highlights, or more significant events.

Another challenge scholars face in interpreting prophecy is whether a single prophecy has dual fulfillment — whether it was or will be fulfilled in two different contexts at two separate times. For example, most scholars hold that Isaiah 17 was fulfilled in the Assyrian invasion in Hezekiah's time, which eventually led to the destruction of the Assyrians (Isaiah 17:14). But this prophecy may also represent a force that invades the land at the time of Jesus's return and is ultimately destroyed.

We cover some of the more notable prophets who addressed the End Times in the sections that follow.

Isaiah

The prophet Isaiah, whose ministry took place between 740 and 687 BCE, wrote the book of Isaiah. He prophesied during the reigns of king Uzziah, Jotham, Ahaz, and Hezekiah. The book of Isaiah contains many *messianic prophecies,* or prophecies about the future Messiah, deliverer of the Jews. However, the following passages are often tied to End Times prophecy:

- ✔ Isaiah 2:1–5 gives a peaceful vision of the End Times in which people will "beat their swords into plowshares."

- ✔ Isaiah 11:11 points to a gathering of Israel (all Jews) and to the Jewish nation's gaining territory in the region.

- ✔ Isaiah 13–14 talks about the destruction of Babylon. Scholars have different views on whether this is a literal or figurative reference to Babylon, especially as it relates to the destruction of Babylon in Revelation 18 (see Chapter 12). Some hold that this section of Revelation indicates that Babylon will actually be rebuilt as a nation in the End Times; others maintain that it's a figurative Babylon, headed up by the Antichrist.

- Isaiah 19 discusses Egypt in the End Times. Isaiah prophesies civil war and judgment in Egypt but says that the country will eventually turn to God; Israel, Egypt, and Assyria (Syria) will become allies and worship together.

- People often call Isaiah 24–27 the *Little Apocalypse* because it seems to parallel what Revelation depicts in the last days. Isaiah 24 talks about the devastation that awaits the earth because of the sinfulness of its inhabitants. Isaiah 25 explains how God will overcome the evil in the world and protect those who are faithful to him. Isaiah 25:7 may allude to the end of the Antichrist's deception (Rev. 13). The salvation of God's people is in Isaiah 25:8–9 (Isaiah 25:8 seems to parallel Rev. 21:4). Finally, many see Isaiah 27's reference to the Leviathan as parallel to the dragon in Revelation 20:2.

- Isaiah 65:17 talks about God's establishing a "new heavens and new earth." Some scholars contend that this chapter describes the Millennium (the period of time depicted in Revelation 20 in which Jesus reigns on earth for 1,000 years). Others point out that Isaiah's imagery seems to nicely parallel Revelation 21:1, which occurs after the Millennium.

- Many scholars who hold to the futurist perspective (see Chapter 4) point to the establishment of the state of Israel in 1948 as the fulfillment of Isaiah 66:8 ("Shall a land be born in one day?").

Ezekiel

Ezekiel was a prophet to the Jewish exiles from 593–563 BCE, during their Babylonian captivity. He prophesied about the destruction of Jerusalem and of its eventual restoration. The book of Ezekiel is nearly all in first-person narrative, and it uses apocalyptic imagery that's similar to John's writing in Revelation.

The first part of the book (Ezekiel 1–24) focuses on the judgment and ruin of Judah (the Jews) by its enemies. The second part (Ezekiel 25–32) prophesies God's judgment and destruction of these same enemies. The final section (Ezekiel 33–48) looks at the future restoration of the Jewish nation.

The following passages are often tied to End Times prophecy:

- Ezekiel 34, 36, and 37 talk about a restored, reunited Israel. Some argue that 36:24 indicates that this gathering is not just the ancient return from Babylon but instead a future return from all over the world.

- In Ezekiel 38–39, Ezekiel prophesies a great battle that will take place. The nations of Gog, Persia, Ethiopia, Put, Gomer, and Beth-togarmah will attack Israel from the north. The rich imagery of Ezekiel 39:17–20 sounds quite like that of Revelation 19:17–21.

  A host of interpretations for these two chapters place this battle before, in the middle, or at the end of the Tribulation (the seven-year period of unprecedented evil that futurists believe will occur prior to the Second Coming of Jesus). Some commentators consider it to be the final battle at the end of the Millennium.

✔ Ezekiel 40–48 describes in a great detail a new Temple, a new sacrificial system, and a new division of land among the Jewish tribes. Some commentators hold that this section prophesies a sacrificial system for Israel during the Millennium. Note that the description of the river in Ezekiel 47:1–12 is similar to that of Revelation 22:1–2.

Daniel

Daniel was a Jew who was taken into captivity at Babylon and amazingly ended up serving as a statesman within the Babylonian court (after spending several years falsely imprisoned). The first six chapters of the book of Daniel contain historical narrative, and the remaining chapters contain apocalyptic visions of future events. People traditionally consider Daniel to be the author of the book of Daniel, though some contend it was written by an unknown author in the second century BCE.

The following passages from Daniel are often associated with End Times prophecy:

✔ In Daniel 7, Daniel prophesies about four beasts from the sea. The first is like a lion with eagle's wings. The second is a bear. The third beast is a leopard with four heads and wings — it has authority to rule. The final terrifying beast has two rows of iron teeth and ten horns. Later in the chapter (Daniel 7:17), Daniel says that these beasts represent four kings who will come to the earth. Some scholars believe this section parallels Revelation 17:7–13. Daniel 7 concludes with the removal of the last king and the establishment of God's reign.

✔ Daniel 8 describes the vision of Daniel in Susa, the capital of Persia. He talks of a two-horned ram (kings of Media and Persia) and a goat (Greece). Many commentators see Daniel 8:5–8 as referring to Alexander the Great and Daniel 8:9–12 as a reference to Antiochus Epiphanes, who desecrated the Jewish Temple in Jerusalem. Others think the Antichrist will fill the "little horn" role in Daniel 8 in the last days.

✔ Daniel 11 vividly describes the actions of historical and future kings. Daniel 11:2–20 discusses historical kings, and many commentators hold that Daniel 11:21–45 prophesies the events pertaining to the future Antichrist ("a despicable person").

✔ Many scholars see Daniel 12 as a description of suffering during the Great Tribulation (Rev. 6–19).

Daniel 9 is one of the most talked about chapters of Old Testament prophecy. We talk about in detail in the section titled "Examining the 70 Weeks of Daniel 9."

Zechariah

Zechariah was a prophet who ministered from 520 to 518 BCE to the many Jews returning from exile to Jerusalem; he called for rebuilding the city and Temple. Zechariah's apocalyptic prophecies clearly point to the coming Messiah and look far into the future to a time in which the people Israel would be removed from their homeland and forced into exile. Some of Zechariah's prophecies that are associated with End Times include the following:

- ✔ Zechariah 1–2 describes the reestablishment of Jerusalem, and it prophesies that the four nations who scattered Judah will be cast out.

- ✔ In Zechariah 4, Zechariah describes a lampstand (menorah) and lamps, which parallels the imagery in Revelation 1. Futurist commentators (see Chapter 4) often interpret the two olive trees in Zechariah 4:11–13 as being the two witnesses from Revelation 11:3–4.

- ✔ Zechariah 6 describes four chariots and horses that are reminiscent of the four horses in Revelation 6.

- ✔ Zechariah 11 describes the destruction of Israel by evil shepherds, the last of which may refer to the Antichrist.

- ✔ Zechariah 12 talks about a Jerusalem threatened by her enemies but eventually protected by God. The same theme carries over to Revelation.

- ✔ Zechariah 13 prophesies that two-thirds of Israel will die but that one-third will be refined and saved, which reflects the effects of judgments that transpire in Revelation.

- ✔ Zechariah 14 talks about God's coming to the rescue of a Jerusalem under serious attack. In the end, the Lord will rule over all nations. Once again, John voices this message in Revelation.

Jeremiah

Jeremiah was a prophet who came about a century after Isaiah. From 628–586 BCE, Jeremiah warned Judah of coming disaster and urged his fellow people to turn back to God. He prophesied that Babylon would overtake Israel (Jeremiah 25:8–11), which would be subject to Babylon's king for 70 years. This happened during his lifetime, as Babylon began taking Jews as captives.

Joel

The book of Joel is divided into two main sections. The first part focuses on a plague of locusts, and the second part (more apocalyptic in nature) focuses on future judgment on the nations of the world. Both images appear in Revelation.

Examining the 70 Weeks of Daniel 9

As you look at prophecy throughout the Bible, one of the most significant yet perplexing passages you're likely to come across is Daniel 9:20–27. Daniel was an old man at the time he wrote the book and had been in Babylon for nearly all his life. However, the 70 years of captivity of Israel by Babylon as punishment for disobedience (Jeremiah 25:8–11) were nearly over.

In the story, Daniel prays to God for mercy on behalf of his people. The angel Gabriel appears and announces that 70 weeks are needed to accomplish several things:

- ✔ To remove and atone for Israel's sins once and for all
- ✔ To establish everlasting righteousness
- ✔ To complete all prophecy
- ✔ To anoint a new Temple

The debate over this passage centers on the meaning and significance of those 70 weeks. Here's how the angel Gabriel breaks them down:

- ✔ **Seven weeks:** "Know therefore and understand: from the time that the word went out to restore and rebuild Jerusalem until the time of an anointed prince, there shall be seven weeks" (Daniel 9:25).
- ✔ **Sixty-two weeks:** "And for sixty-two weeks it shall be built again with streets and moat, but in a troubled time" (Daniel 9:25).
- ✔ **One week:** "After the sixty-two weeks, an anointed one shall be cut off and shall have nothing, and the troops of the prince who is to come shall destroy the city and the sanctuary. Its end shall come with a flood, and to the end there shall be war. Desolations are decreed. He shall make a strong covenant with many for one week, and for half of the week he shall make sacrifice and offering cease; and in their place shall be an abomination that desolates, until the decreed end is poured out upon the desolator" (Daniel 9:26–27).

A variety of views on this passage have popped up over the centuries, but you can boil them down to three main interpretations: dispensationalist, traditional, and critical. I discuss their understanding of Daniel's 70 weeks in the following sections.

Having a long week: The dispensationalist view

Dispensationalists hold that human history is divided into seven "dispensations" (eras), which are represented by the seven churches of Revelation 2–3. They think part of Daniel's prophecy refers to the Great Tribulation period (Rev. 6–19).

The dispensationalist view holds that the "weeks" that Daniel talks about are not actual weeks but a symbolic term for years. Therefore, Daniel is talking about 70 "weeks of years," or 490 years. Dispensationalists make this claim based on three factors:

✔ Daniel lays the groundwork for dealing with years back in Daniel 9:2, when he talks about 70 years of captivity of Israel.

✔ In Daniel 10:2–3, when he is actually referring to days, the prophet goes out of his way to add "days" to his usage of "weeks." In the original Hebrew, the phrase is literally "weeks of days."

✔ Dispensationalists argue that no other time period other than years would permit all the prophetic events to take place.

This section explains how those "weeks" play out and just who the prince and anointed one may be.

Breaking down the timetable

According to dispensationalists, the first 69 weeks took place prior to the crucifixion of Jesus, and the final, 70th week is still coming. Therefore, the entire church age (which began after the life of Jesus with the disciples' establishment of the Christian church) falls in a gap period between the 69th and 70th week.

Many dispensationalists put the starting point of Daniel's 70-weeks prophecy at 445 BCE, when King Artaxerxes permitted Nehemiah to rebuild Jerusalem (Nehemiah 2). The first seven weeks end around the time of the completion of the rebuilding effort in Jerusalem (approximately 400 BCE — see the "A year isn't always a year" sidebar). The next 62 weeks end in approximately 30 CE with Jesus's triumphant entry into Jerusalem just days before his crucifixion. Some dispensationalists have differing timetables, such as the first seven weeks lasting from 587–538 BCE and then the 62 weeks starting in 440 BCE and ending at the birth of Jesus in 6 BCE or at his crucifixion.

A year isn't always a year

If you look at the length of time between the events that dispensationalists mention in their timeline of Daniel's 70 weeks, you may notice that the numbers don't add up. What gives? Can you discount their theory with a few simple strokes on a calculator?

Not so, they say. Some scholars contend that a "prophetic year" is about 360 days, not 365.

Therefore, when you try to calculate the time in a verse like Daniel 9:25, you have to factor in a 360-day year under the Jewish lunar calendar. Using this approach, you can add 69 360-day years to get to Jesus's lifetime. Other people counter that idea, pointing out that Daniel uses "years" in the conventional sense in Daniel 9:1–2.

Dispensationalists may have different takes on some of the dates of the initial 69 weeks, but they all agree on two things:

- ✔ An extended gap comes after the 69th week and before the 70th week. Jesus's crucifixion, the destruction of the city and Temple of Jerusalem in 70 CE, and the entire church age take place in this gap period. The church age continues today.

- ✔ The 70th week is symbolic of the Great Tribulation, the same period depicted in Revelation 6–19. At the beginning of the 70th week in Daniel 9:27, another "prince" from a great empire will enter a covenant with Israel. But midway through the week (3.5 years), he'll break the covenant, stop the sacrifices in the Temple, and desecrate it.

Naming the cast of characters

According to this view, Daniel 9:25–27 refers to both Jesus and the Antichrist. The "anointed prince" and "anointed one" in Daniel 9:25–26 are Jesus, but the "prince" in the last part of verse 26 and then the "he" in verse 27 refer to the Antichrist.

Reading the End Times

Dispensationalists believe in a collaboration among Daniel 9, Revelation 6–19, and Jesus's teaching in Matthew 24, known as his Olivet Discourse (see the "Exploring the Olivet Discourse" section later in this chapter). They hold that Jesus explicitly refers to "the abomination of desolation" from Daniel 9:27 in Matthew 24:15 as a sure sign of the Great Tribulation. Moreover, they also point to Revelation 13's dependence on Daniel 9 in terms of describing the Antichrist. Specifically, both Daniel and Jesus say that the Antichrist will

- ✔ Blaspheme in the temple

- ✔ Make an idol

- ✔ Introduce a reign of terror

> ✔ Have a 3.5-year reign
>
> ✔ Persecute God's people
>
> ✔ Be ultimately destroyed by Jesus

Dispensationalists are convinced that Daniel's 70-weeks prophecy relates to the last days because the universe-changing nature of the prophecy is something that only the return of Jesus can fulfill.

Seeing time as relative: The traditional view

Traditionalists generally believe that Daniel's 70 weeks do not prophesy about the last days but rather point to work of Jesus. In other words, they hold that God gave Daniel a prophecy so that the Jews would recognize the events surrounding the arrival of the Messiah.

Unlike dispensationalists, traditionalists do not look for a week to represent an exact period of time (such as a year). Instead, they see Daniel's 70 weeks as symbolizing an unspecified period. In other words, the events that occur within each "week" are more important than lengths of time — one week may be 200 years; the next may be 1 year; the next, 3 days; and so on.

Checking out the schedule

Many traditionalists believe the starting point of the 70 weeks is when King Darius (Cyrus) of Persia decided in 538 BCE to permit the Israelites to return to Jerusalem after 70 years of captivity and to rebuild the Temple and the city (2 Chronicles 36:23, Ezra 1). The next 62 weeks begin around 400 BCE and end with the birth of Jesus (around 4 BCE).

There's debate among holders of the traditional view, but the final 70th week is usually broken into two parts. The first half of the week ends in 70 CE with the destruction of Jerusalem, and the second half ends sometime in the future with the Second Coming of Jesus. Therefore, the entire church age (from the 30s CE to the present day) is within that second half of the 70th week.

ID-ing the prince and the anointed one

Traditionalists don't believe that Daniel refers to the Antichrist at all in this passage. According to this view, the "prince" and "anointed one" in Daniel 9:25–27 always refers to Jesus, not to multiple people. They also view Daniel 9:26 and 9:27 as parallel verses, referring to the same events. What's more, traditionalists maintain that the "desolation" in Daniel 9:26 refers to the crucifixion of Jesus. The Roman destruction of Jerusalem in 70 CE serves as Jesus's judgment on Israel.

Avoiding the future: The critical view

Criticalists argue that not only does Daniel 9 not prophesy about future End Times events, but it also never "foretells" *any* events. Instead, the critical view claims that the book was written by an unknown author around 164 BCE, describing the events of his day. From this view, "weeks" and "sevens" refers to "weeks of years" (490 years).

Laying out the timeline

According to the critical view, the first seven "weeks of years" (49 years) point to the period 587–538 BCE. However, before the eighth week starts, many proponents push the timeline back 67 years to 605 BCE, when Jeremiah received the prophecy that Israel would go into captivity for 70 years. The next 62 weeks of years last a total of 434 years. The last week of the 70 weeks, according to this view, refers to 171–164 BCE, a chaotic time period in the history of Israel that saw the murder of Onias III (the high priest) in 171 BCE, the desecration of the Jewish Temple in 167 BCE, and the rededication of the Temple in 164 BCE by Judas Maccabaeus.

However, this timeline presents some problems. Although the events noted are significant in Jewish history, saying that sin ended and everlasting righteousness was introduced as a result seems like a major stretch. What's more, Jerusalem and the Temple were not destroyed in 167 BCE but were rather damaged, even if that damage was significant.

Associating characters with historical figures

The critical view tries to match references to the "anointed one" and "prince" to real historical figures. "The anointed one" refers to two different people — high priests Joshua (9:25) and Onias III (9:26). The "prince" in 9:26–27 refers to Greek king Antiochus Epiphanes, who desecrated the Temple.

Exploring the Olivet Discourse: Jesus's Prophecy

As you examine biblical prophecy and the book of Revelation, perhaps no other text in the New Testament is more important to look at than Jesus's discourse on the Mount of Olives in Matthew 24:1–25:46 (see also Mark 13:1–37 and Luke 21:5–36). This message that Jesus gave to his disciples is known as the *Olivet Discourse*. It covers

- ✔ The future destruction of the Temple in Jerusalem
- ✔ A future period of great turmoil and tribulation
- ✔ Signs of Jesus's return to earth

Readers of Revelation often hold one of two major opposing views of the Olivet Discourse:

- ✔ **Preterist:** In simple terms, preterists believe that Revelation refers not to future events but to events that already took place back in the first century (see Chapter 4). Therefore, the preterist view holds that all or nearly all of the prophecy that Jesus describes in Matthew 24–25 was fulfilled when the Romans destroyed Jerusalem in 70 CE. *Full preterists* claim that all the prophetic events have already taken place; *partial preterists* hold that many of the events took place in 70 CE, but the prophecy will be fully completed with the return of Jesus.

- ✔ **Futurist:** Futurists basically believe that Revelation chronicles literal events that will take place on earth sometime in the future (see Chapter 4). The futurist view maintains that although the Temple destruction was fulfilled in 70 CE, most of the prophetic teaching concerns the End Times and the Second Coming of Jesus. What's more, they claim that the particulars of the historical events surrounding the Roman war with the Jews vary too much from the Jesus's prophecies to reflect actual fulfillment.

This section explains the two main interpretations of Jesus's message and how they relate to Revelation.

Noting the signs of the times

As Matthew 24 begins, Jesus tells his disciples that the Temple will be destroyed. The disciples then ask Jesus, "Tell us, when will this be, and what will be the sign of your coming and of the end of the age?"

At the very start, Jesus says that the end of the age won't take place immediately. In Matthew 24:4–8, Jesus warns that before the end of the age even begins, false prophets will claim to be the Messiah, and wars and rumors of wars will arise. However, he goes on to say that the beginning of the end ("birth pangs") will be marked by wars between nations and kingdoms, along with famines and earthquakes. Futurists believe this passage refers to the first 3.5-year period of the seven-year Tribulation and that it parallels the seal judgments of Revelation 6 (see Chapter 9).

Next, in Matthew 24:9–14, Jesus describes a time of great spiritual struggle. On the one hand, Christian followers will be persecuted, martyred, and despised. False prophets will rise up to mislead people. On the other hand, God's people who persevere to the end will help the message (gospel) of Jesus be proclaimed around the world. When the whole world has heard this message, the end will come. Futurists claim this section describes the events of the second half of the Tribulation (Rev. 13:1–18).

Jesus then warns the disciples by specifically referring to the book of Daniel (likely 9:27 and 11:31) in Matthew 24:15 when he says, "So when you see the desolating sacrilege standing in the holy place, as was spoken of by the prophet Daniel [. . .]." *Desolating sacrilege* refers to when the man of sin places his own throne in God's Temple and claim to be God. Preterists think this passage refers to the events surrounding the Roman destruction of the Temple in 70 CE; futurists hold that this refers to the Antichrist, who will be in power during the second half of the Tribulation (Rev. 13).

Continuing on, Jesus tells those who are being persecuted to run for the hills (okay, *mountains*) because there will be great suffering during all these events. He also emphasizes the importance of not being led astray by false prophets.

Witnessing Jesus's (second) big entrance

In Matthew 24:29–31, Jesus describes his Second Coming by painting a vivid picture of the events:

- ✔ The sun and moon become dark, and the stars fall from the sky. (Jesus may be alluding to Isaiah 13:10 or Joel 2:30–31. Some preterists see these references to the Old Testament prophets as Jesus's way of comparing the Romans' future destruction of Jerusalem with the Babylonian captivity of ancient Israel.)

- ✔ The people see "the sign of the Son of Man" and begin to mourn.

- ✔ The Son of Man comes "'on the clouds of heaven' with power and great glory."

- ✔ His trumpet blast sends the angels to collect God's people.

Full preterists claim that these last few points refer to the spreading of Christianity in the Roman world in the early centuries. Partial preterists and futurists counter, saying that a plain reading of the text indicates the literal return of Jesus to the earth.

Futurists also debate the timing of the *rapture* (when God's people are taken up into heaven) in relation to the Second Coming of Jesus. Some commentators believe Jesus doesn't discuss the rapture at all in Matthew 24:29–31. Others, however, argue that the rapture is indicated in 24:30–31 as well as later in the chapter in 24:40–42 (see Chapter 4 for more discussion of the various views).

Keeping your guard up

As if answering the question, "So what do we do in the meantime?" Jesus uses the second half of Matthew 24 and part of Matthew 25 to share several parables aimed at getting his followers to apply a central lesson of his teaching — and of Revelation: *Be ready!* These stories include the following:

- The parable of the fig tree (Matthew 24:32–35)
- The example of Noah (Matthew 24:36–39)
- The lesson of people taken away (Matthew 24:40–41)
- The parable of the faithful house owner (Matthew 24:42–44)
- The lesson of the wise servant (Matthew 24:45–51)
- The parable of the ten virgins (Matthew 25:1–13)
- The parable of the talents (money) (Matthew 25:14–30)

Finally, in Matthew 25:31–46, Jesus tells the story of the judgment of all nations after his return — a time in which he'll separate sheep and goats. In the same way, John warns his readers of the importance of being ready and watchful at all times.

Considering the "generation" gap

Perhaps the verse that sparks the greatest debate in the Olivet Discourse is Matthew 24:34: "Truly I tell you, this generation will not pass away until all these things have taken place." The problem centers on how to define the word *generation*.

Preterists claim that interpreting this passage at face value indicates that Jesus was clearly referring to the current generation, the generation of his audience. If so, then the fulfillment of these prophecies has to have transpired in the short-term — within the lifetime of at least some of Jesu's listeners.

Futurists counter by saying that "this generation" doesn't specifically mean the generation of the disciples:

- ✔ Some commentators argue that you can also translate the original Greek word as "race" or "a common type of people." If so, then Jesus was simply saying that Israel won't pass away before these prophecies are fulfilled.

- ✔ Others hold that "this generation" refers to the generation that sees the events Jesus is describing. In other words, that future generation won't pass away before the Second Coming of Jesus; if you're alive during the "birth pangs" (Matthew 24:8), then your generation gets to witness the end of the world.

- ✔ Others point to the fact that biblical prophecy often wasn't fulfilled within the lifetimes of the original audience. For example, consider the prophecy of Moses in Deuteronomy 18:15: "The Lord your God will raise up for you a prophet like me from among your own people; you shall heed such a prophet." In this case, "you" spans generations. Christians believe it refers to not so much to the ancient Israelites living in the days of Moses but to the Jewish people who lived to see the fulfillment of that prophecy in the earthly life of Jesus.

Part II
Interpreting the Book of Revelation

The 5th Wave   By Rich Tennant

Once again, Alan felt people were avoiding him because of his controversial views on The Book of Revelation.

In this part . . .

Even the world's greatest detectives don't work alone. Batman has Robin; Sherlock Holmes has his plucky assistant Watson. In the same way, allow this book to serve as your trusty sidekick. In this part, we explore the various interpretations of John's prophecy and don our detective hats to figure out the symbolism. Holy apocalypse, Batman!

Chapter 4

Choosing a Perspective for Understanding Revelation

In This Chapter

▶ Looking at interpretation throughout church history

▶ Exploring and evaluating the futurist, preterist, historicist, and idealist interpretations

▶ Highlighting key issues when comparing these four approaches

*I*t's the weirdest thing: Honest people can observe the same event yet draw wildly different conclusions about what they saw. Several people can witness an auto accident and give a handful of contrasting accounts of what really happened. Or if you had gathered Pittsburgh Steelers and Seattle Seahawks fans to watch Super Bowl XL, you would've heard considerable disagreement over whether the Steelers won the contest, the Seahawks lost it, or the refs blew the game.

This same sincere-people-can-disagree principle applies to the book of Revelation. Since the early church, dominant perspectives on how to interpret John's book have emerged, but not even well-intentioned, Bible-based thinkers can reach a consensus. Some argue that John is speaking figuratively, merely expressing spiritual themes relevant in any age. Others, however, believe the symbolic language represents actual events that are going to take place in a literal time period.

Over the span of church history, four major interpretations of the book of Revelation have come to the forefront. In this chapter, you explore this quartet. We begin by taking a brief historical look at how the church has viewed John's book. Next, you dive into each of the four approaches and examine their strengths and weaknesses.

Solving the Revelation Puzzle: Four Solutions throughout History

The debate over the real meaning of Revelation is nothing new. Throughout church history, various perspectives on how best to read, understand, and interpret the apocalyptic letter of John have gained popularity. And although there are more variations and spinoffs than you can shake a stick at, you can group them all under four general categories: the futurist, historicist, preterist, and idealist approaches.

We look at each of these four perspectives in depth in this chapter. This section gives you an overview of their development. To help you follow along, here are in-a-nutshell definitions of how each perspective views the events of Revelation:

- **Futurist:** Everything is going to happen in the future.
- **Historicist:** Some has happened, is happening, and is going to happen.
- **Preterist:** Everything already happened in the past.
- **Idealist:** Nothing literal happens; everything is symbolic.

Okay, we admit these definitions are a bit simplistic, but they define the essence of each perspective reasonably well. Each view falls into a different range along the literal-allegorical continuum (Figure 4-1). What this means is that futurists read Revelation more literally than everyone else and that idealists view the book's message in more spiritual terms than everyone else. The other two positions fall somewhere in between.

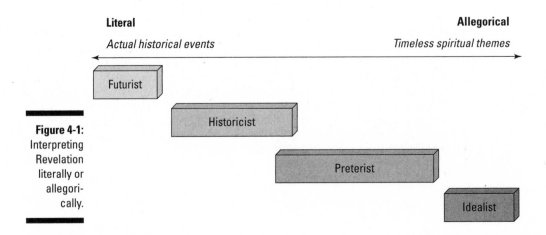

Literal   Allegorical

Actual historical events   *Timeless spiritual themes*

Futurist

Historicist

Preterist

Idealist

Figure 4-1: Interpreting Revelation literally or allegorically.

Early church views

The early church in the second and third centuries usually (though not exclusively) interpreted Revelation in a literal manner, tying John's words into actual events that would take place soon, perhaps within their lifetime. Some of the best-known church fathers during this period — such as Papius, Justin Martyr, Irenaeus, Tertullian, and Victorinus — were outspoken in their beliefs, which today's scholars identify with the premillennial and futurist approaches. (*Premillenial* simply means the belief that all the events from Revelation 1–19 will happen before the Millennium begins — see Chapter 13.)

However, the influential Alexandrian church rejected the literal approach. Instead, Alexandrian leaders, led initially by Origen in the early third century, developed a more figurative, allegorical method of looking at the Scriptures. Tyconius (around 390 CE) articulated this idealist approach for Revelation, and with the backing of Augustine — who was arguably the most influential Christian between the time of the Apostles and the Protestant Reformers — this view essentially became the standard doctrine of the church for nearly 1,000 years.

The Middle Ages and Renaissance

The idealist approach had a virtual monopoly on prophetic interpretation until the historicist method was developed, most concretely by Joachim of Fiore (theologian and founder of the monastic order of San Giovanni in Fiore, Italy) in the twelfth century. He claimed a vision from God led him to look at Revelation in light of actual history. In particular, Joachim argued that many of the judgments prophesied in Revelation were actually fulfilled in the major events of history since John's day.

By the thirteenth and fourteenth centuries, the historicist view gained more prominence, particularly among the Franciscan religious order, as an alternative to the still-dominant idealist approach. However, the Protestant Reformation was what really jump-started the historicist approach. Many reformers, including Martin Luther, came to believe that Revelation 4–22 was a prophetic snapshot of church history and identified the first beast in Revelation 14 as a symbol of the Roman papacy. This historicist approach became the dominant view in the newly emerging Protestant church over the next 300 years, until the mid-nineteenth century.

Into the modern era

During the Reformation era, Spanish Jesuits developed the preterist and futurist approaches, which helped counter the anti-papal (anti-pope) leanings of the historicist approach:

- ✓ Luis de Alcazar (1614 CE) articulated the preterist method, claiming that John's work wasn't talking about current or future events at all but instead was oriented to the early church's battle against Judaism (Rev. 1–12) and Roman paganism (Rev. 13–19). During the nineteenth and twentieth centuries, the preterist view had periodic surges of interest and has recently gained more and more prominence.

- ✓ Francisco Ribera developed the futurist approach in the late sixteenth century. Some in the Roman Catholic Church held his views over the next two centuries, but Protestants rejected futurism until the nineteenth century. However, during the 1830s, J. N. Darby, the founder of dispensationalism, incorporated Ribera's ideas into his framework. (*Dispensationalism* holds that human history is divided into seven "dispensations," or eras, represented by the seven churches in Revelation 2–3 — see Chapters 3 and 13 and the upcoming section "Meaning of the letters to the seven churches.") This futurist approach would soon spread among other groups as well, gaining momentum into the twentieth century, particularly in the Protestant evangelical church.

Throughout the nineteenth and twentieth centuries, the idealist approach to Revelation remained popular in other parts of the church, especially among Roman Catholics and those who embraced a more theologically liberal view of Christianity in this period.

Today, in the twenty-first century, the historicist method has faded significantly in popularity, while futurism, preterism, and idealism all have strong followings. Of these three, the futurist method has emerged over the past half century as the most widely known interpretation in today's culture. It's often portrayed in the media and the arts, as you can see in the bestselling *Left Behind* book series.

Figure 4-2 shows how these four methods of interpretation have grown and weakened in popularity within the church over the years.

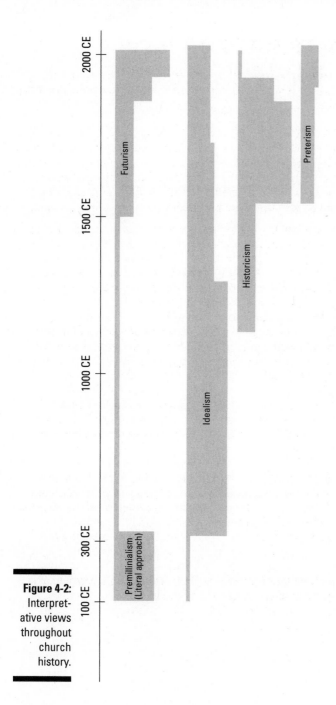

Futurism

Premillinialism
(Literal approach)

Idealism

Historicism

Preterism

2000 CE

1500 CE

1000 CE

300 CE

100 CE

Figure 4-2: Interpretative views throughout church history.

Futurist: Events Will Take Place at a Moment's Notice

Futurists believe that much of John's prophecy, starting with Revelation 4:1, chronicles real events that will take place on this earth sometime in the future. According to this view, John uses Revelation as a platform on which to give specific details of the End Times, including

- A seven-year period of judgment called the Tribulation (Rev. 6–18)
- The Second Coming of Jesus, which immediately follows the Tribulation (Rev. 19)
- A literal 1,000-year of reign of Jesus on the earth (Rev. 20)
- A final judgment of the world (Rev. 20)
- The creation of a new heaven and earth (Rev. 21)

Figure 4-3 shows the futurist's timeline of Revelation.

This viewpoint has risen significantly in popularity over the past 150 years, and you can consider it the mainstream position for many Protestant evangelical churches.

Of the four positions, the futurist method is the most literal in interpretation. While embracing the symbolism in John's work, futurists believe that symbolic prophecy always leads to a literal fulfillment, unless the text specifically states otherwise. Therefore, according to futurists, the numbers used in the book — such as the 144,000 in Revelation 7 or the 1,000-year reign of Jesus in Revelation 20 — should be treated literally, even if they also have symbolic meaning associated with them. So, too, the cosmic disturbances and disasters foretold in the seals, trumpets, and bowls hint at real cataclysmic events while symbolizing political and social upheavals.

However, futurists would add the caution that this principle doesn't mean *every* symbol should be interpreted as a literal description. For example, the "Sodom and Egypt" in Revelation 11:8 is symbolic because the text clearly says (italics added), "Their dead bodies will lie in the street of the great city that is *prophetically* [*allegorically*] called Sodom and Egypt, where also their Lord was crucified."

Futurists don't believe that Revelation's vivid symbolism warrants a fundamental shift in interpretation. They're less likely to look for hidden meanings in the text and instead argue that Revelation tends to be straightforward in its interpretation.

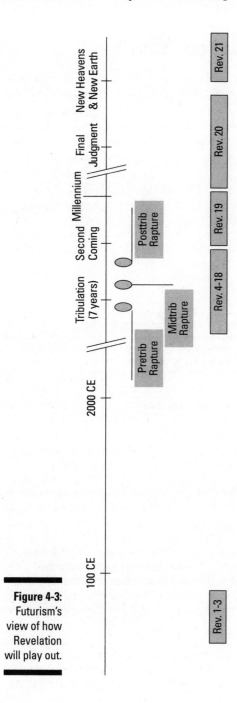

Figure 4-3:
Futurism's
view of how
Revelation
will play out.

Various futurist perspectives

Not all futurists agree on the details of interpretation. In fact, several strands of futurism branch off based on a variety of issues. In this section, we discuss four noteworthy areas of difference.

Meaning of the letters to the seven churches

Futurists differ on how to interpret the letters to the seven churches in Revelation 2–3. Most believe these letters are just what they appear to be: letters from John to the seven first-century churches in Asia Minor.

Another camp of futurists — the dispensationalists — argues that each church represents a period of church history (see Table 4-1 for one interpretation). This approach to Revelation 2–3 is somewhat related to the historicist approach, deviating from a plain reading of John's book for these two chapters (see the upcoming "Historicist: Covering the Entire History of the Church" section).

Table 4-1	Seven Churches Representing the Church Age	
Church Receiving a Letter	*Period Represented (CE)*	*Description of Time Period*
Ephesus	Apostolic church (30–99)	Early New Testament church
Smyrna	Martyred church (100–313)	Roman persecution of Christians
Pergamum	Imperial church (313–590)	Constantine makes Christianity the official state religion
Thyatira	Papal church (590–517)	Leadership the Roman Catholic Church
Sardis	Church of the Reformation (1517–1700)	Protestant Reformation
Philadelphia	Missionary church (1700–present)	Missionaries spanning the globe sharing the gospel
Laodicea	Theologically "liberal" church (1800–present)	Modern church holding less value in Scripture as God's authoritative word

Timing of the rapture

The *rapture* is the point in time when Christians who are still alive on earth will be taken up to heaven to be with Jesus (see Chapter 10). Futurists differ on whether the rapture occurs before, during, or after the Tribulation judgments discussed in Revelation:

- *Pretribulationists* (*pre-tribs*) and dispensational futurists believe that the rapture of the church takes place at the start of Revelation 4. They hold that John's account of being taken up to heaven parallels the rapture accounts in 1 Corinthians 15:52–54 and 1 Thessalonians 4:13–18. In addition, they also point out that the word *church* is conspicuously absent from John's book after the close of Revelation 3.

- *Midtribulationists* (*mid-tribs*) hold that the rapture will take place midway through the Tribulation period.

- *Posttribulationalists* (*post-tribs*) say it'll happen at the end of the judgment period, just prior to the Second Coming of Jesus.

Chronology of Revelation

The majority of futurists believe that, starting at Revelation 4:1, the book largely provides a continuous chronology of events that'll take place during the End Times. Others argue that Revelation actually contains parallel sections (Rev. 4–11 and Rev. 12–19) that provide two descriptions of the Tribulation before the Second Coming.

Timing of judgments

Most people who subscribe to the futurist approach hold that the seal, trumpet, and bowl judgments described in Revelation 6–19 have yet to take place. They represent judgments that are far more severe than the world has ever experienced. In other words, according to classic futurism, you can think of Revelation's prophecy as being in pause-mode, just like on your DVD player. Some of the events (Rev. 2–3) have taken place, but Jesus has yet to unclick the pause button to continue the fulfillment of most of the prophecy in the book of Revelation.

A minority futurist perspective sees the seal judgments as already taking place progressively within the church age, while the others remain in the future.

Newspaper exegesis: The end is near!

One of the criticisms that non-futurists have concerning the futurist approach is its tendency to promote sensationalism and what's called *newspaper exegesis* — interpreting Scripture based on current events. For example, suppose an article on fingerprint and eye-scanning technologies hits the stands, and some futurists become convinced that this technology is a precursor to the mark of the beast (a way in which people are identified by something on their bodies). Or perhaps the European Union is labeled as the modern-day Babylon, and the euro foreshadows a worldwide economy led by the Antichrist. And of course, the Antichrist is whoever is the most notorious villain of the moment.

The important point isn't speculating on whether these theories are true or false but rather recognizing that they are, in fact, *theories*. If the futurist view is correct, then by definition, John's prophecy must truly be fulfilled in actual events. But because Christians believe only God knows the details, people can only play guessing games regarding world events. People in every generation have declared particular world events and leaders or specific dates as definite fulfillments of specific prophecy in Revelation, only to be proven wrong over and over.

Examining the futurist approach

Futurists hold up several arguments to support their position. They say that futurism is consistent with the following:

- ✔ **The history of fulfilled prophecy:** Futurists contend that a literal perspective closely parallels the way in which God fulfilled Old Testament prophecy (see the "Fulfilled Prophesy: Literal or Symbolic?" section in this chapter). Therefore, they argue it's reasonable to assume the same principles apply to Revelation as well.

- ✔ **A plain reading of the judgments of Revelation:** The futurist approach argues that, even if you don't understand the specifics of the End Times judgments, a plain reading of Revelation tells you that they're going to be really, really bad. Therefore, according to futurists, because events of the scope and magnitude of those foretold in Revelation have never occurred in human history, preterism and historicism can't be true.

- ✔ **Traditional scriptural interpretation:** The futurist approach maintains that an accurate reading of Revelation 4–22 shouldn't be much different from the way you approach Revelation 1–3 and the rest of the Bible. Therefore, futurists argue that by following the grammatical-historical method of interpretation, you arrive at a futurist understanding of the prophecy. (See Chapter 17 for some practical guidelines that are part of the grammatical-historical method of interpretation.)

✔ **Early church leanings:** The futurist approach was developed in the Middle Ages as a response to the Protestants' historicist approach. However, the core belief of this approach — a literal interpretation of Revelation — has its roots at least as far back as the early second-century church.

However, critics note some challenges to futurism:

✔ **Futurism requires more effort than the other viewpoints in interpreting John's stated timing of events.** In Revelation 1 and 22, John clearly says that the events he is writing about will "soon" transpire. Critics charge that futurists have to force their translation of that text in order to support their claims. (See the "Are we there yet? or, How soon is 'soon'?" section in this chapter for more on this issue.)

✔ **Much of Revelation becomes less relevant to the seven churches.** If everything after Revelation 4:1 happens in the future, then much of John's book had little relevance for the original readers. (For details on this issue and the futurist response to it, see the later "Who is John really writing to?" section in this chapter.)

Historicist: Covering the Entire History of the Church

The *historicist* interpretation of Revelation sees John's book as revealing the entire course of history during the church age. In other words, the book's prophecy started in the early church and, because there are no clearly defined starting and stopping points, the prophecy is being continuously fulfilled in "real time." The historicist, therefore, sees Revelation as history in the making.

The basic approach

Because prophecy in Revelation is an ongoing process, historicists look at major historical events since the first century and then attempt to map them back to specific prophecies in Revelation (see Figure 4-4). For example, some believe that the opening of the seals in Revelation 6–7 symbolizes the barbarian invasions against the Western Roman Empire, while the locusts of Revelation 9:1 represent the Arabs who attacked the Eastern Roman Empire. Other prophetic events in history range from the Protestant Reformation, to the French Revolution, to such modern issues as the United Nations or U.S. race riots. Although the view is less common today, classic historicists embraced the idea that the papacy (the office of the Roman Catholic pope) was the Antichrist (beast) discussed in Revelation 13:1.

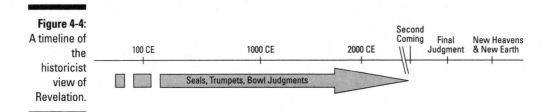

Under the historicist approach, prophecy is fulfilled through real events, but Revelation is also dripping with symbolic significance. In particular, historicists look at the dating discussed in Revelation as key. Specifically, they hold to a *year-day* principle, meaning that one day in Revelation symbolizes one year in actual history (paralleling the year-day relationship in Ezekiel 4:4–6).

The historicist interpretation has an impressive list of proponents from the past, including Martin Luther, John Wycliffe, John Knox, William Tyndale, Sir Isaac Newton, John Wesley, and C.H. Spurgeon. However, like disco music and tapered jeans, the historicist approach is out of style today. Few people in the twenty-first century subscribe to this perspective.

Examining the historicist approach

As evidence for the validity of their interpretation, historicists hold up some rather compelling mappings of real historical events to the prophetic judgments in Revelation.

Critics, however, insist that the matchmaking attempts of the historicist are much like an Internet dating service: Odds are that you'll get an occasional hit, but you'll have many more misses or forced fits along the way. Critics also note these challenges:

- ✔ **No consensus among historicists:** Although historicists may agree on a general interpretative model, this group shows little agreement on the specifics of fulfilled prophecy. This situation raises a practical issue of how useful Revelation would be as prophecy if no one is ever sure about any of the events that happened in either the past or present.

- ✔ **Most historicist models reach too much for a solution:** Non-historicists argue that trying to map history over the past 2,000 years into Revelation's judgments is like trying to fit a round peg into a square hole.

✔ **Fulfillments are too Euro-centric:** Most historicist accounts base much of the fulfilled prophecy on events that impact the European church and overlook the worldwide church.

✔ **Not all timing easily fits into the year-day principle:** Non-historicists point to various parts of Revelation in which the stated timeframes don't seem consistent with the year-day model — in particular, Revelation 11:2, 12:6, 12:14, and 13:5.

One potential danger that historicists (and futurists, too) should recognize is a tendency to become preoccupied with the nitty gritty details of prophetic fulfillment. When this happens, readers risk turning Revelation into little more than a puzzle or math problem rather than the Word of God. Therefore, it's important that Christians not lose sight of the bigger messages that John was delivering — to be faithful and obedient to Jesus regardless of circumstances.

Preterist: Explaining Historical Events from the First Century

Preterists believe that the prophecies discussed in Revelation correspond not to future events but to events that *already* took place back in the early centuries CE. In other words, Revelation is fulfilled prophecy (or at least largely so).

According to the preterist approach, John wrote the entire book of Revelation as a promise of deliverance for the seven churches in the Roman province of Asia that were suffering intense persecution from Jewish authorities and the Roman Empire. The seal, trumpet, and bowl judgments were thus directed at the Jews and the Romans (see Figure 4-5).

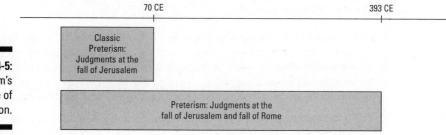

Figure 4-5:
Preterism's
timeline of
Revelation.

70 CE — Classic Preterism: Judgments at the fall of Jerusalem

393 CE

Preterism: Judgments at the fall of Jerusalem and fall of Rome

Classic preterists hold that John's prophecies were fulfilled by the destruction of Jerusalem in 70 CE, though a smaller group of preterists extends this window to include the fall of the Roman Empire in 393 CE. Not surprising, the classic preterist position largely depends on an early dating of John's writing (in the 60s, prior to the fall of Jerusalem in 70 CE). See Chapter 2 for more on the dating of Revelation.

Preterism was formally developed in the Middle Ages and served as a minority opinion for centuries. However, it's recently become a popular model within some scholarly circles. What's more, the preterist approach has a definite appeal to readers who find the futurist's End Times talk too sensationalistic or downright wacky. Preterists see their view as a far more down-to-earth solution, while still holding true to the reliability and divine inspiration of the Bible.

Although preterists would argue that the prophecies were fulfilled as actual historic events, they interpret many of the judgments more symbolically than futurists do. Therefore, the classic preterist holds that the return of Jesus (Rev. 19) is a carrying out of his judgments, not a physical return of Jesus to the earth (because that obviously didn't occur in 70 CE).

Preterists often consider Matthew 24 (also Mark 13 and Luke 17, 21) as a mini-version of Revelation because Jesus discusses many of the same themes of his judgment and return (see Chapter 3). Because this teaching, the Olivet Discourse, is in the first three Gospels but not the Gospel of John, preterists suggest that Revelation may be John's elaboration on what Jesus talked about on the Mount of Olives. They point out that, in context, Jesus's discussion about judgment in the Gospels seems to be related to the destruction of the Temple in Jerusalem. If so, John is following suit in his book of Revelation. (For more on the Olivet Discourse, see Chapter 3.)

Various preterist perspectives

Not all preterists are alike. Here are two notable points of difference:

✔ Timing and nature of Jesus's Second Coming

- *Full (classic) preterists* claim that the prophecies of the entire book — including Jesus's symbolic Second Coming — were already fulfilled back in the first century.

- *Partial preterists* believe that the judgments already took place back in the first century but agree with the idea of a literal Second Coming of Jesus in the future, along with a final judgment.

✔ View of Revelation as prediction versus description

- Many classic preterists affirm the predictive nature of John's writing, believing that these prophecies were fulfilled within years of John's writing.

- Some who call themselves preterists believe John was simply *describing* current events rather than predicting events that would take place in the future. From this perspective, Revelation was the persecuted Christian church's response to the powers that were attacking the church.

Examining the preterist approach

Preterists see several strengths to their interpretative view, including the following:

✔ **Relevance to the original readers:** If John is prophesying about events that will transpire within a handful of years after his writing, then he functions very much like an Old Testament prophet preparing his contemporaries for what to expect shortly. Practically, Revelation also is very similar to other epistles. (See the "Who is John really writing to?" section later in this chapter.)

✔ **Consistency with a plain reading of the timing:** John repeatedly says that the events in the prophecy will happen "soon" (1:1, 22:7, 22:12, 22:20). A preterist can take that word at face value. (See the "Are we there yet? or, How soon is 'soon'?" section.)

✔ **Consistency with the Olivet Discourse:** Preterists hold that the Olivet Discourse (Matthew 24, Mark 13, and Luke 17, 21 — see Chapter 3) tells of the coming destruction of Jerusalem. Given the parallels between Jesus's teaching on the Mount of Olives and Revelation, they believe the two prophecies point to the same events.

Critics of preterism identify several challenges to this viewpoint:

✔ **Dependency on early dating of Revelation:** The classic preterist relies on the early dating of Revelation (before 70 CE). However, as Chapter 2 discusses, the certainty of an early date is no slam dunk.

✔ **Difficulty in seeing all the prophecies fulfilled:** When you compare the fall of Jerusalem (and/or the later destruction of Rome) with the details provided in Revelation, preterists identify remarkable parallels. Specifically, they hold up nonbiblical historical accounts (such as those of the well-known Jewish historian Josephus) that depict stories of suffering and disaster. However, critics argue that even taking those accounts at face value, it remains a stretch to see John's prophecy fulfilled to the extent that Revelation requires.

✔ **Mixture of figurative and literal interpretations:** Critics charge that preterists are selective about what is literal, symbolic, or both. Preterists insist on a plain reading of some of the text, such as the "I am coming soon" wording in Revelation 22, literal references to the Temple in Jerusalem (Rev. 11), and allusions to Nero (Rev. 17). Yet non-preterists argue that preterists run away from a plain reading of the text in other passages. In particular, although futurists and historicists view the white rider in Revelation 19 as Jesus, preterists believe that the image merely symbolizes the carrying out of the Word of God.

✔ **Differences between ancient history and John's prophecy:** Critics insist that if the preterist approach is valid, then church history would've been much different. Instead of suffering continued and pro-longed persecution, early Christians would've received total victory over the Jews and Romans. What's more, they argue that because the final judgment and destruction of evil has yet to occur, then at least some of Revelation is incomplete.

✔ **Origins in a reactionary period of history:** The original proponent of the preterist approach did so in part as a response to the antipapacy claims of Protestant reformers' historicism (see the earlier section "Solving the Revelation Puzzle: Four Solutions throughout History"). By itself, the environment in which preterism developed doesn't nullify the view, but crit-ics believe people should factor potential biases into the whole equation.

Idealist: Identifying Themes, Not Literal Events

The *idealist* position (also known as the *spiritual*, *allegorical*, or *symbolic* approach) looks at Revelation as a figurative description of the constant, cyclical battle between good and evil that exists throughout human history (see Figure 4-6). The idealist, therefore, doesn't look for prophecy to be ful-filled in actual, literal events. You may think of idealists as viewing Revelation as a fictional tale elaborating great spiritual truths.

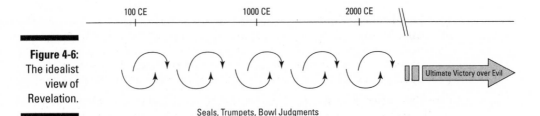

Figure 4-6:
The idealist
view of
Revelation.

100 CE   1000 CE   2000 CE

Seals, Trumpets, Bowl Judgments

Ultimate Victory over Evil

Idealists see Revelation as a book that John wrote to encourage believers in his day of God's eventual victory over evil and to call them to persevere during tough times. The battles discussed refer to struggles that are occurring in a spiritual realm and that the Apostle Paul alludes to in Ephesians 6:12: "For our struggle is not against enemies of blood and flesh, but against the rulers, against the authorities, against the cosmic powers of this present darkness, against the spiritual forces of evil in the heavenly places." The judgments that are prophesied signify the recurrent, natural disasters and political-social problems that humans have always faced. As you'd expect, the idealist approach emphasizes the vivid symbolism of Revelation and downplays its predictive qualities.

Various idealist perspectives

Within the idealist camp, you find a variety of perspectives. Here's the basic tour:

- **Conservative versus liberal idealists:** Most theologically conservative idealists affirm the idea of Jesus's eventually returning to earth, defeating Satan once and for all, and establishing his permanent kingdom. More-liberal idealists maintain that all the talk of a Second Coming in the Scriptures is pure allegory — that Jesus has no intention of an actual, personal return to the earth for a second time.

- **Hybrid idealists:** Some commentators tend to combine the idealist approach with the preterist, forming a hybrid idealist-preterist position (see the earlier section titled "Preterist: Explaining Historical Events from the First Century"). From this perspective, prophecy was fulfilled figuratively within the first century but without any ties to historical events. Other commentators blend the idealist approach with the historicist and even the futurist interpretations.

Examining the idealist approach

Proponents of the idealist approach point to the following strengths of their interpretation:

- **Consistency with the apocalyptic nature of Revelation:** Idealists put all their interpretative eggs in the apocalyptic basket, so to speak. They hold that apocalyptic literature wasn't meant to be taken as a codebook to actual events. Instead, just as artistic expressions like poetry and opera deal with broad moral themes, so, too, does John's Revelation.

- **Relevance in any age:** Because this approach deals with the prophetic messages on a higher, more abstract level, you don't need to try to match up each passage of Scripture with a historical event, as the other approaches do. Therefore, from the perspective of the idealist, all the Scriptures are relevant to every generation of the church, not just a minority of believers facing those events in a specific space and time.

Critics of the idealist approach note several shortcomings, including the following:

- ✔ **Idealism stops short.** Futurists, historicists, and preterists are quick to point out that they can agree with many of the broad symbolic themes that the idealist approach espouses (good will triumph, justice will be served, and so on). However, they argue that idealists make their mistake by not seeing the literal undertones of the text.

- ✔ **An allegorical interpretation waters down Scripture.** A literalist argues that when you interpret the Scriptures allegorically, you reduce their authority because the meaning comes from the interpreter, not the text.

- ✔ **It's less consistent with Old Testament prophecy.** Critics hold that the nonliteral nature of this approach is far less consistent with the normal patterns of Old Testament prophecy. (See the "Prophecy fulfillment: Literal or symbolic?" section in this chapter.)

- ✔ **Symbolism has to turn literal — at some point, anyway.** Christians affirm that God will eventually defeat evil once and for all and usher in a new kingdom that Jesus will reign over forever. If so, then the battle of good versus evil must have actual events play out at some point in history. Non-idealists argue that the concluding chapters of Revelation must have at least some literalness to them, no matter how figurative John's writing may appear to be.

What's Your Angle? Evaluating the Four Approaches

As you examine each of the basic interpretations of Revelation, you can identify several key questions:

- ✔ How consistent are these approaches with the way in which Old Testament prophecy was fulfilled?

- ✔ How relevant was Revelation to the original readers?

- ✔ How consistent are these approaches with John's statements about the timing of fulfillment?

- ✔ Was the persecution of the early Christians serious enough to justify the position that the judgments have already been fulfilled?

We discuss these questions in this section. But first, Table 4-2 summarizes the views that each approach has on the major sections of Revelation.

Table 4-2	Four Major Interpretations		
Interpretation	*Chapters 1–3*	*Chapters 4–19*	*Chapters 20–22*
Futurist	Letters' recipients represent periods of church history	Describes a 7-year Tribulation that is to come	Millennium Final Judgment New heaven and new earth
Historicist	Are actual letters to first-century churches in Asia	Represents events throughout history	Millennium Final Judgment and new earthNew heaven
Preterist	Are actual letters to first-century churches in Asia	Represents conditions in the first century (particularly the fall of Jerusalem)	Represents heaven and God's final victory
Idealist	Are actual letters to first-century churches in Asia	Presents a symbolic conflict of good and evil	Symbolizes victory of good over evil

Prophecy fulfillment: Literal or symbolic?

One of the key debates about Revelation is the degree to which its prophecies are meant literally. In other words, do the prophecies translate into actual historical events? Or do they symbolize key themes that are taking place throughout history?

The way in which the Bible addresses fulfillment of past prophecy can be a valuable guide in determining how best to interpret Revelation. Scholars generally use four ways to describe how any particular prophecy was carried out within documented biblical history:

✔ **Real event, as told through a literal description:** The prophecy describes a real event that took place, and the biblical wording closely matches the historical context. For example, several Old Testament passages offer precise descriptions of real events during Jesus's life, such as his birth in Bethlehem (Micah 5:2) and his ride on a donkey in front of crowds of adoring people (Zechariah 9:9). So too, Zechariah 11:12–13 includes very specific details about the Judas's betrayal of Jesus, prophesying that the price of betrayal will be 30 silver coins and that the money will be used to buy a potter's field. Matthew 27:6–9 says that's exactly what happened.

✔ **Real event, as told through a plainly obvious figure of speech:** The prophecy describes a real event that took place in history but uses a figure of speech; however, as you look back on history, the symbolism in the passage is obvious. For example, Isaiah 53:5 prophesies Jesus's crucifixion: "But he was wounded [pierced] for our transgressions, crushed for our iniquities." Although Isaiah doesn't specifically talk about crucifixion, the symbolism indicates the manner of death that Jesus would suffer.

✔ **Real event, as told through a symbolic description:** A prophecy may foretell a real event but use symbolic language that's less obvious, particularly to the original hearers. For example, consider Jesus's statement in John 2:19: "Destroy this temple, and in three days I will raise it up." Jesus was referring not to the literal Temple in Jerusalem but to himself. Looking back, the symbolism is obvious, though people at the time didn't think so. Or take Psalms 118:22: "The stone that the builders rejected has become the chief cornerstone." This passage is a clear reference to Jesus, but it's more allegorical in nature. Finally, the prophet Ezekiel wrote of angels scattering coals over Jerusalem (Ezekiel 10:1–22), prophesying the destruction of Jerusalem that took place shortly after that (2 Chronicles 36:11–15).

✔ **Real spiritual theme, as told through a symbolic description:** A final category of prophecy is one that provides general themes but has no direct ties to real events, places, or people in history. Some defending the allegorical method would point to God's promises of blessing to Abraham and his descendents (as in Genesis 12:3) as illustrative of the broad, cyclical nature of prophecy.

In general, prophecy that was fulfilled completely within the timeframe of the Old and New Testaments forecasted real historical events that took place in the world. However, the description of the prophecy varies — sometimes very literal (Micah 5:2), sometimes highly figurative (Ezekiel 10:1–22), and quite often, somewhere in between. This literal approach is, by the way, fully consistent with the way in which Old Testament Scripture is used and quoted within the New Testament.

Some prophecies span these categories, such as Isaiah 40:3, which combines the first and second categories in describing John the Baptist: "A voice cries out: 'In the wilderness [*literal description*] prepare the way of the Lord, make straight in the desert a highway for our God [*figurative description*].'"

Therefore, as you consider each of the major interpretations of Revelation, keep these general trends from past prophecy in mind. For more information on whether an interpretation is more literal or figurative, please see Figure 4-1 and the earlier sections on the individual theories.

Are we there yet? or, How soon is "soon"?

In Revelation, John seems to highlight the immediacy of the events that he's prophesying. John kicks off his book telling readers that these events "must soon take place" (Rev. 1:1) and that "the time is near" (Rev. 1:3). John then closes out the book in chapter 22 with not one, not two, but three statements from Jesus saying, "I am coming soon" (Rev. 22:7, 22:12, 22:20).

These statements are like sweet music to the preterist ear. After all, a plain reading of these verses is consistent with this interpretative approach, which insists Revelation has already been fulfilled. The preterist is also eager to jump on Revelation 22:10–11, where Jesus specifically instructs John that he *must not* "seal up" the words of the prophecy, because "the time is near." Preterists contrast this passage to Daniel 12:9, in which God tells Daniel that he *must* "seal up" his prophetic message because it wasn't a message for his lifetime. The preterist then reasons that if John's message were for the church thousands of years later, then Jesus would've told John to seal up his prophetic words as well.

Although a preterist (and a historicist and idealist) can take those words of imminence at face value, the futurist has to work harder:

- Futurists argue that *soon* is best translated in context as *suddenly*. In other words, whenever Jesus does return, the event will happen suddenly and immediately.

- They point out that in apocalyptic literature and biblical prophecy, time is sometimes non-linear: The future is talked about in the present tense and sometimes even in the past.

- They suggest that God's concept of "soonness" is quite different from people's. The Apostle Peter makes this point in 2 Peter 3:8–9: "With the Lord one day is like a thousand years, and a thousand years are like one day. The Lord is not slow about his promise, as some think of slowness."

- Futurists hold up a logical argument that goes something like this: Jesus says repeatedly that he is coming *soon*. However, Jesus has not yet returned to earth. Therefore, *soon* has not yet occurred.

Who is John really writing to?

John identifies the audience of his letter as the seven churches in Asia. However, depending on the approach you take, the actual relevance of the prophecy to this group of people varies greatly.

If you subscribe to the preterist approach, then Revelation reads much like a standard epistle — immediate, practical relevance to the target audience of John's day. As with other epistles — Romans or Hebrews, for example — relevance for later generations, including your own, begins with understanding Revelation's meaning to its original recipients.

However, if you take a futurist or historicist approach, then the bulk of Revelation (4–22) becomes, in a practical sense, irrelevant to the original audience. Consequently, Revelation is written, either partially or completely, as a vehicle intended for a broader audience. As a comparison, consider John F. Kennedy's famous speech at Rice University in 1962. In this address, Kennedy uttered the famous words, "We choose to go to the moon in this decade," in front of a crowd of thousands in Texas. But the speech was for more than the people attending; it was meant for the entire nation. Kennedy was simply using Rice as a venue for a broader purpose.

In addition, critics of the early *rapture* theory (believers' being taken up to heaven in Rev. 4:1) say such a timeline calls into question the very purpose of the book in the first place. They reason that if the church is indeed raptured at the start of Revelation 4, then the prophetic details of the entire Tribulation period would be meaningful only to the unbelieving people "left behind." Pretribulationists (who believe that the rapture will occur before the seven-year Tribulation) counter by saying that God will use the Tribulation period to bring nonbelievers to faith. They add that the events of Revelation 19–22 (Second Coming of Jesus, Millennium, Last Judgment, and new heaven and earth) are relevant to all Christians of any era, regardless of whether they're on the earth at the time that these events transpire.

Was first-century persecution really that bad?

One of the linchpin issues for the preterist position is the extent of persecution that the Christians in the Roman province of Asia were experiencing from the Jews and pagans in the 60s CE. If there was considerable persecution, then this fact helps preterists in the claim that John, in his prophetic judgments, is speaking of the fall of Jerusalem as a judgment on the Jewish people. However, if the persecution of believers was nominal or limited, then the preterist has a harder case to prove.

Overall, evidence of the extent of Jewish persecution of Christians seems to be mixed and inconclusive. Although there's ample proof that frequent persecution of Christians by the Jewish leadership did occur in Jerusalem and Judea, the extent to which that persecution spread beyond the home base of Judaism, particularly into western Asia Minor, is unclear. The Acts of the

Apostles does chronicle Jewish leadership following Paul around and making life difficult for him. It also talks about Jewish attempts to incite persecution among the broader Gentile community. Preterists, in fact, are also quick to point out that the word used in Revelation to refer to the Tribulation (*thlipsis*) is the same word used in Acts (11:19, 14:22) and in 2 Thessalonians 1:4, 1:6.

On the flip side, critics note that the suffering that occurs in Revelation is far beyond anything that occurred in the Acts timeframe. They also point out that the New Testament records the fact that Paul regularly worshipped in synagogues, implying that he was not persecuted as he did so. Further, they argue that in spite of the Jewish dominance in Jerusalem, the Jews simply didn't have a strong influence across the empire.

Finding common ground

When history eventually plays out, one of the four main approaches to interpreting Revelation will, in fact, prove itself to have been the *best*. But until that time, Christians believe they're simply called to faithfully seek the truth under the guidance of the Holy Spirit.

Fortunately, the inspiration, authority, and trustworthy nature of the Bible can remain intact while people identify with any of these four views. In other words, Christians can agree to disagree. Justin Martyr offers a great example of the right attitude regarding how one views Revelation. Though this second-century church father held a premillennialist (futurist) view, he acknowledged that genuine Christians thought differently.

These four approaches differ wildly on the specifics and details of the book of Revelation and the events that it prophesies. However, futurists, preterists, historicists, and idealists can all affirm that Revelation was written, first and foremost, to encourage Christians to persevere during difficult times and to remind them that, even through tough times, the church will persist until Jesus returns.

Chapter 5

Deciphering Symbols with Your Secret Decoder Ring

In This Chapter
▶ Understanding why Revelation uses symbolism in the first place
▶ Surveying the major symbols that John uses in Revelation

*T*he modern mindset is practical. After all, most people lead extremely busy lives — so much so that when they want information on something, they don't want to have to jump through hoops. When it comes to the most popular films of the year, for example, the box-office winners are usually ones with a straightforward plotline. Films rich in symbolism, abstract concepts, and vague imagery usually play only to a few diehards in the art houses.

Not surprisingly, then, people living in the twenty-first century often have difficulty in getting a handle on the symbolic nature of Revelation. The first five books of the New Testament are in a clear narrative style as they depict the ministry of Jesus and the early church. The next set of books — letters by Paul, Peter, and other Apostles — are practical in nature, and you may very easily see them as applicable to your life. But when you get to Revelation, its symbolism can be a shock to the system.

In this chapter, we introduce you to the symbolism and imagery of the book of Revelation. We start off by telling you why John used apocalyptic symbolism (and it really wasn't because he was just being mean or coy!). After that, we survey some of the major symbols you encounter in the book.

Giving John's Readers a Heads-up

People today live in a world of disclaimers. Before you drink a hot cup of coffee, your cup displays *The beverage you are about to enjoy is extremely hot.* Or if you watch a full-screen DVD or video at home, you see the following before the movie begins: *This movie has been modified from its original version. It has been formatted to fit your screen.*

REMEMBER

In Revelation 1:1, John gives readers his own disclaimer — that the letter that they are about to read *will* contain symbolism. In the New King James Version of the Bible, Revelation 1:1 begins, "The Revelation of Jesus Christ, which God gave Him to show His servants — things which must shortly take place. And He sent and *signified* it by His angel to His servant John [. . .]" (emphasis ours).

People often used the Greek word *semainein,* translated as "signified" (or "made it known" in the NRSV), when talking about Delphic oracles in ancient Greece. *Oracles* were prophetic decrees revealed by a priest or priestess, communicated through symbols. The *Septuagint* (the Greek translation of the Old Testament) uses the same word in Daniel 2:45 when talking about the interpretation of a symbolic dream.

In reading the word *semainein,* the original readers would've known right off that John's writing was going to define and convey truth through figurative or imaginative pictures rather than through plain text. In other words, because God "signified" the message, readers should expect God to communicate his message through symbolism. This symbolism was not meant to obscure truth but was simply the mode of communication chosen to convey it.

Given that principle, some commentators go even further in terms of how to interpret Revelation. They suggest that in spotting *semainein,* the original readers would have known, as a general rule, to interpret Revelation figuratively until it's plainly obvious that they should do so literally.

Why Use Symbols?

The simple truth is that almost everyone today would've preferred for John to be Captain Obvious, laying out the Revelation of Jesus in as clear a manner as possible. Understanding the point of the book would be so much easier if specifics such as these were used:

✔ Jesus will be coming back on March 3, 2019. Be there or be square.

✔ Beware, the Antichrist will be named Gilligan. His cohort will be known as the Skipper.

✔ The Millennium is a figurative term meant to represent the Super Bowl halftime show.

In other words, instead of Scripture, almost everyone would prefer a glorified legal document that lists out the complete facts of the last days. After all, with such a document in hand, people wouldn't need to wrestle with the interpretations. If lawyers didn't get involved interpreting the obvious, you'd simply need to decide what to do with the information John presented in his book. But we have what we have.

So why exactly did John write Revelation with a heavy dose of symbolism? We examine several possible reasons in this section.

Following biblical tradition

Although Revelation may be best known for its use of symbolism, the reality is that symbolism is present in many parts of the Old and New Testaments. In the Old Testament, God often speaks though the prophets in symbols. The books of Daniel, Ezekiel, and Zechariah make heavy use of *apocalyptic imagery,* a literary device that employs wild and rich symbolism to represent historical events, nations, and persons.

Jesus may not have used common apocalyptic symbolism in the Gospels, but he did speak through parables, which are, in effect, symbolic stories meant to define and illustrate truth. In Luke 8:10, he says, "To you it has been given to know the secrets of the kingdom of God; but to others I speak in parables, so that 'looking they may not perceive, and listening they may not understand.'" In other words, people who genuinely want to discover his truth will do so, but those who do not will somehow miss out on what exactly he's trying to say.

Those words from Jesus become even more significant when you see the message that Jesus gives to the seven churches in Revelation 2–3 at the end of his personalized messages: "Let anyone who has an ear listen to what the Spirit is saying to the churches."

Adding greater meaning than plain text

You know the old saying *a picture is worth a thousand words.* Well, in the same way, symbolism and imagery can provide greater meaning to define truth than plain words alone. Consider, for example, John's use of the name "Babylon" to describe a great evil power in Revelation. To any Jew, the mere mention of Babylon would have dramatic and emotional significance given the history of what the real-life ancient Babylon did to the Israelites in their history. Therefore, the symbol of Babylon in Revelation had a much greater impact on John's original readers — Jew and gentile alike — than if John would've left it as an unnamed demonic force.

With a twenty-first century Western mindset, symbolism is often considered a form of illustration. In other words, people have a truth or fact and then use a symbol to illustrate or help to explain the concept. For example, consider the truth that, according to the Bible, God sacrificed his son Jesus because God loved the world. A Westerner may explain this by coming up with a story about a father who makes the agonizing decision to let his son die while stuck on the train tracks instead of killing everyone aboard the train by derailing it.

However, from John's mindset, this thinking is reversed. Instead, from a Middle Eastern perspective, parables and symbolism actually *define* meaning and truth; they don't just illustrate truth. In other words, you can glean real insight from discovering the details and essence of the story instead of just trying to summarize the main point of it.

Getting people's attention

The Old Testament prophets and Jesus himself often used symbolism and parables to get the attention of their listeners. Even today, the use of symbolism and imagery gets people's attention more than straight text does. After all, in a church sermon on Sunday morning, the congregation always seems to pay more attention when the pastor or priest provides an illustration or tells a story instead of delivering a straight sermon of bullet points.

Symbolism engages a reader's head and heart. It forces readers to take an image and interpret it by actively considering it in light of their knowledge base and personal experiences. In the process, they make more mental connections and are more likely to remember the image and the message behind it.

John's imagery certainly adds shock value to get the churches out of complacency. For example, describing Babylon as the harlot or prostitute in Revelation 17 can provide a deeper impact than merely writing, "Babylon represents something really bad you need to watch out for."

Reinforcing unity

Symbolism works only if readers have the tools and experience to interpret it. Thus, symbols can help bond the reader and writer and provide continuity among stories.

Connecting the original readers

To the modern-day reader, John's symbolism seems strange and foreign. After all, the reader today is removed in several ways from people of the early church — culture, language, knowledge of the popular literary genres of the day, and so on. In fact, some scholars have compared the symbolism of the modern political cartoon to that of Revelation. A political cartoon, after all, makes little sense unless you understand the symbolism and issues being poked fun of.

In contrast, believers in the churches of Asia Minor would've understood the symbolism because of their knowledge of both the Old Testament and the popular pagan myths of the day in the Roman Empire. To the original readers, the symbolism was not a special "Bible code" for which you needed special expert knowledge.

Tying the Old and New Testaments together

As Chapter 3 describes, the vast majority of symbols that John uses in Revelation originally appeared in the Old Testament from prophets such as Daniel and Ezekiel. Therefore, when you look at the symbols in the context of the entire Bible, then all of God's prophecy and plans begin to make more sense as one cohesive message across the pages of the Bible.

Keeping some secrets

The book may be called *Revelation,* but symbols provide enough ambiguity to keep it from being a tell-all. Some level of mystery protected the original readers and encouraged believers to continue to look to God for guidance.

Protecting the underlying message

When you look at the political and social context of most apocalyptic literature, you see that most of its authors wrote in times of turmoil and distress. Regardless of whether John scribed Revelation during the 60s or 90s CE (see Chapter 2), he certainly wrote during a time of intense trouble and persecution. Therefore, he may have used symbolism to mask his message of hope from potential persecutors. If that's true, then those who really want to discover the truth will do so, but skeptics will never understand.

Encouraging continued reliance on God

Though commentators often fall into the trap of trying to circumvent this fact, the ambiguity of symbolism prevents people from pinning God down on the exact details concerning the last days. After all, consider the major interpretations of the book (see Chapter 4). Preterists read Revelation and see its fulfillment as having already taken place in first century. Futurists look at the way the world is heading and see its fulfillment as happening in the future. Idealists point to cycles of evil throughout history as proof of fulfillment. At the very least, this diversity of opinion should humble people as they seek answers.

Looking for answers

The language of Revelation is filled with symbolism. John uses animals, countries, numbers, lamps, stars, and much more to represent people, places, spiritual events, and the like. In general, you can place symbols into three groups:

✔ **Fully explained symbols:** John explains some of the symbols himself and uses a consistent meaning throughout his text. For example, the red dragon in Revelation 12:3 is clearly defined elsewhere in Revelation 12:9 and 20:2.

✔ **Indirectly explained symbols:** Others symbols aren't explicitly defined in Revelation, but John relies on a reader's Old Testament knowledge to provide an understanding of their meaning.

✔ **Unexplained symbolism:** A final group doesn't have any parallels in Scripture, and John never explains the meaning.

Understanding Common Interpretations

A newcomer to Revelation's imagery may conclude that interpreting Revelation is as easy to do as trying to learn to speak Kanji while you're gagged and blindfolded in a Turkish prison. In other words, pretty difficult stuff! However, although some aspects are challenging and prone to different interpretations (see Chapter 4), there are some common perspectives on many of the symbols you encounter as you read through John's book. Use the rest of this chapter to get a bird's eye view, and then dive deeper into the symbolism in Part III.

Discovering the meaning of the major symbols

The Book of Revelation For Dummies is largely devoted to exploring the symbolism of Revelation. In fact, you can't go a page or two in reading Chapters 6–15 without coming across some discussion of John's imagery. However, to get you started, we provide a brief overview of many of the major symbols in Revelation. Use Table 5-1 as your reference to where you can find complete details on a particular symbol.

Table 5-1	Major Symbols in Revelation	
Symbol	*Reference*	*For Dummies Chapter*
"One like the son of Man"	Rev. 1:13–16	6
24 elders	Rev. 4	8
Scroll	Rev. 5:1	8
Seals	Rev. 6	9
Four horsemen of the Apocalypse	Rev. 6:2–8	9
Martyrs	Rev. 6:9–11	9
Day of the Lord	Rev. 6:12–17	9
144,000	Rev. 7:4	9
Silence in heaven	Rev. 8:1–2	9
Trumpets	Rev. 8:2–12	10
Mighty angel	Rev. 10	10
Two witnesses	Rev. 11:3–11	10
Pregnant woman	Rev. 12	11
Red dragon	Rev. 12	11
Wings of a great eagle	Rev. 12:14	11
Mark of the beast	Rev. 13	11
Babylon	Rev. 14	11, 12
Bowls	Rev. 16	12
Millennium	Rev. 20	13

The scroll

The opening verse of Revelation 5 begins by talking about a scroll: "Then I saw in the right hand of the one seated on the throne a scroll written on the inside and on the back, sealed with seven seals." The scroll proves to be anything but an ordinary document. It's something like a last will and testament because the information revealed on the contents describes the eternal inheritance of those who believe in Jesus. But at the same time, it's a message for God's people right now.

Super sevens and sadistic sixes

Within the Bible, the number seven shows up nearly 400 times to symbolize completeness and perfection. This number is important even in the first two chapters of Genesis, where God creates the world in six days and then rests on the seventh. Genesis 2:3 says, "So God blessed the seventh day and hallowed it, because on it God rested from all the work that he had done in creation." The number seven appears over 50 times in Revelation alone, referring to seven spirits, churches, trumpets, bowls, seals, persons, horns, eyes, thunders, plagues, and signs.

If the number seven is God's number, then the number six symbolizes both humanity and human fallenness. The number six represents humankind's incompleteness and imperfection — falling short of God's perfect number seven.

The seals

In Revelation 6, the seven seals on the scroll are opened one at a time. Therefore, the breaking of each seal is an event — a judgment — that takes place *before* the reading of the scroll's "last will and testament."

Four horsemen of the Apocalypse

The breaking of the first four seals in Revelation 6 reveals four horses, known collectively as the *four horsemen of the Apocalypse;* they're differentiated in part by their colors — white, red, black, and pale green:

- **White horse:** The rider on the white horse, equipped with a bow and adorned with a crown, comes out to kick some booty. Some take this rider to be Jesus himself, symbolizing the spread of the Christian gospel across the world. Others contend the rider is the exact opposite — the Antichrist, wearing the disguise of white but bent on destruction.

- **Red horse:** The rider on a red horse is clearly a bad dude, spreading violence and war wherever he goes.

- **Black horse:** The rider on the black horse symbolizes the famine and starvation that occurs because of the economic inequality that exists between the haves and the have-nots.

- **Pale horse:** The rider of the pale horse is none other than Clint Eastwood. Okay, seriously, the pale rider symbolizes the death that follows in wake of the red and black horses.

The Day of the Lord

The *Day of the Lord* is a key term to understand when you look at Revelation as well as the Old Testament prophets. It refers to judgment, the future time in which God "holds court" and passes judgment on the world. It's also associated with the time in history in which God's will for the world will be fulfilled and complete. The term itself appears 19 times in the Old Testament and 4 times in the other New Testament books. In Revelation, the Day of the Lord is associated with Revelation 6:17 and 6:14. (See Chapter 9 for more on the Day of the Lord.)

Silence in heaven

When the seventh seal is opened in Revelation 8, there's silence in heaven for about half an hour. The silence is noteworthy because it signifies a point of no return for the existing world — the old is passing away and the new is beginning. John reveals the full details of that new world in Revelation 21.

So why 30 minutes? The jury's still out on that one. Some believe that the vagueness of the time "about half an hour" implies that the exact time can't be discerned from the text.

The trumpets

In Revelation 8, John tells of seven trumpets that are played by seven angels. The trumpet was an important symbol in the history of God's people. It was used to direct and lead the Israelites during their desert wanderings as well as during wartime battles. Not only was it a rallying call, but it was also a reminder of God's directing them and fighting on their behalf.

The trumpets in Revelation 8 signify the "amplification" of judgments in the last days leading up to the Second Coming of Jesus; they serve as a reminder that God is leading the fight.

Babylon

Babylon is a dominant military and political power in Old Testament history, but it also appears in Revelation 14. Some believe that readers should take this reference literally, holding that ancient Babylon will rise again in the Middle East as a powerful force in the world and the seat of the Antichrist's power. Others see Babylon as symbolic of first-century Rome. Another view is that Babylon represents the capital of the Antichrist's empire.

The bowls

Like the seals and trumpets that come before them, the seven bowls in Revelation 16 symbolize a set of judgments on humankind during the last days. The seven bowls represent the final, terrible, unprecedented stretch of activity just before the Second Coming of Jesus.

The Millennium

In Revelation, John speaks of a 1,000-year reign of Jesus, a timeframe that's commonly referred to as the *Millennium.* Here are the traditional interpretations:

✔ *Premillennialists* believe that this is a literal 1,000-year period that will take place following the Second Coming of Jesus. Many premillennialists are also *dispensationalists*, who believe that human history is divided into seven "dispensations" (eras), which are represented by the seven churches of Revelation 2–3.

✔ *Amillennialists* believe the Millennium is purely figurative, referring to the current church age or the reign of deceased saints with Jesus in heaven (or perhaps both).

✔ *Postmillennialists* believe the Millennium occurs prior to the Second Coming of Jesus; it's an age in which the world will be transformed by the gospel.

For details on these views, please see Chapter 13.

Assembling the cast of characters

Within Revelation, John provides a memorable cast of characters whose imagery often overpowers the text and brings it to life. Here's a brief look at some of the most significant figures.

The mystery man ("One like the Son of Man")

Early on in Revelation 1, John talks of a vision he had in which a mysterious person stands in the midst of seven lampstands. John describes him in vivid detail:

> "[He was] clothed with a long robe and with a golden sash across his chest. His head and his hair were white as white wool, white as snow; his eyes were like a flame of fire, his feet were like burnished bronze, refined as in a furnace, and his voice was like the sound of many waters. In his right hand he held seven stars, and from his mouth came a sharp, two-edged sword, and his face was like the sun shining with full force." (Rev. 1:13–16)

In this passage, John is speaking of Jesus. The description seems like a rather scary picture of Jesus until you understand the symbolism:

✔ The robe and sash refer to the attire worn by Jewish high priests.

✔ The whiteness of his head and hair symbolizes either Jesus's purity and holiness or his wisdom and dignity.

✔ His fiery eyes depict divine omniscience (complete knowledge) and judgment.

✔ His bronze-like feet contrast with the soiled feet of fallen humankind and the pagan gods' feet of clay.

✔ His mighty voice symbolizes his sovereignty and power.

✔ The seven stars represent the angels of the seven churches (Rev. 1:11), which are the chief focus of Revelation 2–3.

✔ The two-edged sword from his mouth symbolizes the lethal power and penetration of the words of Jesus.

✔ The radiance of his face conveys his divine nature.

The 24 elders

Scholars have several theories about the 24 elders in Revelation 5. Some see them as glorified people who represent the either the entire people of God (Jews and gentiles) or else just the New Testament church (Christians). Others believe they're angelic choirs singing praises to God in heaven. A few contend that John is referring to a 24-point star god of ancient Babylonian mythology.

The mighty angel

The mighty angel in Revelation 10 is a source of debate. Some contend that the mighty angel is Jesus because he's described in terms usually associated with God. Others counter, saying that nowhere else is Jesus depicted as an angel. Instead, they suggest that this reference is talking about an archangel, maybe even Gabriel. Archangels play an important role throughout biblical history.

The two witnesses

Revelation 11 introduces readers to "two witnesses" who will prophesy for 1,260 days while wearing sackcloth. John then refers to these two individuals as "two olive trees" and "two lampstands."

Some interpret the two witnesses as the ongoing witness of the church. Others interpret the passage more literally and see them as two preachers preaching to Jews in Jerusalem. Of course, exactly who that dynamic duo is leads to further debate. Some options include Zerubbabel and Joshua the high priest, the Law and the Prophets, Peter and Paul, Israel and the church, Enoch and Elijah, and Moses and Elijah.

The 144,000

The 144,000 in Revelation 7 has long been a subject of debate and resentment. Some people believe that this group of people symbolizes all Christians. Others think that this refers to Jewish Christians because the passage mentions the tribes of Israel. A final interpretation is that the 144,000 is an elite group of Christians (perhaps martyrs) who have special status because of their devotion.

Pregnant woman

John describes the pregnant woman in Revelation 12 as being "clothed with the sun, with the moon under her feet, and on her head a crown of twelve stars." Once again, people have various perspectives on who exactly this woman symbolizes. Some see her as the people of God since the very beginning (ancient Israel and the church). A second view is that the imagery is a Christianized version of ancient myths. A third view is that the pregnant woman is Domitia, the mother of the Roman emperor Domitian's son; he declared her to be the "mother of God." Some Catholics hold that the pregnant woman is the Virgin Mary, mother of Jesus.

Red dragon

The symbolism of the pregnant woman in Revelation 12 is subject of much discussion, but there's little debate over the red dragon that's menacing the woman. The red dragon, adorned with seven heads and ten horns, is Satan himself.

The wings of a great eagle

When reading about the wings of a great eagle in Revelation 12, you may wonder whether J.R.R. Tolkien picked up on this imagery when writing *The Lord of the Rings*. Some see the creature as the same eagle referred to in Revelation 8:13. If so, then John is talking about an angel providing protection for faithful believers during the last days. Another take is that John is actually speaking of a powerful kingdom that uses an eagle as a symbol.

The beast and his mark

In Revelation 13, John writes about two of the most intriguing symbols in all the book: the beast and the mark of the beast. According to Revelation, the beast, who is a false prophet, will require his followers to receive a number stamped on their right hands or foreheads; the mark is required for surviving in the world economy. That mark, says John in Revelation 13:18, is 666.

Many have long speculated on whether 666 is a literal number or a symbol for something else. Some futurists have speculated that Social Security numbers, bar codes, microchip implants, or some other identification technology is the mark of the beast. Others see 666 as pointing to an address, area code, or the numeric value of a person's name.

Since the early days, many have speculated on the identity of the beast, identifying him as Nero Caesar, Napoleon Bonaparte, and Hitler, as well as modern leaders ranging from Ronald Reagan to Bill Clinton.

Most scholars do believe that the beast symbolizes an actual person. However, they maintain that 666 is symbolic, especially because the number six appears elsewhere in Scripture as a sign of imperfection and fallenness.

Part III

Taking a Grand Tour of the Book of Revelation

The 5th Wave   By Rich Tennant

"Nevermind the preterist view or the futurist view of the Book of Revelation. What's our screenwriter's view of Revelation?"

In this part . . .

Revelation can read much like the movie script of a computer-graphics-laden blockbuster — cataclysmic events and mass panic like *The Day After Tomorrow;* insidious villains like *The Fellowship of the Ring;* and intergalactic wars reflective of *Independence Day.* In this part, you explore the blockbuster plotline of Revelation as we walk through each and every chapter.

Chapter 6

Setting Up the Scope
of the Book (1:1–20)

. . . .

In This Chapter
▶ Looking at features of apocalyptic writings
▶ Understanding John's prologue
▶ Considering the letter format and themes
▶ Reliving John's vision of Jesus
▶ Previewing coming attractions

. . . .

*I*f you suffer a plane crash in the ocean and somehow survive to find yourself stranded on a deserted island, the first thing you have to do is get your
bearings — that is, determine your situation. In a similar way, if you're a first-
time reader of the book of Revelation (or even an infrequent visitor), the task
at hand is essentially the same: How do you make sense of this strange book?

In this chapter, we give you the lay of the land: what apocalyptic literature is,
who wrote the book of Revelation, to whom it was written, why it was written,
and basically what it says. These are all important questions that require an
adequate answer; otherwise, most of the book may fly right over your head.

Declassified! Releasing God's Secrets
in the Apocalyptic Press

John wrote the book of Revelation during the heyday of *apocalypticism*. This
rather obscure term speaks more of a mindset than of a specific literary
genre, though certain works in the period 200 BCE to 200 CE do share some
common literary traits.

Apocalypticism is primarily a view of reality. The Greek word *apocalypsis* (from which we get the word *apocalypse*) denotes action: uncovering, unveiling, disclosing, or revealing something previously hidden or secret. In short, an *apocalypse* is a public disclosure of previously classified information. This section covers its essential features.

Touring God's headquarters and giving away the ending

Apocalypses often include esoteric (secret) information about the workings of the heavenly realms and how this influences the earthly realm. In biblical literature, this information is conveyed to a well-known figure of Jewish tradition — or in the book of Revelation, a Christian — who is transported to heaven and given a heavenly tour. This person then writes down what's revealed and makes it accessible to a larger audience. An angelic guide often explains the meaning of these visions. The Old Testament books of Ezekiel, Daniel, and Zechariah also include apocalyptic sections involving angelic informants (Ezekiel 40:3–4, 43:6–27; Daniel 7:15–28, 8:15–27, 10:10–21; Zechariah 1:9–2:13, 4:1–6:15); in fact, the book of Revelation is indebted to these Old Testament passages.

So what's God's big news? Apocalyptic works claim to inform the reader about certain aspects of an eschatological drama. *Eschatology* is just a big word for the study of the End Times or last days. The grand climax of this drama is imminent — that is, it can happen at any moment. As the prologue of Revelation explains, "The time is near" (1:3).

Choosing sides: Dualism

Apocalypticism takes seriously the notion that two absolute powers or principles operate in the universe. Such a view is called *dualism,* and it can exist on several levels:

- ✔ **Ethical (or moral):** In this case, a fundamental split exists between good and evil. In the book of Revelation, God himself is the ultimate source of all that's good; Satan and free moral agents who refuse to submit to God are the ultimate source of evil. This kind of personal, ethical dualism underlies the basic conflict in the book of Revelation.

- ✔ **Visible and invisible:** This kind of dualism acknowledges that there are two realities. The first is the realm that you can see, touch, and handle — that is, the material world of creation, which is good. But behind the visible is the realm of the invisible, where spiritual beings like God, Satan, and angels of various ranks and orders, both good and bad, exist. Obviously, the book of Revelation assumes this kind of dualism as true, as does historical Christianity.

✔ **Matter and spirit:** In this kind of dualism, matter is associated with evil, and spirit is connected with the good. A religious-philosophical movement called *Gnosticism* advocated such a divide. This system, emerging during the second half of the first century and appearing full blown in the second, offered salvation and escape from the realm of the material, which included the human body, and return to the realm of pure spirit through secret knowledge (hence the name Gnosticism, deriving from the Greek word *gnosis,* meaning "knowledge"). The book of Revelation clearly doesn't share this view.

Christian Gnostics even denied that Jesus, as the Son of God, truly assumed human flesh. In his first epistle, John the Apostle vehemently denounces this idea (see 1 John 2:18–29, 4:1–6). And in Revelation, John may be attacking an early form of Gnosticism in the messages to Pergamum (2:14–15) and Thyatira (2:20–23), where false teachers are encouraging compromise with Christian moral values. The connection with Gnosticism is this: Many Gnostics held that what one did in the body didn't affect the spirit; consequently, they reveled in licentiousness while believing themselves to be the elect people of God.

In short, the book of Revelation embraces two kinds of dualism: the ethical and the visible/invisible.

Christian apocalyptic works assume a struggle for supremacy between Jesus and Satan. Human beings are caught right in the middle of this struggle involving both visible and invisible powers. In other words, behind the imperial power of Rome lurk demonic forces opposed to the kingdom of God. Followers of Jesus (later identified as the Lamb) must make a choice; divided loyalties and sitting on the fence aren't options.

Note that the conflict is truly cosmic in scope. According to the Bible, no one and nothing is exempt or excluded. This struggle is cast in the form of a drama consisting of several acts. Second Esdras and 2 Baruch, Jewish apocalyptic works contemporary with the book of Revelation, have a similar drama that unfolds in stages or acts (2 Esdras 5:21–6:34; 2 Baruch 53:1–74:4).

Being encouraged to stick with it

Apocalyptic writing generally has an exhortatory purpose. *Exhortatory* derives from *exhort,* which essentially means "to encourage." Biblical apocalyptic literature is directed first and foremost to those who make a profession of faith in God.

Christian apocalypses are distinguished from their Jewish counterparts by their insistence that Jesus is the Messiah (the *Anointed One*) and that only he can redeem and restore a fallen world. Thus, the primary purpose of Revelation is practical: to encourage the faithful to hold fast their commitment to Jesus.

Getting the essential message

Every profession has its own lingo. If you've ever hung out with computer geeks, you know that when they get focused on some narrow technical subject, they almost sound like they're speaking a foreign language. They understand each other because they're insiders who know the technical terminology. If you want to understand what they're talking about, you have to have one of them translate the technical terms into layman's terms — more familiar concepts that you can understand.

Much of the book of Revelation is "insider stuff" directed specifically to those who are Christians and who understand the language of faith that's unique to Christian experience. But given the complexity of the metaphors and images, even insiders have trouble fully understanding John's visionary book.

Still, anyone can grasp the basic message: Jesus is going to return to earth, overthrow Satan's evil empire, reward his faithful followers, punish those who reject his lordship, and create a new heaven and new earth. Or as many put it, *Jesus wins.*

In spite of its gloomy assessment and deep pessimism about the present world, viewed as lying under the deadly influence of Satan, Revelation does offer hope: Jesus will ultimately triumph. Therefore, Christian believers are encouraged to cling tenaciously to their faith in Jesus and not defect to Satan.

Probing the Prologue (1:1–3)

The prologue (the opening section of a literary work) provides essential information for understanding the meaning and structure of the book of Revelation. The prologue wastes no time informing you what the book is all about:

> "The revelation of Jesus Christ, which God gave him to show his servants what must soon take place; he made it known by sending his angel to his servant John, who testified to the word of God and to the testimony of Jesus Christ, even to all that he saw." (Rev. 1:1–2)

In this section, we briefly examine the essential information the Apostle John conveys to his first-century readers.

Unveiling the good guy

Revelation is more than mere information: It's a revelation of a person, Jesus. It's somewhat like the unveiling of an official portrait of the President of the

United States or a comparable world figure. Typically, there's a ceremony in which a select audience is invited to view the finished portrait for the first time.

The book of Revelation is a literary portrait of how Jesus appears in heaven and during the End Times. The portrait consists of narrative and descriptive brush strokes depicting a real person. In a sense, you, the reader, are invited to view a newly commissioned portrait of Jesus. You watch as the drape shrouding the canvas falls to the floor, and suddenly an imposing figure, larger than life, directs his gaze right at you.

Checking out John's sources

Deep Throat was the source of key information that brought down the Nixon administration in the Watergate fiasco. For years, no one but the reporters knew who Deep Throat was. But no such mystery surrounds Revelation; according to Revelation's writer, John, God himself is the source of the story. That's a pretty bold claim!

In Revelation, John doesn't get a face-to-face interview with God the Father, but the message comes through some pretty reliable channels. John makes the following assertions:

✔ This unveiling is authorized by God and comes from Jesus himself.

✔ An unnamed angel serves as the mediating or revealing agent who oversees the delivery of the message (vision).

✔ John is the recipient and the recorder (writer) of the message (prophecy).

✔ John receives this revelation (message) through a series of visions.

✔ John testifies that what is in the book is what he has seen. This implies that John is charged with making its contents known to a wider audience. It's not about a private religious experience having only individual significance.

The prologue explicitly claims that what follows in the book is a trustworthy, divine communication. Unless you have prior grounds for accepting this book at face value (that is, you're already a committed Christian), you'll have to suspend judgment on the question of the trustworthiness of the message until you've examined the book in more detail and reflected on its implications. Our task, as your guides, is to help you assess what it says; you can then decide whether you believe it's true.

Receiving blessings

Revelation promises a special blessing to those who read the prophecy aloud (likely during Christian worship services) and to those who listen and put the lessons of its warnings and encouragements into practice (1:3). Reading sacred texts aloud was the prevailing custom in the Ancient Near East as well as during the Greco-Roman period.

Those who read texts silently were sometimes thought to be under the influence of an evil spirit — their lips moved but there was no sound!

The blessing or benediction in Revelation 1:3 is the first of seven scattered throughout the book (14:13; 16:15; 19:9; 20:6; 22:7, 22:14). Each offers encouragement and consolation for Christians who find themselves locked in the struggle with evil. Of course, the number of benedictions is significant: Seven in the Bible represents completeness and perfection. By the time you come to the seventh benediction, the End Times drama has run its course.

Saluting the Saints in Asia (1:4–6)

From 1:4–6, the book of Revelation conforms to conventional letter format of the first century with but slight modification. Salutations typically consisted of four pieces of information:

- The name(s) of the writer or writers
- The name(s) of the recipients
- The greeting
- A prayer of thanksgiving

We run through all four elements in this section.

From John with love: Revelation's writer

Conservative critics make a good case that John, author of Revelation, is the Apostle John, one of the original 12 Apostles of Jesus (see Chapter 2). According to church tradition, this John was a highly respected leader among these churches; the Roman provincial government exiled him to the rocky island of Patmos "because of the word of God and the testimony of Jesus" (Rev. 1:9).

The changing tide of persecution

The Romans viewed the early Jesus movement as one of the sects of Judaism (Pharisees, Sadducees, Essenes). Because imperial Rome recognized Judaism as a sanctioned religion, Jews and Christians were free to practice their religion so long as they were loyal to the empire. Some eastern religious sects were not so recognized and were repressed. What changed for early Christians were two seismic events:

✔ **The fire in Rome in 64 CE:** In order to escape the (probably true) accusations that Nero himself had ordered the burning, the emperor accused Christians of setting the fire. Needing a scapegoat, Nero unleashed a brief but violent campaign against Christians in Rome, killing hundreds.

✔ **The Jewish revolt against Rome in 66–74 CE:** Because Christianity had Jewish roots, was considered a sect of Judaism, and featured leading figures who were Jewish (Jesus himself), the Jewish revolt against Rome necessarily brought Christians again under suspicion. After the revolt, Rome viewed Christianity as a religion distinct from Judaism.

However, not until Domitian's reign (81–96 CE), when loyal citizens were expected to participate in emperor worship (especially in the province of Asia), did a more hostile attitude toward Christians begin to appear.

John was a victim of government-sponsored religious persecution. This circumstance is important for understanding the message of the book of Revelation. The Roman Empire was just beginning to manifest overt hostility toward this rapidly growing phenomenon called Christianity. Prior to this, the Romans had maintained a fairly tolerant attitude.

To whom it may concern: The recipients

Revelation 1:4 reveals that the initial readers were members of Christian house churches in the Roman province of Asia (in southwestern Turkey today — see Chapter 2 for a map). A messenger whom they knew and trusted, a fellow believer named John, wrote the scroll containing what's now called the book of Revelation (Rev. 1:9). Both John and the readers shared commitments to the person of Jesus and his teachings and also a common worldview.

Heaven says hello: Passing on the greeting

The greeting "grace to you and peace" reflects a standard Christian greeting. What's unusual about this greeting is that it comes not from the author initially designated — namely, John — but from three heavenly beings or entities. Here they are now.

God

Revelation's greeting first comes from "him who is and who was and who is to come." This is a title for God, stressing his eternal and self-existent nature. The title is similar to how God describes himself to Moses in the book of Exodus. There, as Moses encounters God through a burning bush in the Sinai desert, God reveals his special name: "I AM WHO I AM" (Exodus 3:14).

Seven spirits

Revelation's greeting also comes from "the seven spirits who are before the throne of God." Later in chapters 4 and 5, the throne room scene, these seven spirits function as worshipers around the throne and as messengers sent out into the world to do God's bidding. We tentatively identify these seven spirits as the seven archangels of Jewish tradition (1 Enoch 20:1–8; Tobit 12:15; 2 Esdras 4:1; and Daniel 10:13; for a further discussion of these beings, see Chapter 8).

However, the seven spirits may be an expression denoting the one Holy Spirit because the number seven in apocalyptic literature often conveys the idea of perfection. However, this view is problematic because the next person mentioned is Jesus. Generally, the members of the Trinity are always listed as God the Father, Jesus the Son, and the Holy Spirit. In no other instance in the New Testament are the members of the Trinity listed in this order (for instance, see Matthew 28:19 and 2 Corinthians 13:14). We think this point tips the scales against the seven spirits representing the Holy Spirit.

Jesus

Finally, the greeting comes from "Jesus, the faithful witness, the firstborn of the dead, and the ruler of the kings of the earth." Each title for Jesus is a window into the message of this book and resonates with hope for the Christians of Asia Minor:

- ✔ **Faithful witness:** The Greek word rendered "witness" is *martys*, from which we get the English word *martyr*. John's Gospel emphasizes the role of Jesus as a witness to God's saving intentions. Through Jesus, God intends that all should have an opportunity to become children of God (John 1:12–13).

  John is noting that in Jesus's earthly ministry, he demonstrated his unflinching commitment at the cross, and he now serves as a role model for the Asian Christians. They, too, must render their witness to Jesus's sacrifice on the cross, even if it means dying on one themselves. Christians must be clear about this: They can't compromise with Rome's religious system, featuring the divine Caesar.

- ✔ **Firstborn of the dead:** This title follows hard on the heels of the former. According to the Bible, here lies the hope of all who commit to the cross: Beyond death awaits a resurrection of the body, just like Jesus's rising from the dead. Throughout Revelation, John repeatedly reminds his readers about this hope. It'll provide backbone for the perilous days ahead.

✔ **Ruler of the kings of the earth:** Talk about being countercultural! This title flies directly in the face of the Roman imperial cult with its claims about the divine Caesar and *Roma* (the Latin name for Rome). John's work portrays the truth as presented in the Bible: All glory and dominion belong to the rightful king (Jesus) — all the more reason for the faithful to remain steadfast.

Singing Jesus's praises: Doxology

In place of a prayer of thanksgiving or a prayer for the welfare of his readers, John substitutes a *doxology* (a hymn or prayer of praise) offering up praise to the central character in the book of Revelation: "To him who loves us and freed us from our sins by his blood, and made us to be a kingdom, priests serving his God and Father, to him be glory and dominion forever and ever. Amen" (Rev. 1:5–6).

This doxology focuses on the biblical claim of Jesus's unique, saving work in the divine plan of salvation: He is the redeemer. As the redeemer, he accomplishes two essential actions:

✔ **Jesus overcomes sin.** This idea presupposes that apart from Jesus's intervention, no one can overcome the deadly effects of sin. The New Testament views sin as a master having complete control over the life of a person outside of Jesus (John 8:34; Romans 6:5–14).

✔ **Jesus ordains believers as priests.** As priests, Christians serve God in worship. A *priest* in biblical thought is one who mediates the blessings of God to others and who intercedes for the needs of the believing community. According to the New Testament, all believers are considered priests and have the privilege of exercising priestly ministry — consisting of prayers of praise, thanksgiving, and intercession (Ephesians 1:3–14; Hebrews 13:15; 1 Peter 2:5–9). Christian liturgy, then, is an indispensable part of what it means to be in the kingdom of God.

The word *liturgy* derives from two Greek words, *le_s/laos,* ("people") and *ergon* ("work"). Thus, *liturgy* is the work that the people of God perform in his presence. Central to Christian liturgy is *Communion,* also known as the *Eucharist* or *Lord's Supper,* in which Jesus's death on behalf of his people is tangibly remembered and made present. The sacrifice of Jesus on the cross is the very heart of Christian worship.

Don't miss the two things attributed to Jesus in this doxology: glory and dominion. This is an implied rebuttal of the claims that imperial Rome made through its elaborate symbolism, rituals, and outward pomp.

Sounding the Theme (1:7–8)

In Revelation 1:7, John suddenly departs from the typical first-century letter-writing style (see "Saluting the Saints in Asia [1:4–6]") and blurts out a startling pronouncement: "Look! He is coming with the clouds; every eye will see him, even those who pierced him; and on his account all the tribes of the earth will wail. So it is to be. Amen."

John's exuberant utterance is both the theme and the conclusion of Revelation, and it combines two Old Testament passages, Daniel 7:13 and Zechariah 12:10–12. Both texts, in their respective contexts, describe the dramatic appearance of a figure whose sudden arrival on earth not only alters history but completes history. John apparently views the "one like a human being coming with the clouds of heaven" in Daniel 7:13 and the "one whom they have pierced" of Zechariah 12:10 as references to Jesus.

John's announcement affirms or implies the following:

- ✔ Jesus's return to earth is a highly visible, public event that will be seen worldwide. Revelation 19 adds more details to this unprecedented event.
- ✔ Jesus's return to earth has relevance and importance for all people living at that time.
- ✔ Jesus's return to earth is, according to the Bible, certain. John adds his *Amen* — "may it be so" — to this confident pronouncement. This announcement that Jesus is coming back frames the entire book: Three times in chapter 22, Jesus himself proclaims, "I am coming soon!" (Rev. 22:7, 22:12, 22:20).

As if to further underscore the certainty of Jesus's return, God now adds his *imprimatur* (approval): "'I am the Alpha and the Omega,' says the Lord God, who is and who was and who is to come, the Almighty" (Rev. 1:8).

Only two times in the book of Revelation does God speak: in Revelation 1:8 and in 21:5–6. In both instances, the point is that he is sovereign over all that is; all of history unfolds under his all-wise and holy counsel. This idea recurs throughout the entire book.

Initiating the Visions (1:9–11)

In typical letters of the first century, after the salutation, greeting, and thanksgiving, the author transitions to the body of the letter. In a way, that's how Revelation 1:9–11 functions: It introduces the main subjects of the rest of the letter; however, the letter format falls away and the document assumes the shape of a typical apocalyptic writing, in which John recounts a series of visions, unpacking the central theme of Jesus's return to earth. (For more on apocalyptic writing, see the earlier section titled "Declassified! Releasing God's Secrets in the Apocalyptic Press.")

John briefly recounts the circumstances and occasion on which he received the first of several (perhaps a total of seven) visions. We call the vision in chapter 1 the *initiating vision*. Here are the salient features of John's first visionary experience.

John's location

John receives his vision on Patmos, an isolated, rocky island about 35 miles offshore from Miletus, on the mainland of Asia Minor (southwestern Turkey — see Chapter 2 for a map). The island itself is approximately 6 miles wide and 10 miles long. More importantly, it was not, in the first century, a luxurious resort or vacation paradise! It served as a place of banishment for political prisoners and other persons deemed to be agitators.

The significance of John's self-ID

John's self-identification carries special meaning for his readers. He's a Christian brother who shares with them three realities:

- ✔ He shares the persecution that goes with being a follower of Jesus.

- ✔ He shares what it means to be in the kingdom. The *kingdom* refers to the present, invisible, spiritual reign of Jesus over his church. Christians believe it'll be succeeded by Jesus's future, visible reign in glory over all creation at his Second Coming.

- ✔ John shares the patient endurance of Jesus. Disciples of Jesus must be prepared to endure suffering for the sake of the gospel. John serves as a positive role model in this regard.

Persecution comes with the territory for those who decide to follow Jesus. Jesus was well aware of this and repeatedly warned listeners to count the cost carefully. In John's Gospel, Jesus issues this warning: "If they persecuted me, they will persecute you" (John 15:20; see also Matthew 5:10–12). The Apostle Paul likewise warns the new converts at Thessalonica: "In fact, when we were with you, we told you beforehand that we were to suffer persecution; so it turned out, as you know" (1 Thessalonians 3:4).

Occasion

John simply states, "I was in the spirit on the Lord's day [. . .]" (Rev. 1:10). The expression *in the spirit* refers to a state of religious exaltation and ecstasy, somewhat like being in a trance. The individual experiences what psychologists would label as a heightened or altered state of consciousness.

This condition has a long history, with notable examples occurring among the Old Testament prophets. Exceptional in this regard was the sixth-century prophet Ezekiel. Several times in his book, he narrates extraordinary, spiritual experiences that involve clairvoyance and levitation (see Ezekiel 1–11). The Apocalypse of John shows many instances of indebtedness to Ezekiel for imagery, symbols, and concepts.

John says the vision occurred on "the Lord's day." This is the earliest documented instance of this expression being used for Sunday, the day set aside by Christians for worship and rest. We know from the Gospels that Jesus rose from the dead on a Sunday following the Jewish Passover (Mark 16:2; Matthew 28:1; Luke 24:1). Not surprisingly, this day of the week held special significance for Christians and was the occasion for their coming together to celebrate the Lord's Supper and the resurrection (Acts 20:7, 20:11; 1 Corinthians 16:2).

Angelic orders

After announcing he was "in the spirit," John explains what really got his attention that day: "[. . .] and I heard behind me a loud voice like a trumpet saying, 'Write in a book what you see and send it to the seven churches, to Ephesus, to Smyrna, to Pergamum, to Thyatira, to Sardis, to Philadelphia, and to Laodicea'" (Rev. 1:10b–11).

John gets a jolt! Like a trumpet, a heavenly voice blares out a commission: He needs to write down what he's about to see. The book must go to seven churches, all located in the Roman province of Asia.

Such a scenario seems surreal to most people in the modern world, but it wouldn't have seemed so to John. He would've viewed himself as being in a succession of prophets for whom divine revelation was a real possibility. The Bible shows that the God of Israel has a long track record of bursting into people's lives — whether they're ready or not — and commissioning them to serve as his ambassadors. Several such commissioning scenes occur in the Old Testament.

Just when John the Apostle's ministry seems to be over, owing to circumstances beyond his control, the Lord intervenes and commissions him for another assignment. And although John probably didn't realize it at the time, the book of Revelation turns out to be the culmination of God's self-revelation in Scripture; it concludes the *canon* (the inspired and authoritative collection of books making up the Bible). Not bad for a 90+-year-old man!

Seeing the First and the Last (1:12–18)

The second half of Revelation 1 falls into two sections: In verses 12–16, you discover what John saw when he turned around to look in the direction from which the voice came; in verses 17–20, you read about John's reaction to what he saw and his consequent commission by the risen Jesus.

These two moments contain the main outline of the book, and they structure the visions that follow in chapters 2–22. This first vision is like a table of contents. It also provides some essential information enabling readers to decode the symbols that occur in the visions of chapters 2–3. In short, John hands you a master key that unlocks the coded apocalyptic language.

Standing among seven menorahs

When John turns around in Revelation 1:12, the first things catching his eye are seven golden lampstands. These are not candlesticks, as the King James Version of the Bible has it, but seven-branched lampstands, called *menorahs* in later Jewish tradition, like those used in the Tabernacle and Temple (Exodus 37:17–24; 1 Kings 7:49). Each menorah consists of seven branches capped with a small bowl that contains olive oil for fuel. The center bowl is the reservoir for the other six, and a wick rests in each bowl, providing illumination when lit.

However, John's attention is quickly riveted to a much more imposing presence — a person.

The human-like figure — Son of God, Son of Man

Standing among the seven lampstands is "one like the Son of Man" (Rev.1:13). The description echoes Daniel's vision of a human-like figure arriving on the clouds of heaven and assuming dominion over an everlasting kingdom (Daniel 7:13–14); this "one like a human being" accepts worship and directly approaches the throne of God. But although he possesses the attributes and rights of God, he also appears very human.

Mystery surrounds this person because he remains unnamed in the book of Daniel. Some Jews in the first century identified this figure as the promised Messiah; you can see this, for example, in a work called the *Similitudes of Enoch,* which probably predates the writing of Revelation.

In Revelation, using descriptive language clearly evocative of Daniel, John identifies this mysterious person as Jesus. Similarly, in John's Gospel, Jesus calls himself the Son of Man: He tells an audience in Jerusalem, "For just as the Father has life in himself, so he has granted the Son also to have life in himself; and he has given him authority to execute judgment, because he is the Son of Man" (John 5:26–27). The title *Son of Man* becomes almost synonymous with *Son of God* in this context.

Understanding the Son's appearance

The Old Testament prophets Ezekiel, Daniel, Isaiah, and Zechariah provide important background material for Revelation. John frequently borrows and reworks ideas and themes from these books. Each feature of the wardrobe and appearance of the "one like the Son of Man" (see Rev. 1:13–16) calls for comment:

- ✔ **"Clothed with a long robe and with a golden sash across his chest":** High priests in the Jewish Tabernacle and Temple wear this item (Exodus 28:4; 29:5). As John has already stated (Rev. 1:5) and makes abundantly clear throughout the book, Jesus offers up his own blood as a sacrifice for sins. He is both priest and sacrifice.

- ✔ **"His head and his hair were white as white wool, white as snow":** The color white is often symbolic of purity and holiness. White hair and a white beard often represent wisdom and dignity. In Daniel 7:9, these characteristics describe the "Ancient of Days," or God. By applying this description to Jesus, John affirms that Jesus is part of the Godhead (which also includes God the Father and the Holy Spirit).

- ✔ **"His eyes were like a flame of fire":** This is a symbol of divine omniscience and judgment. Jesus knows the hearts and minds of all; his gaze penetrates into the deepest darkness. Human beings are an open book before this judge.

- ✔ **"His feet were like burnished bronze":** The high priests of ancient Israel served barefoot in the Tabernacle and Temple. Jesus's feet shine like highly polished bronze, contrasting with the soiled feet of mere human priests; this probably points to the divine and sinless character of Jesus (see Hebrews 7:26–28). The imagery may also imply strength.

- ✔ **"His voice was like the sound of many waters":** This feature emphasizes the sovereignty and power of Jesus. Like the waves crashing against the rocky cliffs of Patmos, Jesus's voice booms out across the universe.

- ✔ **"In his right hand he held seven stars":** John unpacks this symbol in 1:20, so we postpone comment until the section "Decoding the mystery."

- ✔ **"From his mouth came a sharp, two-edged sword":** This image makes a statement about the power and penetration of Jesus's words. The double-edged sword was well-known to John's audience as the *gladius*, a short sword only a couple feet in length and standard issue for Roman legionnaires. It was especially lethal in close, hand-to-hand fighting. Jesus's words, then, effectively accomplish his purposes (Isaiah 49:2, 55:11; Hebrews 4:12).

✔ **"His face was like the sun shining with full force":** John couldn't fail to recognize who this Son of Man was. He had seen him before. The synoptic Gospels (Matthew, Mark, and Luke) all narrate an extraordinary moment called the Transfiguration, when three disciples, including John, see the earthly Jesus begin to radiate with glory. It happens on an unnamed "high mountain" in Galilee (Matthew 17:1). For a brief moment, Peter, James, and John see the divine nature of Jesus of Nazareth unveiled:

> "And he was transfigured before them, and his face shone like the sun, and his clothes became dazzling white. Suddenly there appeared to them Moses and Elijah, talking with him. [. . .] Suddenly a bright cloud overshadowed them, and from the cloud a voice said, 'This is my Son, the Beloved; with him I am well pleased; listen to him!'" (Matthew 9:2–4, 7)

The similarities between the Transfiguration and what John now sees are stunning.

Meeting Jesus face to face

Have you ever met someone really famous whom you admired a great deal? Did you stutter a bit when trying to talk? Did your palms sweat? Did you feel mildly faint? Did your brain shut down, just a bit overwhelmed by the emotion of the event? Well, just imagine meeting the Man Upstairs face to face! The Bible records several instances of human encounters with God:

✔ Abraham, on the night the Lord makes a covenant with him (Genesis 15:12)

✔ Moses, when the glory of the Lord passes before him on Mount Sinai (Exodus 34:8)

✔ Joshua, before the captain of the Lord's army at Jericho (Joshua 5:14–15)

✔ Isaiah, when he sees "the King, the Lord of hosts" on his throne (Isaiah 6:5)

✔ Ezekiel, when he sees the mobile throne chariot of God (Ezekiel 1:28)

✔ The three Apostles Peter, James, and John on the mount of Transfiguration (Mark 9:6)

John's reaction to the presence of Jesus is typical of all who experience a personal *theophany,* or appearance of God: John falls before the feet of Jesus "as though dead" (Rev. 1:17).

Reassuring Jesus's servant

Jesus's reaction to John's collapse is reassuring. He places his right hand on him, probably his shoulder. The right hand in biblical thought is a symbol and sign of power. By placing his right hand on John, Jesus assures him of acceptance and favor.

The gesture is followed by verbal assurance: "Do not be afraid" (Rev. 1:17). Several times, when John the Apostle was a young man, he heard Jesus say these words. The last time was shortly before the crucifixion. Jesus had just informed his disciples that he was leaving them and returning to God the Father. In response to their anxiety, Jesus twice reassured and consoled them: "Do not let your hearts be troubled. Believe in God, believe also in me. [. . .] Do not let your hearts be troubled, and do not let them be afraid" (John 14:1, 14:27). And now in Revelation, John the Apostle, in his old age, once again hears these soothing words spoken by a familiar voice.

Seeing who holds the keys

After telling John not to be afraid, Jesus identifies himself as "the first and last, and the living one. I was dead, and see, I am alive forever and ever; and I have the keys of Death and Hades" (Rev. 1:17–18). The titles Jesus uses for himself are divine titles, the very things that define who God is: the self-existent one, the one who is the source of life itself.

The risen Jesus of the book of Revelation is Lord of life and death, his authority represented by holding the keys. This is really good news for believers because Jesus promises to raise up (resurrect) all who believe in him at the last day (John 5:24–29).

The message of Jesus's triumph over death is a theme that recurs again and again throughout the book of Revelation. Watch for it.

Charting the Course (1:19–20)

The brief section in Revelation 1:19–20 is valuable because it lays out the main sections of the book of Revelation. This occurs within a commissioning scene reminiscent of the Old Testament prophets (Isaiah 8:1; Jeremiah 30:2; 36:2; Ezekiel 43:11; Habakkuk 2:2). Jesus also gives John an interpretive key for understanding the next major section of the book (chapters 2–3). Read on.

Getting a commission to write

The one like the Son of Man tells John, "Now write what you have seen, what is, and what is to take place after this" (1:19). This sentence serves as a table of contents for the rest of the book of Revelation. Notice how it falls into the following three sections:

- ✔ **What you have seen:** This sums up the initiating vision of Jesus granted to John on the island of Patmos, now viewed as a past event (1:9–18).

- ✔ **What is:** The next two chapters consist of seven prophetic messages directed to seven house churches located in the Roman province of Asia (2:1–22).

- ✔ **What is to take place after this:** The *this* refers to what was actually happening in the seven house churches. Beginning at chapter 4, however, John describes his visions of what happens "after this." He is caught up to the heavenly throne room, where he sees Jesus enthroned at the right hand of God the Father. From the throne, Jesus directs the course of history to its grand finale. Everything unfolds in accordance with God's will, symbolized by a scroll of destiny. Revelation 4–19, therefore, by means of a series of visionary experiences, carries the action forward from John's day at the end of the first century until the triumphant return of Jesus at some unspecified time in the future (19:11–16).

Decoding the mystery of the stars

In Revelation 1:20, Jesus explains to John the mystery of the seven stars in his hand: They are "the angels of the seven churches." As for the seven lampstands, they represent the seven churches of Ephesus, Smyrna, Pergamum, Thyatira, Sardis, Philadelphia, and Laodicea, already mentioned in 1:11. The equation of the lampstands as churches seems fairly straightforward. The seven angels are most likely literal angelic beings in God's service on behalf of the churches (see more in Chapter 8).

Chapter 7

Reading the Seven Letters to Conflicted Churches (1:19–3:22)

. . . .

In This Chapter

▶ Appreciating the literary structure of these messages

▶ Interpreting the significance of the seven churches

▶ Unpacking the meaning of each message

. . . .

*G*etting mail has always been popular — even in the first century. In fact, one of the notable achievements of the Roman Empire was the establishment of safe roads over which imperial couriers delivered official letters. Because FedEx and UPS didn't exist yet, travelers and messengers hand-carried personal mail.

After John finished writing the book of Revelation, he sent it to seven churches in the Roman province of Asia, located in what's now western Turkey. As soon as they began reading, these churches would've immediately understood the unusual nature of their mail: It contained seven heavenly messages from Jesus himself, delivered through John.

Jesus addresses these congregations in a stern but compassionate manner. Much is expected of them, but much is promised for those who persevere. They're under enormous pressure to abandon their exclusive commitment to Jesus as Lord and to compromise his high moral standards. In many respects, these seven messages embody the primary purpose of the entire book: to exhort believers to be faithful till the end, even at the cost of their lives.

In this chapter, you explore the content of the seven letters in Revelation 2–3 and gain an increased awareness of the difficulties facing early Christians living in the Greco-Roman world. You also appreciate how each letter is specifically composed for the congregation it addresses, while at the same time addressing all the churches. Readers also get occasional glimpses into the historical background of the cities in which these house churches were located. Finally, you discover some of the foundational beliefs and behaviors of early Christians.

The Symmetry of the Messages

Peeking into Revelation 2–3, one question that immediately comes up is whether these individual messages are really letters. After all, they don't actually follow the typical letter format as seen in the Apostle Paul's New Testament letters and other letters of that era. The closest parallel seems to be prophetic letters and *oracles* (divine messages typically delivered to human beings through prophets), such as those in the Old Testament (2 Chronicles 21:12–15 and Jeremiah 29). In fact, Amos 1–2, with its seven stereotyped judgment oracles, provides the most striking comparison — underscoring the prophetic nature of the book of Revelation. As a result, the best label for these seven letters may be *messages*.

Before diving into the content of the messages, you need to be aware of their structure and pattern. Here's why the organization is significant:

- ✔ Most members of these house churches couldn't read — some authorities estimate that only about 15 percent of the members of a given congregation were capable of doing so. The arrangement of each message falls into a stereotyped pattern consisting of the same basic components, serving as a memory aid to listeners.

- ✔ Carefully structured messages reflect a characteristic of prophetic speech. This confirms John's claim that his work is "prophecy" (1:3).

- ✔ Structuring and patterning also occur regularly in the teaching of Jesus in the Gospels. A quick reading of the Sermon on the Mount displays this feature as well (Matthew 5–7).

In the following sections, we draw attention to this structure.

Surveying the structure of each letter

The basic structure of each message is as follows:

- ✔ **Charge to write:** "To the angel of the church in [. . .] write:"

- ✔ **Identification of sender:** "These are the words of [. . .]"

- ✔ **Commendation or condemnation:** "I know [. . .]"

- ✔ **Pastoral admonition:** "Remember [. . .], Do not fear [. . .], Repent [. . . and so on]"

- ✔ **Pastoral exhortation:** "Let everyone who has an ear listen [. . .]"

- ✔ **Promise:** "To everyone who conquers [. . .]"

Bridging the chapters

John didn't write the book of Revelation in chapter and verse — that organization came later. However, chapters 2 and 3 do have a unique structure, which sets them apart from chapter 1 and kind of provides a natural break. In Revelation 1:20, Jesus decodes the meaning of two primary symbols in chapters 2–3 and prepares the audience for the ideas that lie ahead: "As for the mystery of the seven stars that you saw in my right hand, and the seven golden lampstands:

✔ "[T]he seven stars are the angels of the seven churches,

✔ "[A]nd the seven lampstands are the seven churches."

Jesus, in the midst of the lampstands, sends a message loud and clear: He's present in the lives of believers, both individually and combined, and he's completely aware of what's happening on the ground.

The only deviation from this outline occurs with the last two items; in the last four messages, the positions of the exhortation and promise are reversed. However, the deviations probably aren't significant; they simply reflect the universal desire of authors for some artistic variation!

Yet despite the similar structure, each message is tailor-made for a given church. Here are three features of the messages that call for special comment:

✔ All the messages identify and describe Jesus as the sender, but their descriptions, though based on the initiating vision of Jesus (1:12–16 — see Chapter 6), vary for each individual church. For example, the message to the church at Smyrna identifies Jesus as "the first and the last, who was dead and came to life" (2:8). Given that the believers at Smyrna were about to undergo severe persecution (2:10), they especially needed a reminder of Jesus's power over death.

✔ The pastoral admonitions in the messages are directed at unique situations that exist in each church. Jesus offers encouragement and rebuke as needed.

✔ The promise to each individual church varies, but all the promises point to the same reality: everlasting life. In Smyrna, for example, Jesus promises that the "second death" will not harm them, which is highly appropriate for their circumstances (2:11).

 Although each message is tailor-made for a specific church, its audience isn't limited to that church. On the contrary, the messages are clearly intended for all seven churches because each letter concludes with a summons to hear what Jesus is saying to the churches in plural (2:7, 2:11, 2:17, 2:29, 3:6, 3:13, 3:22).

Considering the order of the messages

On top of each message's basic structure, readers can find an additional pattern that's based on the relative spiritual condition of each church:

- ✔ Churches 1 and 7 (Ephesus and Laodicea) are in grave peril.
- ✔ Churches 2 and 6 (Smyrna and Philadelphia) are the only ones not censured for some shortcoming.
- ✔ Churches 3, 4, and 5 (Pergamum, Thyatira, and Sardis) are okay but not great.

This pattern forms a *chiasm,* a literary device in which parallel ideas or lines of text conform to an half of an X-like pattern: A-B-C-B'-A':

A Ephesus (2:1–7)

  B Smyrna (2:8–11)

    C Pergamum (2:12–17)

    C Thyatira (2:18–29)

    C Sardis (3:1–6)

  B' Philadelphia (3:7–13)

A' Laodicea (3:14–22)

Ephesus and Laodicea are the A and A' elements, Smyrna and Philadelphia are the B and B', and Pergamum, Thyatira, and Sardis correspond to C. This pattern draws attention to the dire need for repentance at Ephesus and Laodicea.

Of course, a glance at a map (see Chapter 2) can clarify an important relationship among the cities: They're all linked by road to Ephesus, the leading city of the province. Perhaps, then, the order of the seven churches in Revelation follows the order of mail delivery in the first century!

Asking about the Audience

Audience is important. After all, when you have something to say, the details you reveal, the support you provide, and the language you use is likely to vary, depending on whether you're chatting with your boss, your great aunt, or the buddies you've known since the sandbox. So for Revelation, the question remains: Who is the audience, and are they real or symbolic? Here's what scholars say.

Angels: Postmen or guardians?

Here's one question you may ask yourself when you read these passages to the seven churches: Just who in the world are these angels that Jesus is referring to when he addresses each letter "to the angel of the church in *x*"?

You may not have seen any of those sorts of creatures hanging around your church. The question is complicated by the fact that the Greek word *angelos* (translated "angel") conveys the idea of a messenger or one sent, but it also has several nuances. Scholars have offered four main explanations. An angel may be

- **The deliverer of the message:** If this is John's meaning, perhaps he's referring to the person who actually delivered the letter — the postman, so to speak. However, the problem with this explanation is that the angel is the *recipient* of the message, not the deliverer. Furthermore, the word *angel* occurs 67 times in the book and, in every other instance outside chapters 2–3, it refers to an angelic being of some kind.

- **A pastor of the church:** A second explanation is that the *angelos* is the pastor of the church. The basic problem with this suggestion is that nowhere in the New Testament, or Christian literature outside the New Testament, does the word *angel* refer to a pastor, bishop, or any other human office-holder in the church.

- **The spiritual attitude of the church:** Some scholars tweak the translation by saying the angel typifies the "spirit" or "attitude" of the church in question.

- **A guardian angel:** The best explanation may be to take John at face value. But is this credible? Do churches have guardian angels? As strange as it may sound, that may just be what John intends. After all, in a few passages, the Bible does speak about angels who assume the role of guardians (Matthew 4:6, 4:11, 18:10, 26:53; Luke 15:10; Acts 5:19, 12:7–15, 27:23), and Paul alludes to angels concerned about proper decorum at Christian worship services (1 Corinthians 11:10).

In John's mind, like that of other New Testament writers, angels appear to be personal agents who watch over and protect the communities of the faithful. Because they're assigned to individual congregations, Jesus addresses them directly, even though they're spiritual representatives rather than visible participants in the life of the churches. This form of address strengthens Christian conviction that divine resources are indeed at their disposal.

The churches as eras of church history

Dispensationalists believe that the churches represent seven different eras of church history. For example, here's one possible scheme:

- Ephesus represents the first Christian century.

- Smyrna represents the era of persecution in the second and third centuries.

- Pergamum represents the age of Constantine, when Christianity became the religion of the Roman Empire.

- Thyatira is the Middle Ages.

- Sardis is the Protestant Reformation.

- Philadelphia is the period of the modern missionary movement.

- Laodicea represents the church of the End Times, which has abandoned its former beliefs and principles.

As intriguing as this may be, we think it oversimplifies church history, which is actually very rich and complex.

The seven churches: Real or symbolic?

Many people look at the structure and pattern of these messages and wonder whether they're messages to seven real churches or whether this is simply a literary device that John uses to address Christians in general. What's more, given the symbolic nature of the number seven (it represents perfection or completeness), many speculate that its usage is a clear tip-off that these letters aren't really addressed to seven actual churches.

Because each church is to read the messages sent to the other churches, the intended audience is at least greater than any one congregation. What's more, the province of Asia contained other churches besides the seven John selected (see, for example, Colossians 4:13). In a very real sense, then, these seven churches represent a much larger constituency.

Still, each message includes too many historical details *specific to that particular church* for a totally symbolic view to be persuasive. Our look at each church in the sections that follow underscores this point.

Good reasons exist for viewing the seven churches as actual churches of the first century, which are typical of churches throughout Christian church history. In short, they're both actual and representative. You can probably find a Smyrna, Philadelphia, and Laodicea, for example, just about any time or era you choose. In fact, you may even catch a glimpse of your own church in one of these snapshots!

Virtues and vices of life in the cities

The following table summarizes the moral and spiritual condition of the seven churches. This chart is selective and representative. It doesn't simply document the various strengths and weaknesses of each church. Rather, it highlights a particular vice and its corresponding virtue. The point is to draw attention to the virtues that, according to Revelation, should characterize Christian congregations at all times.

At Ephesus, for example, the vice is a spirit of contentiousness; what's needed is an infusion of love. The church at Smyrna needs to hear the admonition to exercise courage. It's not as though they had none; they'd been quite courageous to this point. But they did need a reminder not to let fear grip their hearts and thereby undermine their courage.

Church	Vice	Virtue
Ephesus	Contentiousness	Love
Smyrna	Fear	Courage
Pergamum (correct belief)	Doctrinal compromise	Orthodoxy
Thyatira (correct behavior)	Moral compromise	Orthopraxy
Sardis	Overconfidence	Vigilance
Philadelphia	Lack of strength	Endurance
Laodicea	Indifference	Zeal

Getting to Know the Seven Churches Up Close and Personal

A quick read of Revelation 2–3 reveals that all is not well among the house churches of Asia. Although you see a few indications of random violence directed at members of these churches, for the most part, the pressure is more subtle. More than a few Christians are succumbing and lapsing into their pre-Christian lifestyles and vices. It's worth noting what you don't read: nothing about state-sponsored persecution appears in these seven messages — yet. As you move into the central section of the book, however, a quite different scenario emerges. In other words, Jesus addresses these seven churches and challenges them to be faithful for a very good reason: The evil empire — Rome — is about to strike back!

Acts, Artemis, and the silver industry

The book of Acts indicates that Ephesus supported a thriving industry that specialized in making silver figurines of Artemis (the photo shows an image of this fertility goddess). Archeological work at Ephesus confirms the New Testament account. Undoubtedly, women who wanted to get pregnant wore some of these figurines around the neck as a lucky charm.

The Apostle Paul narrowly escaped disaster when disgruntled silversmiths, led by a man named Demetrius, sought to discredit and expel him from the city following his very successful evangelistic campaign. Apparently, because of Paul's preaching, many converts abandoned their devotion to Artemis, so much so that business fell off and the silversmiths found their livelihood threatened (Acts 19:23–27). This led to a huge riot staged in the great theater. Today, tourists can sit in this magnificent 24,000-capacity theater and look out across the remains of the Arcadian way, a colonnaded street leading, in Paul's day, from the theater to the commercial harbor on the shoreline.

Vanni / Art Resource, NY

The second and third centuries are historical periods that saw considerable persecution and martyrdom of Christians who refused to participate in the state religion. This involved venerating the gods of Rome and even some of the deceased Roman emperors, such as Augustus. Christian refusal was considered treason against the empire — a crime deserving capital punishment in the view of most Roman citizens. The book of Revelation, written at the end of the first century, is almost a dress rehearsal for what's coming. Keep this in mind as you read the rest of the story in the later chapters of Revelation.

So what was it like to live as a Christian at the end of the first Christian century in the Roman province of Asia? To help you enter imaginatively into their world, we first provide a brief snapshot of each city in which these believers lived and then reconstruct, as best we can, what the spiritual condition was in the house churches located within them. Bear in mind that early Christians met for worship in private homes.

Probably several houses hosted worship services in each city. Romans 16, for example, mentions "the church in their house" (Romans 16:5) and "the saints who are with them" (Romans 16:15).

Ephesus: Down on love (2:1–7)

Though not the capital, Ephesus was nonetheless the largest and most important city in the province. It even boasted the title *supreme metropolis of Asia*. In fact, the Asian proconsul (Roman official who served as the governor of a province) resided in Ephesus and maintained government offices there.

Ephesus, the city

Ephesus was a splendid Greco-Roman city boasting a population of at least a quarter million. Its geographic location was ideal, beautifully nestled between two mountains close to the Aegean Sea's shoreline. The city was adorned with public and commercial buildings, fountains, gymnasiums, bath houses, stadiums, theaters, and especially, temples. Ephesus was also a commercial powerhouse and transportation hub. If all roads led to Rome, Ephesus was a major intersection on the way.

Besides its location where the Cayster River empties into the Aegean Sea, Ephesus is positioned at the western end of a great road linking western Asia to the Anatolian interior and the Near East (*Anatolia* is the Asian part of modern-day Turkey). Roman milestones on this ancient road calculate the distance using Ephesus as the point of origin. The city is also on a north-south road following the coastline of Asia Minor by way of Smyrna and Pergamum, all the way to Troas (the area around the city of Troy) and the Dardenelles (a strategically important strait). The products of the rich Anatolian lands flowed to the harbor and roads of Ephesus and from there to the larger Mediterranean world.

The crown jewel of Ephesus was the Temple of Artemis, one of the seven wonders of the ancient world. This magnificent structure measured 420 feet long by 240 feet wide, supporting a roof 60 feet high that was upheld by 117 imposing columns. Within the temple, open to the sky, stood a huge statue of Artemis (Diana is the Roman equivalent). Originally the Greek goddess of wild nature, she morphed into a fertility goddess at Ephesus.

The church at Ephesus

Based on what Jesus says to the church of Ephesus (Rev. 2:1–7), their spiritual fervor doesn't match the grandeur of their city.

Revelation notes that believers are doing some things right. Jesus commends them for their hard work and especially their vigilance against false Apostles. Ephesus was a hotbed of false teaching even in the early days following Paul's founding of the church. Paul, in fact, worried and warned about this problem while on his way to Jerusalem during his third missionary journey. He requested the Ephesian elders to come down to the beach and meet with him before he sailed on to the east. In a memorable scene, he predicts future trouble: "I know that after I have gone, savage wolves will come in among you, not sparing the flock. Some even from your own group will come distorting the truth in order to entice the disciples to follow them. Therefore be alert [. . .]" (Acts 20:29–31). Paul was right in his warning. Five years or so later, when Paul writes to his young assistant Timothy who is ministering in Ephesus, a major concern is dealing with false teachers who are upsetting the faith of many (1 Timothy 1:3–11, 4:1–9, 6:3–10).

In Revelation, although Jesus commends the church for examining and rejecting the false teachers, he points to a cancer in their midst: Perhaps as an outgrowth of their zeal to defend the truth, an unloving attitude permeates the Ephesian church. Jesus says, "You have abandoned the love you had at first" (Rev. 2:4). The people have failed to remember the exhortation of their founding father, the Apostle Paul: "But speaking the truth in love, we must grow up in every way into him who is the head, into Christ" (Ephesians 4:15).

According to the Bible, their lack of love is inconsistent with the truth of Christianity and is deadly. After all, John says, "Whoever does not love abides in death" (1 John 3:14). Jesus, however, knows what the solution is: Love must first be directed to him because he's the source of all love. Genuine love for God always overflows as love for others (Philippians 1:9; 1 Thessalonians 3:12). The remedy is immediate repentance. For those who choose to repent, Jesus offers glorious promise — permission to enter paradise.

Smyrna: Faithful under fire (2:8–11)

Smyrna lies 40 miles to the north of Ephesus, just south of where the Hermus River empties into the Aegean Sea. Possessing a well-protected harbor, the city of Smyrna also sits at the western end of a trade route joining the major inland route across Anatolia to the east. Apollonius of Tyana, writing at about the same time as John, describes Smyrna as "the most beautiful of all cities under the sun."

Nixing the Nicolaitans

Jesus commends the Ephesians for hating the works of the Nicolaitans. But who in the world are they? Here's the short answer: We don't know for sure. Mentioned again by name in the message to the church of Pergamum (2:15), they're likely the evildoers and false Apostles referred to in Revelation 2:2. But even this doesn't explain much.

Irenaeus, an early church father of the second century, claims they go back to Nicolaus, a former *proselyte* (gentile convert to Judaism) and deacon in the Jerusalem church (Acts 6:5). Actually, Irenaeus says Nicolaus himself had

taught that one must rigorously hit and strike the body in order to suppress evil desires. Some of his followers, however, radically altered this and held that what one did in the body made no difference whatsoever because the body had no influence on the spirit. This generally led to what believers viewed as an immoral and even lewd lifestyle. Irenaeus's theory may be correct, but there's not enough evidence to come to any certain conclusions. What we can say with some confidence is that the Nicolaitans urged certain compromises with the prevailing culture, a stance that John roundly condemns.

Smyrna, the city

A disaster defined the city of Smyrna. In 600 BCE, Alyattes, king of Lydia (a powerful state in Western Asia), destroyed Smyrna. After the city lay in ruins for centuries, Lysimachus, one of Alexander the Great's generals and successors, resurrected the city in 290 BCE. Once again, Smyrna, with its choice location, became a thriving Greek city with all the trappings. Today, the modern city of Izmir, one of the largest cities in Turkey (3.5 million), stands on the same site. The description of Jesus in Revelation 2:8 as the one "who was dead and came to life" may subtly allude to Smyrna's remarkable return to life.

Of more consequence for early Christians, Smyrna loyally supported Rome in her struggles to gain control of the Mediterranean Sea. In fact, the Smyrneans supplied significant naval support for the emerging Roman Empire. As a consequence, when Smyrna petitioned Rome for the honor of building a temple to the emperor Augustus and his mother in 23 CE, the city received the privilege over 11 other candidates. And even though the Roman Senate never officially deified Tiberius Caesar, the Smyrneans built a temple in his honor. The construction and official support of these temples reveal a city with a culture that took great pride in the imperial cult and zealously insisted on its support from the citizenry. This allegiance to the state presented a major problem for Christians.

The church at Smyrna

Jesus commends but doesn't censor the church in Smyrna. The people are bravely hanging on despite severe affliction and persecution around them. He says sympathetically to the Smyrnean Christians, "I know your affliction and your poverty [. . .]" (Rev. 2:9). But in spite of this, ironically, Jesus calls them rich! Perhaps this echoes Jesus's beatitude: "Blessed are you who are poor, for yours is the kingdom of God" (Luke 6:20). Belonging to the kingdom of God rather than the kingdom of Caesar carries with it riches the world knows nothing about (1 Corinthians 3:21–23; Ephesians 1:7–22).

Imagine how difficult it must have been for the believers in Smyrna to withstand the constant pressure to participate in the *imperial cult* (veneration of the gods of Rome and the deified Roman emperors). Charges of treason and lack of patriotism would be constant issues for them.

Given that religious, civic, and political life were so intertwined in the Greco-Roman world, we wonder how many Christians were expelled from their guild and treated as outcasts and untouchables. If, for example, your guild adopted the emperor as its patron deity, you'd be expected to participate in the sacrifices and suppers held in honor of the divine Caesar. Not to participate would be interpreted as lack of loyalty and friendship. And the same would be true if your guild invoked some of the other Greek/Roman gods and goddesses (of which there were many!) as patron deities. Already in the 50's, the issue of eating meat sacrificed to idols was a major concern of Christian house churches (1 Corinthians 8–10). Ironically, one of the early slanders widely circulated about Christians accused them of being "haters of all mankind."

The Latin phrase for a religion that Rome recognized was *religio licita*. To be unsanctioned was *religio illicita*. During Paul's missionary journeys, he got out of several scrapes because Roman officials viewed early Christianity as one of the sects or parties of Judaism, a *religio licita* (see Acts 18:12–17). However, because of increasing tensions between Jews and the early Christian church, Christianity was downgraded to *religio illicita*.

Jesus forewarns the Smyrneans: Hunker down because you're about to undergo imprisonment. The duration he mentions, "ten days" (Rev. 2:10), probably means a relatively short period of time. No biblical or extra-biblical sources mention this imprisonment, but there's no reason to doubt its reality. As you read this passage, remember the time frame is at the end of the first century (likely 90–95 CE). It won't be long before large numbers of believers experience imprisonment, enslavement, torture, and death because of their refusal to participate in the imperial cult.

Pergamum: Compromising convictions (2:12–17)

Pergamum, 70 miles north of Smyrna, is an impressive city perched high atop a hill overlooking the Caicus River plain and the Bay of Lesbos in the distance. Pergamum, like Smyrna, sided with Rome against the surrounding

Greek city-states in the struggle to dominate the region. For this, the empire amply rewarded Pergamum. In 133 BCE, when Attalus III bequeathed his kingdom to Rome, the city functioned as the official capital of the province of Asia. Today, the city of Bergama in Turkey preserves the ancient name.

Pergamum, the city

Pergamum, a bustling city of some 180,000 inhabitants in John's day, reached its zenith under Eumenes II (197–159 BCE). He transformed the city into an architectural and cultural center. Among its many showpieces was a library of 200,000 scrolls rivaling that of Alexandria, Egypt.

The English word *parchment* comes from a blend of two Latin words: *Parthica (pellis)* ("Parthian [leather]") and *pergam_na* ("parchment"). The latter comes from the Greek word *pergam_n_*, from *Pergam_nos* — that is, "of Pergamum." People used this skin or leather as a substitute for papyrus.

One of the significant architectural monuments of Pergamum was the great altar to Zeus (see Figure 7-1), standing some 40 feet high and crowning the rocky summit of the *acropolis* (a high, fortified part of the city). This altar celebrated the victorious defense of Pergamum against the invading Gauls. Perhaps the comment "where Satan's throne is" (Rev. 2:13) refers to this temple.

Figure 7-1: A reconstruction of the Temple of Zeus.

(c) Wolfgang Kaehler/CORBIS

Many other temples punctuated the city, the most notable dedicated to Dionysius, Athena, Demeter, and Orpheus. However, because of Pergamum's loyalty to Rome, pride of place went to the imperial cult. As early as 29 BCE, citizens of Pergamum venerated the genius of Rome and its emperor by burning incense before a statue of the divine Caesar. This, too, is a good candidate for "Satan's throne."

A thousand feet below, at the bottom of the acropolis, lay a complex dedicated to Asclepius, the god of healing. The Asclepium, or health spa, achieved a far flung reputation as early as 350 BCE. Thousands of people, suffering from a spectrum of disorders, descended on the Asclepium in hopes of a cure. Remarkably, the complex featured individual rooms with the soothing sound of gently flowing water piped into each. Although superstition abounded, the concern and care of the attendants was a point of pride that the patients greatly appreciated.

Today, visitors can view the plaster casts of various body parts that pilgrims left in the sanctuary of Asclepius as testimonials to their healing. Physicians there administered a rather surprising array of medicinal treatments with apparent success. Worth noting in this regard is the fact that Galen, one of the founders of modern medicine, received his medical training at the Asclepium of Pergamum.

The church at Pergamum

In Revelation, Jesus begins by commending the church at Pergamum for their faithful endurance: "Yet you are holding fast to my name, and you did not deny your faith in me [. . .]" (2:13). Clearly, these believers are under intense pressure to participate in the various temple rituals, especially emperor worship, because this was such a point of pride for the city. According to Jesus's message, a believer named Antipas, about whom little is known, lost his life for refusing to participate. He may have even been executed at the temple of Zeus or the temple dedicated to imperial Rome ("where Satan lives").

However, not everything is peachy in Pergamum. Some professing Christians aren't prepared to make the supreme sacrifice that Antipas did. They ask questions like, "Can't we all just get along? If we don't believe it, why not just go through the motions and burn the incense?" Jesus calls this response "the teaching of Balaam" (Rev. 2:14).

So who's Balaam? In Numbers 22–25, Balaam, a greedy false prophet, counsels Balak, the king of Moab, to derail Israel on her march to the Promised Land — by sexually enticing the Israelites to participate in idolatrous rituals, anticipating that God will punish Israel as a result! Balaam nearly succeeds in his diabolical scheme. Some 24,000 Israelites perish in a divine visitation (Numbers 25:9; 1 Corinthians 10:8). Jesus warns the Christians at Pergamum of a similar fate: "Repent then. If not, I will come to you soon and make war against them with the sword of my mouth" (Rev. 2:16).

From Jesus's perspective, participation in idol sacrifices and the imperial cult amount to spiritual prostitution. Either Jesus is Lord or Caesar is Lord — it's a zero-sum game. Furthermore, orgies often accompanied pagan sacrifice, so physical prostitution was never far removed from spiritual prostitution.

The Balaamites probably believed that what's done in the body doesn't affect the spirit (the view of the Nicolaitans — see the "Nixing the Nicolaitans" sidebar). So in their view, illicit sex was a non-issue, a personal decision of no consequence. Some believers in Pergamum were tempted to agree. To those wavering, Jesus issues a stern warning.

However, Jesus promises those in Pergamum who hold fast to their Christian faith many things in Revelation 2:17:

- ✔ **Hidden manna:** This mysterious substance sustained the Israelites throughout their wilderness wanderings after Moses led them out of slavery in Egypt (Exodus 16). It's a symbol of eternal life in Judaism and probably functions in the same way here.

- ✔ **White stone:** In the Greco-Roman world, stones of various kinds served as tickets and admission passes. Here, the white stone admits the holder to paradise — far better than even the Olympics!

- ✔ **A new name:** In the Old Testament, the giving of a name or the changing of one's name carries great significance (Genesis 17:5, 17:15, 32:27–30; Isaiah 56:2, 62:2). In this passage, the new name indicates a completely transformed nature. The fact that no one else knows it suggests that each believer has a unique destiny in eternity.

One final note about this message: The description of Jesus holding "the sharp two-edged sword" (2:12) may allude to the famous Roman short sword that often functioned as a symbol of capital punishment. The fact that Jesus, not Caesar, holds the sword speaks volumes about who really holds the power of life and death.

Thyatira: Dirty dancing with Jezebel (2:18–29)

Thyatira lay on the south bank of the Lycus River in a broad and fertile valley running north and south and connecting the Caicus and Hermus valleys. Today, the Turkish city Akhisar occupies the ancient site.

Thyatira, the city

Thyatira was founded by Seleucus I, one of Alexander the Great's successors. Because of its location guarding the eastern approaches to the great coastal cities like Smyrna and Pergamum, Thyatira was a frontier outpost. Lacking a great *acropolis* (high, fortified part of the city) like Pergamum, Thyatira depended on the determination of its citizens to defend itself against all aggressors. Appropriately, early coins from Thyatira depict the patron deity astride a horse wielding a great battle-axe. Perhaps Jesus's commendation of the church for its "patient endurance" (Rev. 2:19) is an instance where church and city are mirror images of each other.

Perhaps the most significant feature of Thyatira was its large number of trade guilds (akin to modern day trade unions) including woolworkers, linen workers, garment makers, leather workers, tanners, potters, bakers, slave-dealers, and bronze-smiths. Each guild often adopted one of the popular idols as its patron deity to bring luck and bless the business.

Christians in Thyatira would've encountered grave difficulties because of the integral connection between the various guilds and their patron deities. Inscriptional evidence (that is, formal inscriptions on statues, public buildings, tombs, and so forth) indicates that the guardian deity of Thyatira was the god *Tyrimnos,* identified with the sun-god Apollo. No doubt the trade guilds invoked this deity.

The church at Thyatira

Interestingly, the letter to Thyatira is the longest of the seven, and yet in many ways, the city itself was the least well-known and important of the seven.

The start of the letter designates Jesus as "the Son of God" (Rev. 2:18), which is significant because it's the only time the book of Revelation uses that title. It's probably not a coincidence that Tyrimnos (Apollo) and the emperor were both acclaimed as "sons of Zeus." By the reference to Jesus as the Son of God, the Thyatiran believers are reminded that there's only one Son of God, and he's Jesus, not Caesar. What's more, it may be more than mere coincidence that Jesus is also described as having feet "like burnished bronze," especially in a town known for its bronze-working guild. Clearly, the Jesus of Revelation trumps all wannabe gods and goddesses.

According to the message of Jesus, the believers at Thyatira are doing some things right, and they receive high praise for four works:

- ✔ **Love:** This crowning virtue heads the list.

- ✔ **Faith:** Faith, another one of the three Christian virtues (the third is *hope* — see 1 Corinthians 13:13), is also alive and well at Thyatira.

- ✔ **Service:** If the first two items are virtues, the next two are the practical outworking of these virtues. The term *service* can also be rendered as *ministry.*

- ✔ **Patient endurance:** Surviving in the midst of suffering and hard times is a prerequisite for belonging to a house church in Asia Minor. For the most part, this small congregation is withstanding the pressure and receives a passing grade.

On the other hand, Jesus has a beef with their compromises. A formidable female prophetess advocates accommodation with idolatrous rituals, a problem that also bedevils Ephesus and Pergamum. Their challenge is to survive as Christians in a hostile environment in which false religion and economics seem to be intimately intertwined.

Jesus refers to the false prophetess as "Jezebel," likely a reference to the notorious queen of King Ahab in the Old Testament. The original Jezebel promoted the sexually immoral cult of Baal and Asherah and persecuted the true prophets of God (1 Kings 18–19; 2 Kings 9). Thyatira's Jezebel is more subtle — claiming to have received direct insight from God that allows her to encourage Christians to compromise by participating in sexually immoral idol worship. In Revelation, Jesus knows better and describes her insights as "the deep things of Satan" (2:24). In short, she seems to claim that Christians can dance with the devil, so to speak, and not get hurt.

Jesus's warning to the churches of Thyatira is direct and unambiguous: Repent or else! Jezebel and her cohorts will get what they deserve. In place of a bed of sensual pleasure, they'll get a bed of affliction and death.

At the end of the message, Jesus promises the churches two things:

- **Authority to rule:** Victorious believers will share in Jesus's rule over the world to come. However, believers may not coast into the kingdom; they have to be steadfast to the very end.

- **The morning star:** Jesus promises to give his faithful the "morning star." We aren't going to blow smoke here — we don't know for sure what this means! The morning star, the planet Venus, probably refers figuratively to Jesus (see Revelation 22:16 and 2 Peter 1:19). But the precise background is unknown. Perhaps Revelation is reapplying Numbers 24:17 ("a star shall come out of Jacob, and a scepter shall rise out of Israel"), a passage rabbis interpret as a reference to the Messiah.

Because of widespread fascination over this "star's" appearance just before sunrise, Venus serves as a fitting metaphor — the messianic herald of a new world that's coming. Taken together, the two images of authority and morning star may be making the same point: Conquerors — meaning believers who endure to the end — have a vital share and role in the new world.

Sardis: Sleepwalkers in the city (3:1–6)

Located at the junction of routes into the interior of Turkey (30 miles to the south of Thyatira and about 50 miles east of Smyrna), Sardis was an important transportation and commercial hub. Though Sardis was once one of the most prosperous cities in the region, today the ancient site lies abandoned, about 5 miles west of the modern city of Salihi, Turkey.

Hold onto your helmet! Seizing Sardis

Under King Croesus, Sardis ruled over all other Asian cities. But then Cyrus the Great, the king of Persia, began his series of conquests and turned his eyes to the west and wealthy Sardis. Cyrus's army made valiant attempts to storm the citadel but with no success. Just when it seemed Cyrus had to accept defeat and withdraw, one of his soldiers, Hyroeades, spotted a Lydian soldier who had dropped his helmet down the slopes of the precipice and clambered down to retrieve it. Hyroeades watched carefully and marked the place where the Lydian soldier climbed back to the citadel. It was unguarded because it was thought to be so steep no guard was necessary. That proved to be the undoing of Sardis. Cyrus's soldiers were able to force entry and seize the citadel.

The Greek historian Herodotus recounts the siege and capture of Sardis and its aftermath in his book *The Histories* (1.78–93). Surrounding this account, however, Herodotus spins tales about Croesus's rise to power and the splendor of his kingdom (1.25–78). Like a mirror image, Herodotus then narrates Cyrus's rise to power and glory (1.94–141). These two Titans were destined to collide.

Why didn't Croesus prevail? Herodotus attributes his defeat to misplaced confidence in the impregnability of the citadel of Sardis. Perhaps some of this well-known history of Sardis lies behind the message to the church at Sardis: the failure to be vigilant.

Sardis, the city

Sardis had a near legendary past. Once the capital of the kingdom of Lydia, it became a center of fabulous wealth. Its last great king, Croesus (560–546 BCE), was so rich he became a byword: "as rich as Croesus!" Gold and silver coinage was first minted at Sardis, a fitting achievement in a truly golden age.

Sardis was geographically blessed with a grand acropolis: The stronghold of Sardis stood perched atop a steep ridge 1,500 feet above the plain, seemingly impregnable to all assaults. The key word is *seemingly*. The great citadel of Sardis fell to the Persians in 546 BCE.

After Alexander the Great's conquests, Sardis fell under the control of various Hellenistic regimes (*Hellenism* refers to the Greek culture that dominated the Mediterranean basin from the time of Alexander the Great [334 BCE] until well into the late Roman age). Believe it or not, during this era, the citadel of Sardis was seized again and under similar circumstances. In 218 BCE, Antiochus III captured the fortress because no guard was posted above the steep slopes!

The Hellenistic era ended when Attalus III bequeathed Pergamum to Rome in 133 CE. Sardis became an administrative center in the Roman province of Asia. But never again did the city regain the prominence it once held. In fact, in a competition to build a second temple to Rome's imperial cult in 26 CE, Sardis vainly vied for the honor based on its storied past. At this point, the city seems to have had a reputation but no real clout.

The remains of Sardis are impressive. At the foot of the acropolis of Sardis stands a great temple dedicated to Artemis, in imitation of the one at Ephesus. Archaeologists have also uncovered a gymnasium complex featuring a marble court area.

A strong Jewish community inhabited Sardis. Modern visitors to the site marvel at the remains of a beautiful synagogue — about the length of a football field — dating to the third or fourth century. Because Sardis was host to a thriving Jewish community from Hellenistic times, the city doubtless had a fine synagogue in John's day as well.

The church at Sardis

In a sense, the church at Sardis is spiritually sleepwalking — dead on their feet while appearing to be awake — and they're headed for disaster! In his message, Jesus summons these believers from their spiritual slumber: "Wake up!" (3:2). There's still hope! The citadel hasn't fallen yet, and they can still stave off the enemy: "Strengthen what remains and is on the point of death." How? Three commands, barked out like military orders, point the way: Remember, obey, and repent. The book of Revelation leaves no doubt about what they're supposed to remember and obey: the word of God and the testimony of Jesus (1:2, 1:9, 6:9, 12:17, 19:10, 20:4).

The consequences of failure to respond immediately mirror the history of the city. Like previous successful assaults on the citadel of Sardis, Jesus will come "like a thief, and you will not know at what hour I will come to you" (3:3). In short, the local church at Sardis will cease to exist.

But all is not lost. A vigilant minority of people "have not soiled their clothes" (3:4). This vivid metaphor probably refers to compromise with the non-Christian environment. To them, Jesus holds out two glowing promises:

- ✔ **White robes:** Worshipers in temples, whether gentile or Jewish, were required to appear in clean clothes, typically in white linen. Christians are promised that they, too, will worship in the "new Jerusalem" and be dressed in white, a symbol of righteousness and moral purity.

- ✔ **A place in the book of life:** The notion of a registry of the redeemed also occurs in the Old Testament (Exodus 32:32; Psalm 69:28; Daniel 12:1). Jesus promises the conquerors of Sardis — the believers who stick it out — that their names will not be removed from the registry of the new Jerusalem. On the contrary, Jesus himself will announce their names in the presence of God and his angels.

Philadelphia: Holding on 'til the end (3:7–13)

Philadelphia is best known today for the Liberty Bell, Rocky Balboa, and a great cheesesteak sandwich. But another Philadelphia, in the ancient world, resided on the Hermus River Valley at about 30 miles to the southeast of Sardis. Because it was situated at the junction of five roads leading to Mysia, Lydia, and Phrygia, it gained the title "gateway to the East." Besides being a frontier city, linking the interior of Anatolia (Asian Turkey) with the coastal cities (Smyrna was about 100 miles due west), Philadelphia was near an important vine-growing district, and it hosted textile and leather industries. The modern city of Alasehir lies near the same site.

Philadelphia, the city

Philadelphia, the "city of brotherly love," was so-named because of the affection Attalus II Philadelphus (159–138 BCE), the city's founder, felt for his elder brother Eumenes II, the noted king of Pergamum. Before becoming king himself, Attalus II served as a loyal general for Eumenes. In about 140 BCE, Attalus founded Philadelphia in honor of his brother, making it the youngest of the seven cities.

Attalus placed great hopes on this city. He viewed it as a launching point from which Hellenism (Greek culture) might be spread into the barbarian interior of Anatolia. This was partially successful: The Lydian language finally ceased to be spoken by 19 CE, but Phrygian culture itself quite outlived Hellenism.

Greeks and Romans typically viewed other peoples and tribes as substandard and primitive. They used the Latin word *barbarus* and the Greek word *barbaros* for such non-Latin and non-Greek speaking peoples. The Apostle Paul uses the Greek term for non-Greek speakers in Romans 1:14 and Colossians 3:11 but without snobbish, elitist overtones.

The hopes for the city received a jolting setback in 17 CE, when a devastating earthquake leveled the city. Philadelphia, lying close to a major geological fault line, seems to have suffered the brunt of the quake, and successive tremors furthered the damage. According to ancient historians, the danger of collapsing buildings and walls so terrified the populace that most citizens lived outside the city in temporary shelters during these harrowing times. But owing to generous imperial funding made possible by Tiberius Caesar (Luke 3:1), the city made a comeback. Unfortunately, tremors rocked the area for years afterward, making life somewhat chaotic. In spite of this, the city persevered, and in John's day it was relatively prosperous, a testament to their steadfastness.

A major temple in Philadelphia was dedicated to Dionysius, god of merry-making and wine — not surprising in light of the reputation of the surrounding area for high-quality grapes. No archaeological evidence indicates the presence of the imperial cult in Philadelphia during the first century, though such evidence from the beginning of the third century exists. On the other hand, we'd be quite surprised if there were no presence whatsoever of the imperial cult and the widespread trade guilds in John's day.

The church at Philadelphia

Philadelphia, like Smyrna, receives no condemnation or stern warning. What's striking is Jesus's frank acknowledgment of their tough circumstances and his exhortation to hold on at all costs. Like the city in which they lived, the Philadelphian Christians were remaining steadfast in the midst of suffering and hard times. The threat to the church lay not inside its walls but outside of them. In particular, the Jewish community apparently made life difficult.

Jesus identifies himself as the one "who has the key of David, who opens and no one will shut, who shuts and no one opens" (Rev. 3:7). The description probably refers to a passage in Isaiah 22:15–22, in which Shebna, head steward during the reign of king Hezekiah of Judah (716–686 BCE), is replaced by Eliakim. A *head steward* controls the keys giving access to the palace and its rooms. (Palace reliefs from Assyria depict officials having a large wooden key attached to a shoulder.) The point is this: Jesus, like Eliakim, now has the authority to admit or disbar individuals from his kingdom.

The relevance for the church at Philadelphia probably lies in a painful dispute between church and synagogue. Which community is the true Israel, and is Jesus of Nazareth the true Messiah? The Jewish leaders of John's day denied Christian claims and may have even excommunicated (officially excluded) Jewish Christians from the synagogue (see John 7:13, 9:22). For Jewish Christians, this was a bitter blow, cutting them off from their cultural heritage. But Jesus reassures them: "I [like Eliakim] have set before you an open door, which no one is able to shut" (3:7). They're indeed members of the true Israel, and the Jewish community at Philadelphia, like Shebna, will one day acknowledge this transfer of status and authority (3:9).

The message of Jesus in Revelation 3:9 is harsh, so handle with care. It refers to the Jewish synagogue as "a synagogue of Satan" and even denies their claim to be Jews (see also 2:9). Read this passage in the context of a debate among members of the same group. After all, Christianity is a daughter of Judaism. During Jesus's earthly ministry, especially in John's Gospel, Jesus and the religious leadership frequently clash. They challenge his authority; he condemns their unbelief. Because they reject his message and are abusive toward him, he says, "You are from your father the devil" (John 8:43). The Jewish leadership in Philadelphia reacts in a similar way and thus receives his censure. But it's quite another thing for modern Christians to take up this harsh rhetoric and apply it the Jewish people, as was done in the Middle Ages and continues to be done by *anti-Semites* (those who are hostile toward Jews). Christians are taught to leave the matter of people's spiritual status and destiny to Jesus as they bear witness to the gospel. Jesus was not rebuking Jews because of their Jewishness but because of their refusal to accept him and his message.

Jesus offers another promise to this beleaguered congregation: "I will keep you from the hour of trial that is coming on the whole world to test the inhabitants of the earth" (Rev. 3:10). This probably refers to the so-called Great Tribulation of the End Times. (See Chapter 8 for a discussion of the relationship of the rapture to the Tribulation.)

Conquerors may claim two promises from Jesus:

- **Pillars in the Temple of God:** How fitting for believers who live in an earthquake-prone city whose pillars may collapse at any moment! This metaphor speaks of stability and strength. It also speaks poignantly to those cut off from the heritage of the Jewish Temple that once stood in Jerusalem. (It had been destroyed in 70 CE.) They're now members in good standing of the grander and greater Temple of the Lord (Ephesians 2:19–22).

- **New names:** As in Pergamum and Sardis (see the earlier sections on these cities), the notion of receiving a new name plays a prominent role at Philadelphia. But in Revelation 3:12, it's not just one new name; it's three:

  - **Name of God:** Is this the sacred name *Yahweh?* Perhaps. At any rate, the new name emphasizes that believers are part of the family of God. They bear his name as sons and daughters.

  - **Name of the new Jerusalem:** Twice in its checkered history, Philadelphia adopted a new name. More relevant for the church, however, is possession of the name of the new Jerusalem, certifying citizenship in the celestial city.

  - **New name of the Lamb:** Whatever this name is, believers share a new status with the Lamb. He is, after all, "the firstborn within a large family" (Romans 8:29).

Each of the promises point to a new reality: Believers are all in the family, so to speak.

Laodicea: Don't drink the water! (3:14–22)

Laodicea is located in the eastern end of the Lycus Valley, a tributary of the Maeander River. It lies about 40 miles to the southeast of Philadelphia and 100 miles due east of Ephesus on the coast. Antiochus II (261–246 BCE) founded the Hellenistic city in honor of his wife Laodik. The ancient site is near the village of Eskihisar and the large, modern city of Denizli, Turkey (population 800,000).

Laodicea, the city

Located on a plateau 100 feet above the river, Laodicea reached a pinnacle of prosperity during the Roman age. Like Thyatira, Sardis, and Philadelphia, Laodicea lay along the trade routes into the interior of Anatolia and onwards to Syria. It was, accordingly, a military outpost and commercial center. Among the city's assets was a high-quality black wool raised and carded in the region. The city was proud of its medical school and of a locally produced ointment ("Phrygian powder") reputed to cure eye ailments.

Laodicea was also a well-known banking center, with a number of wealthy citizens. The famous Cicero even cashed large bank drafts at Laodicea. Reflecting this wealth, the city minted its own coins and, following an earthquake in 60 CE, rebuilt itself, largely through private donations.

There were, of course, temples dedicated to various gods and goddesses, as witnessed by inscriptions on their coins. The most important deity in the region was Men Karou, a god connected with healing and whose temple lay 13 miles to the west of the city. Within the city itself were temples to Zeus and Augustus, and nearby was a large marketplace where commodities were bought and sold.

Large-scale excavations began in the year 2000, so much of the ancient city of Laodicea remains to be discovered. Nevertheless, the ruins of two theaters, a *nymphaeum* (a Roman building featuring running water, fountains, flower gardens, and statues), an *odeum* (a small public building for music and poetry performances), a gymnasium, a stadium (380 yards long!), and other public buildings are clearly visible to visitors. Of special interest is a triple arch gateway dedicated to none other than the emperor Domitian.

Laodicea did have a downside: The water was lousy. Unlike Colossae, 10 miles to the east, where copious amounts of cool, refreshing water were readily available, Laodicea had to pipe water in from several miles away. By the time the water coursed its way through stone pipes to Laodicea, it was tepid. To make matters worse, it was full of foul-tasting mineral deposits.

The church at Laodiciea

No other church is rebuked as severely — and no other church reflects more clearly the city in which they live — than the Christians of Laodicea.

The spiritual condition of this church is as unpalatable as the water its citizens have to drink. More than a few sermons and commentaries miss the point here. Jesus is not saying that being spiritually lukewarm is worse than being spiritually cold. He's saying the Laodicean Christians are of *no spiritual benefit whatsoever.* Unlike the cool, refreshing water of Colossae or the hot, therapeutic, mineral waters of Hierapolis, 6 miles to the north, the "spiritual water" of Laodicea is worthless and nauseous. The NRSV translation, "I am about to spit you out of my mouth," is too tame (3:16). In reality, the idea Jesus conveys here is, "You're gonna make me puke!"

In addition, Jesus calls them "wretched, pitiable, poor, blind, and naked." What irony! Here's a city proud of its self-reliance, hard-earned wealth, world-famous medical school and ointment, and luxurious clothing. The church reflects a similar complacency. In short, they're oblivious to their spiritual need and completely lacking in zeal.

The remedy for Laodicea is heartfelt and immediate repentance. This is symbolically portrayed in terms of going to the marketplace and making three purchases. All three items speak of salvation through Jesus:

- **Gold refined by fire:** What an appropriate metaphor for a city priding itself on its gold reserves! Pure gold speaks of genuine faith (1 Peter 1:7).

- **White robes:** In place of the chic, black, wool garments, they need white robes, a symbol of the righteousness of Jesus freely granted to repentant sinners.

- **Eye salve:** Once again, you can't miss the irony. These believers are spiritually blind, so Phrygian powder won't help a bit. Turning to Jesus in faith, however, restores spiritual sight to the blind (Luke 4:18).

In one of the most memorable metaphors in the entire book, Jesus stands outside the door of the Laodicean house church and knocks (Rev. 3:20). In other words, he puts the ball in their court: They can either open the door and allow him in or refuse him entrance. The problem at Laodicea is serious: Spiritual indifference threatens their spiritual life. Fling open the door, Jesus urges! Admit him and celebrate his supper (a reference to the Lord's Supper or Communion [Matthew 26; Mark 14; Luke 22] and the End Times marriage supper of the Lamb [Rev. 19:6–9]). In short, they desperately need genuine conversion.

The promise to the conquerors — there were *some* genuine believers at Laodicea ("I reprove and discipline those whom I love" [Rev. 3:19]) — is similar to that of Thyatira (see the earlier section on Thyatira). Conquerors sit on Jesus's throne and share in his reign (3:21). You may be glad to hear that Laodicea did continue to be a center for Christian witness for some time afterward, hosting a famous church council in 363 CE.

Chapter 8

Peeking into the Throne Room (4:1–5:14)

In This Chapter

▶ Surrounding the throne of God

▶ Scanning a sealed scroll: The mysterious book of destiny

▶ Revealing a supreme paradox: The Lion (of Judah) is a Lamb!

*O*ne of the coolest things about the starship Enterprise in *Star Trek* — and there were a lot of cool things — was the capability of "beaming up" or "beaming down." So if Captain Kirk was on the surface of some exotic planet or asteroid and the Enterprise was hovering in the vicinity, he simply issued the famous order, "Beam me up, Scotty," and presto! He dematerialized and vanished. The next thing you knew, he materialized back on the flight deck of the Enterprise. Now that's cool.

"Beaming up" isn't a new idea. In the first two centuries BCE and the first two centuries CE, a number of Jewish writings, designated as *apocalyptic* (because they claim to reveal hidden secrets about the universe and the future), appeared in the Middle East. These writings typically feature an ascent into the heavenly realms by a noteworthy figure from Jewish history and tradition. These visionary ascents end in a visit to the throne room of God himself.

In this chapter, you discover that Revelation 4–5 has striking similarities to these apocalyptic accounts of visionary ascents. But more importantly, as you peek into God's throne room, you dive into the meaning of John's vision and discern how it answers a nagging question for Christians: Who's in charge of all that happens on planet earth? Chapters 4 and 5 of Revelation have an emphatic answer: a book of destiny contains God's unchangeable will for all creation.

Trying to describe God: It ain't easy!

The Bible consistently shies away from describing God in visual terms. Judaism prohibits any images to represent the deity. This edict goes all the way back to the days of Moses, when God tells the Israelites, "You shall not make for yourself an idol, whether in the form of anything that is in heaven above or that is on the earth beneath or that is in the waters under the earth" (Exodus 20:4).

In the Old Testament, whenever God appears to human beings, a brilliant light or fire indicates his presence, but his person is never actually described (Genesis 15:17; Exodus 3:2, 14:24, 19:18; 1 Kings 18:38). Sometimes an angel of God appears in bodily form and speaks on behalf of God (Joshua 5:13–15). Other times, God seems to make himself known to people; Moses and a group of leaders, for example, are said to "see" God in Exodus 24: 9–10. But once again, the text doesn't actually describe him; rather, it tells what's visible "under his feet" — namely, a translucent sapphire-colored pavement. The book of Numbers describes Moses's frequent face-to-face conversations with the Lord (Numbers 12:8). But yet again, Numbers never describes exactly what that form entails. When Isaiah is commissioned to be a prophet, he "sees" the Lord seated on a throne (Isaiah 6:1–3). However, the prophet chooses to focus on the flowing robe and the seraphim who surround the throne, not the actual appearance of God.

Okay, so the Old Testament does dare to describe God using visual imagery a few times.

But the language in these cases is always metaphorical. In the book of Daniel, God is called "the Ancient of Days," and his clothing is "white as snow; the hair of his head [. . .] white like wool" (Daniel 7:9). In a vision of the mobile throne chariot, Ezekiel describes the glory of God as a "figure like that of a man." He also depicts this figure from the waist up as being "glowing metal," and from the waist down, "he looked like fire" (Ezekiel 1:26–27). Significantly, these Isaiah, Daniel, and Ezekiel passages provide the background imagery for John's vision of the exalted Jesus in the throne room in Revelation 4:2–6 (as well as Rev. 1:2–16, 20:11).

The New Testament is consistent with the Old Testament prohibition against representing God the Father in bodily form (John 1:18; 1 Timothy 6:16). However, because Jesus is the Son of God in the flesh (John 1:14; Romans 1:3; Colossians 1:19, 2:9; 1 John 1:1–2, 4:2), the New Testament writings break with their Jewish heritage by affirming that the glory of God is actually seen "in the face of Christ" (2 Corinthians 4:6; John 14:9). It's worth noting, however, that nowhere do the Gospels or other New Testament writings actually give a physical description of Jesus. Perhaps this striking absence underscores an important New Testament concept, which is highlighted in the book of Revelation: Jesus, though born an ethnic Jew (Galatians 4:4), is the redeemer of people "from every nation, from all tribes and peoples and languages" (Rev. 7:9; see also John 3:16).

Focusing on the "Someone" on the Throne (4:1–11)

As Revelation 4 begins, John tells of his ascent into heaven through a heavenly portal: "After this I looked, and there in heaven a door stood open! And the first voice, which I had heard speaking to me like a trumpet, said, 'Come up here, and I will show you what must take place after this.'"

This scene marks a turning point in Revelation. From chapter 4 through chapter 21— which chronicles the grand finale of history — John's perspective alternates between heaven and earth. He experiences a series of visions in which he witnesses various scenes, some taking place in heaven, others happening on earth. All these visions relate in some way to the final triumph of the kingdom of God.

In this section, we follow John on a guided tour of the throne room. He first describes, in highly symbolic language, the one seated on the throne. Then, starting from the outside and working inward, he depicts three different classes of beings who circle the throne.

Seeing who takes the seat

Just after John is transported through the door to heaven, his focus fixes on a throne: "At once I was in the spirit, and there in heaven stood a throne, with one seated on the throne! And the one seated there looks like jasper and carnelian, and around the throne is a rainbow that looks like an emerald" (Rev. 4:2). By the time John completes his tour of the throne room (Rev. 5:13), it's clear that everything in the universe revolves around this magnificent throne.

A throne signifies rule, authority, and power. In theological terms, John's vision of the throne is all about the sovereignty of God. This is the central theme that he emphasizes over and over again in the book of Revelation.

Reflecting his Jewish background, John resorts to traditional images and metaphors to describe the presence of God on his throne. Precious gemstones, a rainbow, thunder and lightning, and a crystal sea all serve to depict God's presence *but not his person*. The invisible God "shows himself" by means of a dazzling light show while his heavenly entourage surrounds him in worship.

Debating when believers go up, up, and away

Okay, this may seem like an odd place to bring this up, but some commentators do attempt to link John's visionary ascent into heaven with what's referred to as the rapture. The *rapture* is the event when all believers (as defined by the Bible) who are living on the earth are taken up into heaven. If you're familiar with the popular *Left Behind* series of books, then you're familiar with the idea.

Linking John's ascent to heaven with the rapture sparks fierce debate. The question is this: *Does* John's ascent correspond to the "rapture of the church"? That is, does John here represent the view that all true believers will be caught up to be with Jesus just before the End Time judgments begin?

The *Tribulation* is usually identified as Daniel's 70th week (Daniel 9:20–27 — see Chapter 3), and it consists of the judgments depicted in Revelation 6–18 under the symbols of seven seals, seven trumpets, and seven bowls (see Chapters 9, 10, and 12 for details). Some people believe the rapture will happen before or after the Tribulation period is complete. Others believe that the rapture will take place during the period of Tribulation. Here, we offer brief summaries of the key arguments for each view.

Making the great escape: The pre-trib rapture

The *pre-tribulation* (pre-trib) teaching, widespread in evangelical circles, holds that before the Great Tribulation, Jesus will remove his people from the earth, sparing them from the judgments that fall on an unbelieving world. It's labeled the *pre-tribulation* view because Jesus returns for the church *prior* to the last seven-year period of earth history. Arguments in favor of this view include the following:

- Pre-trib adherents believe that God wouldn't inflict such suffering and misery on his chosen people. Proponents appeal to texts such as 1 Thessalonians 5:9 for support: "For God did not appoint us to suffer wrath but to receive salvation through our Lord Jesus Christ." This argument generally carries the most weight in pre-trib circles.

- The account of John's rapture (Rev. 4:1–2) immediately follows the messages to the seven churches (Rev. 2–3). Each message was addressed to the angel (or messenger) of that particular church. The angels seem to function as representatives of each church. This may suggest that John himself functions as a representative figure for the entire church in 4:1.

- The word for *church* (*ekkl_sia* in Greek) drops out of the text after Revelation 3:22 and doesn't reappear until the very end of the book at 22:16. Thus, the church isn't explicitly mentioned during the Tribulation (chapters 6–18). Pre-tribulationists believe this silence suggests that the church is raptured before the Tribulation.

- Because Jesus told his disciples his coming would be "like a thief" (Luke 12:39) and "no one knows the day nor the hour," (Matthew 24:36), the rapture supposedly can't follow any known or prophesied event. This leads to what is sometimes called the *any moment* rapture view. The imminence of the rapture rules out any preliminary signs. Therefore, the rapture must take place before the predicted seals, trumpets, and bowls occur. Consequently, John's being caught up to heaven in Revelation 4:1 most likely represents the rapture of the church because it can't be dated and it precedes the judgments that follow. This interpretation preserves the pre-trib insistence on the imminence of the rapture.

Several bestselling authors have promoted the pre-tribulation position over the years. In 1970, Hal Lindsey published a blockbuster book, *The Late Great Planet Earth*, incorporating the pre-trib rapture scheme. More recently (1995), Tim LaHaye (with Jerry Jenkins) burst on the scene with his immensely popular *Left Behind* series.

Staying till the end: The post-trib rapture

Those who hold to the *post-tribulation* (post-trib) view argue that Jesus won't return and the church won't be raptured until after the Tribulation. They offer the following arguments in support:

- ✔ Post-tribulationists agree that God won't inflict his wrath on members of the church. But that's different from saying he'll protect believers from the wrath of the Antichrist. The bowl judgments are all directed at the Antichrist and his followers. Just like the Hebrews in Egypt were protected from some of the plagues (Exodus 8:20–12:30), so God protects his people from the bowl judgments of the End Times. The exhortation to be faithful unto death in the face of the persecution by the Antichrist is directed to the first Christian readers (Rev. 13:9–13). This sounds hollow if in fact no Christians actually experience such a persecution.

- ✔ John's ascent closely resembles Jewish and Christian accounts of other ascents to heaven. In all these other cases, the individual doesn't represent a collective entity, so adherents say the same is true with John's ascent.

- ✔ Although the word for *church* doesn't appear in Revelation 4:1–22:15, post-tribulationists declare that this doesn't mean the church is gone during this period. Clearly, some individuals put their trust in Jesus throughout the period of the Tribulation (Rev. 7:14–17). To call them "Tribulation saints" without acknowledging that they, too, are part of the church seems arbitrary.

- ✔ The imminence of Jesus's coming hardly rules out precursors. Although Jesus specified that one can't know the *day* or *hour,* that's not the same thing as *month* or *year.* Paul seems to indicate that at least two things must first occur before the rapture; namely, a great *apostasy* (a falling away from faith and trust in Jesus) and the appearance of Antichrist (2 Thessalonians 2:1–12). An event that's imminent or impending may quite properly have precursors and yet not be precisely datable.

Clearing out at halftime: The mid-trib rapture

Those who hold to a *mid-tribulation* (mid-trib) view believe the rapture occurs approximately 3.5 years into the seven-year Tribulation, usually identified with Daniel's 70th week (Daniel 9:20–27). As a compromise position, this view incorporates arguments from both the pre-tribulation and post-tribulation views. Distinctive arguments are as follows:

Heaven according to Enoch

An example of a visionary ascent features the patriarch Enoch who, according to the Bible, lived prior to the great flood of Noah. "Enoch walked with God; then he was no more, because God took him away" (Genesis 5:24). Enoch was the perfect candidate for a supposed ascent to the throne room — after all, the Bible implies he was "translated" to heaven.

An anonymous Jewish writer, some two centuries before Jesus, composed *The Book of the Watchers,* which narrates the celestial travels of Enoch. This book, now part of a larger composite work called *1 Enoch,* goes into considerable detail describing the throne room and its surroundings (1 Enoch 14:8–19:3). There are striking parallels to Revelation 4–5.

✔ The last trumpet of 1 Corinthians 15:52 and 1 Thessalonians 4:16 is identified with the seventh trumpet of Revelation 11:15–18. The seventh trumpet in Revelation occurs just after the halfway point of the final seven years. This is based on Revelation 11:3, in which 42 months and 1,260 days equal 3.5 years.

✔ The two witnesses of Revelation 11, who are martyred in the middle of the Tribulation, may symbolize the church and thus mark the moment of the rapture of the church.

✔ According to mid-tribulationists, the seven seals and trumpets of Revelation 6–8 are not judgments; rather, they're the "beginning of the birth pangs" that Jesus refers to in the Olivet Discourse (Matthew 24:8 — see Chapter 3 for more on the Olivet Discourse).

✔ God's wrath doesn't begin until Revelation 11:18, when mid-tribulationists believe the church will be in heaven.

Minority positions on the rapture question

Some tweak the mid-tribulationist view and espouse a *pre-wrath rapture,* occurring just before the bowl judgments of Revelation 15–16 are poured out on the Antichrist and unbelievers.

Others maintain a *partial-tribulationist view,* which agrees with the pre-tribulationist position in regard to timing but differs in one important qualification: Only believers who are walking in fellowship with Jesus are raptured before the Tribulation. Disobedient believers will be "left behind" with unbelievers and not resurrected or transformed until Jesus's Second Coming proper, the so-called "revelation of Christ" at the end of the Tribulation. These last two options are definitely minority positions.

Concluding with a word of advice

Attempting a definitive position on the timing of the rapture is probably much ado about nothing. The book of Revelation begins and ends with a prophecy and a promise that Jesus will return (Rev. 1:7, 22:20), and the church's creeds (statements of belief) proclaim the fact that Jesus will return but don't attempt to set the time of his coming. Debating the precise time shouldn't be an occasion for contention or suspicion. Perhaps a *pan*-tribulation view is best — everything will pan out in the end!

Circling the throne

As Revelation 4 unfolds, John describes the heavenly court that circles the throne (the three distinct groups are in italics):

> "Around the throne are twenty-four thrones, and seated on the thrones are *twenty-four elders,* dressed in white robes, with golden crowns on their heads. Coming from the thrones are flashes of lightning, and rumblings and peals of thunder, and in front of the throne burn seven flaming torches, which are the *seven spirits of God:* and in front of the throne there is something like a sea of glass, like crystal. Around the throne, and on each side of the throne, are *four living creatures,* full of eyes in front and behind." (Rev. 4:4–6)

Thus, John's description of the heavenly court consists of three circles:

✔ Twenty-four elders sit in the outer perimeter, each sitting on his own throne.

✔ A second circle, inside the elders, consists of seven blazing lamps, which John identifies as the "seven spirits of God."

✔ Within this circle lay one last quartet surrounding the throne.

In this section, we explore the occupants of these circles.

The 24 elders

John describes the 24 elders as wearing an interesting combination of priestly and kingly threads — white garments and golden crowns. But who exactly are these 24 elders? On this point, there's considerable disagreement. The most popular theories say that the 24 elders are

✔ Glorified humans who represent the entire people of God, composed of both Jews and gentiles

✔ Glorified humans who represent only the New Testament church

✔ The 24 star-gods of the ancient Babylonian pantheon (a temple of the gods)

✔ Angels patterned after the 24 priestly orders of the Old Testament (1 Chronicles 24:6–19)

✔ Angels who symbolize the 12 tribes of Israel and the 12 Apostles

---

Reflections of heaven

The notion that an earthly sanctuary is a replica of a heavenly one goes back into ancient Near Eastern thought. For example, in a creation epic called *Enumah Elish* dating to the second millennium BCE, the sanctuary of the chief Babylonian god Marduk is patterned after a heavenly prototype.

Closer in time to the book of Revelation are the Dead Sea Scrolls. Among these more than 900 separate manuscripts are the *Songs of the Sabbath Sacrifice*. They refer to a heavenly Temple with elaborate rituals and liturgies carried out by angelic priests. The Qumran community (who maintained the Dead Sea Scrolls) apparently believed their liturgical services mirrored that of the angelic worship above — hence the necessity of doing everything "decently and in order." The Apostle Paul may reflect a similar view in his letter to the Corinthians concerning orderly worship (1 Corinthians 11:10).

The glorified-humans perspective is popular in many evangelical circles. But many scholars argue that the immediate context rules out the idea that the elders are glorified humans because the elders later speak of human beings in the third person (emphasis ours): "You have made *them* to be a kingdom and priests serving our God, and *they* will reign on earth" (Rev. 5:10). This seems to show a clear distinction between the elders and human beings.

The theory that John is referring to Babylonian mythology is even more unlikely. Biblical writers occasionally adapt ancient mythological ideas — indeed, several instances occur in the book of Revelation itself. But the writers use these references only when they're fully consistent with the basic theological foundation of Scripture. What's more, it's quite unlikely that John would feel a need to describe the heavenly throne room in terms of a pagan myth, given his extensive knowledge of the Hebrew Scriptures.

The idea that the 24 elders represent angels receives strong support from a large number of scholars. In Jewish tradition, the Tabernacle was patterned after a heavenly sanctuary in which angelic beings worshiped God. There are many examples of this in the Old Testament, including Exodus 25:9, 25:40, 26:30; Isaiah 6:1–5; and Ezekiel 40–48. This perspective is thus consistent with Scripture by holding that the 24 elders represent heavenly choirs singing praises to God in his heavenly sanctuary.

The seven spirits

John describes the seven spirits as "seven flaming torches" (Rev. 4:5). Exactly who or what they are is highly debated. The Bible often associates fire and dazzling light with God's presence. As a result, these beings almost certainly represent God himself or creatures that serve in the immediate presence of God. Many scholars aren't satisfied with this vague conclusion and thus aim for a more precise definition of the seven spirits. Here are three opinions:

Flights of fancy and the four living creatures

The description of the four living creatures has spawned several far-fetched interpretations over the years. For example, Irenaeus, bishop of Lyons (130–200 CE), thought each creature was one of the four Gospels in the New Testament. Some modern interpreters still see this as a possible interpretation. For example, one widely used commentary suggests the following identification:

✔ **The lion is the Gospel of John.** A lion is a kingly figure, and Matthew presents Jesus as the King of the Jews.

✔ **The ox is the Gospel of Luke.** An ox is a humble, servant figure, and Mark portrays Jesus as the servant of the Lord.

✔ **The man is the Gospel of Matthew.** The man matches Luke's depiction of the humanity of Jesus, the Son of Man.

✔ **The flying eagle is the Gospel of Mark.** The eagle describes John's soaring portrait of the divine Son of God.

From our perspective, John would've been quite surprised by these highly creative interpretations! The four living creatures are part of a standard, Jewish, apocalyptic worldview that John shares and which derives from Daniel and Ezekiel. In neither of these biblical books is there the slightest suggestion that the creatures represent anything other than angelic beings.

✔ Some scholars detect a symbolic significance in the number seven — the number of completeness and perfection — and prefer to identify them as the sevenfold activity of the Holy Spirit as enumerated in Isaiah 11:2.

✔ Others are content simply to identify them as an angelic order like the seraphim and cherubim.

✔ A final group considers the seven spirits to be the seven archangels mentioned in Jewish apocalyptic traditions.

Viewing the seven spirits as archangels parallels the Jewish apocalyptic book *1 Enoch* 20:1–7 (see the "Heaven according to Enoch" sidebar), which lists the archangels' names as follows: Michael, Gabriel, Suru'el (or Uriel or Phanuel), Raphael, Raguel, Saraqa'el, and Remiel (in some manuscripts). These seven angelic beings are explicitly said to stand in the presence of God (*1 Enoch* 9:1, 40:9), which is the same function the seven spirits perform in Revelation 8:2. You can find some other interesting parallels as well. For instance, the Apostle Paul refers to an archangel without giving a name in connection with the rapture of the church in 1 Thessalonians 4:16. Even more significantly, two of the archangels in Enoch are also mentioned in the Bible: Gabriel (Daniel 8:16, 9:21; Luke 1:19, 1:26) and Michael (Daniel 10:13, 10:21, 12:1; Jude 9; and Rev. 12:7).

The four living creatures

The group of four living creatures is closest to the throne. Here is John's description of them:

> "Around the throne, and on each side of the throne, are four living creatures, full of eyes in front and behind: the first living creature like a lion, the second living creature like an ox, the third living creature with a face like a human face, and the fourth living creature like a flying eagle. And the four living creatures, each of them with six wings, are full of eyes all around and inside. Day and night without ceasing they sing, 'Holy, holy, holy, the Lord God, the Almighty, who was and is and is to come.'" (Rev. 4:6–8)

This description seems drawn from two Old Testament prophets: Ezekiel's vision of the mobile throne chariot (Ezekiel 1 and 10) and the seraphim in the book of Isaiah (Isaiah 6:2–3) who constantly worship "the Lord God Almighty." Because Ezekiel 10 explicitly calls the living creatures *cherubim,* this name seems the most likely identification in Revelation 4 as well.

An ode to the one on the throne

As Revelation 4 concludes, the elders sing a hymn to the "someone" on the throne:

> "The twenty-four elders fall before the one who is seated on the throne and worship the one who lives forever and ever; they cast their crowns before the throne, singing: 'You are worthy, our Lord and God, to receive glory and honor and power, for you created all things, and by your will they existed and were created.'" (Rev. 4:10–11)

The praise song in Revelation 4 underscores the central theme of the vision of the throne room vision — namely, the sovereignty of God. In this passage, John says that all creation owes its existence to God and all created beings are obliged to praise him for his glory, honor, and power.

John's original audience — the Christians of Asia Minor — may actually have sung this hymn of Revelation 4:11 in their worship services. A number of modern scholars have drawn attention to liturgical elements (prescribed forms of public worship) incorporated into the book of Revelation.

In the end, the message of Revelation 4 is clear: Believers need not fear what Caesar or any worldly empire may do to them. God is on his throne, and all will be right with the world when all is said and done.

Singing Praise to the Lamb with Scroll-Opening Skills (5:1–14)

As chapter 5 opens, John's attention turns to a sealed scroll in God's right hand, a scroll of immense importance: "Then I saw in the right hand of the one seated on the throne a scroll written on the inside and on the back, sealed with seven seals" (Rev. 5:1). In this section, we describe John's vision of the heavenly scroll and a heavenly person who is qualified to open the scroll. The angelic choirs sing his virtues and achievements.

Examining a mysterious scroll

What kind of document is the mysterious scroll in Revelation 5:1? In the first century, books were in scroll format, not *codex* (a manuscript in book form). Codex, a Christian innovation, did not become dominant until the second century. In this section, we examine this scroll.

Where there's a will, there's a way to open it

Because a scroll, made of papyrus, parchment, or vellum (calfskin), is rolled up when not in use, you have to unroll it to read its contents. This scroll in Revelation is not an ordinary document because it has seven seals along the outside edge (Figure 8-1 shows a sealed scroll). This suggests a very important, probably legal, document (see Jeremiah 32:9–15). A last will and testament fits this description. Such a document would be sealed by the testator (the one who makes the will) and verified by witnesses. Only after the death of the testator would the seals be broken and the scroll unrolled.

Figure 8-1: A papyrus scroll with three seals.

If the scroll is a last will and testament, this throws light on a major purpose of the book of Revelation. A will is a legal document declaring how an individual wishes his or her estate to be distributed after death. To be valid, it must possess two kinds of information:

- ✔ A list of the heirs
- ✔ A description of the estate

Lord of all he surveys: God's cosmic surveillance

At one point in *Return of the Jedi*, episode six of the Star Wars trilogy, the Galactic Emperor, in his Death Star battle station, sits in the control room, surrounded by a battery of video monitors. He views what's going on in various locations of the galaxy. On one monitor, he sees Han Solo and Princess Leia trying to gain access to the shield generator protecting the Death Star. Everything, it seems, is under his surveillance.

The Bible teaches that on an infinitely greater scale, the one on the throne in Revelation is immediately and continuously aware of all that happens in his universe. Psalm 139 celebrates this all-knowing, all-present, all-powerful God who cares deeply for his children. Unlike the evil emperor, God has good intentions and purposes to save his people from sin. The believers in Asia Minor may rest assured: Their heavenly Father is aware of everything happening in their lives.

According to Revelation, exactly that kind of information is eventually revealed. In Revelation 3:5, those who overcome at Sardis (one of the seven churches — see Chapter 7) are promised their names will not be blotted out of "the book of life." John mentions a book of life in Revelation 20:12, at the Last Judgment of the great white throne. This seems to be the scroll listing all the heirs, those who believe in Jesus. Then, immediately afterward, comes an extensive section describing the new earth and the new Jerusalem (Rev. 21:1–22:6) — the real estate and possessions bequeathed to the heirs. All this fits quite nicely the notion that the sealed scroll is a will.

There is, of course, a distinctive twist. In this case, the one who made the will — Jesus, the Son of God — did in fact die; but he also came back to life and now bequeaths his vast estate to those who believe in him. They become joint heirs (Romans 8:17; 1 Corinthians 3:22–23).

Reading the book of destiny

Some things aren't neatly accounted for, suggesting that the scroll is more than a will. After the scroll is opened (Rev. 8:1), you discover that the scroll also includes divine judgments that are poured out on unbelievers before the heirs enter into their inheritance (Rev 8:2–18:24).

In addition to being a will, the scroll is a book of destiny. According to the Bible, what's recorded there must come to pass. This idea of a predetermined course of history is completely in character with apocalyptic thought. The sovereign God is not sitting on his throne, nervously wringing his hands and wondering what on earth is going to happen next. Rather, he's calmly surveying an unfolding story whose every twist and turn is within his knowledge and control. The scroll serves to remind first-century readers of a fundamental Christian conviction: God is the controller of everything that happens.

Double-siding the scroll

The scroll has writing on both sides of the parchment. Ordinarily, one would write only on the side with the fibers running horizontally — the recto side — because the ink goes on more smoothly. This would be the inside of the scroll. The outside or opposite side — the verso — has the fibers running vertically. This means that as you write across the page, the pen must cross minute ridges of the vertically aligned fibers. The writing may not always be as legible on the verso side, with occasional smudges or blots in the ink.

Still, if you needed more space, you could use the verso because parchment was a rare commodity. The significance of this little detail is considerable: The scroll contains so much information that both sides of the parchment must be used (a similar idea occurs in Ezekiel 2:10). The list of the heirs is a long one — many names are "written down in heaven." Revelation 7 confirms this idea as the multitude of the redeemed is so large that "no one could count" its number (Rev. 7:9).

Handling a crisis in the throne room

At this moment, a crisis occurs in John's vision (Rev. 5:2–4). An angel issues a challenge: "Who is worthy to break the seals and open the scroll?" To John's dismay and grief, no one steps forward, nor does he volunteer.

In a visionary trance, the seer's senses are heightened; he or she sees, hears, touches, and tastes more sharply. Emotions are intense. John weeps and sobs openly. Clearly, the scroll must be opened if its contents are to become real. This is the book of destiny containing the course of redemptive history and its completion. If no one opens and reads the scroll, the kingdom of God won't come in all its fullness. No wonder John weeps.

But not to fear! A worthy candidate is waiting in the wings. With a curt command to cease crying, the angel announces the lineage of the worthy one (Rev. 5:5). He is none other than the great Lion of Judah (Genesis 49:9; Numbers 24:17) and the Root of David (Isaiah 4:2, 11:1). These dynastic titles, which refer to the royal house of David, are deeply rooted in Old Testament history. After the collapse of David's dynasty in 586 BCE, they were reinterpreted as references to the promised *Messiah* — who would overthrow Israel's enemies and regather the Jewish people in their ancestral homeland (Jeremiah 23:5, 33:15; Zechariah 3:8, 6:12). By the first century CE, many Jews maintained a hope for one of David's descendants who would rescue and redeem them from oppression. Jesus, as one of those descendents, is sometimes referred to as the *Son of David*.

Varying messianic expectations coexisted within first-century Judaism. Among them was the hope of a Messiah from the house of David. A Jewish writing dating to the mid-first century BCE already gives expression to this hope (*Psalms of Solomon* 17:21–46). Similar sentiments appear in Jewish apocalyptic texts (4 Ezra 11–12; *Testament of Judah* 24:1–5; *Testament of Dan* 5:10–13; and *Florilegium* 1:10–13, 18–19). The New Testament Gospels also witness to this belief among the Jewish people of Palestine in the first century CE (Matthew 2:1–6, 17:10–12, 22:41–45).

Not your ordinary lamb

What John sees next is stunning, and we have to admit, a little weird: "Then I saw between the throne and the four living creatures and among the elders a Lamb standing as if it had been slaughtered, having seven horns and seven eyes, which are the seven spirits of God sent out into all the earth" (Rev. 5:6). Because apocalyptic literature uses metaphors and imagery as symbols, you're correct to assume there's a lot more to this lamb than meets the eye — or *eyes.*

This lamb has been "slain," graphically indicated by its slit throat, the mandated way to slaughter an animal according to Jewish tradition. But this lamb is still very much alive! Miraculously, the lamb survived death and now reigns alongside the One on the throne.

Slain for sins

The background of the slain-lamb image lies in the Old Testament sacrificial system. In ancient Israel, Jews ate meat only after first offering it up in sacrifice to the God of Israel. In other words, the eating of meat (from the herd or flock — that is, a bull, male sheep, or goat) always took place in a ritual/worship context. The worshiper brought a sacrificial animal that was blemish free, the best he possessed. After laying hands on the head of the animal, symbolizing a transfer of guilt, he slaughtered it.

The long-established method of killing the animal was by slitting the carotid artery of the neck, the most painless and humane way to do it. The blood was poured out at the base of the altar (blood wasn't eaten because it served as the cleansing agent whereby the guilt and stain of sin was removed and thus rendered anyone who touched or ingested it "unclean").

The book of Leviticus contains a handbook for priests on how to sacrifice animals and which animals were appropriate for the various occasions and offenses (Leviticus 1–16). If one sinned, the sacrificial ritual, accompanied by genuine repentance, restored the sinner to fellowship with God.

The New Testament is saturated with sacrificial imagery in its depiction of what Jesus did on the cross. By his death, says the Bible, he atones for the sins of the world (1 John 2:2) and reconciles sinners to God (2 Corinthians 5:16–21). Like the Old Testament sacrificial animals and the Passover Lamb, Jesus is without moral blemish. By shedding his blood, he effectively removes the contagion of sin and averts God's righteous wrath against sinners.

Protecting the Israelites

Central to Israel's life and worship was the feast of Passover, celebrating Israel's liberation from slavery in Egypt. The tenth plague, the death of the firstborn, came upon all Egyptians who didn't recognize the God of Israel. The Israelites gained protection from the destroying angel by slaughtering a lamb and daubing its blood on the doorframes of their homes (Exodus 11–13). The plague "passed over" the Israelite homes. By means of the blood of a lamb, without blemish and a year-old male, the people of Israel were saved. The family members then roasted and ate the lamb.

This ancient festival, the longest, continually observed religious festival known to history, provides part of the New Testament imagery that explains what Jesus did for humanity by dying on a cross (John 1:29).

The Lord's Supper (Communion or the Eucharist) reenacts Jesus's death on the cross and powerfully reinforces what Jesus did to save his people. As Christians eat the bread and drink the wine, as in the ancient Passover meal, they celebrate their deliverance from the power of sin and death (Romans 3:21–26). And how can Christians be sure Jesus's death really accomplishes what the New Testament says it does? Because they're convinced that Jesus is alive and well at the right hand of the Father! Jan van Eck's painting (Figure 8-2) from the altarpiece at the Cathedral of Saint Bavon visually depicts the living, slain Lamb in glory.

Figure 8-2:
Jan van Eyck's altarpiece, *Adoration of the Lamb,* in Ghent, Belgium.

Master of the universe

In Revelation, the Lamb stands in the center of the throne. Silence hangs over the throne room. The moment of truth has arrived. The Lamb takes the seven-sealed scroll from the right hand of the one seated on the throne (Rev. 5:7). How does a lamb pick up a scroll? Honestly, we don't know, but perhaps he takes it in his mouth. However he does it, the angelic singers immediately prostrate themselves and erupt in a hymn of praise to the Lamb (5:8–10).

Why is there so much rejoicing by the *heavenly hosts* (the angelic beings who surround the throne)? The description of the Lamb having "seven horns and seven eyes" offers a clue:

- ✔ **Horns:** John doesn't decode the horns, but they're standard apocalyptic terminology for power. The seven horns speak of fullness and perfection of power. In other words, the Lamb possesses the kind of power associated with God himself — he's omnipotent, all-powerful.

- ✔ **Eyes:** The seven eyes are explicitly identified as the seven spirits of God, possibly indicating that the Lamb has authority over the highest angelic beings. Angels function as his "eyes" and convey to him exhaustive knowledge. If, however, the seven spirits represent the Holy Spirit, then the Lamb possesses the Holy Spirit to the nth degree. With either interpretation, the Lamb is aware of everything that transpires on earth; he's omniscient, all-knowing.

Here's the bottom line: The Lamb is a divine being in his own right alongside the one on the throne. Already, in symbolic imagery, you see the outlines of a teaching that's later enshrined in the great creeds (statements of belief) of Christianity — namely, the doctrine of the *Trinity:* three persons (Father, Son, and Holy Spirit) in one God. John's vision of the throne room depicts a profound paradox: The Lamb is a God-man.

John's Gospel and Paul's letters chime in with complementary portraits of a preexistent, divine being through whom all things were made and through whom all things are reconciled (John 1:1–14; 1 Corinthians 8:6; 2 Corinthians 5:19; Philippians 2:6–11; Colossians 1:15–20, 2:9; 1 Timothy 2:16).

The Lamb holds the seven-sealed scroll; he is master of the universe. He determines the course of history and its ultimate outcome. He has a set purpose and goal, namely to create a new people and a new heaven and earth. In short, he intends to make "all things new" (Rev. 21:5).

The chapter concludes with a visual and auditory celebration of the sovereignty of the Lamb (Rev. 5:11–14). John now enlarges the circles around the throne (see "Circling the throne," earlier in this chapter). Beyond the elders, an enormous multitude of angelic beings form an even larger circle. John uses the highest number he can conceive of to convey the magnitude — "ten thousand times ten thousand." They join in the chorus of praise and adore the Lamb who is worthy of a sevenfold tribute — the number of perfection and completion.

Chapter 9

Breaking Seven Seals (6:1–8:1)

. . . .

In This Chapter

▶ Understanding the seals in context

▶ Meeting the four horsemen of the Apocalypse

▶ Witnessing the martyrs

▶ Exploring the Day of the Lord

▶ Interpreting the meaning of the 144,000

. . . .

This chapter has nothing to do with those adorable whiskered aquatic mammals that bark, smack their flippers together, and balance beach balls on their noses. Although these seven seals do sort of bark, they also bite and are not at all cute. Like adhesive flaps on envelopes, these seals serve as locks securing the very serious contents of a special scroll.

Taken together, the seven seals of Revelation 6:1–8:1 are much like a master key to a building. If you have the right master key, then unlocking doors is a straightforward task. But with the wrong key, getting inside may be impossible. That's why we believe unlocking this section of the book of Revelation, discussing the seven seals, is crucial to understanding the entire book. Getting a good grip on the themes and imagery related to the seals helps the rest of the imagery and timelines fall into place.

In this chapter, you discover how the seven seals in Revelation 6:1–8:1 preview the events that lead up to and climax with Jesus's return to earth. You also see how Old Testament references to the End Times and the return of Jesus explain much of the imagery in this section of Revelation. The chapter concludes with suggestions about the meaning of the mysterious 144,000 whom God has sealed on their foreheads.

Unsealing the Beginning of the End

In Revelation 5 (see Chapter 8), the Lamb emerges as the only being worthy to take the scroll, break its seals, and thereby reveal its contents (Rev. 5:5). In Revelation 6, the Lamb now breaks the seals — an act that triggers a series of events leading to his triumph. John watches as one of the four living creatures around the throne calls upon other creatures, each of which plays a part in the unfolding of this cosmic drama.

Exploring the relationship of the three series of sevens

The Old Testament prophets warned that before the kingdom of God triumphs, fearful judgments will impact the earth. They refer to this time of intense suffering as the *Day of the Lord* (Isaiah 13, 34; Jeremiah 4–7; Ezekiel 7, 25; Amos 5:18–29; Zephaniah 1–3). Although John doesn't use that term, his prophecy picks up this concept and organizes it into three series of seven judgments. This section explains how these judgments compare.

The number of judgments in each series may derive from the ancient doom prophecy in Leviticus 26. There, the Lord forewarns his people Israel, "And if in spite of this you will not obey me, I will continue to punish you sevenfold for your sins" (Leviticus 26:18); this warning repeats three more times in the same chapter (26:21, 26:24, 26:28). At any rate, in apocalyptic writing, the number seven typically signifies that which is complete, finished, or perfect. For example, when the last series of seven bowls are about to be poured out, John comments, "For with them the wrath of God is ended" (Rev. 15:1).

Timing

In Revelation, the seven seals are the first of three sevens; the others are the seven trumpets (Rev. 8:6–11:19) and the seven bowls (Rev. 15, 16). A key for interpreting the central section of the book of Revelation is understanding how the three series of sevens relate to each other. Several options are possible:

- ✔ **Concurrent:** The seals, trumpets, and bowls run parallel to each other and end at the same point in time.

- ✔ **Successive:** The seals, trumpets, and bowls follow each other in chronological sequence. On this view, the three series are like an expandable telescope.

- ✔ **Both:** The arrangement of the seals, trumpets, and bowls combines both successive and concurrent elements, ending at the same point.

The third option appears to make the most sense (but you're welcome to disagree!). John designates the sixth seal as the day of the wrath of God and the Lamb (6:16–17). The succeeding series of trumpet and bowl judgments elaborate on the sixth seal, with this exception: All three series end at the same point — the triumph of the kingdom of God. This interpretation means that trumpets 1 through 6 expand on the sixth seal, and bowls 1 through 6 cover much the same ground, though most likely they occur near the end of the sixth seal or Day of the Lord, just before Jesus returns. The upshot is that much of Revelation 8–19 involves the unfolding of the sixth seal. Perhaps the best way to get a handle on this is scheme through the diagram in Figure 9-1.

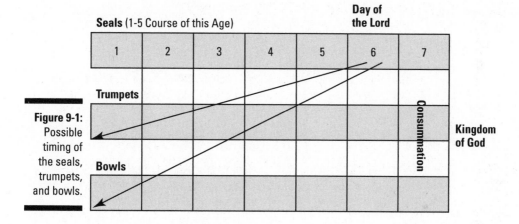

Seals (1-5 Course of this Age)

Day of the Lord

| 1 | 2 | 3 | 4 | 5 | 6 | 7 |

Trumpets

Bowls

Consummation

Kingdom of God

Figure 9-1: Possible timing of the seals, trumpets, and bowls.

Because of the obvious parallels between the judgments in the seven trumpets and the seven bowls, some scholars contend that these are actually parallel passages describing the same events. Although the seven trumpets and bowls are virtually identical in terms of the focus of their judgments, you shouldn't necessarily conclude that these are meant to describe the same events. Rather, these passages appear to best describe a sequence of events — an escalation of severity from a series of partial judgments to a final set of really, really nasty ones. John even refers to the bowls as "the seven *last* plagues" (italics ours) in 15:1, clearly indicating sequence.

Scope

The content of the seals appears less intensive and extensive than that of the trumpets and bowls. The seals affect only a quarter of the earth: "They [Death and Hades] were given authority over a fourth of the earth, to kill with sword, famine, and pestilence, and by the wild animals of the earth" (6:8). By contrast, the trumpet judgments affect a third of the earth (8:7–12), and the bowl judgments are completely global. By then, poor ol' planet earth is maxed out!

Breaking the seals to gain access to the scroll

Visualize how you'd open a sealed scroll. Instead of a book containing a set of bound pages, think of a roll of papyrus (an early form of paper) several feet long. String tied around the scroll prevented it from unraveling. To this was added a clay seal impressed with the owner's signature. An intact seal guaranteed the authenticity of the document and provided evidence that no one had tampered with the contents. See Figure 9-2.

Figure 9-2: A scroll with seven seals along the edge.

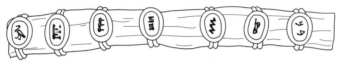

The scroll in Revelation 5–8 has seven such seals. To open the scroll, someone first has to break all seven seals. More than a few interpreters go awry here by failing to realize this rather fundamental point: The seals are not the contents of the scroll! They're *preliminary events* that have to happen before the contents can be read. The sealed scroll is a last will and testament (see Chapter 8). In it are the names of the heirs and a description of their inheritance. Before the heirs receive their inheritance, certain events must first unfold.

Scoping out the seven seals

The seven seals in Revelation 6:1–8:1 fall into four categories:

- ✔ **The first four seals:** Identified as horsemen on four differently colored horses, these seals depict terrestrial events.

- ✔ **The fifth seal:** Though not depicted as a horse and rider, this seal is closely associated with the first four. It provides a heavenly perspective: a brief snapshot of Christian martyrs (killed because of their beliefs) beneath an altar, crying out for justice.

- ✔ **The sixth seal:** This seal brings the reader to a display of terrifying disturbances on the earth and in the heavens, including the sun's turning black, stars' falling to earth, and the moon's becoming red as blood.

- ✔ **The seventh seal:** After a parenthetical section consisting of two explanatory visions, the last seal issues in silence in heaven, a quite unexpected result.

The arrangement of the seals significantly affects the overall interpretation of the section. The evils occurring during the first five seals generally result from human depravity (even famines have a human component in that they're often a byproduct of war). Injustice, inequality, prejudice, hate, greed, lust for power, and lack of self-control contribute to much of the human suffering characterizing the present age. The fourth and sixth seals add so-called natural disasters to the mix. But when the Lamb breaks the seventh seal in Revelation 8:1 and the scroll can at last be opened and read, John delays explaining what happens. We describe the individual seals in detail later in this chapter.

Comparing notes with Jesus

The *synoptic Gospels* (Matthew, Mark, and Luke — every Gospel except John's) provide a key to unlocking the meaning of the seals. In Revelation, everything under the first seven seals parallels a message Jesus gave to his disciples. This teaching — in which Jesus explains what will happen before the end of the world — is commonly known as the *Olivet Discourse* (named after the Mount of Olives, where he gave this teaching); it appears in Matthew 24:3–44, Mark 13:3–37, and Luke 21:7–36. In his teaching, Jesus emphasizes that catastrophic events such as war, famine, earthquakes, pestilence, and persecution will recur throughout the present age.

Table 9-1 shows how the seven seals parallel the teaching in which Jesus outlines the events leading up to and including his return to earth.

Table 9-1	Comparing the Olivet Discourse and the Seals	
Event	*Olivet Discourse (Matthew)*	*Seals (Revelation)*
False Messiah(s)	24:4	6:1–2 First seal
Warfare and bloodshed	24:7	6:3–4 Second seal
Famine	24:7	6:5–6 Third seal
Earthquakes	24:7	6:7–8 Fourth seal
Martyrdom	24:9	6:9–11 Fifth seal
Cosmic disturbances	24:29	6:12–17 Sixth seal
Coming of the Son of Man	24:30–31	8:1 Seventh seal (implied but not stated)

When Jesus lists the events in the Olivet Discourse, he doesn't say they're specific signs of the end (Matthew 24:6); rather, he simply says, "All this is but the beginning of the birth pangs" (Matthew 24:8). The difference is significant. Jewish apocalyptic literature also commonly expected an intense period of suffering, sometimes called the *woes of Messiah,* to precede the Messiah's appearance (1 Enoch 62:4; 2 Esdras 4:42; and Babylonian Talmud: Tractate Sanhedrin 96b–97a). ***Note:*** The Jewish community by and large rejected early Christians' claim that Jesus was the expected Messiah. Most Orthodox Jews (observing the rites and traditions of Judaism) today are still awaiting the coming of their Messiah; meanwhile, non-observant Jews have, for the most part, abandoned belief in a personal Messiah and think instead in terms of a messianic age — that is, a future time of universal peace and prosperity.

In short, the events Jesus foretells in both Revelation and the Gospels aren't simply items on a heavenly to-do list, dates in a calendar of events, or precise indicators of the nearness of the end of time. Life between Jesus's life on earth (that ended with his death and resurrection) and his return to earth is punctuated by disasters and devastating events, none of which is a sure sign of Jesus's immediate return. In fact, he cites only one specific accomplishment that foreshadows his return: "And this good news of the kingdom will be proclaimed throughout the world, as a testimony to all the nations; and then the end will come" (Matthew 24:14).

The First Four Seals: The Four Horsemen of the Apocalypse (6:1–8)

Galloping forth like figures from a Hogwarts School of Witchcraft and Wizardry dinner (think Harry Potter) come four horses and their riders. Each one signifies disaster for the planet. The first four seals in Revelation 6 serve as preliminaries leading up to the earth-shaking events connected with the sixth seal.

Revelation portrays each of the first four seals as a differently colored horse with a rider. John appears to be borrowing the imagery from the Old Testament:

- In Zechariah 1:7–17, four angelic horsemen patrol the earth and are mounted on red, sorrel (reddish brown), and white horses.

- In Zechariah 6:1–8, the prophet has a vision of four chariots pulled by red, black, white, and dappled gray horses, respectively. The chariots (driven by angelic charioteers) are identified with the four winds of the earth, which patrol their respective regions.

✔ Additionally, John may be drawing from Jeremiah's prophecy of four judgments (pestilence, sword, famine, and captivity) and four destroyers (sword, dogs, birds, and wild animals) of the sinful people of Jerusalem (Jeremiah 15:2–3).

✔ Ezekiel likewise prophesied "four deadly acts of judgment, sword, famine, wild animals, and pestilence" against Jerusalem (Ezekiel 14:21).

In this section, we take a close look at John's four horsemen of the apocalypse.

White horse and rider with a bow

This first seal is arguably the most difficult of the seven seals to interpret. In Revelation 6:2, John says, "I looked, and there was a white horse! Its rider had a bow; a crown was given to him, and he came out conquering and to conquer." Commentators are divided between two main interpretations of who this rider on a white horse is:

✔ **Jesus:** This view is linked to Revelation 19:11–16, in which Jesus is depicted riding a white horse in his triumphant return to earth.

✔ **The Antichrist:** This view argues that because the other three horses represent negative, destructive forces, it's more consistent that all four share a common negative character.

So which is it? Well, keep in mind that white horses don't always equate to the good guys in white hats. Generals of armies in the ancient world frequently rode white horses as a sign of prestige, not moral character. Furthermore, it seems inappropriate for an angelic being to summon Jesus to go forth; being summoned is more fitting for someone of lesser status and dignity. Also, the bow in the hand of the rider on the white horse doesn't seem appropriate for Jesus and deviates from the references in Revelation where Jesus has a sword issuing from his mouth (Rev. 1:16, 2:12, 2:16, 19:15). Bows in scriptural imagery frequently convey a negative image of war and destruction (Jeremiah 6:23, 46:9, 49:35; Lamentations 2:4; Hosea 1:5, 1:7; Zechariah 9:10).

As we discuss in the earlier "Comparing notes with Jesus" section, the seven seals seem to parallel Jesus's teaching on the End Times in the Olivet Discourse. There, the first thing Jesus warns his disciples about is false messiahs (Matthew 24:4–5). Many commentators, therefore, suggest that the first rider on the white horse is in fact the Antichrist, the great imitator (see Chapter 11 for more on this bad boy).

In our view, the four horsemen represent conditions and circumstances characterizing human history from the first century until the present. Consequently, the rider is not *the* Antichrist but *false messiahs* (supposed liberators of the Jews) who precede him. These pretenders were already active in the first century; for example, they appear in connection with the Jewish war against Rome in 66–74 CE. The Jewish historian Josephus described several false messiahs leading up to and during this conflict. John, in his first epistle, says, "As you have heard that antichrist is coming, so now many antichrists have come" (1 John 2:18). The false messiahs triggered revolutionary movements erupting in violence. Jewish Christians often suffered persecution from their fellow Jews because they didn't join or identify with these revolutionary movements.

Red horse and rider who removes peace

Opening the second seal reveals another rider and horse. The rider depicted in Revelation 6:3–4 is definitely a negative image: "When he opened the second seal, I heard the second living creature call out, 'Come!' And out came another horse, bright red; its rider was permitted to take peace from the earth, so that people would slaughter one another; and he was given a great sword."

The bright red color of the second horse graphically represents blood. Bloodshed characterizes human history from the first century to the twenty-first. The Roman Empire went through a particularly violent era during the Jewish war of 66–73 CE and the power struggle following Nero's suicide in 68 CE. As many as a million casualties resulted from these conflicts. Though bloodshed was not so widespread during the reign of Domitian, numerous conflicts lay on the horizon. From then until now, the historical record documents a depressing recurrence of death and destruction owing to war. Fast forward to today, where TV and computer screens bombard you with images of violence, acts of terrorism, and oppression around the globe. Clearly, despite the best human efforts, there has never been a golden age in which murder and violence were absent from the world.

Black horse and rider with a pair of scales

As the Lamb opens the third seal, a fearful specter rides forth. In Revelation 6:5–6, John writes, "When he opened the third seal, I heard the third living creature call out, 'Come!' I looked, and there was a black horse! Its rider held a pair of scales in his hand, and I heard what seemed to be a voice in the midst of the four living creatures saying, 'A quart of wheat for a day's pay, and three quarts of barley for a day's pay, but do not damage the olive oil and the wine!'"

In this passage, a famine strikes, but not everyone suffers. The wealthy enjoy luxuries while the poor can't even afford necessities. An entire day's wage (a denarius) is required just to feed one's family — that's an inflation rate

12 times normal! As a result, many enter survival mode and settle for the less-nutritious barley. The disparity in prices and commodities illustrates a distressing feature of human history: inequity and injustice.

Throughout the history of the Roman Empire, famines frequently ravaged the population (Acts 11:27–30). Even today, graphic images of starving children from sub-Saharan Africa regularly haunt our consciences. Never have greater numbers lived on the brink of starvation than the twenty-first century. This illustrates our overriding point that the first five seals characterize human history from John's day to our own. As we see it, they've already been broken and are being actualized in human history. Never have we had an era when famine was not a major concern for multitudes somewhere on the planet. The same goes for each of the five seals.

Pale green horse and Death and Hades

As the Lamb opens the fourth seal, the Grim Reaper rides out on his pale green mount: "When he opened the fourth seal, I heard the voice of the fourth living creature call out, 'Come!' I looked and there was a pale green horse! Its rider's name was Death, and Hades followed with him; they were given authority over a fourth of the earth, to kill with sword, famine, and pestilence, and by the wild animals of the earth" (Rev 6:7–8).

Death and Hades are closely linked: Death is the moment at which physical life ceases; Hades is the continuing post-death existence of disembodied spirits. More specifically, *Hades* is the Greek term for the place of departed spirits, typically regarded as the *underworld*. The New Testament views Hades as a temporary place that's ultimately destroyed at the end of the world (Rev. 20:13–14).

This ghastly apparition speaks for itself. Pale green is chosen as the color of this horse to depict the appearance of a rotting corpse. As a consequence of the red and black horses, Death stalks the land.

Epidemics regularly decimated the Roman Empire. In fact, in Ephesus, plagues felled one-third of the population during the years 165–251 CE. And recall the devastating plagues of the Middle Ages, such as the Black Death of 1347–1351 that swept away one-third of all Europeans. Even in modern times, the great flu pandemic of 1918–1919 accounted for over 675,000 American deaths, far more than in WWI. Today, the AIDS virus infects millions of victims, and the death toll is unthinkable (according to the United Nations, about 33.2 million infected in 2007 with about 2.1 million deaths). Other potential plagues lurk in the dark world of viruses and microbes.

The four horsemen of Notre Dame

On October 18, 1924, Notre Dame football achieved a moment of immortality thanks to a *New York Herald-Tribune* sportswriter named Grantland Rice. Borrowing from the imagery of the Apocalypse, he filed a story following Notre Dame's 13–7 victory over an Army team at the Polo Grounds. Here is perhaps the most famous football story ever penned in sports journalism:

"Outlined against a blue-gray October sky the Four Horsemen rode again. In dramatic lore they are known as famine, pestilence, destruction and death. These are only aliases. Their real names are: Stuhldreher, Miller, Crowley and Layden. They formed the crest of the South Bend cyclone before which another fighting Army team was swept over the precipice at the Polo Grounds this afternoon as 55,000 spectators peered down upon the bewildering panorama spread out upon the green plain below."

George Stricker, a student sports publicist at Notre Dame, capitalized on this characterization. When the team arrived back at South Bend, he arranged with a local livery stable to have four horses available. The four players, quarterback Harry Stuhldreher, left halfback Jim Crowley, right halfback Don Miller, and fullback Elmer Layden mounted up and posed in their uniforms. That picture appeared in the national press and a legend was born.

(c) Bettmann/CORBIS

Putting together the welcoming party

The return of Jesus is called the *Parousia*, a Greek term basically meaning an *arrival, coming,* or *presence.* The term also means a royal visit to a Greco-Roman city. The visit of the emperor or a member of the royal family was a Parousia. The city elected a delegation to meet the emperor and his entourage well outside the city limits and escort him back to the forum in the city center. Much to-do went into preparations, involving general sprucing up, minting of celebratory coins, civic speeches, public festivities, games, and so forth, in order to make a good impression.

The Apostle Paul skillfully adapts the Greco-Roman concept of a Parousia to the return of Jesus. He sees Jesus as the coming King of kings, and the welcoming delegation are believers who are taken up (*raptured*) to "meet the Lord in the air" (1 Thessalonians 4:17). Jesus's entourage includes believers who die before the Parousia. They won't miss out on the festivities; in fact, they have a front-row seat!

The Fifth seal: The blood of martyrs (6:9–11)

Most people believe that the fifth seal, though standing apart from the four horsemen, is closely associated with them. John writes,

> "When he opened the fifth seal, I saw under the altar the souls of those who had been slaughtered for the word of God and for the testimony they had given; they cried out with a loud voice, 'Sovereign Lord, holy and true, how long will it be before you judge and avenge our blood on the inhabitants of the earth?' They were each given a white robe and told to rest a little longer, until the number would be complete both of their fellow servants and of their brothers and sisters, who were soon to be killed as they themselves had been killed." (Rev. 6:9–11)

The connection between this seal and the previous four is simply this: Martyrdom for one's faith, like war, famine, plague, and death on a massive scale, is a recurring historical phenomenon. Religious persecution has never totally disappeared. Based on John's vision, it's unlikely to end until the return of Jesus.

These martyrs, who've died because of their faith in Jesus, rest safely beneath the heavenly altar. In popular Jewish belief, the righteous dwell under God's throne until the day of resurrection. The "rest" promised to the martyrs (Rev. 6:11) speaks of more than mere physical refreshment; it conveys enjoyment of Jesus's presence and anticipation of his complete victory over evil.

Persecution then and now

Ancient historians Tacitus, Seutonius, and Sulpicius Severus captured the gory details of the persecution of early Christians. These historians imply that Nero's actions were designed to deflect the outrage of the citizenry of Rome. In 64 CE, a devastating fire destroyed large portions of the city with huge loss of life. A rumor circulated that Nero himself had set the fire, wanting to rebuild the city in a manner more suited to his taste. Needing a scapegoat, Nero fastened the blame on the Christians.

During the reign of Domitian (81–96 CE), there were periodic outbreaks of persecution, especially in cities of Asia, because Christians refused to burn incense to the divine Caesar. During the second and third centuries, extensive state-supported persecution swept over the empire, and thousands of believers perished.

Throughout the Middle Ages and into the Reformation and Counter-Reformation, violent episodes of persecution erupted, some of it mutually destructive. Christians in Asia Minor, where the seven churches were located, experienced several waves of conquest and persecution in the seventh and eighth centuries, eventually almost dying out entirely.

However, what many people don't realize is that never before in history have there been as many martyrs as there are currently. In many areas of the world, various religious, political, psychological, and economic factors have created a hostile environment for those who follow the teachings of Jesus.

As you explore the fifth seal, keep in mind that John wrote the book of Revelation at the end of the first century. But already in 64 CE, during a brief but bloody episode, Nero Caesar had put a great host of Christians to death. Multitudes died in the arena, torn to shreds by lions. Others were crucified, and some were burned alive at night to serve as torches for Nero's nightly dinner parties.

The Sixth Seal: The Day of the Lord Has Come! (6:12–17)

The events associated with the first five seals are challenges and suffering that humans have encountered over the centuries. However, the description of the sixth seal in Revelation 6:12–17 places it in an entirely different category from the others. A great earthquake accompanied by unparalleled cosmic disturbances (such as literal falling stars!) indicate something off the charts.

Never in recorded history have such phenomena occurred. People in all walks of life cower in caves and cringe as terrible events unfold all around them. What's going on here? It's like Creation returns to its original state of chaos (Genesis 1:2).

Like Old (Testament) times: Going back to the Day of the Lord

Crucial to understanding the sixth seal is the Old Testament notion of the *Day of the Lord*. In this regard, the prophetic books of the Old Testament are essential reading (see Chapter 3). The prophets paint a mural of the last days of earth's history, when the Lord God of Israel holds court and settles all accounts — Judgment Day. Metaphors depicting both its severity and its salvation collide, so get ready for some fire and brimstone.

Amos

The book of Amos is a good example of stark doomsday imagery. In his writings, the prophet Amos tries to correct some common misconceptions. Israelites in Amos's day generally assumed the Day of the Lord would be a time of blessing and light. They believed this solely on the basis that they were Israelites, as if membership in their group brought automatic blessing as a privilege. They disregarded that willfully choosing to disobey God's directives would bring judgment — something they should've known based on the history of their people's interactions with God.

Amos, directed by God, lets them know their wrong behavior has landed them in serious hot water. Just because they're the "children of Israel" doesn't mean they receive a free pass to God's kingdom. Amos graphically attacks their misconceptions. For example, he says that the Israelites are like a man who encounters a lion and bear and escapes both by fleeing to the safety of his home, only to be bitten by a deadly snake hiding in the wall (Amos 5:19). Thinking he's escaped disaster, he is suddenly stricken and dies. What a picture of bitter disappointment! As always, though, God offers an alternative: If the Israelites acknowledge their disobedience and bring their behavior to be in line with God's commands, then the Day of the Lord can be a day of light rather than a day of darkness (Amos 5:18–24).

Isaiah

Other prophets build on Amos's initial sketch of the Day of the Lord, none more graphically than Isaiah. Isaiah sketches a time of terror and trembling: "Enter the caves of the rocks and the holes of the ground, from the terror of the Lord, and from the glory of his majesty, when he rises to terrify the earth" (Isaiah 2:19).

John, in describing the cosmic disasters of the sixth seal, clearly borrows Isaiah's imagery. Isaiah writes:

> "See, the day of the Lord comes, cruel, with wrath and fierce anger, to make the earth a desolation, and to destroy its sinners from it. For the stars of the heavens and their constellations will not give their light; the sun will be dark at its rising, and the moon will not shed its light. [. . .] Therefore I will make the heaven tremble, and the earth will be shaken out of its place. [. . .]" (Isaiah 13:9–10, 13:13)

In the same vein, Isaiah continues, "All the host of heaven shall rot away, and the skies roll up like a scroll. All their host shall wither like a leaf withering on a vine, or fruit withering on a fig tree" (Isaiah 34:4).

Compare Isaiah's description to the following events of Revelation 6:12–17:

- ✔ The sun turns black, and the moon turns red.
- ✔ The stars fall from the sky.
- ✔ The sky disappears "like a scroll rolling itself up."
- ✔ Islands and mountains are no longer in place.

In with the New (Testament): Looking to the Day of the Lamb

The expectation of divine intervention and vindication, as related in the Old Testament's Day of the Lord, became a standard feature of *Second-Temple Judaism,* a term referring to Judaism during 517 BCE–70 CE. Here's how the New Testament relates Jesus to this day of judgment:

- ✔ In the Gospels, Jesus accepts this depiction and further elaborates on some of its features. The distinctive contribution of Jesus lies in his conviction that he, as the Son of Man, plays the pivotal role in the Day of the Lord.
- ✔ In John's Gospel, Jesus is quoted as saying, "The Father judges no one but has given all judgment to the Son" (John 5:22).
- ✔ The Apostle Paul simply expands the Old Testament expression and speaks of "the day of our Lord Jesus Christ" (1 Corinthians 1:8; Philippians 1:6, 1:10, 2:16; 1 Thessalonians 5:2).

For John, this day clearly belongs to both the Lord and the Lamb. In Revelation 6:16–17, as the people flee to the mountains, they call to the rocks, "Fall on us and hide us from the face of the one seated on the throne and from the wrath of the Lamb; for the great day of their wrath has come, and who is able to stand?" Christians often call this time the *Great Tribulation,* a term that comes from Matthew 24:21 and Revelation 7:14 in the King James Version of the Bible.

Sorting out Second-Temple Judaism

First-Temple Judaism means the form of Judaism that existed from the dedication of the first Temple in about 970 BCE until the Babylonians destroyed it in 586 BCE. It was characterized by the great covenant made between the Lord and Israel at Mount Sinai (as recorded in Exodus 19–24). This form of Judaism is basically the one reflected in the Old Testament books.

Second-Temple Judaism means the form of Judaism that existed from about 517 BCE, when the second Temple was dedicated, up to its destruction by the Romans in 70 CE. It was characterized by the traditions of the first Temple, supplemented by the new traditions that arose as Jews interacted with their new Hellenistic (Greek-cultured) environment and their ongoing attempt to adapt the old laws to new settings.

During the Second-Temple period, great controversy arose among the Jews. The various groups — known as Pharisees, Sadducees (as documented in the New Testament), Essenes (as depicted in some of the Dead Sea Scrolls), and others that scholars know about only by inference — arose during this era and had quite different understandings about what constituted genuine Judaism. Of course, the Jewish movement that eventually became known as Christianity also arose during Second-Temple times and added another perspective.

Of the various Jewish groups, only the Pharisees and Christians survived the great war against Rome (66–74 CE). Pharisaism evolved into *Rabbinic Judaism.* This form of Judaism, shaped by the Mishnah and Talmud (authoritative interpretations of the biblical laws of the Old Testament), ended the age of diversity and ushered in a long period of uniformity until the period of the Enlightenment (eighteenth century). Judaism today is once again characterized by great diversity of belief or even unbelief.

Pausing for Effect (7:1–17)

As Revelation 7 begins, John hits the pause button. He feels he needs to elaborate on an important point. As you read through the book of Revelation, several such pauses or interludes occur. These include the following:

- Revelation 7:1–17
- Revelation 10:1–11
- Revelation 11:1–14
- Revelation 12
- Revelation 13
- Revelation 14

These pauses in the action highlight key issues that John considers important. He wants to use the delay to answer the question raised by terrified earthlings who wonder whether *anyone* can escape destruction in the great day of the wrath of God and the Lamb (Rev. 6:17). The reassuring answer unfolds in Revelation 7.

Surveying the survivors

John identifies two groups of people who stand before the throne of God — "the 144,000" (Rev. 7:4) and a "great multitude" (Rev. 7:9). These individuals survive the Day of the Lord for one reason: because God seals and saves them. This salvation is a "God thing," not something they've achieved. As the Apostle Paul says, "For by grace you have been saved through faith, and this is not your own doing: it is the gift of God" (Ephesians 2:8). Seen in this light, the whole Bible is a sweeping, overarching story of mercy showing how God rescues sinful people from otherwise inevitable judgment.

The imagery John uses to depict this salvation is striking. Four angels hold back the four winds of the earth, which represent destructive forces about to be unleashed on the world. But God intends to protect his chosen people just as he did long ago in Egypt (Exodus 8–12).

Another angel places God's seal on the foreheads of 144,000 people, identified as "the people of Israel" (Rev. 7:4). This feature of John's vision recalls a vision of the prophet Ezekiel in 592 BCE. Ezekiel saw six destroying angels about to wreak havoc on the inhabitants of Jerusalem because of their apostasy (abandoning belief in God) and rebellion. Before they're allowed to execute vengeance, however, another angelic being records the names of those who are truly repentant. These he seals with a mark on their foreheads. Only those with the mark escape the impending disaster (Ezekiel 9:1–11).

Suddenly, John sees another group he refers to as "a great multitude that no one could count, from every nation, from all tribes and peoples and languages, standing before the throne" (Rev. 7:9). An innumerable host experiences God's grace and joins the happy throng before the throne. Nothing states that they're sealed by God, but there they are nonetheless.

So what's their story? One of the 24 elders interrogates John: "Who are these, robed in white, and where have they come from?" (Rev. 7:13). John doesn't know, but he knows the elder knows, so John asks the elder. He responds, "These are they who have come out of the great ordeal; they have washed their robes and made them white in the blood of the Lamb" (Rev. 7:14). In short, they're Christians who refused to deny their faith even at the cost of their lives.

Note the paradox of making one's garment white by washing it in blood in this section. For Christian believers, this paradox stands at the heart of the gospel message. In fact, paradox characterizes Christian teaching at many points — *predestination* (God decreed everything that happens) versus human freedom, God's *transcendence* (God is independent of and beyond the universe) versus his *immanence* (God is everywhere present in his creation), and salvation by faith and judgment by works, among others.

A regular feature of apocalyptic literature involves dialogue with a heavenly guide. The seer is either asked a question or asks a question. In this instance, John is asked a question he doesn't know and throws it back to the angel, who supplies the answer (Rev. 7:13–14, 17:6b–7; Ezekiel 37:3; Daniel 7:15–16; Zechariah 1:9, 1:19, 4:1–6).

Identifying the 144,000

John gives a roll call of the tribes of Israel, which results in a tally of 12,000 from each of the 12 tribes listed, for a grand total of 144,000. In short, the total is 12^2 multiplied by 1,000. Considerable speculation and controversy surround the identification of the 144,000. Three major options present themselves.

All Christians

The 144,000 may symbolize all Christians. On this understanding, they're virtually the same group as the great multitude mentioned next in Revelation 7:9–17. The difference is merely one of perspective. The listing of the tribes of Israel here is different from the Old Testament record (the tribes of Ephraim and Dan are omitted), which may support the idea of a purely symbolic nature of the group.

In the New Testament, several passages view the church as a New Israel (Romans 2:28–29; Galatians 6:16). In other words, gentiles and Jews who believe in Jesus make up a new people of God. Take a look:

- This may be reflected in the churches of Smyrna and Philadelphia, where you hear of "those who say that they are Jews but are not" (Rev. 2:9, 3:9). In other words, Christians believe they, not ethnic Jews, are the true Israel.

- The group of 144,000 reappears in chapter 14, and Revelation 14:4 says, "They have been redeemed from humankind as first fruits for God and the Lamb." Proponents contend that this description suggests that the 144,000 — previously described as the tribes of Israel — symbolize the church because "from humankind" refers to gentiles.

- The Apostle Peter refers to gentile believers as "exiles of the Dispersion" (1 Peter 1:1), an application of a Jewish expression to Christians. The same adaptation appears in the Letter of James, where Christians are stylized as "the twelve tribes in the Dispersion" (James 1:1).

Tribe talkin'

The tribes of Israel were groups of people claiming common kinship. Israel traced its ancestry back to the 12 sons of Jacob. These sons in turn became the forefathers of the individual tribes that eventually made up the tribal federation known as Israel (Genesis 12–50). This pattern of organization, widespread in the ancient Near East, is similar to that of Native Americans. They, too, were organized into tribal federations such as the Sioux (or Dakota) and Miami nations.

There are several curiosities in the listing of the tribes of Israel in Revelation 7:5–8. Why is Judah listed first? Why is Dan omitted? Why is Joseph listed along with his eldest son, Manasseh, but not his youngest son, Ephraim? Judah is probably first because Jesus came from that tribe. But as to why Dan is omitted and Manasseh rather than Ephraim is listed, we can only speculate. A few early Christian interpreters (such as Irenaeus in the second century and Commodius during the third) inferred from the omission of Dan that the Antichrist would be a Jew from that tribe. This is mere speculation sometimes laced with anti-Jewish prejudice. (For more on the Antichrist, stay tuned for Chapter 11.)

Jewish Christians

The 144,000 may symbolize Jewish Christians, not Jewish and gentile Christians together. The fact that the tribes of Israel are enumerated accords more naturally with the group being actual Jews who believe in Jesus. Paul speaks of a present remnant of Israel (including himself) who do believe, and he seems to predict that at the end of the age, a wholesale conversion of Jews will occur (Romans 11:26).

Proponents of this view point out that

- People on earth give "glory to the God of heaven" in only one place in the book of Revelation (11:13), and these people appear to be Jews in Jerusalem.

- Jesus promised his disciples that when he comes in his glory, they'll "sit on twelve thrones, judging the twelve tribes of Israel" (Matthew 19:28; Luke 22:30).

- The Apostle Paul seems to envision a future conversion of Jews just prior to the Parousia, or Second Coming of Jesus (Romans 11:26–27).

Perhaps, say proponents, the last chapter of earth's history will include a remarkably dedicated group of Jewish Christians who bear witness to their faith in Jesus as the Messiah. Some interpreters also hold that the two witnesses of Revelation 11 represent Jewish Christians who minister in Jerusalem in connection with the End Times.

An elite group of Christians

The 144,000 may be an elite group of Christians who are especially devoted to Jesus and receive special status as a reward for their commitment. Most often, this group is equated with Christian martyrs. The number is symbolic because there have been many times this number of martyrs in virtually any period of church history you choose. But some religious groups view the number literally and teach that the 144,000 are a spiritually elite group of believers who enjoy exalted status in the final kingdom.

The biggest problem with this perspective is that the elitism such a view implies seems contrary to the clear teaching on equality throughout the New Testament (Galatians 3:28–29; 1 Corinthians 12:13; Colossians 3:11). Moreover, attempts to take the number literally — exactly 144,000 people, not one more or less — ignores the non-literal conventions of apocalyptic writings.

Observing the multitude standing before the throne

Another throne room scene unfolds in Revelation 7:9–17. First, the multitude who have maintained faith in Jesus and who have come out of the great ordeal — commonly known as the *Tribulation* and linked to the Day of the Lord (see "The Sixth Seal: The Day of the Lord Has Come! [6:12–17]") — offer up a confession of faith: "Salvation belongs to our God who is seated on the throne, and to the Lamb!" (Rev. 7:10). This confession underscores that the Bible consistently holds that God saves his people; they don't save themselves.

The angelic choir fills the heavens with a mighty sevenfold song of worship to God: praise, blessing, glory, wisdom, honor, power, and might. Consider that during the time John wrote the book of Revelation, people directed such attributes to Caesar. John is making a clear statement that these attributes befit only a true supreme being, namely God.

Then, combining several Old Testament texts (Isaiah 49:10; Psalms 121:6, 23:1–2; Ezekiel 34:23–24; Isaiah 25:8), the section concludes by describing the blessings that await the multitude of the redeemed, those who have been faithful to Jesus. Like the angelic guardians of the throne, the redeemed surround and serenade the sovereign God. He, in turn, shelters them from the scorching sun. The imagery derives from the figure of an ancient Near Eastern monarch sitting on his throne under a canopy or awning. His subjects are likewise protected from the sun's rays by awnings or something similar, providing shade for the entire court area (see Figure 9-3).

Figure 9-3:
An Assyrian
king on his
throne with
attendants.

John is a master of irony and paradox throughout his writings. As Revelation 7 ends, it offers another striking example of paradox when the Lamb is also designated as the shepherd of the redeemed (Rev. 7:17). This picks up on John's Gospel, where Jesus is both "the Lamb of God who takes away the sin of the world" (John 1:29) and the "good shepherd [who] lays down his life for the sheep" (John 10:11). You can see similar examples of John's use of irony in Revelation 5:5–6, where the lion is a lamb.

The Seventh Seal: Silence in Heaven (8:1–5)

Revelation 8 begins with the opening of the seventh seal. When the Lamb opens it, there's silence in heaven for half an hour. But the drama and suspense quickly rebuild when "the seven angels who stand before God" (Rev. 8:2) receive seven trumpets. Something big is about to go down. Before you hit the fast forward button and hurry to find out what it is, pause and reflect on this delay. What does it signify? Angelic adoration ceases, and silence envelops the command center of the universe.

The significance of the pause is that with the opening of the seventh seal, the old order passes away. God's wrath against sin is spent, and judgment gives way to blessing, just like the prophets said it would (see Amos 9:11–15 and Isaiah 65:17–25). In other words, the future is now, and it's nothing short of a brand new heaven and brand new earth (Rev. 21). John, at this point in his text, deliberately delays a description of the grand finale. He has much more to say about the events leading up to the conclusion.

One of the hallmarks of John's literary technique, in addition to irony, is to postpone the climactic moment of his narrative. He carries the reader along and sustains suspense for as long as possible. John skillfully does this in his Gospel of John, where he narrates the ministry of Jesus by means of a literary device, namely "the hour of his glory," when referring to events related to Jesus and his impending crucifixion. Throughout the Gospel of John, the writer repeatedly informs you that it isn't yet Jesus's hour (John 2:4, 7:6, 7:8, 7:30, and 8:20). Finally, in Jerusalem, during the week of the feast of Passover, John quotes Jesus as saying, "The hour has come for the Son of Man to be glorified" (John 12:23). Ironically, the "hour of his glory" culminates in the death of Jesus on the cross, followed by his resurrection. Perhaps artist Salvador Dali comes closest to visually capturing this glory in John's literary tour de force (Figure 9-4).

Figure 9-4:
The Crucifixion of Christ, one of Salvador Dali's views of Jesus on the cross.

(c) Christie's Images/CORBIS

Chapter 10

Sounding Seven Trumpets (8:2–11:19)

In This Chapter

▶ Connecting the dots between the plagues of Egypt and the seven trumpets

▶ Observing the opening volley against the Evil Empire

▶ Reflecting on God's wrath against evil

▶ Appreciating another interlude before the main event

"Don't make me angry. You wouldn't like me when I'm angry." David Banner uttered that classic line in the 1970s *The Incredible Hulk* television series just before he turned into the Hulk. When we look at Revelation 8–11, we wonder whether God may be saying the same thing. In this section of Revelation, Satan's evil empire is about to experience the opening bursts of the angelic artillery. And this skirmish just softens up Satan's forces for the final bombardment of the bowl judgments (see Chapter 12), reducing Satan's empire to ashes.

The trumpet judgments, cosmic blows that affect a third of the planet, are more extensive and devastating than the seals (see Chapter 9). The trumpet judgments, however, don't impact the people of God; they aim at those still defying the rule of the warrior Lamb.

In this chapter, you explore God's judgment on evil in the world. As you do so, you see how the Old Testament helps you understand what's going on. The account of the plagues on Egypt (Exodus 7:14–10:23) provides a pattern for the trumpet judgments. Here, you also begin to understand why this is a fight to the finish between the two main characters of redemptive history, Jesus and Satan. Both lay exclusive claim to the earth and its inhabitants. Only one will eventually triumph. And the triumph of the one means the demise of the other. (*Harry Potter and the Deathly Hollows* got this right, too — it's either Harry or Voldemort!)

And in this corner . . .

The fight began back in Genesis 3, when Satan (under the guise of a serpent) deceived Adam and Eve. Their disobedience resulted in expulsion from the Garden of Eden, and Satan usurped control over planet earth. The Apostle John, in his first epistle, doesn't mince words when he observes, "the whole world lies under the power of the evil one" (1 John 5:19). Even Jesus, during his earthly ministry, acknowledges Satan's present power and influence: "Now the ruler of this world will be driven out" (John 12:31). The Lord God, however, promises Eve that one of her descendants will crush the serpent's head — that is, deliver a mortal blow (Genesis 3:15).

According to the New Testament, that descendant is none other than Jesus of Nazareth. The Apostle Paul expresses this conviction when he writes to the believers at Rome, "The God of peace will shortly crush Satan under your feet" (Romans 16:20). The fight has turned out to be long and drawn-out, but the book of Revelation narrates the final blow in chapter 20. The trumpet judgments are the beginning of the end for the Dark Lord and his followers. The victor in this cosmic slugfest is not in doubt.

Previewing the Seven Trumpets

Revelation 8 begins with an introduction to the seven trumpets: "When the Lamb opened the seventh seal, there was silence in heaven for about half an hour. And I saw the seven angels who stand before God, and seven trumpets were given to them" (Rev. 8: 1–2).

The trumpets herald the Day of the Lord, the Great Tribulation, the final era of earth history in which the Lamb reasserts uncontested rule of the planet and decisively defeats the forces of evil. The seventh trumpet, like the seventh seal and seventh bowl, transitions to the grand finale, the triumph of the Lamb and his kingdom.

These seven trumpets, like the seven seals (see Chapter 9), fall into four categories:

- ✔ Trumpets 1–4 (Rev. 8:7–12), like the four horsemen (Rev. 6:2–8), form one distinct unit. For the most part, these judgments are directed at nature.

- ✔ An eagle announces trumpets 5–7 and identifies them as the three "woes" (Rev. 8:13–11:19). Trumpets 5 and 6 are demonic in nature and are directed at rebellious human beings.

- ✔ Trumpet 6 is followed by a delay and interlude highlighting specific aspects of the Day of the Lord (Rev. 10:1–11:14).

- ✔ Trumpet 7, like the seventh seal, anticipates the triumph of the Lamb, only to be postponed by another delay and interlude (12:1–14:20).

Preceding the trumpets: Silence and prayer

Before the trumpets begin, Revelation 8:1 notes that heaven is silent for about half an hour (see Chapter 9). After that period of time, activity suddenly fills the heavenly sanctuary. The seven angels who stand before the throne of God prepare to sound their trumpets. This signifies that something big is about to happen. But before the trumpet blasts, a ritual unfolds as related in Revelation 8:3–4: "Another angel with a golden censer came and stood at the altar; he was given a great quantity of incense to offer with the prayers of all the saints on that golden altar that is before the throne."

Incense was a regular feature of non-Christian, Jewish, and Christian worship. The fragrant odor evoked in the worshiper a sense of the presence of the deity and was offered up as an expression of thanksgiving or intercession (requests on others' behalf). Jewish usage goes back to the Mosaic rituals of the Tabernacle and the subsequent first and second Temples. Christianity later incorporated and adapted the Jewish practice for its liturgy. In this passage, John describes the incense drifting over the heavenly sanctuary as a sweet accompaniment to the prayers of the saints — that is, believers in Jesus.

The Bible indicates that believers' prayers facilitate God's will. Does prayer change things? The Bible repeatedly suggests that it does (see Psalm 37:4–5; Isaiah 65:24; Matthew 7:7–8; Mark 11:22–24; Philippians 4:6; Hebrews 4:16; James 5:16). These prayers at the golden altar aren't categorized as to their specific content, but they probably include the prayers of the martyrs, mentioned in the fifth seal (see Chapter 9). In other words, the saints are crying out for vindication, a request about to be answered in a big way.

Making a stormy appearance

The incense burner is hurled down to the earth, signaling the beginning of the heavenly assault: "Then the angel took the censer and filled it with fire from the altar and threw it on the earth; and there were peals of thunder, rumblings, flashes of lightning, and an earthquake" (Rev. 8:5). The storms that follow are considered *theophanic* signs, a fancy theological word that refers to an appearance of God.

To make sense of this episode, take a little trip back in time to review some Old Testament passages that illuminate the text. The Old Testament narrates several theophanies, such as the appearance of God on Mount Sinai. In Exodus 19, *Yahweh* (the personal name of the God of Israel, rendered as *Lord* in most English translations) descends on the mountain accompanied by various earthly and celestial phenomena. Here's how Exodus 19:16, 19:18 describes it: "On the morning of the third day there was thunder and lightning, as well as a thick cloud on the mountain, and a blast of a trumpet so loud that all the people who were in the camp trembled. [. . .] Now Mount Sinai was wrapped in smoke [. . .] the whole mountain shook violently." The similarities of this passage to Revelation 8:5–6 is apparent. John's point is simply this: God is about to reveal himself as he did in the past in order to accomplish the salvation of his people. This is no trivial matter!

Whenever God displays his power on earth, there's a whole lot of fireworks, rocking, and rolling going on (1 Kings 18:38)! Fire from the altar functions almost like a cosmic blowtorch. The Lamb is on the move!

Paralleling the plagues of Egypt

The sequence of trumpets shows some similarities to the plagues that rained down on rebellious Pharaoh and his Egyptian empire, which had been built on the backs of Hebrew slaves (Exodus 7–12). Table 10-1 shows some of the common features between the trumpets of Revelation and the plagues in the Old Testament.

Table 10-1	Comparing the Plagues of Egypt with the Trumpets
Exodus	*Revelation*
First Plague: Water of the Nile River turns to blood (Exodus 7:20–25)	Second Trumpet: A third of the sea becomes blood (Rev. 8:8–9)
Fifth Plague: Livestock disease (Exodus 9:1–12)	First, Second, and Third Trumpets: A third of the trees and grass burn up; a third of living creatures in the sea die; many people die from the wormwood waters (Rev. 8:7, 8:10–11)
Seventh Plague: Hail and thunderstorm (Exodus 9:22–35)	First Trumpet: Hail and fire (Rev. 8:7)
Eighth Plague: Locusts (Exodus 10:1–20)	Fifth Trumpet: Locusts (Rev 9:1–11)
Ninth Plague: Dense darkness (Exodus 10:21–29)	Fourth Trumpet: A third of all celestial light darkens (Rev. 8:12)

You may notice that the plagues and trumpets aren't sequentially parallel, nor do all the plagues have a trumpet counterpart. But the events are too close to be accidental, and it seems likely that John borrows the plague imagery to describe what unfolds in his vision. Comparing the trumpets to the plagues is helpful because it enables readers to make theological sense of both sets of judgments. In the case of the Egyptian plagues, the Lord is trying to break Pharaoh's will as well as punish him for crimes against humanity — well before anything like an International Court of Justice at the Hague existed.

Worshiping the god of light: One-god Egyptians

Philo the Jew, a writer in the first century, interprets Exodus 12:38 as proof that some Egyptians embraced *monotheism,* the belief in one god: "These were [. . .] those who, reverencing the divine favour shewn to the people, had come over to them, and such as were converted and brought to a wiser mind by the magnitude and the number of the successive punishments" (*On the Life of Moses* 1.147).

The reign of Akhenaton may show further evidence. Akhenaton ruled Egypt after the time of Thutmose III and Rameses II — the two most likely candidates for the Pharaoh of the Exodus. Inexplicably, Akhenaton departed from a millennia-long, polytheistic (many-god) tradition and affirmed a form of monotheism. Akhenaton spoke of Aton, the sun-god, as a unique, transcendent, and everlasting deity, remarkably similar to the biblical depiction of Yahweh. What prompted such a radical move? It may have been memory of the plagues on Egypt and the contest between Pharaoh and Yahweh, in which the gods of Egypt were shown to be inadequate.

Pharaoh isn't a pawn in a predetermined power play; he has an opportunity to repent. According to the Bible, God allows people to make their own choices. Pharaoh refuses, but at least some Egyptians choose to believe in God. In fact, according to Exodus 12:38, a few believing Egyptians even leave Egypt with the Hebrews and cast their lot with them.

The same applies to the trumpet judgments. According to the Scriptures, God takes no delight in judging defiant sinners. But he does allow evil to overtake those who embrace it. He also allows repentance up until the last possible moment. In that light, the trumpet judgments aren't merely a punishment but also a warning to those who don't believe in God. They serve the same remedial function as the plagues on the ancient Egyptians.

Admitting problems of interpretation

As you look at the trumpet judgments, you have to consider two nagging problems: How should this passage be viewed, and how does what happens fit into the portrayed character of God?

The literalness of events

Is all this trumpet imagery purely symbolic, or is it intended to be taken at face value? Or is there a middle position? A literal interpretation of the trumpets doesn't make much sense in hard scientific terms. We can argue that God can do whatever he wants, but it's difficult to understand how only a third of the light from heavenly bodies can be darkened.

Some argue that although God occasionally breaks natural laws, he generally operates in accordance with the laws and forces that he put in place. These people suggest that these judgments are unprecedented but still within the parameters of known laws of astrophysics and earth sciences.

Those who interpret these trumpets symbolically point out that the trumpet judgments are at home in the standard apocalyptic imagery that prophets used to depict God's judgment on evildoers in the End Times.

The character of God

How can a loving God inflict wide-scale suffering, even on his rebellious human creation? Is God sadistic? Does God get off the hook simply by saying these people deserve what they get? This is, of course, a long-standing theological problem that extends beyond the pages of Revelation. The technical name for this issue is *theodicy* — that is, justifying God's actions and attitudes.

We don't pretend to have a definitive answer. We will, however, point out that the underlying theme of the Bible is that God is holy, just, righteous, gracious, loving, and merciful (Exodus 34:6–7). The consistent testimony of God's people through the ages is that all God does is good and right.

When trying to understand any single chunk of the Bible, view it in the context of the entire Bible. Try to set your own biases aside instead of imposing them on what you're reading. Does the resulting interpretation accord with reality, and does it cohere with the biblical perspective? See Chapter 17 for tips on sorting out Scripture properly.

Honing in on the horns of old

Trumpets played an important role in biblical history as well as in the Roman world of the first century:

- ✔ **Direction:** In the Old Testament, the Lord instructs Moses to make two silver trumpets (Numbers 10). These trumpets serve as directional and inspirational devices. For example, during the wilderness wanderings, the children of Israel assemble, pack up, and move out when they hear a distinctive blast from the trumpets. They stop and set up camp when they hear a different call (Numbers 10:3–8).

- ✔ **Military commands and morale:** During war, the trumpets indicate attack, retreat, and so forth. The sound of the trumpets also constantly reminds Israel that the Lord fights on their behalf (Numbers 10:9).

- ✔ **Dates:** The blowing of trumpets heralds various appointed festivals, the beginning of months, and the new year (Numbers 10:10, 29:1; Leviticus 23:24).

- ✔ **Royal crownings:** Trumpets sound at the coronation of Israelite kings (1 Kings 1:34, 1:39; 2 Kings 9:13).

Perhaps the most famous episode involving trumpets is at the battle of Jericho during the invasion of Canaan, the Promised Land (Joshua 6). Seven priests with seven trumpets blowing continuously lead the army of Israel around the city for seven days. On the seventh day, after circling the city seven times, blowing the trumpets continuously, the priests blow one final blast as the people shout to the Lord — and the walls of Jericho collapse. The parallel to the trumpet judgments of Revelation seems unmistakable. Like Jericho, the evil empire is going to tumble down.

Like the Israelites, the Roman army used trumpets as a tactical device during battle. Legionnaires performed certain maneuvers at the sound of trumpets. One of the keys to Roman success was the well-coordinated movements of the various military units. Perhaps this feature of mighty Rome also lies behind John's vision. The angelic legions are being unleashed against the inhabitants of earth.

The single, most important fact for understanding the trumpet judgments is this: They're *eschatological trumpets*. That's a fancy way of saying that they herald the day of God's wrath against sin. This theme is reflected in the Old Testament and in several apocalyptic works of roughly the same period as the book of Revelation, as well as in the New Testament (1 Corinthians 15:52; 1 Thessalonians 4:16).

The First Four Trumpets: Fire, Blood, and Hail

Revelation 8:7–12 describes the sounding of the first four trumpets:

> "The first angel blew his trumpet, and there came hail and fire, mixed with blood, and they were hurled to the earth; and a third of the earth was burned up, and a third of the trees were burned up, and all green grass was burned up. The second angel blew his trumpet, and something like a great mountain, burning with fire, was thrown into the sea. A third of the sea became blood, a third of the living creatures in the sea died, and a third of the ships were destroyed. The third angel blew his trumpet, and a great star fell from heaven, blazing like a torch, and it fell on a third of the rivers and on the springs of water. The name of the star is Wormwood. A third of the waters became wormwood, and many died from the water, because it was made bitter. The fourth angel blew his trumpet, and a third of the sun was struck, and a third of the moon, and a third of the stars, so that a third of their light was darkened; a third of the day was kept from shining, and likewise the night."

These first four trumpets focus directly on the planet earth. The Old Testament prophets speak of the dire consequences of sin on the environment and predict environmental repercussions for failure to keep covenant with God (Isaiah 24:4–13; Hosea 4:3). Because of massive noncompliance on the part of humanity, it's now zero-hour, and earth reels under a heavenly bombardment.

Trumpet 1: Plague on the land

"Hail and fire, mixed with blood" descend upon earth when the first angel blows his trumpet (Rev. 8:7). This seemingly incongruous mixture may describe, in graphic imagery, violent thunderstorms in which lightning and hail result in huge loss of life. Whatever its nature, the results are devastating.

Don't insist on a literal understanding of the fraction one-third. Fractions like one-third are a regular feature of apocalyptic imagery (see Zechariah 13:8–9; Ezekiel 5:1–2).

The takeaway point is this: Vegetation of all kinds is completely wiped out in large portions of the earth. If the third and fourth seals depict the ravages of famine *in the course of* world history (Rev. 6: 5–8 — see Chapter 9), this first trumpet results in famine on an unprecedented scale at the *end of* world history. Wealth is of little help now. Obviously, both domesticated and wild animals perish in vast numbers. The consequences are unimaginable. Human beings realize, too late, how dependent they are on the plant and animal kingdoms.

Trumpet 2: Plague on the high seas

When the second angel blows his trumpet, "Something like a great mountain, burning with fire, was thrown into the sea" (Rev. 8:8). One perspective is that this refers to an asteroid or comet slamming into the earth. After all, such things have occurred in earth history with devastating consequences. Alternatively, is it a reference to volcanic activity in the Mediterranean? In 79 CE, Mount Vesuvius erupted and buried the inhabitants of Pompeii and Herculaneum alive. As many as 10,000 people died in that disaster.

This imagery is typical of that found in other Jewish apocalyptic writings. John's vision, then, in keeping with apocalyptic imagery, seems to depict a planetary disaster involving a large portion of the oceans. The "sea" as the location for the impact of this asteroid-like object probably reflects the fact that the Roman Empire was essentially the land areas surrounding the Mediterranean Basin. This was, for all practical purposes, the extent of the known world at that time. The implication, then, is that this is a truly world-wide disaster. The impact is staggering, and the fallout, in terms of ecology, economics, and human life, is enormous.

Trumpet 3: Plague on fresh water

Compounding an already desperate situation, much of the freshwater sources of the planet are suddenly rendered toxic when the third angels blows his trumpet. As Revelation 8:10–11 says, "A great star fell from heaven, blazing like a torch, and it fell on a third of the rivers and on the springs of water. The name of the star is Wormwood."

A literal reading suggests something like an asteroid or comet. The problem here is the name given to the star. *Wormwood* — a type of bitter, poisonous herb (Jeremiah 9:15, 23:15) — almost makes it sound like a person whose name personifies what happens. Furthermore, in Jewish apocalyptic literature, stars are frequently associated with angelic or demonic beings. Following this tack suggests an angelic being who in some way degrades vast tracts of freshwater sources. The result is sobering: "Many died from the water" (8:11).

Some modern commentators, endorsing a literal interpretation of Revelation, draw attention to the increasing danger posed to world peace by inadequate drinking water. They entertain various scenarios involving international conflicts over the availability of drinkable water and cite this section of Revelation as support. Without denying the increasingly dangerous situation of adequate drinking water, we think this really misses the intent of John's vision. These are divine judgments without parallel in human history.

Trumpet 4: Plague on sources of light

The fourth trumpet involves something inexplicable in terms of known laws of physics. The light output from heavenly bodies diminishes one-third. Even worse, during a third of normal daylight hours and nighttime, total darkness reigns. This recalls the ninth plague of darkness upon Egypt (Exodus 10:21–22). The impact of such a reduction in light would be catastrophic. Besides the psychological effects (paralyzing fear and biological clocks completely out of synch), the consequences for earth's living creatures (death of plant life and animals that feed on it) are mind boggling. The bottom line is this: Panic paralyzes the planet.

In the Old Testament, judgment is depicted in terms of darkness. The Old Testament prophet Amos likens the Day of the Lord to a day of darkness (Amos 5:18). The prophet Joel chimes in with a similar conviction: "a day of darkness and gloom, a day of clouds and thick darkness!" (Joel 2:2). Jesus also predicts that "the sun will be darkened, and the moon will not give its light" (Mark 13:24).

But the darkness has an even darker side. In Scripture, darkness sometimes symbolizes the demonic. The fourth trumpet may foreshadow worse things to come. In this case, it points toward the fifth trumpet, which depicts a demonic invasion. The Dark Lord and his demons are about to prowl the planet, and before they do, it gets dark — really dark. In his Gospel, the Apostle John has a keen eye for this sort of symbolism. It's no coincidence in his Gospel when, after Satan possesses Judas during the Last Supper, John ominously informs his readers, "And it was night" (John 13:30).

Wailing the Woes of the Last Three Trumpets

At the end of Revelation 8, John hits the pause button, saying, "Then I looked, and I heard an eagle crying with a loud voice as it flew in mid-heaven, 'Woe, woe, woe to the inhabitants of the earth, at the blasts of the other trumpets that the three angels are about to blow!'" (Rev. 8:13). These "woes" are named appropriately: They're aimed directly at humanity itself.

The dark side now enters the arena: demonic invasion. No, the Martians aren't coming, nor are UFOs with strange-looking creatures — the situation's actually a lot worse than that. Demons from the bottomless pit are about to be unleashed on the Earth. Who you gonna call? Ghostbusters won't be any help this time!

Trumpet 5: Demonic locust plague

In Revelation 9:1–3, an angel blows the fifth trumpet. John sees a star fall from heaven to earth, and it receives a key to the bottomless pit (in some English translations, rendered "Abyss"). The fallen star then opens a shaft, allowing smoke and locusts to escape and envelop the earth (Rev. 9:1–3).

No, the star is most likely not a little twinkling star gone bad. Instead, in keeping with standard apocalyptic imagery, the star is probably an angel, just as Revelation 1:20 and 2–3 identify seven stars as the angels of the seven churches of Asia. The bottomless pit or abyss is another standard apocalyptic expression for the underworld, the place of the dead and demonic spirits.

Meeting the swarm

As for the locusts, these are really nasty creatures (Rev. 9:4–11). The imagery is related to the prophecy of Joel in the Old Testament. Joel envisions locusts descending upon the land of Judah in massive numbers. At first he seems to be describing the well-known and dreaded locusts that periodically infest the Middle East (Joel 1:1–7). But then his prophecy takes a bizarre turn, and he describes locust-like creatures that do the Lord's bidding. In this case, they wreak total destruction on the land. The prophet describes this plague as occurring during the Day of the Lord. Apparently, these are no ordinary locusts but an end-times mutant, even more terrifying than the normal ones (Joel 2:1–11).

The ancient Near East was subject to periodic locust infestations. Locusts occasionally experience a tremendous population explosion and form massive swarms. They then go in search of vegetation. The ancients were helpless in the face of such a plague. Today, aerial and satellite surveillance pinpoint such swarms, and pesticides head off potential disasters. The last major locust invasion in Israel occurred in 1916.

John echoes Joel's ancient prophecy by describing a demonic invasion under the figure of a locust invasion. These locusts are certainly not your typical, garden-variety locusts — they prefer humans to vegetation! The demons are permitted to torture those who lack the seal of God but are forbidden to kill them. The suffering is so intense that those stung attempt to commit suicide but are unable to.

John's depiction of these demonic locusts almost defies description. They're likened to powerful war horses having human faces (reminiscent of Ringwraiths from the J. R. R. Tolkien's book series *The Lord of the Rings*). The locust-demons wear crowns like kings and princes, and they have long, flowing hair like women and teeth like lions. Covered in scale armor, these creatures possess a scorpion-like tail with a stinger that inflicts intense agony (Rev. 9:7–10). The imagery combines to create a truly terrifying specter.

If there's a bright spot in this ghastly portrayal, it's this: The assault is limited to five months, the lifespan of ordinary locusts. The fact that God determines a limit points to the remedial aspect of the judgment: Rebellious sinners still have an opportunity to repent and switch allegiance to the Lord of light (Rev. 1:16). It also shows that God permits evil to carry out his own purposes. This is reminiscent of Isaiah 10:5–11, in which the Lord allows the cruel empire of Assyria to punish rebellious Israel and Judah. Later, the Lord punishes Assyria for its arrogance and excessive cruelty.

Debating demonic invasions

Is such a thing really conceivable? Theological assumptions play an important role in this question. If you believe that demons are real and that demonic possession is possible, then this scenario isn't off-the-wall. Jesus, the Apostles, and the church fathers, after all, believed in the reality of demons and demonic influence and possession (see Mark 1:32, 3:15, 7:26–30; 1 Corinthians 10:20–21).

Joel 2:1–11, along with Exodus 10:1–20 (the eighth plague against Egypt) and possibly Genesis 6:1–4, serve as the backdrop for the text in Revelation 9:1–11. A destroying angel leads the assault: "They have as king over them the angel of the bottomless pit" (Rev 9:11). John gives him a descriptive name: the double name of Abaddon (Hebrew for *Destruction*) and Apollyon (Greek meaning *Destroyer*). The Destroyer orders his horde of demons from the bottomless pit to assault the earth.

The great flood and the first wave of invasions

One school of thought is that Revelation 9:1–11 refers to a second great demonic invasion of earth. Supporters of this theory believe the first invasion occurred before the flood of Noah and was the reason for the destruction of all living things. In this perspective, the "sons of God" of Genesis 6:1–4 refer to fallen angels or demons who take possession of human beings and coexist with them. The result is a monstrous hybrid, the *Nephilim* (Genesis 6:4). In this scenario, the Lord intervenes with a cosmic judgment and initiates a new beginning (Genesis 7–8). Both demonic invasions occur prior to cosmic destructions: The world that was (the pre-flood world) perished by water; the post-flood world perishes by fire (2 Peter 2:4–10; 3:1–13). It bears repeating: The sealed saints aren't subject to this demonic assault (Rev. 9:4). The Dark Lord can't take any of the Lamb's followers (John 10:28–29).

Trumpet 6: Demonic cavalry

A divine command kicks off the sixth trumpet and second woe: "Release the four angels who are bound at the great river Euphrates" (Rev. 9:14). In Jewish and Christian apocalyptic tradition, angels perform various regulatory functions in connection with the cosmos. Evil angels are also depicted as bound or restricted to certain locations, sometimes in subterranean caverns, sometimes in a watery abyss. The four angels of Revelation 9:14 appear to fall into this latter category, only in this case, they're bound somewhere at the Euphrates River. This great river, because of its fame and importance, is often simply referred to as "the river" or "the great river" in the Old Testament.

The Tigris-Euphrates River Valley is significant because it was one of the two great "cradles of civilization" in the ancient Near East (the other being the Nile River Valley). It was also the eastern border of the Roman Empire. To the east lay the threatening kingdom of the Parthians, today the area of eastern Iraq and western Iran.

Perhaps the action of released angels, which isn't explicitly described here, is related to the sixth bowl, in which the Euphrates River dries up, allowing the kings of the east to invade the Holy Land (Rev. 16:12–16) (see Chapter 12 for details on the bowls). But for now, the four angels unleash an even more devastating demonic invasion, resulting in the torture and death of one-third the world's population (Rev. 9:15).

In keeping with apocalyptic traditions, the exact hour, day, month, and year of this conflict is predetermined, but only God knows when that is (see Daniel 12:7, 11–12). Jesus tells his disciples that the exact day and hour of his coming is also known only by the Father; not even he nor the angels know the exact date (Mark 13:32).

The fact that Jesus seems not to know the exact date of his return has prompted more than a little theological controversy. How can he truly be divine if he's limited in knowledge? The traditional response has been to say that during his earthly ministry, Jesus voluntarily laid aside certain divine attributes such as omniscience. Now, in his exalted state at the right hand of God the Father, he fully exercises all his divine attributes and knows exactly the day and hour of his return.

Commentators differ considerably on the occasion and combatants in the slaughter following the sixth trumpet (see Chapter 4 to discover the four basic approaches to the book of Revelation):

✔ **Idealists:** Idealists simply speak in generalities, namely that world conflict will result.

✔ **Historicists:** Historicists have championed a number of warmonger candidates, running the gamut from Genghis Khan to T. E. Lawrence (of Arabia).

✔ **Preterists:** Preterists most often suggest a Parthian invasion. Parthia, a kingdom lying east of the Euphrates River and stretching across Iran, was the eastern frontier of the Roman Empire. The Parthians were a feared opponent, having more than once bloodied the eastern legions. John pictures this vast army as cavalry, and the Parthians were famous for their swift horses.

✔ **Futurists:** Futurists of an earlier generation expected a literal cavalry, 200 million strong, to descend on Israel during the Tribulation. More recently, many have identified China as the invader. This invasion will supposedly force the Antichrist to intervene in the Middle East.

Modern futurists take the references to sulfur, fire, and smoke — and the enormous casualty rate — as evidence of thermonuclear weapons. In fact, some authors find allusions to a whole host of modern weapon systems in the book of Daniel, Ezekiel, and Revelation, including attack helicopters armed with a tail mount that sprays chemical and biological weapons!

Overall, many commentators argue in favor of a literal demonic army because the description exceeds anything known to human experience. Horses with lion-like heads and death-dealing mouths and tails, the latter having heads like serpents, probably indicate you're dealing with something supernatural. This connects the army with the fifth trumpet, the locusts, which most interpreters identify as demons.

Greek mythology includes a bizarre monster called Chimera (the name means *she-goat*). Chimera is a three-part creature, being like a lion in front, a snake behind, and a fire breathing she-goat in the middle. Perhaps John's vision adapts this mythological imagery.

Whether these creatures are literal or figurative, the havoc they wreak is real. Yet in spite of these demonic judgments, the survivors "did not repent of their murders or their sorceries or their fornication or their thefts" (Rev. 9:21).

Trumpet 7: Not just yet

The seventh — and last — trumpet, like the seventh seal (see Chapter 9), is delayed. Before moving on to the seventh and final trumpet, John describes two more intervening visions. Why the delay? In part because there's still more to relate concerning certain aspects of the End Times, and in part because when the last trumpet sounds, just like when the fat lady sings, it's over. Well, almost . . .

The First Interlude: The Angel and the Little Scroll

Like a commercial that comes right before you hear whether a contestant is going to win on a TV game show, an interlude appears at the beginning of Revelation 10 — it's time for a word from our sponsor. Destruction, judgment, and chaos are momentarily set aside to, among other things, announce no more delays!

But the more significant role of this vision of the angel and the little scroll is that of a re-commissioning. John is divinely directed to continue his role as prophet to the nations. He must warn them, like a watchman on a castle wall, of impending disaster.

Looking at a mighty angel

Emerging from the heavens in brilliant sunlight, an angel takes center stage:

"And I saw another mighty angel coming down from heaven, wrapped in a cloud, with a rainbow over his head; his face was like the sun, and his legs like pillars of fire. He held a little scroll open in his hand. Setting his right foot on the sea and his left foot on the land, he gave a great shout, like a lion roaring. And when he shouted, the seven thunders sounded. And when the seven thunders had sounded, I was about to write, but I heard a voice from heaven saying, 'Seal up what the seven thunders have said, and do not write it down.' Then the angel whom I saw standing on the sea and the land raised his right hand to heaven and swore by him who lives forever and ever, who created heaven and what is in it, the earth and what is in it, and the sea and what is in it: 'There will be no more delay, but in the days when the seventh angel is to blow his trumpet, the mystery of God will be fulfilled, as he announced to his servants the prophets.'" (Rev. 10:1–7)

Notice that John now appears to be viewing the action from the earth. Prior to this — after he was taken into the heavenly throne room (Rev. 4:1) — his vantage point was from heaven looking down on the earth. This alternation between heavenly and earthly perspectives is typical of apocalyptic literature, in which the seer moves easily between these two vantage points. This provides the reader with behind-the-scenes information and thus a more comprehensive picture of what's really going on than is accessible to outsiders.

At this point, John describes the descent of a powerful angelic figure to the earth as though he's looking upward. Perhaps it's fitting that he's on earth for this portion of the vision, because he's now re-commissioned to proclaim the End Time judgments. Like the prophets who preceded him, he ministers to his fellow humans.

ID-ing the angel

But who is this mighty angel referred to in Revelation 10:1? Is it Jesus? An archangel? Or neither? Well, it's most likely either Jesus or an archangel. Here are the arguments for each:

- ✔ **Jesus:** Because the description of the mighty angel in Revelation 10 includes items sometimes associated with deity, some commentators conclude that the angel is Jesus. For example,

  - "Wrapped in a cloud" describes God in Psalm 104:3.

  - "With a rainbow over his head" reminds readers of the rainbow above the throne in Revelation 4:3.

  - "His face was like the sun" recalls Revelation 1:16, where the risen Jesus is so described.

  - "His legs like pillars of fire" is similar to Revelation 1:15, where Jesus's feet are "like burnished bronze, refined as in a furnace."

  This, at first glance, is rather convincing. The problem, however, is that nowhere else in the book of Revelation is Jesus referred to as an angel. Furthermore, it seems inappropriate that the Lord of all creation should take an oath to God as the mighty angel does in Revelation 10:6. Also, there's no biblical support for the notion that humans actually *become* angels in heaven; they're only said to be *like* them in a few specific ways (see Matthew 22:30).

- ✔ **An archangel:** Most likely, the mighty angel belongs to one of the classes of angels mentioned in the Bible and in Jewish literature. Archangels, in particular, are very powerful and perform critically important roles in redemptive history. In Jewish tradition, the archangel Uriel is associated with light and the luminaries, and he carries out a number of important divine missions. You can also make a good case for Gabriel, who comes to Daniel's assistance and explains the meaning of a vision (Daniel 8:15–16). Gabriel is also the messenger who informs Zechariah and Mary of their key roles in the births of John the Baptist and Jesus (Luke 1:11–20, 1:26–38).

Keeping secret things

When the mighty angel straddles the planet and shouts, seven thunders resound, apparently with an intelligible message. As John is about to record the message, a divine voice restrains him: "Seal up what the seven thunders have said, and do not write it down" (10:4). Such a command is another standard feature of apocalyptic literature:

✔ Daniel is instructed not to let the contents of his prophecy be known to his generation (Daniel 7:28; 8:26; 12:4, 9).

✔ The Apostle Paul is forbidden to disclose the details of his visit to the throne room (2 Corinthians 12:4–7).

✔ In John's Gospel, Jesus cries out, "Father, glorify your name" (John 12:28). In response, "A voice came from heaven." Some who are present that day think "it was thunder." Others claim "an angel has spoken to him" (John 12:29). But none of them really understands what was said and what it means. In this instance, only for believers is the veil of secrecy removed. But even in the case of believers, some things remain hidden and secret, beyond comprehension. Such is the case here in Revelation 10:4. As Deuteronomy 29:29 says, "The secret things belong to the Lord our God."

One thing is quite clear: The end is imminent. When the seventh trumpet sounds, "the mystery of God will be fulfilled" (Rev. 10:7).

Tasting a bittersweet book

John is summoned to take a small scroll from the hand of the mighty angel and then eat it:

> "Then the voice that I had heard from heaven spoke to me again, saying, 'Go, take the scroll that is open in the hand of the angel who is standing on the sea and on the land.' So I went to the angel and told him to give me the little scroll; and he said to me, 'Take it, and eat; it will be bitter to your stomach, but sweet as honey in your mouth.' So I took the little scroll from the hand of the angel and ate it; it was sweet as honey in my mouth, but when I had eaten it, my stomach was made bitter. Then they said to me, 'You must prophesy again about many peoples and nations and languages and kings.'" (Rev. 10:8–11)

Visualizing this scene isn't easy. Imagine a gigantic angel straddling the continents and seas and John apparently zooming upward and asking for the scroll.

Similar to what happens with the Old Testament prophet Ezekiel (Ezekiel 2:10–3:3), John is told to eat the scroll. He's warned that at first it will taste sweet, but then it'll turn bitter in the stomach. The text itself gives no explanation for this turn of events. Perhaps it refers to how God's word is sweet if it's believed, but if ignored, it becomes a bitter word of judgment. The fact that the prophet ingests the scroll implies that the message itself becomes a part of the prophet's life. Being a true messenger of God involves living out its message, and sometimes that message is harsh and bitter. Judgment is hard to digest.

The Second Interlude: Two Star Witnesses in Jerusalem

In Revelation 11, a second interlude (which is also the second of the three woes) further delays the blowing of the seventh trumpet. John is transported to the streets of Jerusalem to witness a remarkable example of street preaching. Two Jews-for-Jesus make a big splash in the Holy City! In fact, they get the attention of the ultimate bad boy himself, the Antichrist. Here are a few of the highlights of this second interlude (see Rev. 11:1–11):

- John is told to measure the Temple.
- John is told about two witnesses who appear and prophesy for 1,260 days.
  - Fire comes from their mouths to kill any attackers.
  - They can stop rain and turn rivers into blood.
  - They can release any manner of plague anywhere on the earth.
- John is told about a beast from a bottomless pit that comes and kills the two witnesses.
  - The people of world celebrate the deaths of the witnesses.
  - After 3.5 days, the two witnesses return to life and go up into heaven.
- John is told about an earthquake that destroys one-tenth of the city.
  - 7,000 people die.
  - The survivors give praise to God.

In a mere 11 verses, you see an incredible story with multiple plot twists, populated by fantastic creatures and people with superpowers! Revelation may be complex, but it's definitely not a boring book of the Bible!

Measuring the Temple

Remember how the three ghosts of Charles Dickens's *A Christmas Carol* transported Ebenezer Scrooge through past, present, and future scenes? Scrooge could see and hear all the people around him, but they couldn't see him. That's sort of what happens to John in Revelation 1:1–11.

He has been transported to Jerusalem some time in the future, where he visits the Temple and sees all that takes place. But before the two witnesses show up, John is told to take a special measuring stick and measure the Temple of God and the great altar in front of it, as well as count the worshipers. This, of course, prompts a number of questions.

What is this Temple?

Bear in mind that at the time John wrote this vision, the second Jerusalem Temple had already lain in ruins for over 20 years (unless you opt for an early dating, in the 60s CE, for the book of Revelation — see Chapter 2 for details). Readers must either imagine a third Temple or use a symbolic interpretation. If you opt for a literal understanding, this lands you right in the middle of a highly controversial, politically charged issue! Will there be a third Temple? And if so, what happens to the Mosque of Omar, the famous Dome of the Rock that was built over the site of the original Temple? Christians affirm that God alone knows.

The New Testament includes one other place that some people interpret as a reference to a third Jewish Temple: Paul's passage describing the coming of the Antichrist, whom he calls "the lawless one" (2 Thessalonians 2:3–12). There, Paul says, "He [the Antichrist] takes his seat in the *temple of God*, declaring himself to be God" (2 Thessalonians 2:4). But there's considerable disagreement about what Paul means, and in other places, he says that believers themselves are the Temple of God (1 Corinthians 3:16, 6:19). Ultimately, it's an open question.

Why do measurements even have to be taken?

The background of John's action in measuring the Temple recalls a similar task undertaken by two Old Testament prophets, Zechariah and Ezekiel.

In Zechariah 2:1–5, the prophet observes an angelic surveyor taking a measuring line to determine the dimensions of a restored and rebuilt Jerusalem. Jerusalem had been burned to the ground by Nebuchadnezzar's army in 586 BCE. Living in the era of return and restoration, before the rebuilding of the walls by Nehemiah (444 BCE), Zechariah is informed by his angelic guide that the city will swell and sprawl beyond its historic boundaries.

Ezekiel assumes a rebuilt Jerusalem, but more importantly, given his priestly perspective, focuses on a blueprint for a greatly enlarged Temple replacing Solomon's structure (Ezekiel 40–48). His detailed measurements make up the bulk of this section of his book. An angelic being does the actual measuring with a 6-cubit-long reed (just over 10 feet long); Ezekiel writes down the measurements.

John echoes these prophetic accounts for his own purpose. The point seems to be a divine promise of protection for the people of God. That which God measures for restoration is safe from all alarms. This protective measure chimes in with Revelation 7, where John describes the sealing of God's people prior to the trumpet judgments (see Chapter 9).

Deciphering who or what the witness are

Who are these two witnesses of Revelation 11? This is the question everyone wants an answer to! From our experience, this section is one of the most difficult chapters to interpret in a book already notorious for its complexity.

A survey of commentaries reveals a dizzying array of candidates for the two witnesses. At least commentators agree that the number two is significant: This was the minimum number of required witnesses to sustain a charge in a court case (Deuteronomy 19:15). Beyond that, unanimity disappears. Here are some of the leading options:

- ✔ **Zerubbabel and Joshua the high priest:** Revelation 11:4 identifies the two witnesses as "the two olive trees and the two lampstands that stand before the Lord of the earth." This phrasing comes from Zechariah 4:3–14, where it refers to the two leaders of the post-exile Jewish restoration movement at the end of the sixth and beginning of the fifth centuries BCE. (This was a movement among dispersed Jews to return to their ancient homeland and rebuild a Jewish colony). However, it's more likely that John simply borrows the imagery and applies it to some other individuals or group.

- ✔ **The Law and the Prophets (Scripture):** In the first century, the Old Testament Scriptures were often referred to as "the Law and the Prophets" (see Matthew 5:17; John 10:34; Romans 3:31). Although the Scriptures serve as a witness to the truth, this hardly seems appropriate to the context of Revelation 11. The two witnesses, after all, are martyred and raised to life again!

- ✔ **Peter and Paul:** Advocates of an early dating for the book of Revelation (preterists) are more likely to suggest this option because both Apostles were martyred at about the same time during the latter part of the reign of Nero Caesar (64–68 CE). Highly problematic for this view, however, is the obvious fact that neither Apostle was brought back to life.

✔ **Israel and the Church:** This option capitalizes on the fact that both Israel and the Church (Christians) have a mission as witnesses to the nations (Isaiah 42:6–7, 49:6; Acts 1:8). Although martyrdom has often befallen Israel and the Church in their respective histories, and you can speak metaphorically of a "resurrection" for both in their ongoing mission, you have to ignore the details of Revelation 11 rather wholesale on such a view.

✔ **Enoch and Elijah:** These two are selected because both were raptured (taken up) to heaven and did not experience death (Genesis 5:24; 2 Kings 2:11). Because Hebrews 9:27 says, "It is appointed for mortals to die once," some expositors hold that these two prophets are required to return and experience death like all mortals before being resurrected and raptured again.

✔ **Moses and Elijah:** The context of Revelation 11 fits these two better than any previously mentioned. For example, take Revelation 11:5: "And if anyone wants to harm them, fire pours from their mouth and consumes their foes" corresponds to an episode in the life of Elijah (2 Kings 1:9–12), as does Revelation 11:6: "They have authority to shut the sky, so that no rain may fall during the days of their prophesying" (1 Kings 18). The last half of Revelation 11:6 says, "They have authority over the waters to turn them into blood and to strike the earth with every kind of plague, as often as they desire," recalling Moses and the plagues on Egypt (Exodus 7–12).

But is it credible to hold that these two individuals actually return to earth and carry out a witnessing ministry in Jerusalem? We can't rule this out. After all, according to the Gospels, Moses and Elijah appeared with Jesus to Peter, James, and John on the mount of Transfiguration (Matthew 17:1–8; Mark 9:2–8; Luke 9:28–36). Still, that appearance is hardly the same thing as the ministry described in Revelation 11. It's also true that the prophet Malachi spoke of Elijah's coming before "the great and terrible day of the Lord," in a context mentioning Moses (Malachi 4:4–5). In fact, there was an expectation among the Jewish people that Elijah would return and announce the coming of Messiah (see Matthew 17:10). To this day, observant Jews leave a special chair empty during the Passover ritual, giving tangible expression to the hope that Elijah will return and announce the coming of Messiah.

On the other hand, Jesus seems to identify John the Baptist as coming in the spirit and power of Elijah and, in that sense, he was Elijah (Matthew 11:14, 17:11). This seems to tip the scales against the notion that Moses and Elijah actually return for one more mission.

The answer to this question is tough. We think you can marshal a credible case for a more or less literal interpretation, involving two actual individuals who powerfully witness to the gospel during the first 3.5 years of the Great Tribulation in Jerusalem. Whereas many take a symbolic view of the "great city," we cautiously suggest that Jerusalem will indeed be the scene of this remarkable ministry. Our reasoning is that John's prophecy accords with Old

Testament prophecy placing Jerusalem right in the thick of things during the tumultuous Day of the Lord (see Zechariah 12–14). But, as is true with other parts of Revelation, no one knows the specific answer until it happens. You could say that John has written the ultimate cliffhanger!

A rising beast, raptured witnesses, and a deadly earthquake

The ministry of the two witnesses of Revelation 11 is cut short by "the beast that comes up from the bottomless pit" (Rev. 11:7). Interpreters agree that the beast is the Antichrist. The abrupt introduction of a key figure in apocalyptic literature is not unprecedented. Fortunately, John lingers later with another interlude (Rev. 12–13), adding more details to the portrait of this bad boy.

At this point, John is content to inform the readers briefly about a power encounter in Jerusalem. The two witnesses seem invincible. A divine aura protects them from enemies (11:5), and they possess unprecedented power over nature (11:6). Who can stand up to them? The answer is a bit frightening. Satan, the Dark Lord, conjures up a person who can not only take them on but defeat them. Arising from the bottomless pit, this satanically energized person kills the two witnesses and leaves their bodies exposed as an act of humiliation and intimidation. None dare oppose the beast from the bottomless pit without mortal consequences! But apparently, most earth-dwellers are quite happy with the outcome: Global celebrations over the demise of the two prophets take place.

Does the Dark Lord get the last word? No. After 3.5 days, the bodies of the two witnesses are raised and raptured (taken up) to heaven in plain view of eyewitnesses. In fact, their rapture is a command performance in response to God's command: "Come up here!" (11:12). This is followed by a most unsettling phenomenon for the inhabitants of Jerusalem: A devastating earthquake occurs, leveling a tenth of the city and resulting in 7,000 deaths.

The response of the survivors is instructive. This is the only time in the sequence of seal, trumpet, and bowl judgments that indicates a positive reaction. Though filled with terror at what had happened, John says they "gave glory to the God of heaven" (11:13). This is in stark contrast to the reactions to prior judgments, where the people cursed God. This is also the conclusion of the second woe mentioned in Revelation 8:13.

Calculating with prophetic years

John's vision in Revelation 11 draws heavily upon the book of Daniel. Two time periods signal this: "forty-two months" and "one thousand two hundred sixty days" (Rev. 11:2–3; see Daniel 7:25, 9:27, 12:7, 12:11–12).The book of Daniel equates these time periods with "three and one half years."

John takes over a chronological scheme in the book of Daniel and incorporates it into his framework for the Great Tribulation or Day of the Lord. Daniel contains a prophecy of a succession of world powers (symbolized by various predatory beasts) leading to the eventual arrival and triumph of God's kingdom (Daniel 7). In this sequence, the seer discovers that a particularly evil king reigns during the fourth kingdom "for a time, two times, and half a time" (Daniel 7:25). In the context of the book (see Daniel 4:16, 36), a "time" equals one year.

Furthermore, Daniel reinterprets Jeremiah's prophecy that after 70 years elapsed, Jews would return back to their ancestral homeland (Jeremiah 25:11–12). Daniel transposes the 70 years into 70 weeks of years, in which a "week" equals seven years. This, then, amounts to 490 years (70×7). Daniel sees that when the 490 years finally elapse, transgression, sin, and iniquity are put to an end and everlasting righteousness arrives (9:24). His primary focus, however, is on the seventh week of seven years. Apparently this "week" is divided equally into two segments of 3.5 years. During the second segment, an evil person commits outrage and abomination in Jerusalem. John apparently accepts this framework for his description of the last "week" of the prophetic calendar. Like Daniel, John paints a portrait of an evil person who commits blasphemy and persecutes God's people for 3.5 years.

In other words, the Tribulation is calculated to last one prophetic week — that is, seven years, in keeping with Daniel's chronology. Putting this all together, John pictures a scenario in Jerusalem in which two witnesses proclaim the gospel for 3.5 years before being martyred — the midpoint of the final seven years of earth.

Beginning of the End: The Seventh Trumpet

In Revelation 11:15, the seventh trumpet blast sounds, the last of the three woes mentioned in 8:13. The angelic choir again raises an anthem of praise. The keynote of fulfillment resounds in the heavens: "The kingdom of the world has become the kingdom of our Lord and of his Messiah" (Rev. 11:15). Seemingly, everything's ready for the grand celebration! The 24 elders intone the significance of this moment: "You have taken your great power and begun to reign" (Rev. 11:17).

As the great doors of the heavenly sanctuary open, John catches a glimpse of the Ark of the Covenant resting inside the Temple (Rev. 11:19). In both the Mosaic Tabernacle and the first and second Temples, the Ark resided in a special room called the *holy of holies,* whose dimensions formed a perfect cube. Accompanying this disclosure are features regularly associated with a theophany, or appearance of God: lightning, thunder, earthquake, and hail (see Exodus 19:16–19; Psalm 18:7–15).

Not to be confused with Noah's gigantic animal-filled boat, the Ark of the Covenant was the central piece of furniture in the Tabernacle, cloistered in a cubical room (15 × 15 × 15 feet; see Exodus 25:10–22). The *Tabernacle,* where the priests offered worship to God, was actually a very elaborate tent (Exodus 26). The Tabernacle was disassembled and reassembled over and over during the 40 years that the Children of Israel wandered in the desert after leaving Egypt.

The Ark (see Figure 10-1) was made according to the pattern God showed Moses on the mountain. In construction, it's essentially an acacia wood chest with a lid, covered in pure gold (see Figure 10-2). On the lid of the chest are two golden cherubim, angelic figures, facing each other with outstretched wings that touch above the Ark. Inside are the book of the covenant, containing the Ten Commandments (Exodus 24:12), a golden bowl of manna (Exodus 16:32–34), and later, Aaron's staff (Numbers 17:2–10). The Ark functions as Yahweh's footstool (1 Chronicles 28:2; Psalm 99:5), and a bright luminescence hovers over it.

Figure 10-1:
One artist's representation of the Ark of the Covenant.

The Jewish Museum, NY/Art Resource, NY

So, where is the Ark? What happened to it is a mystery. Most scholars think the army of the Babylonian king Nebuchadnezzar destroyed or melted it down in 586 BCE. Persistent Jewish traditions, however, claim that the priests or Jeremiah hid the Ark and that it remains hidden to this day. Several "arke-ologists" in modern times claim to have seen it or photographed it, but these claims are all fraudulent. The mystery surrounding the disappearance of the Ark, however, makes for a great movie, even though you can be sure it's not really stowed somewhere in a warehouse in Washington, D.C., as depicted in *Indiana Jones and the Raiders of the Lost Ark!*

The reappearance of the Ark in this moment functions as a symbol of God's faithfulness to his covenant promises. The people of God need a strong reminder of this because in the short run, they're about to experience the wrath of Antichrist.

Chapter 11

A Woman, a Dragon, Two Beasts, and More! (12:1–14:20)

In This Chapter

▶ Examining redemptive history in the story of the woman and the dragon

▶ Seeing the emergence of two beasts

▶ Reassuring the saints in the face of satanic opposition

*T*he climactic moment in the long struggle between good and evil begins, and the church is put on full alert. Revelation 12–14 can be viewed as describing a period of despair bracketed by a beginning and ending of hope. Revelation 12 reverberates with hope and victory for the believers, those who trust in the Lamb (Jesus) for their salvation.

Revelation 13, the middle section, is the rock bottom for the people of God. The forces of darkness and evil close in for the kill. Satan's Antichrist appears to crush all resistance. But suddenly, just when all seems lost, in chapter 14, the Lamb counterattacks with devastating effect. The forces of evil completely crumble and collapse. All this is crammed into three chapters in order to help the church cram for its last test.

In this chapter, you explore the topic of the Antichrist and why the Bible maintains that believers have no need to fear in face of satanic opposition.

Heavenly Drama: The Dragon Falls, the Woman Is Saved (12:1–17)

A skilled writer, John borrows imagery from the Old Testament and various pre-Christian traditions and weaves them into a new tapestry displaying distinctly Christian threads. In Revelation 12, he draws upon ancient, mythological traditions from Babylon, Egypt, Greece, and Rome, and of course, the Hebrew Bible. Out of these, he creates a mini drama about cosmic redemption.

The drama that unfolds is essentially the age old conflict between Jesus and Satan. The plot features a child of destiny, Jesus, who comes to planet earth to rule over all the nations. For his part, Satan resists this liberation movement by attempting to kill the infant Jesus. Failing this, he unleashes his venom against the historic people from whom Jesus descended (the Jewish people) and those who profess allegiance to him (the church). The warfare that rages in this conflict is truly cosmic in scope involving the celestial (heavenly) as well as the terrestrial (earthly) realms. After the last battle, a new heavens and a new earth emerge from the smoke of this protracted struggle (Rev. 21–22).

In composing this mini-drama, John incorporates imagery and concepts drawn from pre-Christian mythology and legend as window dressing. These borrowings are part of the shared traditions common to the Greco-Roman world to which John's audience belonged. By employing them, John adds vividness and luster to the basic storyline. C. S. Lewis does much the same in his Narnia books. The essential Christian message is dressed up in the language of myth and fable. In neither John's nor Lewis' case are they affirming belief in the window dressing; they are simply creatively retelling the familiar gospel story.

John sets up his dramatic vignette by depicting the leading characters under the guise of "portents." These "portents" signify something of great importance for understanding redemptive (biblical) history. In the following discussion, we offer our take on the identity and meaning of these portents.

Meeting the cast of characters

John's mini-drama involves three leading characters; two others appear in minor roles. Each of these figures appearing on stage convey important realities about redemptive history and thus are described as "portents" (omen). Because John and his first century audience share a common cultural heritage, which is not our own, the imagery and symbolism requires decoding.

Pregnant woman clothed with the sun

The first character to appear on the stage is "a woman clothed with the sun, with the moon under her feet, and on her head a crown of twelve stars" (Rev. 12:1). She speaks no intelligible lines but cries out in pain as she gives birth (Rev. 12:2).

As is common in apocalyptic literature, John depicts characters who function as symbols. A good example is an apocalyptic portion within a Jewish book called 1 Enoch, dating to a period before the beginning of Christianity. It retells the story of Israel using animals like cows, sheep, bulls, and rams as symbols for the leading characters (1 Enoch 83–90). For this reason, modern scholars designate this section as the "Animal Apocalypse." If one knows the story of Israel in the Bible, the various symbols are rather easily identified.

Matters are not so cut and dried in Revelation 12—considerable disagreement arises among scholars about the symbolic meaning of the woman. Here are four differing perspectives:

✔ **The people of God:** A majority of scholars identify the woman as the people of God — Israel of the old covenant and the church of the new covenant. One reason for this connection lies in Genesis 37:9–11, which shares some common features. In a dream, the 17-year-old Joseph sees the sun, moon, and eleven stars bowing down to him. His father Jacob, whose name was changed to Israel (Genesis 32:28), interprets this to mean that he and Rachel, Joseph's mother, will bow down and submit to Joseph's authority.

In John's adaptation of this vision, the twelve stars represent the twelve tribes of Israel (Jacob's 12 sons became the 12 tribes of Israel, as narrated in Genesis 29 through Exodus 1). Furthermore, in several poetic passages, prophets refer to Israel in the figure of a woman (Jeremiah 2–3; Ezekiel 23; Hosea 1–3) and, especially significant for this passage, as a woman in childbirth (Isaiah 26:17–18, 66:7; Micah 4:10, 5:3).

✔ **A Christianized version of ancient mythology:** Another possible source for John's imagery comes from the world of Babylonian, Egyptian, and Greco-Roman mythology. For example,

- From ancient Babylon comes a creation myth in which Marduk, the national god of Babylon, defeats the seven-headed, primeval dragon Tiamat.

- From Egypt comes a myth in which Set-Typhon, a red dragon, pursues Isis, a mother-goddess, only to be killed later with fire by her son Horus.

- Greek mythology provides perhaps even a closer parallel in the story of the pregnant goddess Leto. She is pursued by the dragon Python but escapes to the island of Ortygia.

Because his original readers were aware of these mythological traditions, John may have been borrowing some of the trappings. His finished product, however, is thoroughly Christianized, as seen in this line: "But they have conquered him by the blood of the Lamb" (12:11).

✔ **Domitia, the mother of God:** An intriguing possibility relates to the emperor Domitian. In the year 83 CE, Domitian's 10-year-old son died. In his grief, Domitian proclaimed his deceased son a god and his mother, Domitia, the mother of god. Coins from this period give expression to Domitian's fantasy. One coin, for example, displays Domitia enthroned, holding a scepter and wearing a diadem (a crown). The inscription reads "Mother of the Divine Caesar." Another coin depicts the child playing with the seven stars and sitting above the heavens. Still another coin shows Domitia on one side and the moon and six planets on the other (see Figure 11-1). On this view, John counters imperial ideology by indicating who the true Lord of heaven and ruler of all the kings of the earth really is.

✔ **Virgin Mary:** A very popular view during the medieval era and today in conservative Roman Catholic circles interprets the woman as the Virgin Mary. The correspondence in some of the imagery and storyline is obvious. Whether this is what John intended, however, is debatable. For the reasons stated in support of the first option, most Catholic scholars today agree that the woman symbolizes God's people of both the Old and New Testaments. One could, however, combine both views, in which case the Virgin Mary typifies or embodies the true people of God.

Figure 11-1:
A rendering of a Domitia coin.

Alicia South.

Red dragon with seven heads and bad attitude

Among scholars there's very little disagreement on who the red dragon from Revelation 12:3 represents. In fact, you can hardly miss the symbolism. The "great red dragon, with seven heads and ten horns, and seven diadems on his heads" is generally believed to be none other than Satan. In fact, John decodes this big, bad dragon in Revelation 12:9 — "The great dragon was thrown down, that ancient serpent, who is called the Devil and Satan, the deceiver of the whole world" — and later in Revelation 20:2.

Male child with iron scepter

The identity of the male child in Rev 12:5 seems an obvious reference to Jesus. Jesus is the one who will "rule all the nations with a rod of iron." In many translations, rod is translated as *scepter,* a symbol of power and royalty. John's opening salutation describes Jesus as "the ruler of the kings of the earth" (1:5), and to the conquerors at Thyatira Jesus promises, "I will give authority over the nations; to rule them with an iron rod" (2:26–27). And, says John, when Jesus finally returns, "he will rule them [the nations] with a rod of iron" (19:15). All this is based on Psalm 2:8–9, a Psalm given a messianic interpretation by some Jews well before the time of Jesus (see the sidebar, "Document 4Q174") and taken over and applied to Jesus by early Christians (Hebrews 1:2).

Document 4Q174

In 1947, a shepherd was herding his flock near Qumran, which is located near the Dead Sea. As the story goes, the shepherd thought some sheep had wandered into one of several caves in the area. He tossed a rock into one, hoping to scare the sheep out. Instead of bleating sheep, he heard the sound of breaking pottery. Going into the cave, he discovered several clay containers that held seven ancient scrolls. The year was 1947, and it marked the beginning of the further discovery of hundreds of documents in nearly a dozen caves; these documents are known as the Dead Sea Scrolls.

One of those documents provides evidence that some Jews interpreted Psalm 2 in terms of the Messiah. The reference appears in a sectarian, probably Essene, document, called *Midrash on the Last Days* and given the designation 4Q174. The Essenes are designated as a sectarian group because they broke away from the more influential and dominant group in first century Judaism, the Pharisees. A midrash is an interpretation or paraphrase of a biblical text. The text quotes Psalm 2:1 and then offers this comment: "The meaning is that the nations shall set themselves and conspire vainly against the chosen of Israel [a title for the Jewish Messiah] in the Last Days. That will be the time of persecution that is to come upon the House of Judah, to the end of sealing up the wicked in the consuming fire and destroying all the children of Belial [another name for Satan]. Then shall be left behind a remnant of chosen ones, the predestined."

So what does 4Q174 mean? This code is easy to break! The number 4 means this document was found in cave four (there were 11 in all) and the Q means it was found at Qumran, a site along the northwestern shore of the Dead Sea. The number 174 is an inventory number given by the researchers who studied the various documents. The total number of manuscripts found in these caves is thought to be between 800 and 900. The settlement was inhabited by an ascetic group of Jews called the Essenes. They rejected both the Sadducees and Pharisees as incorrect interpreters of the law of Moses. They consequently withdrew into the Judean desert to await the coming of two Messiahs — one from the line of David and the other from the priestly line of Zadok. They expected a decisive battle against evildoers (which included the Sadducees and Pharisees!) in the End Times.

Michael the mighty archangel

Revelation 12 speaks of Michael the archangel (Rev. 12:7), a regular character in Jewish and Christian apocalyptic writing. He is typically the defender of Israel (Daniel 12:1) and the leader of the angelic army loyal to God (Daniel 10:13, 10:21; Jude 9). In the Dead Sea Scrolls he appears ten times and functions as the great protector of God's people and as one who administers judgment upon the wicked forces allied against Israel. He also conveys heavenly mysteries and explains their meaning to a visionary like Enoch (See 1Enoch 9:1; 10:11; 20:5; 24:6). He may be the unnamed archangel the Apostle Paul had in mind when he described what would happen at Jesus' second coming (1 Thessalonians 4:16).

With the wings of an eagle

Does Revelation 12:14 refer to an eagle or just its wings? If it's an eagle, could be this the same eagle that announces the three woes back in Revelation 8:13? If so, the eagle may represent an angelic being.

Or perhaps John depicts some powerful king or kingdom under the figure of an eagle. A passage in Ezekiel may shed some light. In Ezekiel 17, the prophet gives an allegory involving two powerful eagles. The first represents the Babylonian monarch, Nebuchadnezzar. The second is Psammetichus II of Egypt. Judah sought, unsuccessfully, to resist Nebuchadnezzar by forming an alliance with Psammetichus (Jeremiah 37:5).

In this regard, it's perhaps worth noting that the Roman legions had an eagle on top of their standards. John's first readers may have immediately thought of Rome. A number of prophecy buffs today see a reference to the United States of America symbolized in the American bald eagle.

Most likely, the passage means only the wings, not the whole eagle, related to the imagery of Exodus 19:4 and Deuteronomy 32:11. This would mean you can view the eagle as representing God's protection for the faithful remnant of the End Times. This may, of course, involve angelic agency, here depicted as a great eagle.

Unpacking the plot and viewing the action

Now that the leading characters appearing onstage have been identified, we're ready to let the drama unfold. The drama consists of three acts arranged in a logical, if not chronological sequence. The first act is necessary to understand what happens in the second and the second is essential for grasping what happens in the climactic third act. The bottom line is this: We learn why the dragon is so filled with rage. Despite his best efforts, he can't thwart the kingdom of the child destined to rule the nations. He can cause carnage, but he can't keep control of planet earth.

Act one: The great escape

Act one opens with an immediate, life-threatening danger: a woman in the throes of child birth confronted by a red dragon intent on devouring her new-born! The dragon is backed up by fallen angels (or demons). One thinks here of the Death Eaters in Harry Potter: "His tail swept down a third of the stars of heaven and threw them to earth" (Rev 12:4).

Amazingly, the child escapes. All you're told is that he is "snatched away and taken to God and to his throne" (Rev. 12:5). So, who is this child? As mentioned above, most commentators understand this as a reference to Jesus. However, a few express doubts that a Christian writer like John would tell the story of Jesus in such a compressed way, without even mentioning the cross and resurrection. Moving from birth to ascension leaves out incredibly important parts! But that shouldn't be seem as a great problem. John is selective and creative. He doesn't feel compelled to "give the whole ball of wax" because his audience is already aware of the details.

For example, the original recipients of Revelation would be aware of the Gospel of Matthew, which provides a fuller account of the birth of Jesus. According to Matthew, eastern astrologers (magi or wise men) arrive in Jerusalem (Matthew 2:1–12). They're convinced from observations of a certain "star" that the promised Messiah has been born in Judea. Unfortunately, they go straight to the man in charge, the paranoid and cruel Herod the Great, and ask where the child is. Herod pretends to sincerely desire to show homage to this heir to the kingdom. Having asked the religious experts where the Messiah was prophesied to be born and learning it was Bethlehem (Micah 5:2), Herod dispatches the magi with instructions to let him know when they find the child. Herod's intention is to murder the infant in order to eliminate any potential threat to his power.

Providentially, God steps in to save Jesus' life. That is, God oversees the course of history down to the smallest details. In this instance, by means of a dream, the wise men are warned not to return to Herod. Then an angel alerts Jesus' father Joseph to the mortal danger and Joseph flees to Egypt with his family just in the nick of time. When Herod realizes he's been outsmarted, he orders a massacre of all males two years old or younger in the village of Bethlehem, adding to his already long list of atrocities.

John's vision summarizes the same event but from "behind the scenes." In other words, behind all the plotting of the paranoid Herod, the devil is at work. John's vision unmasks the ultimate culprit. Satan works through people who fully embrace evil to achieve their own ends (similar to the tragic story of Faust, who sold his soul to the devil).

Act two: A cosmic slugfest

Act two quickly ensues in Revelation 12:7–12. Satan (appearing as a dragon and later as a serpent) has been outwitted. An all-out heavenly war erupts between the good angels under the command of Michael and the evil angels led by the dragon. This cosmic slugfest results in the ousting of Satan and his evil cronies. They're consigned to the earth. This seems to be a case of good news/bad news. The good news is that Satan has no more influence in heaven; the bad news is that planet earth becomes his base of operations.

In this mini-drama, the final chapter of earth history is characterized by a cosmic power struggle. In John's vision, a loud voice from heaven spells out what this all means: "Rejoice then, you heavens and those who dwell in them! But woe to the earth and the sea, for the devil has come down to you with great wrath, because he knows that his time is short!" (Rev. 12:12). A determined and desperate devil digs in for "the last battle." He wants to take as many with him as he can.

However, in spite of all the threatening talk about Satan, Satan suffers two stunning setbacks in this section. Michael and the angels oust him from the heavenly court and the saints on earth also defeat him. How do they, so much weaker in virtually every way, manage to overcome the powerful red dragon? The answer is once again expressed in Johannine paradox: "they have conquered him by the blood of the Lamb and by the word of their testimony" (Rev. 12:11). They trust in the death of the Lamb on their behalf and remain faithful to him even to the point of death (12:11b).

Act three: Satan on a leash

Act three returns the woman to center stage. The dragon directs his rage at the woman who gave birth. But Satan is on a leash; he doesn't have unlimited power. God providentially protects the woman — the people of God (see the earlier "Meeting the cast of characters" section) — from Satan's assaults. This is the message John wants the church of his day to hear — a message relevant for the church throughout the last days.

From the New Testament perspective, "the last days" began at Pentecost (Acts 2:17–21; Hebrews 1:2) and continue until the Parousia (the second coming of Jesus).

Remarkably, Revelation 12:12–16 describes an extraordinary rescue operation. It's as if the woman drank an energy drink that literally gave her wings! How cool is that? So, what can you make of these mysterious eagle wings that carry the woman away to a wilderness retreat, "where she is nourished for a time, and times, and half a time" (three and one half years or 42 months or 1,260 days)? Then the dragon tries to drown the woman with a flood of water issuing from his mouth. But the earth comes to the woman's rescue and swallows up river. Once again the dragon is prevented from destroying the woman, the people of God. Admittedly, this is another difficult passage, and interpreters diverge in keeping with the degree of literalness they employ. Here a couple of interpretations:

- **Literal view:** On a more-or-less literal reading, the woman represents the Jewish people of the End Times. They come under satanic attack led by the Antichrist (the beast of Rev. 11:7 and Rev. 13). God providentially rescues them (perhaps by aircraft?) and transports them to a sanctuary in the Negev (a wilderness area of southern Israel).

  One expositor of an earlier generation, Dr. Louis Talbot, believed the rose-red city of Petra (in modern-day Jordan) would serve as a safe haven during the great tribulation. Following up on this conviction, he arranged to have Gospel pamphlets printed and stashed in Petra in anticipation of that time! Needless to say, this goes well beyond what the biblical text actually says.

Tim LaHaye, in his novel *Desecration: Antichrist Takes the Throne* (the ninth book in his *Left Behind* series) takes the woman to represent "tribulation saints" — that is, individuals, both Jewish and Gentile, who are not believers when the rapture occurs but come to faith in Jesus during the great Tribulation. They're part of a resistance movement dubbed "the Tribulation Force." LaHaye sketches a scenario in which a million believers, including many Israelis, escape the Antichrist's wrath by also fleeing to Petra. This planned escape is called "Operation Eagle," based on Revelation 12:14.

✔ **Symbolic view:** Those holding a symbolic view explore the imagery drawn from the whole of Scripture. They believe this passage resonates with echoes of the story of the Exodus from Egypt. For example, notice the following items:

- Just like the red dragon who pursues the woman, so Pharaoh pursued the Israelites when they left Egypt (Exodus 14:8).

- The reference to the two wings of an eagle recalls the words of the Lord in Exodus 19:4: ". . . I bore you on eagles' wings and brought you to myself."

- Perhaps readers hear an echo of Pharaoh's charge to drown Hebrew babies (Exodus 1:22) when the serpent pours forth water like a river in order to drown the woman.

- The opening of the earth to swallow up the water may allude to the episode in the wilderness when the rebellious house of Korah was swallowed up by the earth (Numbers 16:31–33).

The bottom line is this: The imagery emphasizes God's providential protection for his people during the great Tribulation. This doesn't mean they're spared the wrath of the Antichrist. Rather, it means the Antichrist can huff and puff as much as he wants, but he won't be able to blow the house down. Those who believe in Jesus will emerge victorious whether by life or death. After all, Jesus himself promised that "the gates of Hades will not prevail against it [the church]" (Matthew 16:18).

Two Beasty Boys Join the Dragon to Make Their Mark (13:1–18)

As Revelation 13 begins, John describes how the dragon (Satan) spawns and empowers two henchmen who set out to deceive the world and destroy the *Fellowship of the Lamb*. In this chapter, you are introduced to the members of the unholy trinity and how they manage to take control of planet earth. You see how through a counterfeit miracle, a mock resurrection, the beast from the sea (antichrist) secures economic and political control of the world. The beast from the earth, the antichrist's minister of propaganda and high priest, installs a false religious system requiring worship of the beast. A worldwide identification scheme, the infamous number of the beast, 666, is implemented. Only those bearing the number and thus cooperating and participating in this godless cult can buy or sell. The fellowship of the Lamb is on the brink of extermination.

Monster mash: The Antichrist, beast of the sea

In ancient mythology and in the Hebrew Bible, the sea often represents an unruly force echoing the chaos that existed prior to the creation of the earth (Genesis 1:2). One version of a creation story from Babylon, called *Enuma Elish*, speaks of the primeval sea waters as a great dragon called Tiamat. In this epic myth, Tiamat and Marduk (see Figure 11-2), the young, powerful god of Babylon, engage in hand-to-hand combat. Psalm 74:13–14 borrows the imagery of this primeval duel but changes the names: It's not Marduk but Yahweh who overcomes the chaos monster Leviathan. Just before this trial by arms, Tiamat spawns a massive army of dragons. (If you're a *Lord of the Rings* fan, think Sauron and his Orcs.) In keeping with that imagery, the dragon of Revelation now conjures up the ultimate chaos monster; "a beast rising up out of the sea, having ten horns and seven heads; and on its horns were ten diadems, and on its heads were blasphemous names" (Rev. 13:1). This monster shows up again in Revelation 17–18.

Figure 11-2: The ancient dragon Tiamat and the Babylonian god Marduk.

John's description of the beast also incorporates important information from the book of Daniel. The beast from the sea is a composite beast displaying features of a leopard, bear, and lion. Daniel uses these three animals to depict a sequence of four world empires that precede the final kingdom of God (Daniel 7). Many conservative scholars understand this sequence accordingly:

1. The lion represents Babylon under the authority of Nebuchadnezzar.

2. The bear represents the large and powerful kingdom of Persia launched by Cyrus the Great.

3. The leopard represents the lightning-fast conquests of the Macedonian Greeks under Alexander the Great.

4. The nondescript beast who supplants all previous kingdoms is either Rome or the final kingdom of the Antichrist.

5. The little horn with human-like eyes and arrogant mouth is either Antiochus IV Epiphanes (215–163 B.CE) or the Antichrist. Some interpreters see this as a case of typology. Typology is a way of linking persons, events or institutions from one biblical era to a later one, especially the Old and New Testaments. This is usually stated in terms of a foreshadowing. It assumes that there is a correspondence or pattern that unfolds within salvation history. In this particular case, Antiochus IV of the second century B.CE (the era of the Maccabean Revolt) foreshadows the final Antichrist of the end times.

In John's vision, the beast from the sea is so terrifying and hideous he incorporates all the evils of the wicked world empires preceding him. The most alarming fact about this beast is his source of power and authority: The dragon energizes the beast and authorizes him to act on his behalf. This is Satan's most cunning creature ever — it's not a physical beast, like Godzilla walking around and terrorizing the earth. He's a human being, no doubt possessing charm and charisma, who cobbles together an immense, international, economic and political coalition, all under the direct control of Satan. John, however, describes him under the guise of ferocious beasts in order to expose his real character and intentions.

The dragon cons the world into believing the beast is invincible. Receiving an apparently mortal blow to one of his heads, the beast recovers. It seems to be a miracle. In fact, it's a parody of the resurrection of Jesus. The world is amazed and responds with worship and adulation directed to both the dragon and his protégé: "They worshiped the dragon . . . saying, 'Who is like the beast, and who can fight against it?'" (Rev. 13:4). The answer seems to be *no one.*

A reign of terror ensues. The beast seizes power and authority over the entire planet. For the first time since the Tower of Babel (Gen. 11:1–9), a one-world government arises. God is ridiculed and debunked in the new regime. The beast claims he is God. This seems to be the same event the Apostle Paul describes in 2 Thessalonians 2:4: "He opposes and exalts himself above every so-called god or object of worship, so that he takes his seat in the temple of God, declaring himself to be God." For 42 months (three and a half years) the beast holds the reins of power. The church and all others are unable to stop him. But believers aren't powerless. They refuse to worship the beast or receive his mysterious mark. John inserts a word of admonition and exhortation, noting the pointlessness of mounting a violent resistance (Rev. 13:9–10). The exhortation has special relevance for believers in the first century confronting the blasphemous claims of the imperial cult. But it also has relevance for succeeding generations who must likewise resist false ideologies that supplant God. One thinks of Christians like Dietrich Bonhoeffer who resisted, at the cost of his life, the Nazi ideology during WWII. The primary reference, however, is for that last generation of Christians who are called upon to resist the onslaught of the antichrist. Believers, however, should not lose their cool. This is all foreseen by God. He knows precisely what's happening. The saints must do the one thing in their power left to do: They must continue to be faithful to the Lamb even if it costs them their lives. As John says in Revelation 13:10, "Here is a call for the endurance and faith of the saints."

Head of PR: The false prophet, beast from inner earth

In Revelation 13, the dragon (a.k.a. Satan) conjures up a second beast, this time from the depths of the earth, that has two horns like a lamb and speaks like a dragon (Rev. 13:11). Like many of the beasties and other odd critters found in Revelation, this beast is not a literal monster but rather is a symbol. In this case, the beast is an individual who heads up a world government.

Ancient and apocalyptic mythologies speak of two primeval monsters: a sea monster called Tiamat or Leviathan and a land monster, sometimes called Behemoth (1 Enoch 60:7–10; Isaiah 27:1; Job 20:15). John may draw upon these two primeval monsters in his portrayal of the Antichrist and his false prophet.

Although we don't know exactly what form this beast will take, we do have some good clues as to its character:

- **It has two horns like a lamb might have**. This could imply an attempt to appear like the Lamb of God. In apocalyptic literature, animals with horns, like sheep and goats, are regularly used as symbols of strength and power (See Daniel 8).

- **The beast speaks like a dragon**. This doesn't mean he speaks in some kind of mythic language only other dragons can understand. It refers rather to the nature or substance of what he has to say. Because Satan has already been characterized by John as a dragon, it's a safe bet that this beast's words will be deceptive and dangerous.

Combining the two character traits symbolized by the lamb-like horns and dragon tongue, what you get is a real beastly wolf in sheep's clothing! He's the consummate false prophet, and, in fact, is so designated later (Rev. 16:13; 19:20; 20:10). A charismatic figure, the beast from the earth serves as the minister of propaganda for the beast from the sea. He performs miraculous signs like a modern Moses or Elijah and thoroughly hoodwinks a credulous world. In short, the beast from the sea functions as an unholy spirit. Together, beast one (from the sea) and beast two (from the earth) represent the Antichrist and the false prophet.

The false prophet seeks to glorify the Antichrist in the eyes of the unbelieving world by setting up a blasphemous cult featuring a speaking image of the beast. The beast must be worshiped as a god, and the penalty for disobedience is death. There's no escape for members of the Fellowship of the Lamb. A worldwide registration system comes online, the notorious "mark of the beast."

As early as the days of Caligula (41 B.CE), a near-crisis occurred when Caligula insisted that his statue be worshiped in the Jerusalem Temple. The Jewish people were prepared to resist his decree to the death. Fortunately, he was assassinated before the command was carried out. In John's day, worship of the divine Caesar was mandatory in some Asian cities, and at least one Christian, Antipas, suffered martyrdom for disobeying (Rev. 2:13). The imperial cult is doubtless the lens through which John portrays the false prophet's ministry (for more on emperor worship in Ancient Rome, see Chapter 2).

Beastly markings: 666

Perhaps no single feature of the book of Revelation has intrigued readers as deeply as the mark of the beast and its mysterious number, 666. The false prophet (beast from the earth) institutes a registration system whereby followers of the sea beast all receive a number stamped on either their right hand or forehead. Without this number, no one can buy or sell. Survival literally depends on having this number, which is "the name of the beast or the number of its name."

So, what is this mysterious number and whom does it represent? Given that John states, "This calls for wisdom: let anyone with understanding calculate the number of the beast" (Rev. 13:18), you'd almost think all you need to do is pull out a calculator and go at it! Some people have tried that approach, which has yielded some pretty offbeat conclusions. Like a Gordian Knot, the problem of perpetual motion, and Colonel Sander's secret blend of 11 herbs and spices, the number of the beast has kept scholars scratching their heads for ages. Here's a sampling of proposed explanations for the identity and mark of the beast.

Nero Caesar

The early church Father Irenaeus, in the second century CE, mentions that people were already suggesting many candidates for the role of Antichrist. One in particular was at the top of the list — and with good reason. Nero Caesar's brief but bloody persecution of Christians in the aftermath of the fire in Rome (64 CE) qualified him because Revelation 17:6 describes a woman (closely identified with the beast) as "drunk with the blood of the saints and the blood of the witnesses to Jesus."

A rumor that became a legend circulated to the effect that Nero either had not died (the official report said he committed suicide), or that he died but would come back from the dead. Supposedly he was alive and well in Parthia (Rome's bitter rival in the east) and would soon return and wreak vengeance on Rome. This became known as the *Nero redivivus* legend. Perhaps a majority of modern scholars think John had this in mind when he penned this section, even if he only borrowed the legend in order to depict an eschatological (end times) figure.

Here's where the story gets interesting and somewhat involved: If one takes the name of Nero Caesar, converts it into Hebrew letters, and then takes the numeral value of the letters according to their order in the alphabet, the sum is 666. This kind of calculation is part of a system of interpretation called *gematria* and was popular not only in Jewish circles but in Roman culture as well. Examples of *gematria* can be seen on the walls of the Roman city Pompeii.

Irenaeus, however, warns his readers not to engage in idle speculation. The number can be known only when the antichrist actually arrives on the scene. For now, he notes, only God knows what the number means and who the antichrist is. Yet, in spite of Irenaeus's warning, scholars have tried their hand at breaking the code, with astonishingly different results!

The pope

The Reformers, locked in an often-violent struggle over control for the hearts and minds of European Christians, readily found ammunition for their apologetic cannons by pillorying the pope as the antichrist. The primary source for this identification comes later in Revelation 17–18. The mention of the seven mountains (Rev. 17:9) seemed to point to Rome, the center of papal power. Mention of being clothed in purple and scarlet, gold and jewels, along with a golden cup of abominations (thought to be an allusion to the doctrine of *transubstantiation*, the Roman Catholic teaching that the bread and wine of the Eucharist actually become the body and blood of Christ when consecrated by the priest) seemed quite sufficient for the Reformers to erase all doubt: The pope was indeed the antichrist.

The number 666 was accordingly viewed as symbolic of the evil papal system. Because six falls short of perfection (seven), it is suitable as the number for fallen humanity. Thrice six simply intensifies the evil of this wicked person and institution. The first edition of the Church of England's *Westminster Confession of Faith* (1646) says, "There is no other Head of the Church, but the Lord Jesus Christ; Nor can the Pope of Rome, in any sense be head thereof: but is that Antichrist, that Man of sin and Son of Perdition, that exalteth himself, in the Church, against Christ, and all that is called God" (Chapter XXV, VI). This section of the book has long since been deleted. Today, only a tiny minority of commentators hold this view.

Napoleon Bonaparte

During the upheavals of the late eighteenth and early nineteenth centuries, more than a few commentators and preachers identified Napoleon Bonaparte, the Corsican corporal himself, as the antichrist. His return from exile in Elba (the wound that seemed mortal, Rev. 13:3) and mobilization of another army (Rev. 16:14–16) seemed to unfold according to the script. Then there was Waterloo, exile in St. Helena, and death — but no return to life. Another candidate faded from memory.

Assorted modern dictators and tyrants

In more recent times, a number of Bible teachers and preachers went into print claiming that Adolf Hitler and Benito Mussolini were the antichrist, or perhaps together, were the beast and false prophet. In fact, if one added Japan's emperor Hirohito to the equation, you had the three, self-designated Axis powers, a kind of unholy trinity from the perspective of the Allies! Needless to say, the Axis perpetrated enough heinous crimes to merit the dubious distinction. But that terrible time fell far short of fulfilling John's prophecy. Joseph Stalin, Mao Tse-tung, Pol Pot, Saddam Hussein, and Osama Bin Laden, among others, merit mention in this infamous "Hall of Shame" for ordering or otherwise causing the deaths of so many. Each of them displayed a measure of cunning and cruelty that Revelation's antichrist no doubt possesses in unprecedented measure.

World-renowned leaders

We mention the following people because they illustrate only too well the need for Irenaeus's warning about speculation. A few Bible prophecy buffs, following the old theory that the antichrist is a Jew, latched onto one of the most charismatic and enigmatic political figures of the twentieth century, Henry Kissinger, Secretary of State under President Richard Nixon. More than a little whiff of anti-Semitism can be detected in this supposed identification. Still others pointed to Mikhail Gorbachev, whose only real "credential" — besides that fact that he was the General Secretary of the Communist Party and President of the Soviet Union (some believe that Communism is a tool of Satan and will eventually be controlled by the Antichrist) — was a rather prominent birthmark on his forehead!

Buildings, phone numbers, and computer codes

Speculation still runs rampant about the number 666. Bar codes and microchips provide a field day for 666 sleuths! The Internet abounds with theories, and new sightings regularly surface. A prominent building in New York City bears the address 666; rumors persist that it serves as the future office for the antichrist. When a new computer system came online in Europe with the code name 666, the prophecy experts were all over it! And when a telephone company assigned the area code 666 to a part of the Bible Belt in Kentucky, the uproar was sufficient to have it changed! One "expert" observed that Ronald Wilson Reagan's full name has six letters in each name; to top it off, when he left Washington, the number of his new address was originally 666. He had it changed to 668. So what's in a number? Apparently a lot!

The PIN of the antichrist

Most scholars in the premillennial tradition (Jesus returns to the earth and reigns a thousand years before the final judgment and the new heavens and earth) believe the beast from the sea represents an actual person who heads up an evil empire. They further contend that 666 symbolizes who this person is, a kind of personal identification number (PIN). They claim that the notion of six as the number of imperfection and fallen humanity makes sense. In the Bible, seven is often referred to as representing perfection, so six would be imperfect, and thus 666 emphasizes three times over the evil and depravity of the person and his kingdom. But as to his specific identity, most believe that only when he is actually revealed may his identity be known with certainty.

Many historical figures and regimes have embodied some of the features of the antichrist (despotic cruelty and oppression for example) but none have come close to matching the scale of deception and devastation depicted in Revelation 13. Does he, she, or it exist somewhere on the earth right now? Only time will tell! How's that for a definitive non-answer to the mystery of 666?

The Lamb and the 144,000 (14:1–5)

Revelation 14 opens with an image that gives comfort to all people of God: The Lamb is standing on Mount Zion with the redeemed. By sharing a short celebration that includes thunder, harps, and a new song, John assures believers that ultimate victory belongs to the Lamb.

The 144,000 (the number is symbolic) first mentioned in Revelation 7 (see Chapter 9) reappear in John's vision — this time on Mount Zion, with the Lamb, around the throne of God. Etched on their foreheads, as opposed to 666, is the name of the Lamb and the Father speaking to the character and status of those who bear it. These are sons and daughters of God. None of them have the dreaded mark of the beast. They've resisted the most intense pressure and persecution imaginable. Their unswerving loyalty and commitment is expressed in the following biblical imagery:

✔ **Virgins, or those who kept themselves pure:** This description draws attention to spiritual fidelity and chastity. In the Old Testament, Israelites frequently turned away from God and worshipped other gods, committing a kind of spiritual adultery. In the New Testament, believers are warned about mixed loyalties (Matthew 6:14; 1 John 2:15, 5:21). In this context, the redeemed are called virgins (some translations are more descriptive, indicating they avoided sexual relations) because they acknowledge and confess that only Jesus is Lord: "These follow the Lamb wherever he goes" (Rev. 14:4). True believers in Jesus are, figuratively, the pure bride of Jesus.

In the first century CE, Christians had to make a choice: Is Caesar Lord or is Jesus Lord? Those who chose Jesus ended up as macabre entertainment and food for lions. According to Revelation, the End Time generation will have to make a similar choice: Is the beast of the sea Lord or is the Lamb Lord? The redeemed choose the Lamb and celebrate their choice by singing a song of redemption that only they can sing.

✔ **First fruits:** In the Old Testament, Israelites were commanded to bring a portion of the early harvest of the land to the Temple of God as an act of thanksgiving and gratitude for the full harvest to follow (Leviticus 19:23–25, 23:9–21; Deuteronomy 26:1–11). These first-fruit offerings also supplied the priestly and Levitical families (those belonging to the tribe of Levi and assigned to assist the priests at the tabernacle as specified in Numbers 3–4) who ministered before the Lord at the sanctuary and were not able to spend the time in the fields themselves. Metaphorically, the expression refers to that which is first (Jeremiah 2:3) and that which belongs solely to the Lord. In the New Testament, believers are referred to as first fruits (James 1:18; 2 Thessalonians 2:13; Romans 8:23).

✔ **Blameless:** The 144,000 reflect their status as followers devoted completely to the Lamb by virtue of their virtue. Transparent integrity characterizes these redeemed. John probably alludes to a prophetic text in Zephaniah 3:13: ". . . the remnant of Israel; they shall do no wrong and utter no lies, nor shall a deceitful tongue be found in their mouths." The stark contrast to the deceit and deception of the dragon and the beasts is unmistakable.

This vision of the Lamb on Mount Zion surrounded by 144,000 bearing his name stands in splendid contrast to the previous section. By the time chapter 13 concludes, one wonders how the fellowship of the Lamb can possibly survive such an onslaught .Yet here there are singing a new song in the presence of the Lamb! The bottom line is this: faith in the Lamb triumphs over demonic deception, economic deprivation, and brute force. John says in prose in his first epistle what he here depicts in imagery: "And this is the victory that conquers the world, our faith. Who is it that conquers the world but the one who believes that Jesus is the Son of God?" (1 John 5:4).

Three Angels with Three Messages (14:6–13)

Have you ever seen a school production of *Peter Pan* or some other play requiring actors to "fly" by means of "invisible" wires? What John witnesses is way better! Three wireless angels appear in mid-air, each with a special message. These announcements anticipate and summarize the last series of seven judgments, the seven bowls of God's wrath. These bowls, when finally poured out, finish off the antichrist's kingdom headquartered in Babylon the great (14:8). All those who follow the beast suffer the same fate: They must drink the wine of God's wrath. This entails a fiery punishment whose smoke "goes up forever and ever" (Rev. 14:11).

Proclaiming an eternal gospel

The first announcement is in Revelation 14:6–7: "Then I saw another angel flying in mid-heaven, with an eternal gospel to proclaim to those who live on the earth — to every nation and tribe and language and people. He said in a loud voice, 'Fear God and give him glory, for the hour of his judgment has come; and worship him who made heaven and earth, the sea and the springs of water.'"

The eternal gospel is more broadly based than the good news of Jesus' atoning death. This message spoken by the angel addresses the fundamental offense human beings commit: failure to acknowledge God as Creator. This primal offense (Genesis 3) replicates itself in every human heart and leads to our alienation from him and all others. The Apostle Paul is making the same point in Romans when he says: ". . . for though they knew God, they did not honor him as God or give thanks to him, but they became futile in their thinking, and their senseless minds were darkened. Claiming to be wise, they became fools; and they exchanged the glory of the immortal God for images resembling a mortal human being or birds or four footed animals or reptiles" (Romans 1:21–23).

Proclaiming the fall of Babylon

A second angel announces the soon-to-happen collapse of Babylon the great: "Then another angel, a second, followed, saying, 'Fallen, fallen is Babylon the great! She has made all nations drink of the wine of the wrath of her fornication'" (Rev. 14:8). That doesn't sound like a very appealing vintage! In Chapter 12, we go into more detail as to the identity of Babylon. But for now, all you need to know is that Babylon is not necessarily a literal city but could be a political power. Here's a sampling of the leading views on what this angelic message means (for more on general ways to read Revelation, see Chapter 4):

- ✔ **Literal approach:** People adhering to a strictly literal approach insist that ancient Babylon (which is located in Iraq) will rise from the desert sands and become the global capital of the Antichrist's evil empire. Back in the 1990s, when Saddam Hussein began restoration work on the ancient site of Babylon, prophecy buffs were buzzing. Needless to say, the initial enthusiasm has cooled in light of more recent events. Still, some of the faithful continue to teach that ancient Babylon will literally be rebuilt.

- ✔ **Symbolic approach:** Those holding a symbolic approach argue that Babylon is more likely to be a code name for Rome. An apocalyptic work contemporaneous with the book of Revelation uses Babylon as a symbolic name for Rome. On this view, John is encouraging the faithful of his day by predicting the demise of imperial Rome.

- ✔ **Futurist approach:** A moderately futuristic approach understands John to be using first-century imperial Rome as the lens through which to focus on the ultimate power center of the Antichrist. John borrows prophetic language from the Old Testament prophet Isaiah that predicts the fall of historic Babylon for destroying Jerusalem and the First Temple in 586 B.CE (Isaiah 21:9). John reapplies this prophecy to Rome of the first century CE God will judge Rome, the new Babylon, for destroying Jerusalem and the Second Temple in 70 CE It's possible, however, that Rome represents that ultimate Babylon the great, the capital of Antichrist's empire. Where this will be located is, like the identity of the Antichrist himself, to be known only at the end.

Proclaiming a warning with assurance

All who accept the mark of the beast are destined to experience God's wrath. There's simply no way to soften this. The third angel delivers a somber warning that makes this pretty darn clear: "'Those who worship the beast and its image, and receive a mark on their foreheads or on their hands, they will also drink the wine of God's wrath, poured unmixed into the cup of his anger, and they will be tormented with fire and sulfur in the presence of the holy angels and in the presence of the Lamb. And the smoke of their torment goes up for ever and ever. There is no rest day or night for those who worship the beast and its image and for anyone who receives the mark of its name'" (Rev. 14:9–11).

The imagery employed for this punishment derives from the Old Testament and is related to undiluted wine, fire, and sulfur — not a tasty blend of flavors. The first metaphor stresses the potency of God's judgment (Jeremiah 25:15–16, 51:7), and the second recalls the devastation of Sodom and Gomorrah (Genesis 19:24). What is especially difficult is the seemingly unending nature of the judgment: "And the smoke of their torment goes up forever and ever" (Rev 14:11). We look more closely at this judgment in Chapter 13.

That's the bad news; now the good news: On a brighter note, the angel ends with a word of exhortation to the faithful, encouraging them to "hold fast to the faith of Jesus" (Rev. 13:9–10). A voice from heaven affirms this encouragement with a benediction or beatitude (a blessing): "Blessed are the dead who from now on die in the Lord" (14:13). Who does this voice belong to? Most likely it's the voice of Jesus. This is strengthened by the fact that the Spirit responds. This is one of those biblical passages that suggest the threefold nature of God (Father, Son, and Holy Spirit).

Revelation 14:13 is the second of seven beatitudes or benedictions ("Blessed are") interspersed throughout the book of Revelation. The others are in Revelation 1:3, 16:15, 19:9, 20:6, and 22:7, 14.

Harvesting and the Grapes of Wrath (14:14–20)

A two-part, multi-layered, harvest-themed vision caps off Revelation 14:

- ✔ In the first harvesting, an angel tells someone sitting on a cloud and holding a sickle to reap the harvest of the earth.
- ✔ In the second harvesting, another angel tells a different angel holding a sickle to harvest grapes, which are then thrown into a winepress and trampled.

Are these two scenes positive or negative images? Or is one positive and the other negative? A majority of commentators agree that the second harvesting is a picture of divine judgment. Considerable disagreement, however, surfaces over the nature of the first harvesting. Following the harvestings is an image of warfare.

Reaping the earth

In most agrarian settings, and throughout the Bible, harvest time typically denotes a joyous time of thanksgiving. In this passage of Revelation, however, what is reaped (that is, to gather a crop in by cutting) is not corn, wheat, or any kind of grain. Human beings are reaped. Consequently, some interpreters understand the reaping imagery as the ingathering (or rapture) of the church. This view is strengthened by the fact that the one sitting on the white cloud who does the reaping is said to look like "the Son of Man," which is another title for Jesus.

Two takes on one judgment

John apparently borrows the imagery for both the wheat and the grape harvestings from the Old Testament prophet Joel. In Joel 3:13, in a context of impending divine judgment on the nations, the prophet says, "Put in the sickle, for the harvest is ripe. Go in, tread, for the wine press is full. The vats overflow, for their wickedness is great." The last line, many scholars observe, casts a quite different perspective on *both* the first and second harvestings. From this perspective, both would seem to represent divine judgment. John's vintage scene is introduced by describing an angel who performs the action: "And he too had a sharp sickle" (Rev. 14:17). This seems to link closely the two sickles, and clearly, the second conveys a negative image. Therefore, many commentators conclude that both harvestings, in this context, depict God's End Time judgment on an unbelieving world.

Jesus' parable of the sower (Mark 4) may offer further support for this view. In the parable, some "hear the word and accept it and bear fruit, thirty and sixty and a hundredfold" (Mark 4:20). Even closer in thought is the parable in which a farmer sows a field with seeds. Afterward, it sprouts and yields ripe grain. The farmer "goes in with his sickle, because the harvest has come" (Mark 4:29). But even closer yet is John's narrative of the Samaritan woman in his Gospel. Jesus says to his disciples, "'But I tell you, look around you and see how the fields are ripe for harvesting. The reaper is already receiving wages and is gathering fruit for eternal life, so that sower and reaper may rejoice together'" (John 4:35–36). Not surprisingly, then, some expositors take a positive view of the first harvesting of the earth.

Treading the grapes (of wrath)

The second harvesting involves gathering and then stomping on symbolic grapes. The grape vintage is typically another joyous occasion in biblical times. The entire family would participate with singing and games while crushing the grapes barefoot in the wine press.

But in some passages, treading grapes serves as a terrifying metaphor of God's judgment. In fact, John seems to borrow the imagery from Isaiah 63:1–6. There, in a startling word picture, the prophet describes the Lord's coming upon the land of Judah bedecked in garments stained crimson. When asked why his royal robes are red, he replies, "I have trodden the wine press alone . . . I trod them in my anger and trampled them in my wrath; their juice spattered on my garments, and stained all my robes. For the day of vengeance was in my heart, and the year for my redeeming work had come. . . . I trampled down peoples in my anger, I crushed them in my wrath, and I poured out their lifeblood on the earth." Most likely, then, the image of squeezing out the juice, like blood, vividly conveys another picture of God's wrath poured out on unbelievers during the great Tribulation.

"The Battle Hymn of the Republic" — the source of the title of John Steinbeck's *The Grapes of Wrath* — also refers to Isaiah 63:1–6.

Battle-spilled blood as high as a bridle

Chapter 14 ends with a grisly one-sentence depiction of death: "Blood flowed from the wine press, as high as a horse's bridle, for a distance of about two hundred miles" (Rev. 14:20). This is another dramatic image that most commentators don't take literally. Several accounts of ancient battles employ hyperbole in order to impress upon the reader the enormity of the loss of life. Josephus in his epic *The Jewish War* is a prime example. Similar exaggeration appears in Jewish accounts of the fall of Bar Kokhba's fortress to the Romans in 135 CE (Bar Kokhba was the leader of the second revolt against Rome [132–135 CE]and declared to be the Messiah by Rabbi Akiva). It seems likely that John is using hyperbole to describe his vision as well. Having said that, don't minimize the main point — namely, the immense loss of life.

Notice that the wine press is trodden "outside the city" (Rev. 14:20). What city? Does John mean Babylon the great, whose collapse he more fully describes in Revelation 18? Or does he mean Jerusalem, where the two witnesses ministered? Probably he means Babylon the great, a code name for Rome and the lens through which John projects the ultimate imperial city of the beast.

Chapter 12

Seven Angels, Seven Bowls, and a Final Smackdown (15:1–18:24)

In This Chapter

▶ Pouring out God's wrath

▶ Arming for Armageddon

▶ Getting up close and personal with the great whore

▶ Watching Babylon burn and sink

*T*he book of Revelation can seem like endless rounds of a heavyweight, world championship boxing match, with a dash of extreme fighting and tag-team wrestling thrown in and a lot more characters in the ring. And some of the characters are way weirder than any that show up on WWE Friday Night SmackDown. But in this match-up, the fix is in, and the favorite is none other than Jesus. Based on the claims of Scripture, the outcome of the match has never been in doubt. Babylon and the beasties are going down for the count.

This chapter explores the final outpouring of God's wrath on rebellious humanity, spurred on by the unholy trinity: the dragon, the beast, and the false prophet (see Chapter 11). The imagery and metaphors draw heavily from the Old Testament story of the plagues on Egypt and judgment oracles found in the Hebrew prophets. The driving metaphor is that of bowls filled with God's wrath. Like a highly toxic liquid, these bowl judgments affect the entire planet. The upshot is a planet rendered almost uninhabitable.

In this section of Revelation, John also tantalizes the reader with more clues to the identity of both the beast and Babylon. Then, in the longest chapter in the book of Revelation, he composes a dirge (song of mourning) over the collapse of Babylon the great. Ironically, the saints are encouraged to join in and rejoice over Babylon's demise. Ladies and gentlemen, take your seats — the bell is about to sound on the final round.

A Preamble to God's Final Wrath (15:1–8)

Revelation 15:1–8 prepares readers for the final onslaught of God's wrath. The action unfolds in the form of a heavenly liturgy, or worship service. John first glimpses the faithful martyrs worshiping God around a sea of glass (15:2–4).

Seven angels then solemnly emerge from the heavenly Temple, probably also the throne room, the very presence of God (15:5–6). One of the four living creatures invests the seven angels with seven golden bowls containing the wrath of God (15:7). They prepare to pour out the contents, just like priests in the Jerusalem Temple regularly poured out drink offerings on the great bronze altar standing in front of the Temple (1 Kings 7:50; 2 Kings 12:13). In the book of Revelation, however, the bowls are poured out on the earth, not an altar. The significance seems to be that these bowls function as a purification ritual. Fittingly, the scene concludes with the heavenly Temple filled with God's glory. None may enter its precincts until the purification is complete. The theological point, conveyed by means of priestly and liturgy imagery, seems to be this: God's ultimate intention is to render his creation holy — that is, completely set apart for his worship and service.

Preparing for the end

As Revelation 15 opens, John views proceedings from heaven. The first time John's perspective shifts to heaven occurs in Revelation 4, when he is raptured (caught up) to the heavenly throne room. This remains his vantage point until Revelation 10–11, in which John is apparently back on earth. But Revelation 12 once again describes the action from a heavenly perspective, followed immediately by Revelation 13, in which John is back on the ground to witness the rise of the beast and false prophet. Revelation 14 presents another visit to heaven, where he remains in Revelation 15.

Alternation between heavenly and earthly perspectives is characteristic of apocalyptic writings. Note that the book of Exodus, chapters 19–40, reveals Moses making several ascents and descents of Mount Sinai in the course of the narrative. Perhaps this fundamental event, the Sinai theophany (appearance of God), establishing the children of Israel as the Lord's chosen people, served as a model for later visionary experiences during the Second Temple period (517 BCE–135 CE). In other words, the various recipients of visionary experiences (Enoch, Ezra, Baruch, and so on), like Moses, alternate between being in God's presence and being on earth among their fellow human beings.

For only the second time in Revelation, John describes a portent, or omen (the first mention of a portent is Revelation 12, with the woman and the red dragon; see Chapter 11). Now, John sees seven angels who administer the seven final plagues. This is an omen of imminent destruction. That's the bad news.

If we can even speak of the good news, it's this: "With them the wrath of God is ended" (Rev. 15:1), meaning after the bowls are empty, the punishment ends.

Fulfilling two covenants

John sees what appears to be a sea of glass mixed with fire (Rev. 15:2). He also mentions the sea of glass in Revelation 4:6, indicating that it's situated directly in front of the throne of God.

By the Roman era, glass-making techniques were such that translucent glass vessels were readily available. John seems to describe glass having a highly polished glaze. John's reference to "glass mixed with fire" may describe the reflection and refraction of light coming from the throne of God.

Understanding the two covenants

A *covenant* is a mutual arrangement and agreement defining a relationship between two parties. In the Bible, God enters into a special relationship with certain individuals, such as Abraham (Genesis 15:18) and David (2 Samuel 7), and with a particular people, namely, Israel. A covenant specifies certain obligations imposed upon the covenant partners.

The covenant between the Lord and Israel, made at Mount Sinai, was mediated by Moses (Exodus 24). It called for Israel's faithful observance of the moral and ritual commandments recorded in Exodus, Leviticus, Numbers, and Deuteronomy. For his part, the Lord promised to be their God and to bless and preserve them as a nation. Israel repeatedly broke this covenant and placed its continuance in jeopardy (Hosea 1–2).

Nonetheless, the prophets foresaw a new covenant being enacted between the Lord and Israel. The new covenant would be superior to the old one because the Lord would write it on Israel's heart so that Israel would faithfully carry out its obligations (Jeremiah 31:31–34; Ezekiel 34:25, 34:30–31, 36:25–27).

According to the New Testament, Jesus establishes this new covenant by his death, which atones for sin (Luke 22:14–20; 1 Corinthians 11:23–26). By the Holy Spirit, there's now a faithful obedience on the part of the new people of God, the new Israel (Galatians 6:16), composed of both believing Jews and Gentiles (Romans 3:21–26, 8:1–4).

Surrounding this surreal sea are the saints who remain steadfast in their commitment to the Lamb. They sing a song named after two key players in redemptive history: Moses and the Lamb. Moses represents the old covenant made at Mount Sinai with Israel (now embodied in the Old Testament), and the Lamb represents the new covenant made at Mount Calvary between Jesus and all who believe in him as Savior and Lord (now embodied in the New Testament).

Both the old and new covenants share a common view of atonement: removal of the stain and guilt of sin requires shedding blood (see Hebrews 9:22). The blood of an innocent and blameless victim serves as the cleansing agent in both covenants.

Especially relevant for the study of Revelation is the borrowing of the Passover imagery from the old covenant:

✔ The old covenant festival of Passover features a Lamb whose blood is smeared on the lintel (top of the doorframe) and doorposts of Hebrew homes so that the destroying angel benignly passes over, sparing the lives of the inhabitants (Exodus 12:7). The ritual also reminds Israel of the Lord's promise to lead them into the Promised Land (Exodus 13:3–10). In the book of Revelation, believers in Jesus are spared the bowl judgments containing the wrath of God (7:1–17, 14:9–10, 15:2).

✔ The new covenant features the ultimate fulfillment of this Old Testament ritual in Jesus, who is "the Lamb of God who takes away the sin of the world!" (John 1:29). It's more than coincidence that the primary image for Jesus in the book of Revelation is that of "a Lamb standing as if it had been slaughtered" (Rev 5:6). At a critical point in the action, the Lamb stands on Mount Zion with the redeemed (Revelation 14:1). Like the Lamb, the redeemed are now described as "blameless" (14:5). In the Apostle Paul's words, Jesus "rescues us from the wrath that is coming" (1 Thessalonians 1:10). This promise sustains believers through the ordeals described in Revelation (Revelation 14:12–13). The Promised Land of the old covenant becomes the New Jerusalem of the new one (Revelation 21–22).

The short anthem that the victors sing in Revelation 15:3–4 echoes the words of the Song of Moses in Exodus 15:1–18 and Deuteronomy 32, capturing this essential message: The holy God deserves all worship and glory. The anthem is in fact a mosaic of Old Testament texts skillfully pieced together. Not to be missed in this song is the clear implication that Jesus is the true king of the earth and the Lord God Almighty himself.

Clearing out of the Temple

A sobering scene ensues in Revelation 15:5. The portals of the heavenly sanctuary, here called "the temple of the tent of witness," open ominously. Proceeding from the sanctuary of the Temple are seven angels. These may be the seven archangels, seraphim (see Isaiah 6:2–3, 6:6), or cherubim (Ezekiel 10:3–4). They're robed like officiating priests — white linen and golden sashes. The priestly garb draws attention to an important aspect of the heavenly throne room: the nearly constant worship rendered by the angels in the presence of God. The book of Hebrews, also manifesting apocalyptic features, describes angels as "spirits in the divine service" (Hebrews 1:14).

Giving God some alone time

Two times in the history of Israel, the glory of the Lord prevents human beings from ministering in the sanctuary. After Moses finishes building and dedicating the Tabernacle (narrated in Exodus 36–40), the text says, "Moses was not able to enter the tent of meeting because the cloud settled upon it, and the glory of the Lord filled the Tabernacle" (Exodus 40:35). Likewise, after Solomon builds and dedicates the first Temple, the text says, "And when the priests came out of the holy place, a cloud filled the house of the Lord, so that the priests could not stand to minister because of the cloud; for the glory of the Lord filled the house of the Lord" (1 Kings 8:10–11).

Furthermore, two prophets of Israel, Isaiah and Ezekiel, experience visions in which they see the heavenly sanctuary filled with smoke, symbolizing God's presence (Isaiah 6:4; Ezekiel 10:3–4). God's presence is simply overwhelming.

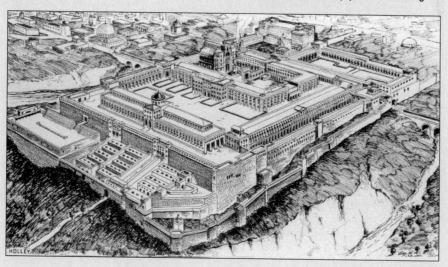

©CORBIS

One of the four living creatures, those angelic beings who stand closest to the throne of God (see Rev. 4:6), hands each angel a golden bowl full of the wrath of God. Immediately, God's glory, the *Shekinah* — a Hebrew word meaning *Divine Presence* — fills the Temple like thick smoke, and it's declared off-limits until the contents of the bowls are poured out and God's wrath is spent. God's reaction to human sin and rebellion is no light matter.

Although the notion of God's wrath is not popular these days, Scripture insists that God's holiness and glory can't be upheld without reinstating his legitimate right — even necessity — to punish those who ultimately refuse and reject him as Lord. The point of this passage in Revelation 15 is to insist that God's judgment reveals his glory as surely as does his mercy (see Romans 2:4–11, 3:3–8).

Pouring Out the Seven Bowls (16:1–21)

In Revelation 16:1, a loud voice from the heavenly temple orders the pouring out of the bowls, the final series of divine judgments. Though the voice is not identified, ultimate authorization comes from God and the Lamb. In the verses that follow, seven angels pour out the contents of their bowls—the wrath of God.

In contrast to the seals and trumpets of Revelation 6–8 (see Chapters 9 and 10), the sequence of seven bowls has no distinct subdivisions, nor do any interludes separate the judgments. They're poured out without interruption. The only deviation from this flow of events occurs between the third and fourth bowl, during which an angel adds a brief commentary on the judgment, justifying God's action (Rev. 16:5–7).

Interpreting the bowls: Four views

Interpreters understand the bowl judgments in rather different ways. You may distinguish among four main views, corresponding to the four major approaches to the book as a whole. Following is a brief overview (for a more detailed discussion of these approaches, see Chapter 4):

✔ **Preterist:** Preterists (those who interpret the book of Revelation solely from the perspective of the first century) try to connect these bowls with various historical events or features known to John's first readers. For example, the sixth bowl, the drying up of the Euphrates to prepare for the kings from the east, is often linked to the Parthian threat (this kingdom lay just to the east of the Euphrates and was hostile toward the Roman Empire). A legend that Nero would return to life and lead a Parthian invasion of Rome circulated widely during the latter part of the first century. Preterists don't agree, however, on the interpretation of the other bowls.

- ✔ **Historicist:** Historicists (those who interpret the book of Revelation as if it depicts Christian history from the first century to the Second Coming of Jesus) diverge even more than preterists on the particulars. The reason is fairly obvious: There's much more to consider and therefore so many more possibilities!

  Typically, historicists find most of their "connections" in the Middle Ages and Reformation. The bowl judgments were often related to the religious wars that swept Europe in the sixteenth and seventeenth centuries.

  Protestant historicist commentators, from the Reformation period through the nineteenth century, often identified the great whore, mystery Babylon, as the Roman Catholic Church and the papacy — a view rightly rejected by the overwhelming majority of Protestants today. A major criticism of historicism is its nearly complete omission of church history outside Europe. Western bias is apparent.

- ✔ **Idealist:** Idealists aren't committed to discovering what possible historical connections lie behind the bowls, because they view the book of Revelation as an essentially symbolic book depicting the ongoing struggle between good and evil. The various symbols are simply stock figures drawn from Jewish apocalyptic literature. On this understanding, the message of the book is applicable to any time and place and not rooted in the historical circumstances of the first or any other century.

  The problem here is the reductive nature of the approach. On a face value reading, the book proclaims more than timeless principles; it announces the victory of the Lamb *in real history*.

- ✔ **Futurist:** Futurists hold that Revelation 4 (John's being taken up to heaven) signals a transition from John's day in the first century to the events of the Day of the Lord — that is, the Great Tribulation — the end of the age. On this understanding, the bowl judgments occur just prior to the Second Coming of Jesus. Futurists are fairly uniform in interpretation of the specific details, but once again, hardly any agree completely with their fellow futurists.

The majority of modern interpreters recognize some element of truth in each approach. Perhaps the decisive question is whether the book of Revelation describes historical events or depicts principles and ideals. We think it's a both-and, not an either-or scenario. Without denying that timeless principles are present, we think a moderate futurism makes best sense of the text. That is, the book begins at the end of the first century in chapters 1–3 and concludes with the return of Jesus in chapters 19–20 and the inauguration of the new heavens and earth in chapters 21–22. But from chapter 4 onward, the focus is on the last brief period of time leading up to Jesus's return, the so-called Great Tribulation. The book of Revelation itself suggests that this period lasts seven years.

In our understanding of the relationship among the three series of sevens, the trumpets and bowls fall within the general time frame of the sixth seal, unleashing the Great Tribulation, which corresponds to the Old Testament Day of the Lord (see Chapter 9). This constitutes the final period of earth history, in which the Lamb decisively intervenes and judges human rebellion and wickedness. The number seven applied to the seals, trumpets, and bowls fittingly sums up the notion of completion and finality.

Checking out the bowls' contents

The plagues that come from the bowls, like the trumpets, are reminiscent of the plagues on Egypt. The most notable difference is the scale and intensity of these bowl judgments; they're simply off the Richter scale of seismic judgments and are truly global in their impact. In rapid succession, the contents of the seven bowls rain down on the evil empire and obliterate all resistance.

Bowl 1: Foul and painful sores erupt

The first angel pours his bowl of sores on the earth. This plague, reminiscent of the sixth plague of boils in Egypt (Exodus 9:10–11), affects only those who bear the mark of the beast (Rev. 13:16–17; see Chapter 11).

Bowls 2 and 3: The sea and fresh water turn to blood

The second angel pours his bowl into the sea. This time, the entire sea turns to blood, and all life in it perishes. The third angel pours his bowl into the fresh waters, and they, too, turn to blood. Notice that bowls two and three correspond to the first plague on Egypt, which turned the Nile River to blood (Exodus 7:19–21).

At this point comes a momentary interruption in the sequence of judgments. The angel of the waters justifies God's actions in Revelation 16:5–7:

> "'You are just, O Holy One, who are and were, for you have judged these things; because they shed the blood of saints and prophets, you have given them blood to drink. It is what they deserve!' And I heard the altar respond, 'Yes, O Lord God, the Almighty, your judgments are true and just!'"

The principle invoked is deeply rooted in the Old Testament notion of justice: The punishment should fit the crime. This is known as *lex talionis*, the law of retaliation — the well-known eye-for-an-eye, tooth-for-a-tooth principle (Exodus 21:23–25).

Bowl 4: The sun scorches the earth

The fourth angel pours his bowl on the sun, causing it to increase in heat, which scorches the earth. Talk about global warming! Like a solar blowtorch, the sun bears down on earth's inhabitants with deadly intensity.

The highest recorded temperature on earth to date is 136 degrees Fahrenheit on September 13, 1922, at El Azizia, Libya. The highest in the United States is 134 degrees Fahrenheit on July 10, 1922, at Death Valley, California. No doubt this plague far exceeds those temperatures.

How do the inhabitants of earth react to this "act of God," as so-called natural phenomena are sometimes referred to by insurance companies? They curse God and refuse to repent.

What about believers in Jesus? Aren't they affected as well? Remember that the trumpet and bowl judgments recall the Egyptian plagues, and the Hebrews weren't affected by all the plagues (Exodus 8:22, 9:6, 9:26, 10:23, 11:7). Presumably, that's also the case with the bowl judgments of Revelation. God seals and protects his people against his wrath.

Bowl 5: Darkness falls

The fifth angel pours his bowl on the throne of the beast. The very epicenter of the beast's empire is stricken with total darkness. This is no rolling blackout. In fact, the darkness is so complete it's palpable.

Paying up for sin

In first-century Roman culture, people commonly used libation (pouring) vessels in religious rituals honoring the gods. Drink offerings were poured out to the gods on an altar. But Revelation's source for the bowl imagery probably stems from Old Testament rituals connected with Tabernacle and Temple. In particular, golden bowls were used to catch the blood of sacrificial animals, which was then literally thrown against the base of the altar, where fire totally consumed it (Exodus 24:6; Leviticus 1:5, 3:2, 7:2).

There's a profound theological connection between *expiation* (making amends or reparation for wrongdoing and guilt) and retribution (punishment for wrongdoing). God's holiness, like a refining fire, totally consumes the blood

offered as an atonement on the altar. In the fulfillment of this Old Testament ritual, Jesus offers his blood as the atoning sacrifice. The book of Revelation makes this point repeatedly (1:5, 5:6, 12:11, 19:13), and it runs like a scarlet thread throughout the entire New Testament (see Romans 6:10; Hebrews 7:27).

However, if sinful human beings refuse God's offer of atonement through blood shed on their behalf, the Bible says they face "a fearful prospect of judgment" (Hebrews 10:26) because "God is a consuming fire" (Hebrews 12:29). Clearly, according to the Bible, that same divine holiness consumes the unrepentant sinner (Rev. 20:14–15, 21:8). The bowls in Revelation serve a different purpose: They're vessels not of *expiation* but of punishment.

This blackness only exacerbates the previous plagues and ratchets up the misery index to nearly unbearable levels. Although some commentators prefer to interpret the darkness symbolically, many see no need to depart from a more-or-less literal reading because the previous four bowls appear to be physical realities. Once again, the plague has no effect — the inhabitants curse God and refuse to repent.

Bowl 6: Kings arm for Armageddon

The sixth bowl, in Revelation 16:12, has striking similarities to the sixth trumpet (Rev. 9:14). In both cases, the Euphrates River figures prominently in the action, and demonic activity stirs up a final and decisive showdown between the dragon and the Lamb. The sixth bowl dries up the Euphrates, apparently allowing the army of an eastern coalition to cross easily.

The sixth bowl, however, doesn't relate to a return to the Holy Land (Promised Land) by the Jewish people; it involves an invading force sweeping in from the east and finding a potential barrier suddenly removed. Presumably, these forces have a hostile intent toward the Land of Israel.

Turning seas and rivers into dry land

The Euphrates River allows easy access to the Holy Land for an invasion force coming from the east. Similar to what's depicted in Revelation 16:12, twice in the Old Testament does a formidable body of water dry up to allow passage:

✔ During the Exodus from Egypt, the Red Sea parts and the Israelites escape certain retribution and recapture by Pharaoh and his crack chariot corps (Exodus 14).

✔ In the days of Joshua, the Israelites have to cross the Jordan River in order to attack Jericho, the eastern gateway to Canaan, the Promised Land. The Jordan, however, is in flood stage, and the Israelites lack any means of negotiating the flood plain. The God of Israel stops the flow upriver, allowing the army of Israel to cross and initiate their invasion (Joshua 3–4).

A vision of the prophet Isaiah recorded in Isaiah 11 describes what the Lord God of Israel is going to do "on that day," a synonym for the Day of the Lord or Great Tribulation. Among those items detailed is a two-fold drying up of bodies of water playing prominent roles in redemptive history:

✔ **The Red Sea:** In short, Isaiah envisions a new exodus. As in days of old, so in the future, says the prophet — God enables his people to escape bondage and make their way through the desert to the Promised Land. You can find this motif of a new exodus in a number of New Testament texts (such as Colossians 1:13).

✔ **The Euphrates River:** Remarkably, Isaiah also says that the Lord "will wave his hand over the River [that is, the Euphrates] with his scorching wind; and will split it into seven channels, and make a way to cross on foot; so there shall be a highway from Assyria for the remnant that is left of his people, as there was for Israel when they came up from the land of Egypt" (Isaiah 11:15–16).

Some interpreters think that this military incursion prompts the beast (see Chapter 11) to intervene and stave off the attack. The beast then proceeds to invade the Holy Land himself and proclaim himself God in the Jerusalem Temple. This perspective is based upon a futuristic (and debatable) interpretation of Daniel 11:40–45 and Ezekiel 38–39, along with Paul's comments about "the lawless one" in 2 Thessalonians 2:1–12.

TECHNICAL STUFF

Battleground: You say Megiddo, I say Armageddon

The term *Harmagedon* (NRSV) or *Armageddon* (most English versions) refers to the ancient site of Megiddo, a strategic city guarding the main north-south route from Egypt to Syria. This road, later called the Via Maris ("Way of the Sea"), passes through a low ridge of hills into the fertile Jezreel Valley. Hebrew kings from Solomon onward fortified the site because it serves as a choke point controlling traffic and commerce along this important artery. Whoever controls Megiddo controls much of Canaan, the Promised Land.

As early as the sixteenth century, Pharaoh Thutmose III fought a battle against a Canaanite coalition at this site. Megiddo figures in the famous battle between the Canaanites and Israel in the days of Deborah the prophetess and judge (Judges 4–5). The Assyrians and later the Babylonians assaulted and conquered Megiddo in their brutal conquests of the kingdoms of Israel and Judah. Even Napoleon Bonaparte won a convincing victory at Megiddo, and General Allenby, during World War I, defeated the Ottoman Turks there as well.

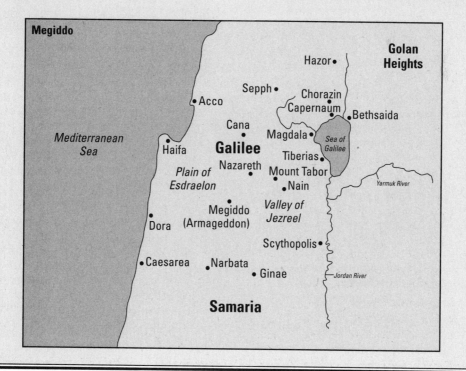

The sixth bowl describes the last battle, the location of which has become a household word: Armageddon. The unholy trinity — the dragon, beast, and false prophet — send forth demonic emissaries to mobilize the forces of the earth against the Lamb. The demonic spirits look like frogs and are reminiscent of the second Egyptian plague of frogs (Exodus 8:1–6). The demons are successful in their war propaganda. A massive army assembles at a site laden with memories of former battles: Megiddo in the Jezreel Valley of Israel (see the sidebar "Battleground: You say Megiddo; I say Armageddon.").

Many scholars prefer to view the reference here in Revelation symbolically, seeing Megiddo as an assembly point for the coalition forces allied with the beast but not the site for the final battle. This may be, but you can also make a good case for a literal reading that the warfare takes place at this location. The Old Testament prophets Joel and Zechariah located the main action of the Day of the Lord in the Holy Land, particularly in Jerusalem (Joel 3:1–21; Zechariah 12–14). A massive invasion of Israel would almost certainly involve Megiddo because of its strategic importance.

Bowl 7: An earthquake and hailstones shake things up

When the seventh angel pours his bowl into the air, John doesn't delay in describing what happens next (in contrast to the seals and trumpets in Revelation 6–8; see Chapters 9 and 10): An unprecedented earthquake convulses the planet, and a massive hailstorm pounds great Babylon and the entire planet with 100-pound hailstones! The devastation is complete; the evil empire collapses like a house of cards. Babylon splits into three parts, and all the cities of the world fall in ruins.

You may wonder how anyone could survive such an onslaught, but apparently many do. Still, though, rather than call upon God for mercy and forgiveness, they curse him. John reverts to form and gives readers another interlude in Revelation 17–18. In so doing, he provides an up-close-and-personal perspective on the mysterious Babylon, the great whore.

But First, a Word from Our End-Times Sponsor, the Lamb (16:15)

Tucked into the vision of the sixth bowl is a brief word of exhortation in Revelation 16:15: "See, I am coming like a thief! Blessed is the one who stays awake and is clothed, not going about naked and exposed to shame." In the style of the messages to the seven churches (see Chapter 7), John inserts a word of prophecy from the Lamb himself. Though the Lamb isn't directly mentioned in Revelation 16, you can be sure he's on the scene. The Lamb leads the charge against the evil empire and orchestrates its total destruction.

But this little word of prophecy isn't about the beast and his allies; it's intended only for believers. The message is essentially this: Don't despair at what appears to be the success of the dragon, beast, and false prophet. Don't desert from the ranks of the Lamb and go over to the dark side. Remain steadfast and faithful to Jesus.

The imagery of the prophetic exhortation is similar to Jesus's teaching during his earthly ministry (for example, Matthew 24:42–44). The unexpected, open-ended timing of the return of Jesus requires constant vigilance.

The notion of nakedness refers to a state of being spiritually unprepared. On the occasion of the first sin in the Garden of Eden in Genesis 3, after disobeying God's explicit command, Adam and Eve suddenly sense that they're naked. That is, they're aware of guilt and recognize they're liable to punishment. In psychological terms, they feel exposed and open to scrutiny. So, too, says the Bible, followers of the Lamb who defect under pressure may be exposed in the end. The followers of the Lamb are thus both warned and exhorted to stay the course.

This prophetic exhortation reminds readers of the underlying purpose of the entire book: to build a firm, steadfast commitment to what Christians saw as the true message of Jesus over against all counterfeits, whether they be the imperial (Roman) cult of the first century or its End-Times counterpart during the reign of the Antichrist.

Exposing the Mystery of Babylon the Great (17:1–18)

Revelation 17–22 is essentially a tale of two cities. No, we didn't borrow this from Dickens; he actually borrowed it from the Bible! The two cities, of course, are Babylon (Rome) and the new Jerusalem — not London and Paris as Dickens wrote about. The descriptions of these two biblical cities couldn't be more opposite. John devotes two chapters to Babylon and two chapters to new Jerusalem. Babylon passes away; the new Jerusalem lasts forever. Another way of looking at this section portrays the two cities under the guise of two women: the great whore and the bride of the Lamb. Again, the contrast is both stunning and stark.

Calling her names: Harlot on seven hills

In Revelation 17, John hits the rewind button. The seventh bowl in Revelation 16 ends with the utter collapse of Babylon. Now, he backs up and reviews the career of this wicked city, portraying it as a notorious prostitute. One of the seven angels in charge of the seven bowls becomes John's guide. John is transported from the heavenly sanctuary back down to earth to "a wilderness."

Almost certainly John borrows the imagery of Isaiah 21:1–17, a judgment oracle upon Babylon of the sixth century BCE. The setting of Isaiah's prophecy is southern Iraq and Kuwait, a desolate desert region brought vividly to television screens in recent history. John reapplies this prophecy to Imperial Rome as it existed in John's time, the template for the ultimate God-defying empire of the Antichrist.

A whore who's a city who is another city: Seeing behind the imagery

John takes the reader behind the scenes and exposes political intrigues and treachery that eventually bring down Babylon the Great. You gain an insider's view of the relationship between the beast and Babylon — what you may call a twisted version of *Beauty and the Beast!* In the end, the beast betrays "beautiful" Babylon and brings about her destruction.

John's description of Babylon (a city) contains clues pointing to her identity as the city of Rome (another city):

- ✔ **"Seated on many waters":** The city of Rome and the empire of which it was the center controlled the waterways of the Mediterranean. In fact, by the end of the first century, the Mediterranean Sea was virtually a Roman lake. The imperial navy had numerous ports of call such as Syracuse (in Sicily), Corinth and Thessalonica (in Greece and Macedonia), Troas and Ephesus (in modern Turkey or Asia Minor), Seleucia (in modern Syria), Alexandria (in modern Egypt), and Cyrene (in modern Libya), to name but a few. Rome plied the sea lanes to her commercial advantage, siphoning natural resources away from far flung provinces and importing luxury items for the upper classes. Rome was the leading commercial emporium of the known world.

  John calls Babylon "the mother of whores" (17:5). John describes her commercial activity as "fornication" because of its unjust and immoral nature. Literal prostitution was also a major industry in the empire.

- ✔ **"Sitting on a scarlet beast":** The fact that the empire sits on the beast points to the person who really wields the power. The emperor and the imperial cult (emperor worship) drive this vast political and mercantile enterprise. Many commentators hold that John's description transcends any particular Roman emperor — though Nero Caesar certainly provides a chilling template — and embodies that ultimate dictator and tyrant, the Antichrist.

- ✔ **"Drunk with the blood":** The Roman Empire reveled in luxury and sensuality (17:4–5), all the while exhibiting extreme cruelty. Utter indifference to human need and dignity characterizes the moral climate. John draws special attention to the role of Rome in persecuting believers in Jesus. The image is appalling: "The woman was drunk with the blood of the saints and the blood of the witnesses to Jesus" (17:6).

Rome by any other name

Most New Testament scholars think Babylon is a code word for Rome. Just as Babylon, under Nebuchadnezzar II, destroyed Jerusalem and the first Temple and gloated over it, so Rome would play a similar role in the complete destruction of Jerusalem and the second Temple.

In Jewish literature of the late first century, Rome is labeled as Babylon (2 Esdras, 2 Baruch, and Sibylline Oracles), recalling its ancient role as nemesis and persecutor.

Even Peter concludes his first epistle (letter), written to primarily Gentile Christians in Asia Minor, by saying, "Your sister church in Babylon, chosen together with you, sends you greetings; and so does my son Mark" (1 Peter 5:13). Is Peter living at the ancient site of great Babylon? Probably not. So why doesn't Peter just come right out with it and mention Rome by name? Well, the first epistle probably dates to just after the bloodbath that Nero initiated in 64 CE. Thousands of Christians perished. Peter is sensitive to the fact that another wave of persecution is possible. He doesn't want his letter to fall into the hands of government informers and be misconstrued as anti-government propaganda.

In the book of Revelation, Babylon functions symbolically as the ultimate center of power for the Antichrist. Freely borrowing language and imagery from Old Testament prophetic texts speaking of historic Babylon, John reapplies these to its first-century counterpart, the great city of Rome. Babylon and Rome are mirror images of each other — both dens of injustice and wonders to behold. They embody, in the words of a Clint Eastwood movie, "the good, the bad, and the ugly." In that respect, the original Babylon and Rome anticipate the appearance of that final Babylon: organized, rebellious humanity, oblivious to or pitted against the kingdom of the God and the Lamb.

Unlocking the interpretation

John doesn't leave you to your own imagination for interpreting the passage about the whore of Babylon. Actually, an angelic informant reveals the key, and John records it in Revelation 17:7–18.

Seven heads

The scarlet beast's seven heads serve a twofold function: They're both seven hills and seven kings:

- ✔ **Hills:** This piece of information almost certainly identifies the city as Rome, long famous for its seven hills. The seven hills are Palatine, Capitol, Aventine, Caelian, Esquiline, Viminal, and Quirinal. References to these famous seven hills abound in the writings of historians and literary figures of the ancient world.

- ✔ **Kings:** The seven heads represent seven kings. Interestingly, five of them have already died at the time of John's writing, one is currently in office, and the sixth is coming but has a very short tenure.

An eighth king, says John, belongs to the seven and is none other than the beast from the bottomless pit — the one who was, is not, and is yet to come. In short, the eighth king is the Antichrist, who appears to die and returns to life. This correlates closely with the description of the beast in Revelation 13.

Some commentators argue that John is referring to the Roman emperors in this passage — and claim that the eighth king was Domitian. After all, if you begin with Augustus Caesar, generally reckoned as the first emperor, the chronological sequence is as follows:

1. Augustus (27 BCE–14 CE)

2. Tiberius (14–37 CE)

3. Gaius [Caligula] (37–41 CE)

4. Claudius (41–54 CE)

5. Nero (54–68 CE)

6. Vespasian (69–79 CE)

7. Titus (79–81 CE)

8. Domitian (81–96 CE)

After Nero committed suicide in July of 68 CE, three men unsuccessfully laid claim to the title: Galba, Otho, and Vitellius. All three were assassinated after very short tenures. Vespasian, who had been in the Holy Land subduing the Jews during the first Jewish revolt (66–73 CE), was acclaimed emperor by his legions in Palestine. He quickly returned to Rome and secured his hold on the empire. This turbulent period was called "the year of the four emperors." Many scholars leave the three wannabes out of the reckoning because their stints were too short to qualify them as emperors.

The problems fitting this historical sequence of emperors into John's scheme are considerable:

- ✔ The only one on the list who fits nicely with John's scheme is number seven, Titus: "When he comes, he must remain only a little while." (Rev. 17:10).

- ✔ Julius Caesar was actually the first to be called *imperator* (emperor). If you begin with him, this throws off the entire scheme in that Domitian now becomes the ninth.

- ✔ Three claimants to the throne — Galba, Otho, and Vitellius — were actually considered legitimate emperors by the Jewish historian Josephus, as well as by a first-century work called the *Sibylline Oracles*. Including them makes Domitian the twelfth emperor.

> ✔ John indicates that the king who is currently reigning is the sixth. According to the numbered sequence, the sixth king is Vespasian. But most scholars opt for the reign of Domitian as the time of writing, and we concur. In order for the actual sequence to fit John's scheme, Domitian needs to be the sixth king.

But perhaps you shouldn't even try to harmonize John's scheme with the list of Roman emperors. Given the symbolic nature of the number seven, this may only suggest the complete power and dominance of these kings. The beast is identified with these kings in that he, too, embodies virtually absolute authority over his subjects. In that sense, he is one with them and thus the eighth.

Despite problems and uncertainties, John's essential point seems clear: Imperial Rome, with its seriously flawed emperors, is mystery Babylon. But as many commentators claim, John may be using imperial Rome as the lens through which to portray that ultimate Babylon, the tool of the beast from the bottomless pit, the Antichrist.

Ten horns

The beast's ten horns refer to a separate coalition of kings who ally themselves with the beast. In biblical thought, the horn of a bull, ram, or goat symbolizes strength and power. In apocalyptic writings, an animal horn frequently represents powerful kings or generals (see, for example, Daniel 8). This alliance of ten kings was not yet in existence in John's day — that remains for a designated time called "one hour" (Rev. 17:12).

John draws this imagery from the book of Daniel, in which a fourth and final earthly kingdom, described as "terrifying and dreadful and exceedingly strong," is also depicted as having ten horns (Daniel 7:7). Later in the same chapter, Daniel discovers that the ten horns represent ten kings that arise in connection with an insolent person who speaks against God and persecutes believers (Daniel 7:24–25). This fits rather closely with the beast of Revelation, the Antichrist. Ominously, John informs the reader that the ten kings join in the war against the Lamb. However, they're unable to carry out their objective, and the Lamb carries the day.

Waters

The waters represent a multinational, multiethnic empire. This empire is forged by the beast as a tool for achieving his own ambitions and, of course, those of the great dragon who energizes and eggs him on. This interpretive key points to imperial Rome as the template for the final evil empire.

The Roman Empire, at the end of the first century, was the largest and most diverse empire the world had ever known. Lest there be any lingering doubt or confusion in his readers' mind, John makes it crystal clear who the woman is: "The great city that rules over the kings of the earth" (Rev. 17:18). No other city but Rome fills the bill. End-Times Babylon exercises the same clout and sway as imperial Rome did in the first century.

Turning on her: The beast bites back

As the chapter ends, John mentions something that comes as a shock: "And the ten horns that you saw, they and the beast will hate the whore; they will make her desolate and naked; they will devour her flesh and burn her up with fire. For God has put it into their hearts to carry out his purpose by agreeing to give their kingdom to the beast, until the words of God will be fulfilled."

In spite of using Babylon (Rome) to achieve his own ends, the beast and his allies (ten kings) harbor deep hatred for the imperial capital. They actually plot and carry out its complete destruction. The book of Revelation doesn't say precisely why, but remember that these kings are ambitious politicians who loathe to share power and glory more than they have to. They likely envy the wealth and influence of Babylon the Great and want it all for themselves. As witnessed so many times in human history, evil is self-destructive.

What is clearly stated, however, is that God decrees the total destruction of mystery Babylon. This destruction is portrayed as a burning up (19:3), the fate of most ancient cities sacked by invading armies. In this case, however, the burning is depicted as everlasting in duration, a sure indicator of divine, not human retribution.

Loveless in the Ruins: Celebrating Babylon's Fall (18:1–24)

Remember that old nursery rhyme that goes, "London bridge is falling down, Falling down, Falling down. London bridge is falling down, My fair lady"? The reference is actually quite grim. Historians trace it back to the medieval period when London bridge was ruined multiple times by war, tornado, and fire. The "fair lady" may refer to the practice of burying a dead virgin in the foundation of a bridge to ensure its strength and longevity. Or she may be Queen Eleanor of Aquitaine, the mother of two kings of England, Richard the Lionhearted and John Lackland.

Uncovering the real Babylon

The story of Babylon begins in the book of Genesis, when the hero Nimrod founds a city named Babel (Genesis 10:10). The name means *gate of god,* perhaps already hinting at the city's self-claims to fame. At any rate, the city first appears in the historical record when Sharkalisharri (about 2250 BCE) mentions that he moved dirt from Babel to Agade, thereby transferring Babel's authority and sanctity to the new location.

During the second millennium BCE, the city of Babylon achieved new heights of prosperity under the guidance of Hammurabi (1792–1950 BCE), famous for his Code of Hammurabi, one the earliest written law records. He greatly enlarged the city and extended its commercial ties.

The first millennium BCE found Babylon at the center of power struggles between the Assyrians (north of modern-day Iraq) and the more southerly tribes of Babylonia. Sargon II, king of Assyria and conqueror of Samaria (2 Kings 17:6), the northern kingdom of Israel's capital city, swept into Babylon in 710 BCE. Babylonia didn't regain independence until about 626 BCE.

The city came into its own under the leadership of the Babylonian superstar Nebuchadnezzar II (605–562 BCE). After claiming the throne in 605 BCE and defeating an Egyptian and Assyrian coalition at Carchemish, Nebuchadnezzar headed the most powerful military in the ancient Near East. Judea finally fell after rebelling against being a servant state of Babylon. Nebuchadnezzar is notorious as the destroyer of Jerusalem and the first Temple in 586 BCE. He used Judean craftsmen and builders to enlarge and beautify Babylon. The massive Ishtar gates, hanging gardens of Babylon, soaring temples and ziggurats (towers), and waterways and palaces made it the most impressive city the world had yet seen. Hebrew prophets like Isaiah (Isaiah 13) and Jeremiah (Jeremiah 50–51), however, prophesied her fall because of cruelty to Judah.

And Babylon did fall — with no shots fired! Cyrus the Persian entered the city after diverting the Euphrates River that flowed right down its middle. By night, his soldiers simply walked up the now empty river bed right into the heart of the city. The city itself welcomed Cyrus as a liberator, and he assumed the title "King of Babylon" (539 BCE). For Jews, Babylon became a byword for all that's cruel and evil. Later, when Rome became master of the Mediterranean, Jews used Babylon as a code word for Rome. A famous Jewish oracle *(Sibylline Oracles)* gleefully prophesies the demise of this "new Babylon." As you can see in the book of Revelation, early Christians shared a similar sentiment with regard to Rome.

Persian monarchs after Cyrus the Great, like Xerxes, neglected Babylon. This lasted until Alexander the Great swept across Asia Minor and into the heartland of the Persian Empire. After he defeated the Medes at Gaugamela, the city of Babylon welcomed him as a liberator (331 BCE). Alexander had great plans for the city, but he didn't live long enough to realize them. In the power struggles between Alexander's successors, Babylon fared poorly. Eventually, a new city, Seleucia, became the seat of government, and Babylon declined in importance. Though not totally abandoned, the city never regained its former glory. During New Testament times, a small town rested in the vicinity of the ancient site. Today, ancient Babylon is uninhabited; it is, however, an archaeological site of great importance.

Seen in this light, the nursery rhyme actually has two things in common with Revelation 18: Both recount a catastrophic collapse, and both feature a *femme fatale*. In Revelation 18, the spotlight falls on Queen Babylon, the great whore (17:1–2). John allows her to speak on stage in a soliloquy, affording a window into her thoughts: "I rule as a queen; I am no widow, and I will never see grief" (Rev. 18:7). She revels in her power and considers herself invincible, a mistake many powerful people make.

Nebuchadnezzar II was once swept away by his own self-importance and achievements as he surveyed the great city of Babylon: "Is this not magnificent Babylon, which I have built as a royal capital by my mighty power and for my glorious majesty?" For his vanity, God visits Nebuchadnezzar with a serious mental illness. Later, when he recovers, he makes quite a different confession: "I blessed the Most High, and praised and honored the one who lives forever. For his sovereignty is an everlasting sovereignty, and his kingdom endures from generation to generation" (Daniel 4:34). Before his fall from power, Saddam Hussein expended great sums to restore and reconstruct the ancient site of Babylon. He even had gigantic statues of himself portrayed like Nebuchadnezzar! Like these two dictators, Queen Babylon never gets the point and pays dearly for her arrogance.

Singing stinging sarcasm

A mighty angel announces the fall of Babylon the Great. This section is composed as a dirge, a lament sung at funerals:

> "Fallen, fallen is Babylon the great! It has become a dwelling-place of demons, a haunt of every foul spirit, a haunt of every foul bird, a haunt of every foul and hateful beast. For all the nations have drunk of the wine of the wrath of her fornication, and the kings of the earth have committed fornication with her, and the merchants of the earth have grown rich from the power of her luxury." (Rev. 18:2–3)

In popular imagination, undesirable creatures, whether animal or demonic, haunted the abandoned ruins of ancient cities. Isaiah 13:21–22 gives expression to these fears: "But wild animals will lie down there, and its houses will be full of howling creatures; there ostriches will live, and there goat-demons will dance. Hyenas will cry in its towers, and jackals in the pleasant palaces [. . .]" Such places were avoided, and frightening tales told about the horrible things that happened there reinforced the stigma. Ghosts and ghouls hover in the rubble of formerly magnificent buildings. Such is the portrait of once-great Babylon in Revelation 18:2.

The reference to "the wine of the wrath of her fornication" is difficult to interpret. It seems to combine two ideas:

- ✔ Strong passion (the basic meaning of the Greek word *thumos*) aroused by the seductive power of Queen Babylon.
- ✔ God's wrath (divine punishment), which comes as a consequence of participating in the corrupt, immoral, and oppressive economic system of the great whore

This is a lament with a twist, however. It's actually a taunt song, a mocking dirge. That is, it celebrates the demise of a tyrant or wicked regime under the guise of a funeral lament. The wording of Revelation 18:2–3 draws on the language of several Old Testament taunt songs (Isaiah 21:9; Jeremiah 50:39, 51:8). Significantly, one of the most famous Old Testament taunt songs celebrates the death of a Babylonian dictator (Isaiah 14:3–21).

Revelation 18:3 serves to justify the treatment of Babylon. Why does she experience this fate? Using the language of the Old Testament prophets, John fastens on the damning sin of this vast political, economic, and military enterprise. The key word is *fornication.*

To *fornicate* often means, to the Old Testament prophets, to break faith with the God of Israel and follow other so-called gods. It amounts to disloyalty, the fundamental sin of the Ten Commandments: "You shall have no other gods before me" (Exodus 20:3). Babylon the Great proclaims another god: the god of consumption, wealth, pleasure, and self-indulgence. Her motto is essentially *spend your way to happiness.* In short, the great sin of Babylon is to prefer creation to the Creator. In his letter to the Romans, the Apostle Paul provides an apt commentary on this section: "They exchanged the truth about God for a lie and worshiped and served the creature rather than the Creator, who is blessed forever! Amen" (Romans 1:25).

Fleeing the scene to safety

Revelation warns believers to escape from Babylon and to have nothing to do with her (18:4). The passage functions as a summons to believers. Drawing on language similar to that used by Jeremiah in the sixth century BCE (Jeremiah 51:45), John applies it to Rome, the Babylon of his day. Many scholars believe Rome serves as the template for End-Times Babylon, that final world empire utterly opposed to God and the Lamb.

John warns believers not to become enmeshed in the attitudes and lifestyle of Queen Babylon. To do so is to betray the values of the Lamb and his kingdom. Christians during the first century constantly struggled with the difficulties of making a clean break from the idol-worshipping Greco-Roman culture in which they lived and worked. Several New Testament passages highlight

the temptation to slide back into their previous lifestyle (see 2 Corinthians 6:14–18; Galatians 4:8–11; Ephesians 4:17–24, 5:6–14; 1 John 2:15–17).

Shedding no tears for the fallen

In Revelation 18:5–8, John justifies the harshness of the sentence on Queen Babylon. Babylon deserves what she gets. In fact, her sins "are heaped high as heaven" (a phrase drawn from Jeremiah 51:9). Because of her self-indulgence and refusal to acknowledge God, she receives a sentence twice as harsh as might be expected, "double for her deeds" (see Jeremiah 50:29; Isaiah 40:2).

We think of Queen Marie Antoinette prior to the French Revolution. Quite oblivious to human needs just outside the royal palace, she occupied herself in trivial pleasures and luxurious living. Queen Babylon is likewise totally absorbed in sensual enjoyment — a sure recipe for spiritual disaster.

Reeling from markets' collapse: Goods gone bad

In Revelation 18:9–20, John describes what amounts to a first-century version of SkyMall magazine — a catalog featuring the wares and finery of the very best stores in Rome. This long list of goods, imported from the far flung corners of the empire, illustrates the insatiable appetite of the rich and powerful upper crust of Roman society. But instead of a tale in which money buys happiness, the passage reads like a wake.

Lamenting market loss

Kings, merchants, shipmasters, seafarers, and sailors, standing at a safe distance, lament the demise of this mercantile marvel. The political leaders are the first to intone their regret and shock: "Alas, alas, the great city, Babylon the mighty city! For in one hour your judgment has come" (Rev. 18:10). They're stunned. No one saw this coming.

Next, the merchants of the earth express their distress and grief in weeping and wailing. No more sales! No more profits! They can't comprehend that their livelihood has been suddenly snatched away: "All your dainties and your splendor are lost to you, never to be found again!" (Rev. 18:14). Americans who experienced the Stock Market Crash of 1929, Black Tuesday, can probably best appreciate the feeling of these distraught merchants.

The merchant marines next offer their condolences. The scope of destruction is beyond their comprehension. First-century Rome was like a magnet attracting an unending flow of goods arriving on a vast network of waterways. Needless to say, the volume of commerce created a huge transportation

industry. Following Middle Eastern funeral customs, the mariners throw dust on their heads as a sign of extreme grief and sorrow (Rev. 18:19). They, too, are completely caught off-guard by the suddenness of this disaster: "For in one hour she has been laid waste" (Rev. 18:19).

Ill-gotten gains

The bottom line is that with the fall of Babylon, the movers and shakers lose control of their economic and political empire. But before you feel too sorry for them, look more closely at how that wealth was acquired and spent. Most of the imports were forcibly taken from subject peoples; furthermore, the items listed in Revelation 18:1–13 are, for the most part, luxury items. The great majority of citizens and non-citizens of the empire could never afford them, anyway. Here's what the Roman socio-economic pyramid looked like:

- ✔ **Slaves:** Anywhere from one-third to one-half of the population of imperial Rome were slaves. Not to be overlooked in this catalogue of goods are the last two items: "slaves — and human lives." Slave trafficking was a common evil in the economic fabric of the empire (Rev. 18:13).

- ✔ **Freedmen:** These were individuals who were either born free or were able to work themselves out of slavery. Most of these folks, who made up a fairly large segment of Roman society, were craftsmen and day laborers who did the grunt work for the empire.

- ✔ **Nobility and upper-class families:** These minorities controlled the wealth and resources of the empire.

In reality, then, only a small proportion of society directly benefited from this immense wealth. To be sure, the wealthy and powerful often acted as bene-factors and provided public works and programs for the masses. But this was little more than an appeasement, and it didn't significantly lower the misery index for the average citizen, freedman or slave.

According to John, this system is fundamentally immoral. It must be disman-tled and replaced. The book of Revelation envisions a vastly superior world to come. The other woman in the story, Queen Jerusalem, the beautiful bride of the Lamb, offers a truly "Great Society."

Ding-dong! The witch is dead!

One segment of society doesn't lament the demise of Queen Babylon. The people of God, designated as "saints and apostles and prophets" (Rev. 18:20), say goodbye and good riddance to this "mother of whores." It's a day of rejoicing. The setting for this portion assumes a courtroom. Queen Babylon is in the dock. She is arraigned for a wide array of crimes and offenses, not the least of which is the murder of many saints (Rev. 17:6, 18:24). The verdict comes down from God, the supreme judge. Babylon is guilty as charged and sentenced to extinction (Rev. 18:20).

The imagery describing Babylon's end is striking. A mighty angel tosses a huge millstone into the sea and gives voice to this dramatic symbolic action: "With such violence Babylon the great city will be thrown down, and will be found no more" (Rev. 18:21). (If this seems to conflict with the earlier image of destruction by fire, remember that this is poetry, not prose — strict logic need not apply.) The point is clear enough: Babylon sinks to the bottom of the sea, a fitting end to a city and system conjured up from the depths of the abyss.

John probably borrows his imagery from Jeremiah's prophecy against the Babylon of Nebuchadnezzar's day in the sixth century BCE.: "When you finish reading this scroll, tie a stone to it, and throw it into the middle of the Euphrates, and say, 'Thus shall Babylon sink, to rise no more, because of the disasters that I am bringing on her'" (Jeremiah 51:63–64).

The dirge that accompanies the symbolic action opens another window into the life and times of first-century Rome. The reader glimpses musicians, artisans, and merchants, along with bridegrooms and brides. The language draws heavily from two Old Testament passages:

- ✔ **Jeremiah 25:10:** The first, ironically, is a prophecy directed against Judah and Jerusalem, predicting that Nebuchadnezzar of Babylon will most certainly destroy the land. John, however, reverses the recipient of destruction: Babylon, not Jerusalem, falls this time.

- ✔ **Ezekiel 26:13:** The Ezekiel passage is a judgment oracle uttered against the city of Tyre (located in modern Lebanon just to the north of Israel). Once again, Nebuchadnezzar is the agent of retribution against this ancient city, notorious for its greed and corruption. John simply borrows the imagery of destruction to make his point: No music, no creativity, no business and commerce, no joys and pleasures of life animate great Babylon; instead, she sits silent and solitary in the darkness at the bottom of the sea. She'll never seduce anyone again.

Chapter 13

Coming of the Kingdom
(19:1–20:15)

The focal point of Revelation 19 is the long-awaited return of the King. Revelation 19 also juxtaposes two suppers and sketches more details about the battle of Armageddon and the Lamb's stunning triumph before the end.

Next, Revelation 20 features a golden age, an idyllic time, in which the Lamb and his followers reign on earth for a millennium, 1,000 years. However, the exact meaning of the Millennium has generated considerable debate through the centuries. In this chapter, we sort out the differences of belief.

Finally, we explore another mystery in Revelation 20. Satan, the ancient archenemy and antagonist, is bound at the beginning of the Millennium. Inexplicably, at its conclusion, he's released from his prison. True to form, he sets about doing what he's always done: deceiving people and stirring up rebellion. He enlists another army more powerful than even the beast and the ten kings could muster in Revelation 19. They assault the very center of the Lamb's kingdom, the beloved city. The response to this attack is devastating and decisive: Fire consumes Satan and his army.

When the smoke clears, a great white throne dominates the scene. It's the last judgment, popularly called Doomsday. In the end, there are only two options: the new Jerusalem or the lake of fire. John indicates the basis for judgment and the outcome.

In this chapter, we run through these events. And at the end, we take a closer look at some theological takes on hell and the Millennium.

Returning as Promised (19:1–21)

In Revelation 19, five angelic anthems or acclamations herald the imminent return of the Jesus, the King. Each one provides additional commentary on the demise of Babylon the Great and the defeat of the beast and false prophet. Four different titles for the Lamb appear in this section, each adding luster to the character and status of Jesus.

This part of Revelation essentially describes what happens to the beast, the false prophet, and their vast army of ten kings. A sharp sword issuing from the mouth of him who is called "Faithful and True" and "the Word of God" destroys the allied forces. As for the beast and false prophet, they're captured and consigned to the lake of fire. Believers, on the other hand, are invited to the marriage supper of the Lamb and his bride.

Having a roaring good time

A massive heavenly choir leads off the celebration with a *doxology* (a giving of praise or blessing to God). The anthem begins with a rousing "Hallelujah!" This keynote captures the mood of the heavenly courts.

The choir voices the reason thanksgiving and praise are so appropriate. In short, God acts in accord with his faithfulness and justice (Rev. 19:2). He upholds his promises, and his character never changes. Because this is so, the great whore receives her just "reward." She, by contrast, reveals her true character as unfaithfulness. Not only does she break faith with God, but she also viciously persecutes his covenant partners, the people of God.

A second hallelujah rings out, declaring the duration of her punishment: "forever and ever" (Rev. 19:3). This raises some hard theological questions, which we explore in the section titled "Struggling to understand hell," later in this chapter.

Another word for booyah!

Hallelujah! Christians the world over, who otherwise may not know Hebrew from Hindi, regularly sing, chant, pray, shout, or whisper this Hebrew word. Meaning literally *praise the Lord,* it resonates with deep spiritual and emotional overtones.

By the time you get to Revelation 19, you see that the people of God are shouting *Hallelujah!* all over the place in the wake of the Lamb's total victory over the unholy trinity (dragon, beast, and false prophet) and their allies.

The 24 elders and the four living creatures bow deeply before God's throne and add their voices to the heavenly liturgy (public worship): "Amen. Hallelujah!" (Rev. 19:4). The word *amen* comes from Hebrew, and it conveys the notion of that which is firm, established, and true. The angelic beings closest to God's throne thus affirm and agree with God's judgment.

Next, an unidentified voice "from the throne," perhaps one of the four living creatures, sings a solo part: "Praise our God, all you his servants, and all who fear him, small and great" (Rev. 19:5).

The angelic choir responds, antiphonally (singing in alternating parts) and in unison. The sound is overwhelming. Like waves crashing against a rocky shoreline during a thunderstorm, the concluding anthem resounds through the heavenly sanctuary. Two events are the subject of this song:

- ✔ **The Lord reigns:** All resistance crumbles. The ringleaders of the Dark Lord's kingdom are incarcerated. The fulfillment of the Lord's Prayer is a reality: "Your kingdom come. Your will be done, on earth as it is in heaven"(Matthew 6:10).

- ✔ **The saints prepare for a wedding:** The imagery is striking but not unique; it draws upon a rich tradition in which Old Testament Israel is compared to a bride and God (Yahweh) is her husband (Isaiah 54:6–8; Jeremiah 2:1–3; Ezekiel 16:8–14; and Hosea 2:14–23). John now applies it to the Lamb (the groom) and the Church (the bride), as he also does in his Gospel (John 3:29). The bride dresses in white as a symbol of purity.

Avoiding angel worship

In Revelation 19:9, John writes,

> "And the angel said to me, 'Write this: Blessed are those who are invited to the marriage supper of the Lamb.' And he said to me, 'These are true words of God.' Then I fell down at his feet to worship him, but he said to me, 'You must not do that! I am a fellow-servant with you and your comrades who hold the testimony of Jesus. Worship God! For the testimony of Jesus is the spirit of prophecy.'"

The authenticity of the invitation is certified: "These are true words of God." No need to check with Sotheby's auction house on the genuineness of this invitation! This is the fourth of seven beatitudes or blessings John records in his book. (See Rev. 1:3; 14:13; 16:15; 19:9; 20:6; 22:7; 22:14.)

You can't crash this wedding

Jesus uses the metaphor of a wedding banquet in his ministry. In Matthew's Gospel, a parable about a king who prepares a lavish wedding banquet for his son only to be humiliated by the invited guests' refusal to come, highlights the spiritual blindness of the religious leadership of his day (Matthew 22:2–10).

Jesus takes the parable further by sketching a scenario in which a person does show up at the wedding banquet but without the appropriate attire. The point is clear: One must be an invited guest to attend — no wedding crashers allowed! (Matthew 22:11–12). The point of Revelation 19:9 is similar: A state of spiritual blessedness and fulfillment awaits those who belong to the fellowship of the Lamb, the true bride of Jesus.

Once again, the prophet John interacts with his heavenly guide. This time, he prostrates himself (bows low) with the intent of worshiping the angel. Perhaps he thought it was the Lord himself. At any rate, John is sharply rebuked: "You must not do that!" (Rev. 19:10). This episode may serve as a warning to congregations in Asia (the seven churches; see Chapter 7) against the veneration of angels.

Paul's letters to the Colossians and Ephesians (both in the province of Asia) and the anonymous letter to the Hebrews suggest that venerating angels and alleged visionary ascents to the heavenly throne room to participate in angelic worship were potential sources of error and false pride (Colossians 2:18; Ephesians 1:20–23; and Hebrews 1:4). The corrective is clear: "Worship God! For the testimony of Jesus is the spirit of prophecy" (19:10). This affirmation links the Old and New Testaments. In short, Jesus is the central biblical figure of redemptive history, as is stated at the outset of the Book of Revelation (Rev. 1:2; see also John 1:1–3, 1:14; 1 John 1:1–3).

Making a grand entrance

In Revelation 19:11, John writes, "I saw heaven opened, and there was a white horse!" For only the second time in the book, the heavens open. In the first instance, John himself ascended to the heavenly throne room and began recording his visions of "what is to take place after this" (1:19). This time, there won't be an ascent but a dramatic descent: King Jesus comes down on a white horse, followed by the armies of heaven. These two openings frame the action in chapters 4–20.

Determining who's on this white horse

The white horse in Revelation 19:11 is reminiscent of Revelation 6:2, where the first seal also features a rider on a white horse. Some commentators believe that Revelation 6's white horse refers to Jesus and the preaching of the gospel.

However, even though both riders are on white horses, they don't necessarily both represent good guys. Other commentators believe that Revelation 6's white horse refers to the spirit of the Antichrist, already present at the end of the first century, exercising his influence through deception and error (see 1 John 2:18–25). If this is the case, the two riders on white horses frame Revelation 6–20 and provide a dramatic contrast. The last rider on a white horse trumps the first. No rivals stand against Jesus.

Getting four names for one rider

Four names identify the rider on the white horse. Of course, John's readers already know who this is. These names speak to the character and qualifications of the King. Each name of Jesus highlights certain attributes or characteristics that qualify him to be the redeemer and rightful ruler of humanity:

- ✔ **"Faithful and True":** The faithfulness of Jesus is a keynote in the Book of Revelation. He is "the faithful witness" (Rev. 1:5, 3:14). There's no falsehood in him, so he stands in stark contrast to the beast and false prophet, who specialize in deceit.

- ✔ **Name known only to the rider:** This title reminds the reader that because Jesus is God, there are dimensions of his being and person that are inaccessible to mere mortals.

- ✔ **"The Word of God":** This title connects the book of Revelation with the Gospel of John and is one of the indicators of common authorship. John doesn't elaborate on the pre-existence and creative activity of Jesus in Revelation as he does in his Gospel (John 1:1–5). But he does allude to it. Jesus strikes with a sword from his mouth. This figure of speech means that he simply speaks a word of command, and it happens.

Knowing God's name

Widespread in the ancient Near East was the notion that knowing a deity's name granted special power or favor. The Bible does reflect the conviction that knowing the name of the deity brings one into personal fellowship and relationship, but not in a magical sense (Exodus 33:12, 18–19; John 17:6). The Bible is emphatic, however, that knowing God's name doesn't amount to controlling God; on the contrary, the name of God controls all that is (Genesis 32:29; Exodus 3:13–15; Judges 13:17–18; Acts 19:13–16; Philippians 2:9–11).

✔ **"King of kings and Lord of lords":** This title answers a central question posed in the book of Revelation: Who's in charge? The repetition in the title (King of kings) reflects a characteristic of the Hebrew language: using repetition to emphasize something superlative or unique. In short, Jesus is a king and a lord without peer. Even though John writes in Greek, you can still detect here and there the influence of the Hebrew language on his Greek.

Of interest is the location of this title. The image appears to be that of a long robe trailing out behind the rider. The title is emblazoned both on the robe and upper leg, where warriors typically wear their sword. Perhaps the sword itself bears this title.

The robe has another distinctive mark: It's dipped in blood (Rev. 19:13). Does this refer to Jesus's sacrificial death, or is the image that of a warrior whose garment is stained with the blood of fallen enemies? Perhaps both images are intended; both ideas are rooted in biblical thought (see Rev. 1:5, 5:6, 5:12, 7:14, and 12:11 on the sacrifice idea, and see Isaiah 42:13, 63:3–6; Habakkuk 3:11–14; and Zephaniah 3:17 on the conquering hero image).

Taking multiple, descriptive names is a traditional practice among monarchs, both ancient and modern. At their coronation, leaders often assume throne names, which become part of the royal ideology. For example, Isaiah 9:6 lists four throne names of the prophesied Messiah: "Wonderful counselor, Mighty God, Everlasting Father, Prince of Prince." Each name is a fitting description of John's Jesus, the returning King.

Taking up throne titles

Here's a sampling of the throne titles of two ancient kings:

✔ **Ramses II of Egypt:** King of Upper and Lower Egypt, Son of Re, Giver of life forever, Beloved of Amon-Re, Lord of the Two Lands, Appearing on the Horus-throne of the Living, like his father Har-akhti forever

✔ **Sennacherib of Assyria:** Sennacherib, the great king, the mighty king, king of the world, king of Assyria, king of the four quarters, the wise shepherd, favorite of the great gods, guardian of right, lover of justice, who lends support, who comes to the aid of the destitute, who performs pious acts, perfect hero, mighty man, first among all princes, the powerful one who consumes, the insubmissive, who strikes the wicked with the thunderbolt

Modern monarchs continue the tradition! Here are Queen Elizabeth II's throne titles: Elizabeth the Second, by the Grace of God, of the United Kingdom of Great Britain and Northern Ireland and of Her Other Realms and Territories Queen, Head of the Commonwealth, Defender of the Faith.

Readers of the King James Version (KJV) of the Bible may object, noting that there are five, not four names in Isaiah 9:6. The KJV places a comma after the word *Wonderful,* distinguishing it from the following word *Counselor,* making it appear as a separate name (that's also how the passage appears in the "Hallelujah Chorus" of Handel's *Messiah*). There are, however, good arguments for taking *Wonderful Counselor* as one title. Jewish scribes, called the Masoretes, added punctuation and vowel points (marks indicating how a syllable is to be pronounced) to the ancient Hebrew text, which had only consonants, about 700 CE. According to their understanding, the text consists of four titles composed of two words each. The result is a nicely balanced unit.

Picking the bones clean and taking prisoners

John rewinds the tape of the last days' events as Revelation 19 concludes. He wants to show the battle scene at Armageddon one last time. The vision features another invitation to a banquet called "the great supper of God" (Rev. 19:17). But what a contrast to the marriage supper of the Lamb! If the former is glorious — a white-robe only affair — this one is gory, a macabre feast of decaying flesh. An angel summons scavenger birds, like vultures, to the scene of the battle. They're the clean-up crew. So ends the army recruited by the beast and false prophet. We think of those photographs of the aftermath of Civil War battles that so shocked the American public — bloated, blackened, stiff corpses litter the fields.

Attention now shifts to the ringleaders themselves. What happens to the beast and the false prophet? Both are captured: "These two were thrown alive into the lake of fire that burns with sulfur" (Rev. 19:20). No mention of who captures them or how it's accomplished. Perhaps that's the point: They're defenseless against the Lamb. But how did their army perish so suddenly? The sword issuing forth from the mouth of the rider on the white horse kills them. That is, by a mere word of command, they die. God (the Lamb), who called the worlds into existence by a mere word (Genesis 1), can also operate in the other direction.

Dawning of the Millennial Age (20:1–6)

Revelation 20:1–6 pictures an unprecedented time in human history. The arch deceiver, Satan, bearing four descriptive titles, is unmasked and incarcerated. Here are some of his aliases:

- ✔ **Dragon:** This descriptive title, perhaps indebted to an ancient Near Eastern myth in which a chaos monster threatens to destroy the created order, depicts Satan as a dragon. As such, Satan is the archetypal chaos monster.

- ✔ **Serpent:** This title may also reflect ancient Near Eastern mythology in which a snake tricks humanity and prevents their obtaining immortality. But even more relevant is the account of the serpent's deception of the first human couple in Genesis 3. Revelation 20:3 explicitly states why Satan is cast into the bottomless pit: "so that he would deceive the nations no more."

- ✔ **Devil:** The Greek word *diabolos*, translated as "Devil," means "one who slanders." Characteristic of the Devil's tactics are his slanderous accusations brought against God and his people (see Job 1–2; Revelation 12:10).

- ✔ **Satan:** The basic meaning of this word is "adversary." This pretty much sums up Satan's mode of operation: he resists, obstructs, and subverts all attempts to realize God's kingdom on earth. He is the "mother of all adversaries."

As soon as the Devil is locked up, the Lamb takes charge! Jesus brings back to life those who were martyred for their faith, and they reign with him for 1,000 years. A special blessing is pronounced upon all who participate in this golden age (Rev 20:6). In this section, we go over the downfall of the dragon and the resurrection of the martyrs.

Seizing the dragon

Checkmate! The Devil has no moves left on the cosmic chessboard. An unidentified but obviously powerful angel, "holding in his hand the key to the bottomless pit and a great chain," drags the Devil off to prison. In the pit, he no longer practices his trade: deceiving the nations. Revelation states the length of his sentence twice: 1,000 years (20:2, 20:3). But then comes the ominous statement: "After that he must be let out for a little while" (Rev. 20:3). At least one last event in the career of Satan is to play out later in the chapter.

Reigning with the Lamb

A new administration takes charge. John turns to thrones containing individuals entrusted with the authority to dispense justice. Though John doesn't identify them, they're clearly followers of the Lamb. In the Gospels, Jesus promises his disciples that they'll occupy positions of leadership and judgment when his kingdom fully arrives: "Truly I tell you, at the renewal of all things, when the Son of Man is seated on the throne of his glory, you who have followed me will also sit on twelve thrones, judging the twelve tribes of Israel" (Matthew 19:28; see also Luke 22:29–30, and compare 1 Corinthians 6:2–3 for Paul's contribution to the subject).

John's attention fastens on one particular group of Jesus's followers: those who pay the ultimate price for their commitment to the Lamb. John sees the souls of the Christian martyrs who were beheaded by the beast. Earlier, during the fifth seal, John saw "the souls of those who had been slaughtered for the word of God and for the testimony they had given" (Rev. 6:9). They were located under the altar, and they cried out for justice. That day has now come, and they collect their reward for faithfulness.

These souls are suddenly embodied — that is, they receive new, physical bodies, just like Jesus did in his resurrection: "They came to life and reigned with Christ a thousand years" (Rev. 20:4). This event is designated as "the first resurrection" (Rev. 20:5), and it constitutes the fifth of seven blessings recounted in the book. To experience resurrection places one beyond death; immortality is now an inherent and irreversible attribute. Added to this unending life is the privilege of serving as a priest of God and Jesus. These believer-priests, seated on thrones, reign with Jesus throughout the millennial era — that is, the period of 1,000 (Rev. 20:6).

Notice the brief editorial comment concerning the fate of nonbelievers who die before Jesus's millennial reign. They, too, experience a resurrection of sorts, but its nature is drastically different from that of the saints; it receives a fuller discussion later in Revelation 20 (see "Termination of Death and Hades," later in this chapter).

Perhaps no single passage in the Book of Revelation captures readers' imaginations more than the description of a 1,000-year reign of Jesus on earth, as described in the opening verses of Revelation 20. Hopes for a millennial, golden age have stirred the hearts and minds of reformers, politicians, theologians, and poets for generations. Popular media resonate with millennial aspirations under varied figures and images. The question continually resurfaces: Will there truly be a prolonged period of peace and prosperity? Is a golden age in our future? We examine some of these issues in detail at the end of this chapter.

Letting Satan Loose (20:7–10)

Surprisingly, after 1,000 years of lockup, Satan actually gets paroled! Why does God allow this fiend to go free? We can only speculate.

Perhaps the point is to demonstrate once and for all how deeply sin affects the human heart. Even though Jesus himself personally reigns over the earth during the Millennium and Satan is unable to incite rebellion, as soon as Satan is released, he finds willing accomplices. Perhaps the prophet Jeremiah gives the best possible explanation: "The heart is devious above all else; it is perverse — who can understand it?" (Jeremiah 17:9). At any rate, Scripture affirms that "all things work together for good for those who love God, who are called according to his purpose" (Romans 8:28). Somehow, Satan's parole fits into God's plan.

In this section, we explain how Satan spends his last great escape.

Reverting to form

Satan, as portrayed in the Bible, is incorrigible. Many theologians think redemption is provided for human beings only, not angels, and Satan himself is a fallen angel (see Job 1:6–12; Ezekiel 28:11–16; Luke 10:18).

In the Bible, angels, like humans, are free moral agents who can decide for or against God. Maybe when Satan leads the primeval angelic rebellion (see 2 Peter 2:4; Jude 4), those who side with him are confirmed in wickedness (this idea appears, for example, in the Jewish apocalyptic work 1 Enoch 15–16). Perhaps this is so because of the enormity of their offense in light of their exalted privilege and position. In the case of angels, God seems to require perfect obedience. Satan and his minions opted out and are now, by nature, utterly opposed to the good.

At any rate, once released from his prison, Satan wastes no time. He immediately sets about duping the crowning achievement of God's creation, human beings. It's shocking how easily he accomplishes his aim. He's a master of deception with a vast repertoire. Added to that, he knows humans — the sons and daughters of Adam and Eve — better than they know themselves.

Googling Gog

More mysterious figures enter the fray: Satan goes to the *four corners of the earth* (an expression meaning the entire planet) to summon Gog and Magog to battle. Who are they?

Finding other biblical references

The name Gog appears in three separate texts: 1 Chronicles 5:4, Ezekiel 38–39 (ten times), and Revelation 20:8:

- ✔ In 1 Chronicles 5:4, Gog is a son of Joel of the tribe of Reuben. Obviously, he's not under consideration in Revelation 20.

- ✔ Ezekiel 38:2 mentions a Gog, "the chief prince of Meshech and Tubal." This text is doubtless the background of John's thought. In Ezekiel 38–39, *Magog* is a region to the extreme north of the land of Israel (Ezekiel 38:6). Gog of Magog, lured by the Lord, leads a coalition invasion force against Israel. In Ezekiel's vision, the Lord destroys this vast army on the mountains of Israel.

The name Magog occurs five times: Genesis 10:2; 1 Chronicles 1:5; Ezekiel 38:2, 39:6; and Revelation 20:8. According to Genesis and 1 Chronicles, *Magog* is one of the sons of Japheth, the ancestor of non-Semitic, Euro-Asian peoples.

Discerning what John meant

Although there undoubtedly was an ancient people known as Magog living far to the north of Israel, we don't think John's intent was to be politically and geographically correct. In Revelation, he wants to depict an evil alliance, embracing peoples traditionally considered to live at the farthest corners of the world. This End-Times "axis of evil" seeks to unseat the Lamb from his throne. In short, most scholars conclude that Gog and Magog (G&M) are symbolic names, not literal, which was the standard interpretation of the expression among the Jewish rabbis.

The *aim* of this G&M coalition, however, is far from symbolic. Once again, Satan orders a frontal assault, this time on the city of Jerusalem, the abode of the redeemed. They attack the rider on the white horse and his army (Rev. 19:19), but G&M are stopped in their tracks — but not cold in their tracks! "And fire came down from heaven and consumed them" (Rev. 20:9). Talk about blunt force and trauma! The battle is short and, thankfully, the last.

No sympathy for the devil. His sentence is swift and severe. He joins his creations, the beast and false prophet, in the lake of fire and sulfur (Rev. 20:10). From his first appearance in the Bible in the Garden of Eden (Genesis 3), Satan has consistently sought to frustrate the purposes of God. He's responsible for an incalculable amount of suffering, and his punishment corresponds to his crimes: "tormented day and night forever and ever." The curtain comes down on the final act of his career.

Coming from Russia without love?

Some students of Bible prophecy claim that Gog is a symbolic name for the leader of Russia and that Magog is an ancient tribal name for that region. They claim that because Russia is far to the north of Israel, this fits geographically. Furthermore, they claim that Meschech and Tubal (Ezekiel 38:2) are equated with the Russian cities Moscow and Tobolsk.

Going a step further, they suggest that *Gog* should not be translated as "chief prince" in Ezekiel 38:2 but as "Rosh." (The Hebrew word *Rosh* usually means "head, leader, commander," and so forth.) They take it as a proper name and appeal to the fact that one of the leading tribes in Russian history is the *Rus*. From this, they infer that Russia invades the land of Israel in the End Times. A difference of opinion surfaces, however, as to the

placement of this invasion. Some locate it before the Millennium, at the battle of Armageddon (Revelation 9:13–19, 16:12–17), but others follow the order of Ezekiel 38–39 and place it, like Revelation 20:7–10, after the Millennium. Still others entertain several different options in order to harmonize Ezekiel with Revelation.

Today, most scholars are wary of identifying ancient biblical names for various tribal, ethnic groups with modern nation-states. Understanding the genre of the book of Revelation is crucial: John employs these ancient tribal names symbolically in order to depict a final coalition of peoples opposed to the kingdom of Jesus. Beyond that, readers have to be very cautious about making bold predictions involving contemporary nations and states.

Standing at the Great White Throne (20:11–15)

An awe-inspiring vision unfolds in the last third of Revelation 20. A great white throne dominates the scene, speaking of authority and sovereignty. John doesn't have to say who sits on the throne — that point is clear: God the Father and the Lamb preside over this court.

The New Testament attributes Judgment Day to both the Father and the Son (see John 5:22; 2 Corinthians 5:10; Romans 14:10; and 2 Timothy 4:1). This final judgment differs from a number of other divine judgments that occur within history:

✔ Adam and Eve's expulsion from the Garden of Eden (Genesis 3:22–24)

✔ Cain's banishment for murdering his brother Abel (Genesis 4:12)

✔ The flood in the days of Noah, destroying the entire earth because of human and demonic wickedness (Genesis 7:11–24)

✔ The destruction of Pharaoh's empire for infanticide and forced slavery (Exodus 7:14–12:36)

✔ The extermination of the Canaanites for their extreme depravity and cruelty (Joshua 1–12)

Judging art

Many artists and writers have tried to imagine the moment of the Final Judgment in Revelation 20:11–15. Michelangelo completed his fresco rendition of "The Last Judgment" in the Sistine Chapel at Rome. Dante Alighieri expressed the Judgment to great literary effect in *The Divine Comedy,* especially in the first *cantica* (section), "Inferno." And Mozart's opera *Don Giovanni* ("the most perfect opera ever written," according to theologian Søren Kierkegaard) gives a musical interpretation when the notorious seducer descends into the fires of Hell. These artists are all indebted to the primary description of Doomsday in Revelation 20. This scene is unsettling. Standing before God to be judged for is indeed cause for concern!

These historical judgments pale in comparison to this the final righting of wrongs and vindication of the righteous. According to the Bible, all human beings must give an account for their deeds before God (Romans 14:10–12; 2 Corinthians 5:10; 2 Timothy 4:1; 1 Peter 4:5). For that reason, this scene is properly called the *Last Judgment.*

John's vision shares some features with Daniel's earlier vision of the Last Judgment: "As I watched, thrones were set in place and an Ancient One took his throne. [. . .] The court sat in judgment, and the books were opened" (Daniel 7:9–10). Almost as an afterthought, John mentions that earth and heaven flee from the presence of the one on the throne (Rev. 20:11). John returns to this rather startling idea in Revelation 21:1. The issue at center stage in this paragraph is the Final Judgment.

In this section, we explain who is judged, the standard and basis for judgment, and the two diametrically opposed outcomes.

Judgment by the books

The judgment process appears to involve two books. To be more precise, Revelation speaks of a collection of books and a single, very likely large book (20:12). Scholars hold three main views with regard to the correlation between the two:

> ✔ **Only the names of the redeemed are listed in the book of life, and only nonbelievers are listed in the books of deeds.** This view, however, runs contrary to the teaching of Scripture that even believers will be judged on the basis of their deeds (2 Corinthians 5:10; Romans 14:10).

✔ **Only the names of the redeemed occur in *both* the books of deeds and the book of life.** On this understanding, the deeds of believers simply demonstrate the presence of saving faith. Obviously, nonbelievers aren't listed in the book of life, and their deeds likewise testify against them that they don't possess genuine faith. In short, faith produces good works (James 2:14–26).

✔ **Those whose names are missing from the citizen list, the book of life, may appeal to the books of deeds.** Perhaps, proponents argue, some may even be admitted to the heavenly city at this late hour, testifying to an implicit trust in God and his Messiah. The Apostle Paul is sometimes cited in support of this conjecture:

> "When Gentiles who do not possess the law, do instinctively what the law requires, these, though not having the law, are a law to themselves. They show that what the law requires is written down on their hearts, to which their own conscience also bears witness; and their conflicting thoughts will accuse or perhaps excuse them on the day when, according to my gospel, God, through Jesus Christ will judge the secret thoughts of all." (Romans 2:14–16)

We leave the interpretation an open question. What's clear in both the Old and New Testaments, however, is that salvation is not based on works; salvation is by *grace* (unmerited favor from God) through faith. Furthermore, good works are the fruit of genuine faith (Ephesians 2:8–10), and believers are judged on the basis of their works with regard to reward or loss of reward in the new Jerusalem (1 Corinthians 3:10–15).

Looking at the books of deeds and the people before the throne

John says, "And I saw the dead, great and small, standing before the throne" (Rev. 20:12). The collection of books contains an account of all their works.

On a premillennial understanding of Revelation, these dead include all the people who have ever lived and have *not* responded to God's offer of salvation — in other words, the great majority are nonbelievers. Premillenialists assume that believers prior to the Millennium have already been judged at Jesus's judgment seat and received their rewards for faithful service or suffered loss for failure to do so (see 1 Corinthians 3:10–15; 2 Corinthians 5:10; and Romans 14:10–12). But many people survive the Great Tribulation and enter the millennial era. They and their descendants born during the Millennium must make a personal decision to trust Jesus as Savior. Presumably, many of them do and, presumably, they're included in this judgment scene. But obviously, many do not because Satan is able to deceive a great host at the end of the Millennium. So nonbelievers from the millennial age are present as well.

On an amillennial approach to Revelation, things aren't so complicated. Everyone, believers and nonbelievers alike, participate in this final court session because no interim earthly kingdom precedes the eternal state.

Salvation in the works?

According to the Bible, good deeds alone don't assure a place in heaven. *Not fair!* cries the reader. What if a person has an admirable record of good deeds? What orthodox Christians have always affirmed, in light of the total message of the Bible, is that essential, good works are a result of believing in Jesus but aren't the key to heaven. Here's what noted theologians have reasoned from the Bible for centuries:

✔ **No one is *saved* on the basis of good works.** The reason is that even noble deeds can be carried out with impure or false motives; the human heart is deceitful (Jeremiah 17:9). The Apostle Paul's exposé in Romans 3:9–18 builds to this conclusion: "For no human being will be justified in his sight by deeds prescribed by the law, for through the law comes the knowledge of sin" (Romans 3:20). He then summarizes his argument with this indictment: "For there is no distinction, since all have sinned and fall short of the glory of God" (Romans 3:23). The verdict is certain: Innumerable offenses litter everyone's personal transcript.

✔ **If judgment is on the basis of works, the flip side is that salvation is by grace through faith in Jesus (Ephesians 2:8–9).** Those who truly come to Jesus recognize their shortcoming and cast themselves on the mercy of the court. The work of the Holy Spirit in the heart, what theologians call *regeneration* or the *new birth* (see John 3:3–10), is such that good deeds follow as a natural consequence. Indeed, good deeds are an outward indicator of an inner work of grace but are not sufficient to secure salvation (Galatians 5:6, 6:15; 1 Corinthians 7:19).

✔ **Salvation comes down to a relationship, not human effort (Galatians 2:15–16).** Those who trust in Jesus are reconciled to God and become part of his spiritual family; they enjoy the privileges of being his children (Galatians 4:6; Romans 5:1, 5:6–11, 8:12–17) and show the fruit of the Spirit in their lives (Galatians 5:16–26). In short, those with admirable deeds turn out to be those who are spiritually reborn and have their names in the book of life. At the end of the day, then, the two sets of books in Revelation are in harmony.

Searching in the book of life

The *book of life* is a listing of all the heirs of God and joint heirs of Jesus (see Romans 8:12–17). In a sense, Jesus is the sole heir of God; however, he willingly shares his inheritance with the redeemed. Believers thus become joint heirs with their elder brother. The sealed scroll in Revelation 5:1–10 seems to function like a last will and testament. A will indicates who is to inherit the estate, and now you discover who the beneficiaries are.

Perhaps first, a search is made of the book of deeds. The life of the individual is, so to speak, an open book. The transcript speaks for itself. But the crucial question is this: Is a person's name also found in the book of life? A listing in the book of life, biblically, indicates that a person is a certified believer. According to Revelation 20:15, this is decisive: "And anyone whose name was not found written in the book of life was thrown into the lake of fire."

Termination of Death and Hades

John's readers may have wondered what happens to those who die at sea. And though he doesn't mention it, readers may also wonder about those whose bodies were cremated. Does this prevent any possibility of resurrection?

Though John doesn't spell it out, his vision is in harmony with the biblical view that *everyone* experiences a bodily resurrection before the Final Judgment. The quality of the resurrection of the righteous, however, differs drastically from that of the unrighteous. The root of this conviction goes back to the Old Testament book of Daniel. There you read, "Many of those who sleep in the dust of the earth shall awake, some to everlasting life, and some to shame and everlasting contempt" (Daniel 12:2). Jesus reaffirms this teaching:

> "Do not be astonished at this; for the hour is coming when all who are in the graves will hear his voice and will come out — those who have done good, to the resurrection of life, and those who have done evil, to the resurrection of condemnation." (John 5:28–29)

John personifies the realm of the departed under the twin names of Death and Hades. *Hades* is a Greek term for the place and condition of those who experience the separation of body and spirit called death. Dramatically, John sees the realm of the dead virtually emptied out and poured into the lake of fire. He adds this editorial comment: "This is the second death, the lake of fire" (20:14). With this statement, John closes the books, so to speak, on redemptive history. His next series of visions usher the reader into a new earth and a new Jerusalem.

Sorting Out Two Theological Issues

In this section, we briefly discuss two difficult theological problems — namely, the nature of final punishment and the nature of the Millennium. Instead of arguing for a specific position, we try to describe fairly and accurately the various options. We do, however, indicate our preferences.

Struggling to understand hell

Christians and others struggle with the idea of hell. What are you to make of the idea of eternal punishment of nonbelievers in the lake of fire? Is such a teaching really compatible with the core doctrines of Christianity, especially the love and mercy of God for all human beings?

We don't pretend to have definitive answers. Much more competent theologians have grappled with this question and admitted failure in resolving the problem satisfactorily. We simply present some of the views of respected Christian thinkers.

A traditional view: No rest for the wicked

Traditionally, hell is viewed as a condition of eternal, conscious torment. Most Christian theologians through the ages have held this view. However, many of these same theologians haven't insisted on a *strictly* literal interpretation of the lake of fire.

Rather than press the language in this way, they've instead preferred to stress the essential nature of hell as exclusion from God's presence. Nonbelievers are cast out or excluded from the blessings and joy of God's presence, the source of all that's truly good. The torment experienced by the impenitent (those who are viewed biblically as unrepentant sinners) is understood as primarily mental and spiritual anguish and remorse.

A minority view: Being wiped out of existence

Some scholars are troubled even by the notion that God would inflict an eternal punishment. They raise questions such as the following:

- ✔ How can you avoid calling such a thing torture, and how can this be worthy of God?
- ✔ Can't he forgive his enemies as he commands people to do?
- ✔ Doesn't this present an enormous philosophical and theological problem in that this place or condition of punishment exists forever?
- ✔ How can there be an ultimate solution to the problem of evil if this pocket of punishment always exists?

In light of these questions, they suggest that the lake of fire represents *annihilation*. That is, nonbelievers cease to exist, kind of like being blasted by some sort of space gun. Because they no longer exist, they're not conscious and suffer no pain. A slight modification of this view agrees that there's a time of conscious torment for nonbelievers, but it's limited in duration. After their deserved punishment, they cease to exist. The philosophical and theological advantage for those holding the annihilation view is that it eliminates the continuing presence of evil in the universe.

A more radical view: Everyone's forgiven

A more radical solution to what some see as the "problem of hell" affirms that God eventually pardons and receives virtually everyone into fellowship with himself — except, perhaps, for the devil and his angels! This position is often labeled as *universalism*. A few Christian theologians have dared to champion this position. One of the most noteworthy was the brilliant scholar and churchman Origen (who died 254 CE). His view, however, was later condemned in 553 CE at the Fifth Ecumenical Council in Constantinople (an *ecumenical council* is a private meeting of representative leaders from the entire church having authority to define doctrine and practice for all Christians).

No simple answers

Many Christian scholars see aspects of annihilation and universalism as attractive, but they note weighty objections. The Scriptures seem to treat the destiny of believers and nonbelievers as parallel in duration. That is, believers are pictured as enjoying the new Jerusalem forever. Nonbelievers are pictured as being in the lake of fire forever. Does limiting the extent of the one jeopardize the other?

Perhaps the fundamental problem is the limitation of human language to describe spiritual realities. Scripture employs a range of conventional, even contradictory, figures and expressions to describe hell (for example, fire and darkness). But as with any analogy, these shouldn't be pressed too far.

Don't charge the suffering of the impenitent to God's account. The biblical case is that this is what they've chosen for themselves; you are what you choose to be, and God allows you to make that choice — and to reap the consequences. The Bible resounds with warnings about the reality of final judgment. It insists that there's "a fearful prospect of judgment, and a fury of fire that will consume the adversaries" (Hebrews 10:27).

Mulling over the meaning of the Millennium

Five times in six verses, John mentions a 1,000-year reign. But how are you to interpret this chronological notation? Symbols, figures, metaphors, and images abound in the Book of Revelation. Is the Millennium simply another symbol for a spiritual reality? This question has generated considerable debate in Christian circles for a long time. Perhaps the best way to proceed is simply to lay out the respective viewpoints and their arguments.

Pessimistic premillennialism: A literal 1,000 years

The earliest documented approach to the celebrated millennial passage (Rev. 20:1–6) is dubbed *premillennialism*. This view, as the name suggests, holds that Jesus returns to earth and then establishes an earthly kingdom, reigning for 1,000 years with his saints. Hence, the name premillennial describes Jesus's return — that is, before the Millennium. Here are the chief arguments supporting it:

✔ It's based on a literal reading of the text and coheres with a similar reading of the Old Testament prophets, who proclaim a very this-worldly future kingdom in connection with the Day of the Lord (see, for example, Amos 9:11–15; Joel 3:18–21; Isaiah 2:1–4, 4:2–6; and Jeremiah 31:38–40).

✔ The earliest church fathers who write on matters dealing with the End Times appear to be premillennialists. Among these are Papias, Irenaeus, Justin Martyr, Tertullian, and Victorinus. Although such an argument is hardly decisive, neither should it be dismissed. Papias and Justin Martyr are quite close to the apostolic age (when John wrote Revelation), and it's difficult to imagine they already misunderstood the nature of the 1,000 years.

✔ The mention of resurrection, specifically designated as "the first resurrection," is most naturally understood as the resurrection of the body, not a spiritual resurrection. The physical nature of the resurrection seems to require a corresponding physical dimension to the 1,000-years reign — in other words, an earthly kingdom.

Premillennialism is typically not optimistic about converting the great majority of the world's population to the gospel ("good news" of Jesus). Premillennialists have always been in the forefront of world missions but have not imagined that their evangelistic efforts would ultimately lead to a truly Christian world. Rather, premillennialism holds that at the end of the age, the Dark Lord and his evil emissaries succeed in deceiving a majority of people then-living to accept the mark of the beast (see Matthew 24:10–14).

Some critics, especially postmillennialists (see that view later on), find fault with premillennialists for not having more confidence in the power of the gospel to convert the great majority. Premillennialists respond that Jesus and the apostles never teach that most will accept the gospel. Jesus and the apostles do, however, command that the gospel be preached to all the nations of the world.

Premillenial dispensationalism: Two separate destinies

Dispensationalism is a highly influential variant of premillennialism (see the preceding section). The distinguishing feature of dispensationalism is the conviction that there are two separate peoples of God: Israel (the Jewish tribes) and the church (all Christian believers). The mission and destiny of these two peoples are quite distinct:

✔ The ultimate destiny of the Jewish people is to be regathered in their historic homeland and be restored as a nation. They're also to put their faith in Jesus of Nazareth as their promised Messiah. Dispensationalism believes that all the Old Testament prophecies about the restoration of Israel are fulfilled literally during the Millennium of Revelation 20. They hold that the literal fulfillment of the Old Testament–covenant promises to Abraham and his descendants is the primary purpose of the Millennium.

✔ The church does not share in this future program but rather is raptured out of this world (taken up to heaven) prior to the Great Tribulation. For this reason, another *pre-* gets added to the mix! Dispensationalists are almost exclusively *pre-Tribulationalists* — that is, they believe Jesus returns for the church prior to the "70th week" of Daniel, the Great Tribulation, the Day of the Lord. The church is a heavenly people and has a destiny different from Israel's, reigning with Jesus in the heavens, not on the earth in a literal Jerusalem. (See Chapters 3 and 9–12 for details on the Great Tribulation.)

The linchpin for dispensationalists is the steadfast insistence upon a strictly literal interpretation of biblical prophecy. If you do adhere to such a strict literalness, you'll most likely arrive at a view very close to that advocated by dispensationalists.

Dispensationalists share, perhaps even accentuate, the premillennial pessimistic view that the gospel will not convert the whole world before Jesus returns.

Negative amillennialism: A long, spiritual reign

The prefix suggests that *amillennialists* reject the notion of a Millennium. This is somewhat misleading. To be sure, they don't believe in an earthly, interim kingdom before the new heavens and new earth (Revelation 21). On the other hand, they do believe in a figurative Millennium, referring to the present gospel era, the reign of deceased saints with Jesus in heaven, or both. In this sense, they affirm a Millennial age. The arguments for this approach may be summarized as follows:

✔ Amillenialists refer to the figurative use of threes, sevens and multiples of seven, and twelves and multiples of twelve throughout the book. Nowhere else in the Bible is a literal, 1,000-year reign of the Messiah over the earth mentioned. In the book of Revelation, where symbols abound and numbers carry a spiritual rather than a literal significance, the 1,000 years simply conveys the idea of a long period of time (on this point, many premillenialists agree). Amillenialists view the 1,000-year reign in a spiritual, not an earthly, sense.

✔ To amillennialists, the notion of an earthly, interim kingdom seems to be a backward step. The trajectory of Scripture, according to amillennialists, encourages people to see a movement from the earthly to the heavenly, from types and shadows to fulfillment and reality, from the temporary to the eternal. Amillennialists definitely reject the dispensational type of premillennialism (see the preceding section) because it seems to undercut the unity of one people of God that's so important to the covenant concept found in the Bible. The distinction between Israel and the church is flatly rejected and often viewed as heretical! Old Testament–Israel *is* the church, and the New Testament church *is* the new Israel — ultimately all one group.

✔ The reference in Revelation 20:4 to those who "came to life and reigned with Christ a thousand years" is interpreted as a spiritual resurrection. That is, it's really a figurative way of speaking about conversion, about being born again. Thus, the "first resurrection" of Revelation 20:5 is the entire era during which the gospel is preached until Jesus returns. Amillennialists understand the second resurrection to occur in Revelation 20:11–14, when Jesus returns and all the righteous and the wicked are resurrected and stand at the great white throne of judgment (see the earlier section "Standing at the Great White Throne [20:11–15]").

Amillennialists point out that this is certainly a cleaner, simpler position than the premillennialist stance, which involves two resurrections and two different judgments. The dispensational variant, they say, is even more convoluted, with two different "second comings" of Jesus: the pre-Tribulational rapture *for the saints* before the Great Tribulation and the return (or revelation) of Jesus to the earth *with the saints* seven years later.

✔ Amillenialists frequently call attention to a literary technique that John uses. Several times, he recaps the storyline or flow of the narrative. He backs up and looks in more detail at certain pivotal persons or events. Amillenialists often insist that Revelation 20:1–6 is another instance of recapitulation. After describing Armageddon (Rev. 19:17–21), John backs up and surveys the entire gospel era prior to the last battle. In their view, then, Revelation 20 offers no support for a literal Millennium.

Optimistic postmillennialism: Jesus's fashionably late return

As the prefix suggests, *postmillennialism* holds that Jesus returns *after* the Millennium. Here's a summary of this position:

✔ Postmillennialists do not typically insist on a literal 1,000 years; they believe the expression simply means an extended period of time.

✔ In agreement with premillennialists and contrary to amillennialists, postmillennialists hold to an actual, earthly kingdom. In contrast to premillennialists, however, Jesus is not physically present on earth during this golden era. He is present spiritually, and by the power of the Holy Spirit, the gospel transforms society so that Christianity dominates the world. For this reason, you can consider this view optimistic.

✔ Postmillennialists appeal to the power of the gospel to convert and transform — and accuse premillennialists and amillennialists of not having enough confidence in God's saving power. Postmillennialists cite Biblical texts in which believers are commissioned to tell the good news to the ends of the earth. If the world is the mission field, then God must intend to save the great majority of the world, so the argument runs (see Matthew 28:19–20; Acts 1:8; and Romans 1:16). In particular, people who hold this view appeal to where John sees "a great multitude that no one could count from every nation, from all tribes and peoples and languages, standing before the throne and before the Lamb, robed in white, with palm branches in their hands" (Rev 7:9).

Postmillennialism is not a widely held view. Although its confidence in the power of the gospel is commendable, the Scriptural support is slim. A number of texts from Jesus and the Apostles rather strongly suggest that the world won't be Christianized, nor will a majority embrace the gospel (see Luke 18:8; Matthew 24:3–31; 2 Thessalonians 2:3–12; Revelation 13). The actual course of history in the 20th century and the beginning of the 21st century offers little encouragement that the gospel is transforming society. The overall misery index shows no sign of improvement.

The primary contenders in this debate are really premillennialists and amillennialists. The relative merits and deficiencies of the arguments are difficult to assess, and the reader with no vested interest in the outcome may be forgiven for thinking it's just a tempest in a teapot! None of the great ecumenical creeds (statements of belief) render a verdict on this question, so we won't either. What do you think?

Chapter 14

Seeing the New Jerusalem and a Triumphant Church (21:1–22:6)

In This Chapter
▶ Exploring a new heaven and new earth
▶ Walking in the streets of the new Jerusalem
▶ Returning to the Garden of Eden

*O*ut with the old, in with the new. A new world now replaces the old! In fact, the Greek word that John uses (*kainos*) stresses a quality of newness that means *unused, unprecedented, unworn, uncommon.* Although the old world is destroyed, God doesn't leave it in ashes.

In this chapter, you walk through the glorious newness of Revelation 21–22. John first describes the new heaven and earth in Revelation 21:1–8. Then his attention zeroes in on the centerpiece of this new world order: the new Jerusalem. He takes readers on a virtual tour of the celestial city (so-called because its origin is in heaven), noting some of its features and landmarks along the way (Rev. 21:9–22:6).

Finally, we explore John's imagery, which provides a fitting conclusion not only to his book but to the entire Bible. In short, he portrays the new Jerusalem as a garden of Eden (22:1–5). In fact, John Milton, the seventeenth-century English poet, picks up on this theme in his epic poem, *Paradise Regain'd:* God's people return to the garden.

Exploring a New Creation (21:1–8)

In Revelation 20:11, John says "the earth and the heaven" flee from the presence of the one on the great white throne, and "no place was found for them." As Revelation 21 begins, John describes the nature of the new earth and what life on it will be like for believers. Interestingly, though he says there's a new heaven, it remains shrouded in mystery. Instead, he fastens onto a few features of the new earth. This section unpacks these new features.

Understanding the heavens

For modern readers, the Bible may seem to be quaint and quite out-of-date when it comes to the natural order. This shouldn't be worrisome. The Bible was written long before the scientific method of hypothesis and empirical observation, which was first developed in the seventeenth century. Remember that the Bible reports on the physical world in terms of simple observation, unaided by telescopes or microscopes. Only the portion of creation visible to the naked eye appears in the creation account in Genesis 1.

From the perspective of the Bible and later Jewish and Christian tradition, heaven consists of three main divisions (the Hebrew word for heaven, *shamayim*, is plural in number, in keeping with its three primary meanings):

✔ The first heaven is the atmosphere above the earth in which the birds fly (Genesis 1:20), the winds blow, the clouds float, and from which rain and snow fall (Genesis 9:14; Judges 5:4; Isaiah 55:9–10). According to Genesis 1:6–8, God made a dome (rendered as "firmament," "expanse," or "vault" in other English translations) separating the waters of the sea from the waters above the dome or atmosphere (see also Psalm 148:4). Genesis 7:11 says this reservoir above the dome was a major source of the flood waters; the other source was subterranean waters upon which the dry land of the earth was supported by the "foundation" and "bases" of the earth (Job 38:4–6; Psalm 102:25; 104:5). Apocalyptic works like *1 Enoch* (chapters 72–82) devote much attention to how the wind, rain, snow, sleet, and hail fall upon the earth through windows in this atmospheric dome.

✔ The second heaven refers to the celestial heaven: the planets, sun, moon, and stars (Genesis 15:5; Matthew 24:29). This is the realm of outer space. *1 Enoch* (chapters 72–82) also goes into great detail about how the sun, moon, and stars move across the second heaven and appear through various portals in the dome below. Their movements occur in a predetermined sequence, thus causing the daily, monthly, and yearly cycles of life.

✔ The third heaven is above the first two. There, God resides on his throne, surrounded by his angelic retinue. The Apostle Paul says he "was caught up to the third heaven" in a vision (2 Corinthians 12:1–4). It's this latter meaning that's most often in view in John's visions. For example, he, too, is caught up to the third heaven in Revelation 4:1, because there he's able to view the throne room (Rev. 4:2–5:14). Occasionally, however, John refers to heaven in the sense of meanings one or two (see 8:13, 14:6, and possibly 10:6).

Despite its nonscientific understanding, the biblical notion of multiple heavens adequately depicts God's relation to his creation. After all, even sophisticated astrophysicists still speak about beautiful "sunsets"! The Bible affirms that God "made heaven, the heaven of heavens, with all their host, the earth and all that is on it, the seas and all that is in them" (Nehemiah 9:6; see also Genesis 1:1; 14:19; Psalms 8, 19; John 1:1–3; Colossians 1:15–20). Not only did he make all things, but he also sustains all things. Furthermore, he intends to recreate all things for his own glory (2 Peter 3:13).

Scrapping the old world

John merely states that the first heaven and earth pass away without explaining how this actually happens. The Apostle Peter, on the other hand, provides a graphic description of the end, which is the culmination of the judgments poured out on the earth described earlier in Revelation (see Chapters 10–13). Peter writes, "But the day of the Lord will come like a thief, and then the heavens will pass away with a loud noise, and the elements will be dissolved with fire, and the earth and everything that is done on it will be disclosed. [. . .] The heavens will be set ablaze and dissolved, and the elements will melt with fire" (2 Peter 3:10).

Some speculate that this kind of global wipeout results from a human-inflicted nuclear mishap or perhaps even from a gigantic meteor strike. This is unlikely. From his Jewish background, John knows that God spoke the original world into existence *ex nihilo* (out of nothing). In this regard, see Genesis 1, in which God creates simply by voicing a command (see also Hebrews 11:3). So bringing the old world to an end and recreating a new world is no big deal for God!

Reaching the end of the sea

Some wish John had spent more time describing the new creation. What he says is tantalizing, but it raises as many questions as it answers. John says simply, "The sea was no more" (Rev. 21:1). What does this mean? Does the new earth lack oceans, a feature distinguishing the present earth from all known planets?

Taken literally, the new earth radically differs from the old, increasing the amount of land available by almost 2.5 times (because approximately 71 percent of the earth's surface is presently covered in water). And perhaps this is what John intends to say. If so, it suggests a very large number of God's people and a very spacious dwelling place (see John 14:2; Revelation 7:9).

On the other hand, apocalyptic writings frequently describe the sea in figurative terms. In some poetic passages in the Old Testament, the sea is likened to the primeval chaos — the earliest period of earth history — and speaks of that which is restless and unruly (see Genesis 1:2; Job 16:12; Psalms 74:13, 89:9, 107:23–29). John has already spoken of the sea as the source of the dragon's great counterfeit: the beast, or Antichrist (Rev. 13:1). Perhaps, then, John's statement is just another way of saying that all that's potentially threatening is no longer present in the new creation.

Making a fresh start

Long before John's vision on Patmos, the Old Testament prophet Isaiah foresaw a new heavens and a new earth. As a matter of fact, the Apostle John almost certainly borrows some of Isaiah's language and imagery. In a key passage, Isaiah speaks in the name of the Lord himself: "For I am about to create new heavens and a new earth; the former things shall not be remembered or come to mind" (Isaiah 65:17; see also 66:22–23).

Another key Isaiah text depicts a wonderfully transformed world order: "In days to come the mountain of the Lord's house shall be established as the highest of the mountains, and shall be raised above the hills" (Isaiah 2:1). Jerusalem becomes a magnet for world pilgrimage and worship. The nations cease their warfare, and the Lord arbitrates their disputes (Isaiah 2:3–4).

Not just another makeover?

You may wonder why God has to make a new creation. Couldn't he simply fix up the old one? In fact, some theologians think renovation is precisely what God does. On this understanding, the dissolving of the elements that Peter mentions in 2 Peter 3:10 doesn't mean matter disappears; rather, matter is reconstituted or reconfigured. (By the way, Peter isn't thinking of the modern periodic table when he refers to the elements. Rather, he assumes the ancient Greek notion, widely accepted in the Near East by the first century, that the world is made up of four fundamental "elements" — earth, fire, water, and air. At any rate, Peter's point is that the present world is seriously flawed.)

The list of things gone wrong in the world is deeply disturbing: war, ethnic cleansing, genocide, murder, theft, robbery, rape, injustice, dishonesty, pollution, waste, exploitation, greed, poverty, starvation, indifference, selfishness — and on and on. The Old Testament prophets were right: The created order suffers because of human sin (Isaiah 24:4–13).

The magnitude of evil is such that only a brand new creation is appropriate for the redeemed people of God. The Apostle Paul personifies the created order and depicts it as longing to be set free from its bondage:

"For the creation waits with eager longing for the revealing of the children of God; for the creation was subjected to futility, not of its own will but by the will of the one who subjected it, in hope that the creation itself will be set free from its bondage to decay and will obtain the freedom of the glory of the children of God. We know that the whole creation has been groaning in labor pains until now. [. . .]" (Romans 8:20–22)

Apocalyptic thought, clearly reflected in the New Testament and especially the book of Revelation, radiates with a long-term optimism: God restores the fallen world to a pristine state. In fact, he does better than that — he recreates a perfect world.

Yet another passage from Isaiah describes the Messiah, the great descendant of the house of Jesse, and his righteous reign over the earth. Remarkably, his reign transforms even the animal kingdom:

> "The wolf shall live with the lamb, the leopard shall lie down with the kid, the calf and the lion and the fatling together, and a little child shall lead them. The cow and the bear shall graze, their young shall lie down together; and the lion shall eat straw like the ox. The nursing child shall play over the hole of the asp, and the weaned child shall put its hand on the adder's den. They shall not hurt or destroy on all my holy mountain; for the earth will be full of the knowledge of the Lord as the water cover the sea." (Isaiah 11:6–9)

If you take this passage literally, even the predatory cycle of nature (the big ones just eat the little ones) is transformed. Some theologians believe that before Adam and Eve ate the forbidden fruit, the garden's natural animal order was not lion-eat-sheep. On this view, the new earth reinstates the primeval, non-violent character of the garden of Eden. On the other hand, Isaiah may simply be employing figurative language in order to depict sweeping, moral transformation in the human sphere. Either way, it highlights the radical newness of the new earth.

Welcoming a city from the sky

Immediately after his cryptic statement "the sea was no more" (Rev. 21:1), John's attention is totally absorbed by a truly awesome scene. Almost like a spacecraft coming in for a landing, the holy city, the new Jerusalem, descends upon planet earth (see Figure 14-1). John is quite clear about it: It comes "down out of heaven from God" (Rev. 21:2). This rings a bell. In John's Gospel, Jesus reassures his distressed disciples that he is going away to prepare a place for them (John 14:3). That "place" is doubtless the new Jerusalem that John now sees and describes in Revelation 21. The really significant thing to note in Revelation 21 is where the new Jerusalem finally docks. John's city isn't up there in space, nor does it orbit planet earth. It comes down to the new earth.

Figure 14-1:
The New Jerusalem descending, from the *Cloister Apocalypse,* an early fourteenth-century illustrated manuscript.

© 1994 The Metropolitan Museum of Art

In heaven or on earth?

A new earth with a new Jerusalem raises some questions regarding where believers will end up. Will they be up in heaven, or will they take up residence down on the new earth? The New Testament is somewhat ambiguous on this point and so, not surprisingly, Christian theologians arrive at different positions:

✔ Many hold that believers spend eternity in heaven with God, the Lamb, and the holy angels. Biblical support for this view comes primarily from the Apostle Paul's letters. In two passages, he sketches a scenario in which, at death, the believer passes immediately into the presence of Jesus in heaven:

> "For we know that if the earthly tent we live in is destroyed [a metaphorical expression for death], we have a building from God, a house not made with hands, eternal in the heavens. [. . .] We would rather be away from the body and at home with the Lord." (2 Corinthians 5:1–8)

> "[. . .] My desire is to depart and be with Christ, for that is far better. [. . .] But our citizenship is in heaven, and it is from there that we are expecting a Savior, the Lord Jesus Christ." (Philippians 1:23; 3:20)

Thus, many theologians assume that Christians spend eternity in heaven, a view similar to that found in a Jewish apocalyptic writing called *2 Baruch*. This is by far the majority view among Christians. It's often embellished by incorporating the mention of harps in the book of Revelation (Rev. 14:2, 15:2). Popular culture encourages all sorts of supposed delights for this celestial jam session!

✔ Others think believers spend eternity on a new earth. In this view, the passages cited from Paul's epistles refer not to the eternal state but to an intermediate state that gives way to an eternal reign with Jesus on a new earth, either at the Second Coming of Jesus (amillennialism) or after the Millennium (premillennialism and postmillennialism). Evidence from Revelation in support of this is in the passage describing the fifth seal. There, disembodied souls of the martyrs are depicted under the heavenly altar and are very much conscious of what is going on (Rev. 6:9–11). Furthermore, this view is in keeping with Jewish apocalyptic writings like *Jubilees* and *4 Ezra,* in which a new Jerusalem descends from heaven and replaces the old Jerusalem.

We think the latter view better fits all the evidence. Paul argues in 1 Corinthians 15 that God intends to raise up believers in physical bodies, even if those bodies are considerably souped-up versions (1 Corinthians 15:42–49)! It's hard to imagine why God bothers to bestow new bodies for a purely heavenly existence. Life on a new earth is more in line with the original creation mandate to rule over earth (Genesis 1:26–30) and the this-worldly prophetic vision of the new heavens and new earth in Isaiah 65:17–25 and books of other Old Testament prophets (see Amos 9:13–15 and Jeremiah 31). In short, the popular view probably owes more to Plato, with his disdain for the material, than to the Bible.

Getting ready to see the bride

John uses what may seem like an odd image to describe the holy city as it descends, saying it's "prepared as a bride adorned for her husband" (Rev. 21:2). The original recipients of John's Revelation would've readily understood this description.

The Old Testament occasionally compares Israel to the bride of the Lord (see Isaiah 62:5; Jeremiah 3:1–13; Ezekiel 16:6–14). A marriage bond or covenant shares many similarities with the covenant the Lord made with Israel at Mount Sinai (Exodus 19 and 24); in both cases, mutual obligations must be fulfilled. One prophet, Hosea, who divorced his wife Gomer for unfaithfulness, uses his own crisis as a powerful metaphor to describe how Yahweh is also going to divorce Israel for her covenant unfaithfulness (Hosea 1–2). Thankfully, Hosea prophesies that, in the end, Yahweh takes Israel back and reconciles with her (Hosea 3).

God's city

In the Bible, human beings' desire to form a society began shortly after the fall into sin and the consequent alienation from God (Genesis 3–11). To compensate for his rejection by his fellow humans, Cain built a city (Genesis 4:12–17). Following the great flood of Noah (Genesis 7–8), the descendants of Noah came together to build the great city of Babel (Genesis 11:4) as an act of defiance against God's command to disperse and replenish the earth (Genesis 9:1–7).

These early attempts to create community were followed by an endless succession of great cities: Nineveh, "that great city," (Jonah 1:2); Babylon, of which Nebuchadnezzar boasts, "Is this not magnificent Babylon, which I have built as a royal capital by my mighty power and for my glorious majesty?" (Daniel 4:30); Athens, the cradle of democracy and taproot of Western civilization; and Rome, boasting over 1 million inhabitants and the lens through which the Apostle John depicts mystery Babylon, the great whore. Today, the global community is dominated by sprawling metropolitan centers, the top 20 all exceeding 10 million persons. A new word was coined to describe this modern phenomenon: the *megacity*. Human aspirations haven't changed all that much! Still, none of these attempts succeeded in building the truly great society.

The Bible refers to another city, a city that God is building. The letter to the Hebrews describes this city in these words:

> "But you have come to Mount Zion and to the city of the living God, the heavenly Jerusalem, and to innumerable angels in festal gathering, and to the assembly of the firstborn who are enrolled in heaven, and to God the judge of all, and to the spirits of the righteous made perfect, and to Jesus, the mediator of a new covenant, and to the sprinkled blood that speaks a better word than the blood of Abel." (Hebrews 12:22–24)

The Apostle Paul reminds his Gentile converts in Galatia that they belong "to the Jerusalem above; she is free, and she is our mother" (Galatians 4:26). He also alludes to this when writing to the Philippians: "But our citizenship is in heaven, and it is from there that we are expecting a Savior, the Lord Jesus Christ" (Philippians 3:20). In both of these texts, Paul views Jerusalem as a heavenly reality to which people belong, even though it hasn't yet descended to earth. He makes the same point in Colossians 3:3 without explicitly mentioning the heavenly Jerusalem: "[. . .] For you have died, and your life is hidden with Christ in God. When Christ who is your life is revealed, then you also will be revealed with him in glory."

The church father Augustine, in the fourth century, wrote a book entitled *City of God*, contrasting the human attempt to build community with God's great building project. Augustine's thesis is this: Christians don't truly belong to this world; they're part of the community of faith having its citizenship in heaven. This is the ultimate destination of believers, and this idea must shape values and behavior. John Bunyan, the Baptist minister imprisoned for being a non-conformist to the Church of England, also captured this vision in *The Pilgrim's Progress*. All these believers testified that God is creating a community of redeemed people who fully experience what it means to be part of a truly great society.

The New Testament likewise presents the spiritual relationship between the Lord and his redeemed people in marital terms (1 Corinthians 11:2). The most notable instance is in Paul's famous passage about Christian marriage in Ephesians 5:25–32, where the church is likened to the bride of Christ. In order to be the bride of Jesus, however, the church must dress the part — that is, reflect the requisite virtues worthy of Jesus's bride.

The word *adorned,* in Greek, is the word from which English speakers get the word *cosmetics.* Of course, in Revelation, John envisions a Jewish wedding in which the adorning of the bride is a very costly and elaborate affair. Much time is given over to the preparation of her appearance, apparel, and accessories. Her complexion must shine with a luster like marble. Her hair is braided and interwoven with jewels, gold, and pearls. She is decked with all the precious stones and gems that the family inherited from previous generations and, if need be, borrowed from friends and neighbors. The bride leaves her father's house in all her finery, with a crown on her head and perfume wafting about her person.

John couldn't have chosen a better way to describe the splendor of the holy city. The prophet Isaiah depicts the Lord's bride in similar terms: "[The Lord] has clothed me with the garments of salvation [. . .] as a bride adorns herself with her jewels" (Isaiah 61:10). The Apostle Paul rhapsodizes on the church as the bride of Jesus in these words: "[. . .] so as to present the church to himself [Jesus] in splendor, without a spot or wrinkle or anything of the kind — yes, so that she may be holy and without blemish" (Ephesians 5:27).

Moving in with God

In the new world order, God is continuously and intimately present — and that sort of closeness hasn't happened since God walked with Adam and Eve in the garden of Eden (and Jesus walked the earth). John says simply, "See, the home of God is among mortals. He will dwell with them; they will be his people and God himself will be with them" (Rev. 21:3). This encounter is sometimes called the *beatific vision* because of its utter bliss and blessedness. Clearly, this city is not so much a place as it is a community.

The progression in John's thought is significant. First, he says that the "home of God is among mortals." This contrasts with earlier phases of redemptive history, in which the degree of closeness was markedly less. After being kicked out of the garden of Eden, the first human couple no longer had daily visits with God "at the time of the evening breeze" (Genesis 3:8). Instead, during the primeval era (the early period of earth history, as recorded in Genesis 4–11) and the patriarchal era (the time of the founding fathers of the Israelites in the second millennium BCE, as recorded in Genesis 12–50), there were infrequent *theophanies,* appearances or manifestations of God through heavenly representatives, in dreams or visions, and so on.

But then, the Bible says, a child is born to a Jewish virgin in Bethlehem (around 6 or 5 BCE). He is a descendant of King David and is named Jesus, meaning "the Lord saves." John offers the theological meaning of this birth in his Gospel: "And the Word became flesh and lived among us, and we have seen his glory, the glory as of a father's own son, full of grace and truth" (John 1:14). Note that the Greek word translated as "lived" in John 1:14 is the same Greek word that's translated as "dwell" in Revelation 21:3. A very literal rendering of this Greek word would be he *tabernacled* among us. For John's original readers, the connection to the Old Testament Tabernacle (the portable tent Moses erected in the Sinai desert to house the Ark of the Covenant, as recorded in Exodus 25–40) and this new Temple is unmistakable. (See Chapter 10 for more on the Ark of the Covenant.)

Enjoying a new existence

John notes that life in the new world (whether it's in heaven or on earth) is radically different and way better. He states that crying and pain end and that water (better than bottled!) is freely available, and people can enjoy a special inheritance.

Relishing the end of suffering

Characteristics of life as you now know it are banished from the new earth and the new Jerusalem (Rev. 21:4):

- ✔ **No more death:** For many, death is the ultimate human tragedy. Why must loved ones be taken away? Why can't we continue to live with the vitality and energy of youth? The author of the Old Testament book of Ecclesiastes claims, "All go to one place; all are from the dust, and all turn to dust again" (Ecclesiastes 3:20). But that's not the end of the story, says John: Death will be no more!

- ✔ **No more mourning or crying:** Tears speak of the whole array of human tragedy. Grief, rejection, failure, disappointment, frustration, suffering, and persecution characterize life outside the Garden of Eden. Who knows how many tears have been shed during the long, dark night of human history? Once again, Ecclesiastes gives expression to the human condition: "Again, I saw all the oppressions that are practiced under the sun. Look, the tears of the oppressed — with no one to comfort them!" (Ecclesiastes 4:1). Thankfully, human responses to tragedy are no longer needed in the new world order.

- ✔ **No more pain:** The word John uses for *pain* is typically used in Scripture to refer to hard, exhausting work. It's labor so strenuous it saps all one's strength. It's the kind of toil the Israelites experienced during their bondage in Egypt (Exodus 1:13–14).

> But John may also mean that physical pain itself no longer exists. If so, this points to a radically different kind of existence after the resurrection. In the present, earthly bodies, pain is essential to long-term survival. Without it, people would be unaware of many life-threatening situations. But with immortal bodies (1 Corinthians 15:42–44), this is no longer an issue. (The superiority of the spiritual body that the Apostle Paul describes sounds better and better with each passing year to those of us who are part of the AARP crowd!)

Having a drink

John fastens on one fundamental human need that answers the question of death. In Revelation 21:6, the one on the throne says, "To the thirsty I will give water as a gift from the spring of the water of life." This metaphor has deep roots in the Old Testament and in the teaching of Jesus. Isaiah the prophet is the root of this idea. In a short hymn, the prophet portrays redeemed Israel in this word picture: "With joy you will draw water from the wells of salvation" (Isaiah 12:3). In a generally arid land, where water was often a matter of life and death (Isaiah 21:14), it's no surprise that water becomes a symbol of spiritual life.

In John's Gospel, Jesus tells a Samaritan woman he can give her "living water" (John 4:10). To her bewildered response, Jesus adds, "The water that I will give will become in them a spring of water gushing up to eternal life" (John 4:14). No wonder she jumps at the chance!

The supreme moment in which Jesus employs the symbol of water occurs during the festival of Booths in Jerusalem (John 7:1–43). This feast included a seven-day ritual in which the priest carried a golden pitcher of water from the Pool of Siloam up to the Temple. This was a reminder of the miraculous supply of water when the Israelites wandered in the wilderness (Exodus 17:1–5). Dramatically, on the last day of the festival, Jesus cries out to the assembled multitudes, "Let anyone who is thirsty come to me and let the one who believes in me drink. As the scripture has said, 'Out of the believer's heart shall flow rivers of living water'" (John 7:37–38). *Living water* symbolizes eternal life, and this is what John is referring to in Revelation 21:6. All inhabitants of the new Jerusalem possess this inexhaustible resource.

Inheriting an eternal treasure

John declares, "Those who conquer will inherit these things, and I will be their God and they will be my children" (Rev. 21:7). "These things" affirms all the items previously mentioned: the banishment of all evil and the presence of all that's truly good. The ultimate heritage of believers is belonging to God's family (Romans 8:14–17).

And what happens to those who aren't part of this inheritance? There are some sad consequences. We discuss the issue of judgment in more detail in Chapter 13.

The end-all, be-all, from A to Z

Three times, the book of Revelation uses the divine title "Alpha and Omega." In Revelation 1:8, it refers to God the Father. In Revelation 21:6 and 22:13, it indicates Jesus. So what does it mean?

Alpha is the first letter of the Greek alphabet, from which we get the English letter *a*. *Omega* is the last of the 24 letters in the Greek alphabet and is equivalent to the English *o*. In English, when you want to speak of the entire range of possibilities, you can use the expression *from A to Z*. In Greek, you can express that same idea

as *alpha and omega*. When coupled with "first and last," and "the beginning and the end," the meaning is something like this: that which comprehends and contains everything else. In this case, that something is *someone*. The Bible says only God is before and after all things and is the source of all that is (see 1 Corinthians 8:6). What's important in applying this title to Jesus is the implication that all that God is, Jesus is. In short, this title affirms the full deity of Jesus.

Taking a Virtual Tour of the New Jerusalem (21:9–27)

Time for a virtual tour of this new city! Most interpreters of the book of Revelation recognize that John's description, although it conveys spiritual realities, shouldn't be squeezed into a literal mold; symbolism and imagery abound. We don't mean to deny that John has a real city in mind; however, readers should acknowledge that he employs stock images from the apocalyptic thesaurus in order to depict certain features of this city that are especially noteworthy, such as splendor, security, and sanctity.

An angel John has seen before takes him on a tour of the new Jerusalem, called "the bride, the wife of the Lamb" (Rev. 21:9). The contrast of Jerusalem (the Lamb's bride) with "Babylon the great, mother of whores and of earth's abominations" (17:5) is deliberate. The two images symbolize two opposing societies. Their completely different stories dominate Revelation 17–22.

John is caught up by the Spirit in order to get a good look at the holy city. In accordance with apocalyptic conventions (see Ezekiel 40:2; *1 Enoch* 17:2), the seer is whisked off to a high mountain that provides a spectacular viewpoint. From there, he watches the holy city descending from heaven to the earth and provides a detailed description.

His first impression of the city is its glory, its sheer radiance. The city possesses a luminescence that overwhelms the senses; it's the ultimate "crystal cathedral"! John resorts to mentioning precious gems and jewels in order to convey the splendor of the new Jerusalem.

This section examines the city, including its gates, foundations, and walls. John dutifully records the height, number, names, measurements, and materials used in their construction.

Admiring the architecture: Walls, gates, and foundations

The city itself is surrounded by a massive wall built on 12 foundations and entered by 12 gates. The gates are named after each of the 12 tribes of Israel, and the foundations are named after the 12 Apostles. Taken together, the gates and foundations emphasize the continuity and unity of the people of God.

In the book of Exodus, 12 pillars are set up at the foot of Mount Sinai to represent each of the tribes of Israel as part of the covenant ratification ceremony (24:4). In the wilderness, the Tabernacle forms the center of the Israelite camp. Arrayed around it in a specific order are the 12 tribes, three on each side (Numbers 2:1–34). A portion of the land of Canaan is distributed to each tribe after the conquest (Joshua 13–17). The fact that there are 12 gates named after each of the 12 tribes of Israel conveys a clear theological message in Revelation: The Old Testament people of God, the 12 tribes of Israel, are a vital part of the new Jerusalem. Those who put their trust in the God of Israel will be there.

The 12 foundations are named in honor of the 12 Apostles of the Lamb. The 12 Apostles were the appointed successors of Jesus, the guardians of the gospel. Paul wrote that believers in Jesus are "built upon the foundation of the apostles and prophets, with Christ Jesus himself as the cornerstone. In him the whole structure is joined together and grows into a holy temple in the Lord [. . .]" (Ephesians 2:20–21).

Siege warfare often involved undermining the foundations of walls. City walls are only as strong as their foundations, so builders put enormous effort into constructing walls on solid bedrock. Thus, the 12 foundations memorialize the role of the Apostles and attest to their strength.

Considering dimensions and shape

The city is a massive cube with all streets intersecting at right angles. Its dimensions are 1,500 miles in length, width, and breadth. (This is the English equivalent of the Greek expression "twelve thousand *stadia*." The NRSV thus obscures the fact that another 12 actually occurs in the Greek text.) The thickness of the walls is 144 cubits (about 216 feet), which is 12^2.

The cube, composed of perfect squares, features prominently in biblical history. The Holy of Holies (inner sanctuary) of the Tabernacle constructed in the wilderness was a cube, being about 15 feet in each dimension (Exodus 26). In Solomon's Temple, the Holy of Holies was also a cube (20 cubits, or 30 feet in each dimension). In Ezekiel's vision of a new Temple, the Holy of Holies was 34 feet per side (Ezekiel 41:3–4).

What's so radically different about John's vision is that *the entire city is a cube*. In theological terms, the city of God, which is also the bride of Jesus, is where God himself dwells with his people. The cubic nature of the new Jerusalem symbolically proclaims its perfection. What John portrays symbolically, Paul describes metaphorically by comparing believers to a "holy temple in the Lord" (Ephesians 2:21–22).

Scoping out the building materials

John's description of the city defies precise analysis. Although the wall is built of jasper, the city itself is composed of translucent gold. Added to that, each of the 12 foundations is adorned with 12 different precious stones, and the 12 gates consist entirely of gigantic, single pearls. The streets, like the city, are "pure gold, transparent as glass" (21:21). John's language symbolizes spiritual realities.

In the Old Testament and Apocrypha, precious stones provide a standard recipe for depicting splendor and glory. Isaiah the prophet describes a restored Jerusalem in the following way: "I am about to set your stones in antimony, and lay your foundations with sapphires. I will make your pinnacles of rubies, your gates of jewels, and all your wall of precious stones" (Isaiah 54:11–12).

Apocrypha: Now where'd we put those books?

The *Apocrypha,* a word meaning "hidden or esoteric," refers to 14 books appearing in the Old Testament portion of Roman Catholic and Greek Orthodox Bibles. The Roman Catholic Church recognizes 11 of them as canonical — that is, as inspired and authoritative. Protestants admit none of the 14 to the canon of Scripture. Palestinian Jewish rabbis didn't reckon these works as inspired Scripture, and thus, they don't appear in the Hebrew Bible. Protestants accept this determination as valid, though many (such as Martin Luther) acknowledge that the apocryphal works contain enriching material.

The prophet Ezekiel, in a funeral song over the fall of the king of Tyre, compares the deposed dictator to a cherub (an angelic being) in Paradise before its fall from grace. Consider the description of his splendor: "You were in Eden, the garden of God; every precious stone was your covering, carnelian, chrysolite, and moonstone, beryl, onyx, and jasper, sapphire, turquoise, and emerald; and worked in gold were your settings and your engravings" (Ezekiel 28:13).

In the apocryphal book of Tobit, dating to about the third century BCE, the anonymous author describes Jerusalem's future greatness and glory in these terms: "The gates of Jerusalem will be built with sapphire and emerald and all your walls with precious stones. The towers of Jerusalem will be built with gold, and their battlements with pure gold. The streets of Jerusalem will be paved with ruby and with the stones of Ophir" (Tobit 13:16).

One more piece of information fills out the picture. The 12 stones of the foundations seem modeled after the breastplate worn by the Israelite high priest, according to the description of it in Exodus 28:15–20. After detailing the 12 different precious stones, the text concludes by saying, "There shall be 12 stones with names corresponding to the names of the sons of Israel; they shall be like signets, each engraved with its name, for the 12 tribes" (Exodus 18:21).

John's description of the holy city is especially indebted to the breastplate. The new Jerusalem is a priestly city, and all the people of God — the 12 tribes, the new Israel — are priests of God, precisely what Jesus intended for the fellowship of the Lamb: "To him who loves us and freed us from our sins by his blood, and made us to be a kingdom, *priests serving his God and Father* [. . .]" (Rev. 1:5–6, emphasis ours). View the precious stones in light of this symbolism.

Recognizing what's not there

The new Jerusalem is defined as much by what isn't there as by what is. Revelation 21:22–22:5 details five items or groups of items that aren't there. When you add these five to the two that John has already mentioned, you arrive, not surprisingly, at the magic number seven: The city is the epitome of perfection! Here's the complete list:

- ✔ No sea (21:1)
- ✔ No death, mourning, crying, or pain (21:4)
- ✔ No Temple (21:22)
- ✔ No need of sun and moon (21:23)
- ✔ No night (21:25)
- ✔ Nothing unclean (21:27)
- ✔ No curse (22:3)

The lack of a Temple is quite surprising because the Temple was central to Jewish tradition. The Apostles Paul and Peter both use Temple imagery to describe the present church (1 Corinthians 3:16–17, 6:19; 2 Corinthians 6:16; Ephesians 2:21; 1 Peter 2:5). The Old Testament prophet Ezekiel spends eight chapters describing and extolling the glories of a third Temple he seems to envision on the site of the first and second Temples (Ezekiel 40–48).

The first Temple was built by Solomon, and it stood from about 970 BCE until it was destroyed by Nebuchadnezzar II in 586 BCE. The second Temple was dedicated in 517 BCE and was greatly enlarged and enhanced by Herod the Great beginning in 20 BCE. The Romans destroyed the second Temple in 70 CE, near the end of the first Jewish revolt against Rome, only some 20 years before John wrote the book of Revelation. In Jewish literature of this period, prayers for a new and glorious Temple appear frequently.

Furthermore, in the book of Revelation, the conquerors in Philadelphia are promised, "I will make you a pillar in the temple of my God; you will never go out of it" (Rev. 3:21). And Revelation includes numerous references to a heavenly Temple (7:15, 11:19, 14:15, 15:5–8, 16:1, 16:17); most people would just assume that it must have a counterpart in the new Jerusalem. Consequently, it's unexpected that the new Jerusalem lacks one. On the other hand, John's explanation makes perfect sense: There's no Temple building because all that the Temple stood for in the past is now realized by the very presence of God: "Its temple is the Lord God the Almighty and the Lamb" (21:22). God dwells with his people face to face.

Item four is also hard to imagine: no more sun or moon! The city is so suffused with glory it actually illuminates itself. The glory of God and the Lamb are a perpetual source of light (Daniel 12:3; 2 Thessalonians 1:10; Romans 8:30; 2 Corinthians 3:18). Add to that, there's no more night. Physicists and cosmologists may speculate about how the new earth operates, but in the end, John's explanation suffices: "The first things have passed away" (Rev. 21:4).

Coming Home to the Garden (22:1–6)

The culmination of the vision Jesus gave to John is like stepping back into the garden of Eden — only it's better than the original. The long, dark night of banishment is over at last; cherubim no longer guard the garden's entrance with a flaming sword (Genesis 3:24). If you're a C.S. Lewis fan, you'll appreciate a comparison to Narnia; the wicked witch of the North is deposed, the snow melts, and springtime returns!

In this section, we revisit John's description of Paradise. It features a crystal clear river with life-giving properties; its banks are lined with 12 kinds of fruit dispensing healing for the nations. The single most important feature, however, is the two people who have made it all possible. Planted squarely in the middle of the garden is the throne of God and the Lamb, surrounded by their willing and worshiping servants. Only the redeemed may see them because only the redeemed are there. And there's no more night, a fitting metaphor for salvation.

Dipping into the river of life

In Revelation 22, the first image that the angel points out to John is a river; and what a river it is! The river symbolizes spiritual life. No innate human need is more urgently felt and essential than water. The symbolism of this river is so special it requires further unpacking.

So what's the source of the mysterious river of life, with its water as bright and clear as crystal? Right in the very center of the city stands the throne of God, and this marvelous river flows from it. The theological point is that God is the true source of life.

The origin of this word picture lies deep in the Old Testament Scriptures. In the book of Genesis, the narrator explains that "a river flows out of Eden to water the garden, and from there it divides and becomes four branches" (2:10). John's new Jerusalem incorporates features of the garden of Eden; in other words, biblical history comes full circle. Genesis 2–3 and Revelation 21–22 are like bookends, framing redemptive history between them — or to change the analogy, they're like two massive towers of a bridge on opposite banks of a river, suspending the roadway between them. Apocalyptic thought often includes the hope of a return to the original, pristine world.

But John's description owes the most to Ezekiel 47:1–12 (see also Joel 3:18). In this passage, Ezekiel describes a river that springs from beneath the threshold of a rebuilt Temple in Jerusalem. It flows eastward "below the south end of the threshold of the temple, south of the altar" (Ezekiel 47:1). Particularly striking about Ezekiel's river is the rapid increase in volume and depth as it courses its way from the Temple courtyard toward the Dead Sea. After the river exits the Temple compound on the east side and flows 150 feet, it's ankle-deep (Ezekiel 47:3). Another 150 feet, and the river is knee-deep (Ezekiel 47:4). And by the time it's gone a further 150 feet, the river is waist-deep (Ezekiel 47:4). Finally, 150 more feet brings Ezekiel to a place where the river is so deep it "could not be crossed" (Ezekiel 47:5).

No known river increases in volume so rapidly, but this is no ordinary river. It's a symbolic river that speaks of God's power to cleanse the guilt and pollution of sin, sin that affects not only individuals but the entire universe. In Ezekiel's vision, the water transforms the desert into an oasis, and the Dead Sea (so named because the salt content is so high that only the most highly adapted organisms live in it), known as the *Salt Sea* in the Old Testament, is converted into a sweet-water lake teeming with fish and lined with trees along its shore. In fact, an abundance of fruit trees line this channel of life. Ezekiel notes that "their leaves will not wither nor their fruit fail. [. . .] Their fruit will be for food, and their leaves for healing" (Ezekiel 47:12). John sketches the river of life in the new Jerusalem using Ezekiel's vision as template. (See the earlier section titled "Having a drink" for more details on water symbolism.)

Recovering the tree of life

John's description of the garden changes Ezekiel's many trees with fruit (Ezekiel 47:12) into one tree having 12 kinds of fruit (there's another 12!) — one for each month of the year. In short, there are no non-productive months.

John wasn't the first to come up with the notion of a tree of life. The concept has a long history going back into antiquity. Ancient Mesopotamia already gave evidence of a myth about a magic tree that granted life to those fortunate enough to discover and eat its fruit. The Chinese and Egyptian cultures also gave visual and written evidence of a mythological tree of life. This testifies to longstanding reflection on the human plight and the hope that, somehow and someway, people may achieve immortality.

John is primarily indebted to the Hebrew story of the Garden of Eden and its two, most important trees (Genesis 2:8–3:24). In the center of the Garden of Eden is a tree that provides knowledge of good and evil. Its fruit is off-limits and not to be eaten — or touched (Genesis 3:3). On the other hand, there's also the tree of life, which is accessible. The story of the fall into sin concludes with these words: "See, the man has become like one of us, knowing good and evil: and now, he might reach out his hand and take also from the tree of life, and eat, and live forever" (Genesis 3:22). (***Note:*** The *us* in this verse is likely either an implied reference to the Trinity or a council of angelic beings.) To prevent this unthinkable outcome — living forever in alienation from God, like Satan and the fallen angels — Adam and Eve are expelled from the garden and its entrance is sealed. The tree of life is no longer accessible. Redemption is necessary, and as the book of Revelation makes clear, the sacrificial death of the Lamb is the remedy.

Against that backdrop, John's vision brings salvation history to a satisfying conclusion. The garden is once again open, and all citizens have full and equal access to the tree of life. And the Lord God resumes his daily walks with the crown of his creation! "They will see his face, and his name will be on their foreheads. [. . .] And they will reign forever and ever" (Rev. 22:4).

Chapter 15

Promising to Return (22:6–21)

In the movie *The Terminator* (which, by the way, is an End Times story), Arnold Schwarzenegger's character utters the famous phrase, "I'll be back." In relation to the return of Jesus, that sentiment is the central point of the closing verses of Revelation.

All good things must come to an end — or must they? As John wraps up his prophecy, he reminds the faithful of some basic promises Jesus intends to keep. Not only does Jesus vow to return, but he also promises to reward everyone's work. Good will prevail and last forever in the celestial city. The faithful must hold on because it won't be long in coming.

In this chapter, you see John recap the essential message of his entire prophecy. He issues one last invitation to accept the good news of salvation through Jesus and a stern warning against tampering with the finished product. Prophecies are no light matter!

Verifying the Source of the Message (22:6–8)

Most Christians generally accept that the entire Bible is a divine revelation. To examine the research and arguments regarding the authenticity and authority of the Bible is well beyond the scope of this book. However, what's striking is the unshakable conviction of biblical prophets, sages, psalmists, and the Apostles that God's word, the Bible, is *self-authenticating*. Listen to John's wording: "These words are trustworthy and true, for the Lord, the God of the spirits of the prophets, has sent his angel to show his servants what must soon take place" (Rev. 22:6).

According to John, God authenticates the message that both comes from and reveals Jesus. The message is delivered by means of an angel, apparently the same angel mentioned in a similar capacity in Revelation 1:1. John now adds his personal stamp of certification to the process: "I, John, am the one who heard and saw these things" (Rev. 22:8).

Getting to the End on Time (22:7)

In Revelation 22:7, John quotes Jesus as saying, "I am coming soon." The problem is that we're almost 2,000 years removed from the time of Revelation's writing and Jesus hasn't returned yet! For many, Jesus passed the fashionably-late mark ages ago, and this seeming tardiness may call into question the credibility of the message. For centuries, people have asked over and over again, "Is he here yet?"

The Old Testament prophets who spoke of the End-Times Day of the Lord (see Chapter 3) also describe it as imminent, impending, even threatening. For example, Isaiah, speaking in the name of God, proclaims, "For soon my salvation will come, and my deliverance be revealed" (Isaiah 56:1). Through Ezekiel, the Lord promises "they [the exiled people of Israel] shall soon come home" (Ezekiel 36:8). Many similar passages make the same point.

The New Testament adopts the same note of imminence about Jesus's Second Coming — the day of the Lord Jesus Christ (see Romans 13:12; James 5:8; 1 Peter 4:7; 1 John 2:18). At the very least, there's a consistency of expectation between the two Testaments: Both Testaments view the Day of the Lord as imminent.

So what's the holdup? Perhaps, as many commentators point out, the real problem is one of perspective. From humans' limited point of view, 2,000 years seems incompatible with the notion of imminence. On the other hand, from God's eternal perspective, 2,000 years is a mere blip. As the psalmist says, "For a thousand years in [God's] sight are like yesterday when it is past" (Psalm 90:4).

Just about 2,000 years after God promised Abraham that he would have as many descendants as the stars in the sky (Genesis 15:5, 22:17) and the sand on the seashore, Jesus appeared on earth and the Christian church was launched (Galatians 4:4; Acts 1:8; 2:1–47). The Apostle Paul describes those who believe in Jesus as Abraham's spiritual children (Romans 4:1–25). It's now about 2,000 years after Jesus first walked the earth. We're not making any predictions, just pointing out this very interesting fact!

John himself may well have thought that Jesus would return in his lifetime. But John doesn't, nor does any other New Testament spokesperson (not even Jesus himself! See Matthew 24:36), teach that Jesus *will* return in the writer's lifetime (1 Thessalonians 5:1–11).

The sixth beatitude of Revelation — "Blessed is the one who keeps the words of the prophecy of this book" (22:7) — returns to the theme of the first blessing (Rev. 1:3). It emphasizes the importance of actually *doing* what is enjoined in the book. The first and sixth beatitudes, like bookends, frame the entire book of Revelation.

Knocking "Other" Worship (22:8–9)

Perhaps as an almost involuntary response to the enormity of all that John has witnessed, he falls down to worship at the feet of the angelic messenger (22:8–9). For this he is again curtly reprimanded (see Rev. 19:10).

Some commentators believe that John was so distracted by the awesomeness of all he had witnessed that he did what he did without thinking. Regardless of why John did it, the angel's reprimand does serve to make a point to the Christians in Asia Minor, and by extension, all Christians in all times and places. Only God is to be worshipped — not angels, emperors, or anyone or anything else in all creation.

Leaving the Scroll Unsealed (22:10–15)

Many refuse to join the Fellowship of the Lamb. They make their own bed and now must lie in it. The angel instructs John not to seal the scroll. Let its contents lie open for inspection and reflection. This stands in contrast to the book of Daniel (and standard apocalyptic literature), where Daniel is told several times to "seal up" his visions in a scroll because they refer "to many days from now" (Daniel 8:26; see also Daniel 12:4, 9). In the case of John's message, the time is short and the churches need to hear the message now.

In antiquity, scrolls were sealed and often stored in jars for safekeeping (see Chapter 8 for more on scrolls and seals). In Revelation, there's no need to reseal the scroll because the churches have immediate need of its message.

In this section, we observe how John begins to draw out the practical implications of what he has seen in his visions. He spells out what is going to happen on the day of reckoning. Decisions must be made one way or the other — one is either for or against the Lamb. The consequences of each person's choice are mutually exclusive. And God makes no mistakes in the sorting-out process; the God of eternity, who knows the end from the beginning, dispenses perfect justice.

Making your own choices

At first sight, Revelation 22:11 seems callous: "Let the evildoer still do evil, and the filthy still be filthy, and the righteous still do right, and the holy still be holy." Doesn't God care what people do? Is he really indifferent to whether or not they repent?

The verse has a proverb-like ring to it. It seems to be saying that most people, given the shortness of time left, simply won't change their attitudes and commitments — they won't switch horses mid-stream! By this time, those who have decided against the kingdom are unlikely to have a change of heart; on the other hand, those who have counted the cost and committed to the Fellowship of the Lamb are unlikely to opt out — they stay the course to the end.

Looking to an eternal judge

Jesus says, "See, I am coming soon; my reward is with me, to repay according to everyone's work. I am the Alpha and the Omega, the first and the last, the beginning and the end" (Rev. 22:12–13). You hear from the Lamb himself.

The message is crisp and to the point — everyone may expect to be treated with complete fairness and justice. Each receives precisely what his or her work merits. At first sight, this message may sound contrary to the New Testament teaching that salvation is by grace through faith, not works (Ephesians 2:8–9). The resolution to this seeming contradiction is this: Genuine faith produces good works (Ephesians 2:10; Galatians 5:6). Lack of good works points inevitably to lack of saving faith (James 2:14–26). In the end, there's no real conflict.

How can the Lamb assume such responsibility? Here's the short answer: He's God. *Alpha* and *omega* are the first and last letters of the Greek alphabet, and together, they're one way of expressing the notion of eternity, an attribute only God possesses. The Lamb can be an impartial judge because he's not subject to the varying opinions of time and place about what constitutes justice and fairness. From everlasting to everlasting, he knows what's right and wrong, just and unjust.

Reaping reward

The final blessing of Revelation reads, "Blessed are those who wash their robes, so that they will have the right to the tree of life and may enter the city by the gates. Outside are the dogs and sorcerers and fornicators and murderers and idolaters, and everyone who loves and practices falsehood" (Rev. 22:14–15). This text presents two starkly contrasting outcomes. The first is couched in language previously used to describe the new Jerusalem: a return to the Garden of Eden and access to the tree of life (see Rev. 22:1–3 and Chapter 14). The reward amounts to everlasting life and unending companionship with the Lamb and the saints.

Friends forever

Can a state of friendship really exist forever? The Bible says so. On the way to the garden of Gethsemane, just before Jesus was arrested, the Gospel of John reports Jesus saying to his disciples, "I do not call you servants any longer, because the servant does not know what the master is doing; but I have called you friends, because I have made known to you everything that I have heard from my Father" (John 15:15). Then a bit later, in what's often called the *high priestly prayer,* Jesus requests, "Father, I desire that these also, whom you have given me, may be with me where I am, to see my glory, which you have given me because you loved me before the foundation of the world" (John 17:24). The duration of the relationship is clearly stated: "This is eternal life" (John 17:3). For believers in Jesus, this is not just a possibility; they "have the *right* to the tree of life" (Rev. 22:14, emphasis ours).

Blood-washed robes, the ticket inside

What qualifies a person to be a friend of Jesus? A familiar metaphor reappears in Revelation 22:14: Ones' robes must be washed in the blood of the Lamb. As seen earlier in the book of Revelation (5:9, 7:14, 12:11, 19:13), this figure of speech portrays a spiritual transformation. The notion of washing one's robes invokes the symbolism of baptism, a cleansing initiation ceremony.

Very early in the Christian church, a special ritual during baptism gave visible expression to this "washing of one's robes." The baptismal candidate came to the baptismal font and took off his or her outer garment. After being immersed in the water, the candidate was clothed in a white robe.

Figure 15-1 shows a delicate carving that features three objects: a lamb, a cross, and a dove. The Lamb has its muzzle inserted into the arm of the cross, reminding the viewer that the blood of the Jesus the Lamb, voluntarily shed on a cross, is what washes away sins. The dove is a symbol of the Holy Spirit and has in its mouth a wreath of victory. The Lamb wins! Every time Christians celebrate the Lord's Supper, they "proclaim the Lord's death until he comes" (1 Corinthians 11:26).

Figure 15-1:
An artist's rendering of The Lamb of God (Agnus Dei) based on an early Christian sarcoph-agus.

Don't miss the seventh and final benediction of the book (Rev. 22:14). The first thing the book of Revelation praises Jesus for doing is freeing "us from our sins by his blood" (1:5). Fittingly, the book concludes with a blessing upon those who benefit from that gift. What's unspoken but assumed in this blessing is clearly stated in Revelation 7:14 (emphasis ours): "They have washed their robes *and made them white in the blood of the Lamb.*"

Facing punishment: The outsiders

Those who reject the Lamb forfeit entrance into the new Jerusalem. The ominous word *outside* says it all. As we discuss in Chapter 13, the teaching of final punishment is best expressed by the notion of exclusion.

You may wonder, however, who the dogs are in Revelation 22:15. In the book of Deuteronomy, the Hebrew word for *dog* is rendered as "male prostitute" (23:18). This may be what John means. Also, calling someone a dog was a common insult. It was a term Jews used to refer to Gentiles. Generally, how-ever, it indicated anyone who was "unclean" by the standards of Jewish ritual purity laws (as found in the Old Testament books of Exodus, Leviticus, Numbers, and Deuteronomy and further expanded and elaborated on in the *Mishnah,* a compilation of rabbis' interpretations of these laws).

John doesn't give a complete listing of those excluded from God's presence. After mentioning behaviors widespread in Greco-Roman society — occult practices and magic, sexual immorality, murder, and idolatry — he inserts a generalizing description: "and everyone who loves and practices falsehood." In many ways, this comes right to the heart of the matter. Paul analyzes human rebellion in much the same way: "They [Gentiles] exchanged the truth about God for a lie and worshiped and served the creature rather than the Creator, who is blessed forever! Amen" (Romans 1:25).

So how can sinners even be "outside" the city if supposedly they've already been cast into the lake of fire (Rev. 20:15)? Most likely, John is simply using conventional language to make his point: They won't, in fact, be there.

And Now, In Conclusion (22:16–21)

The concluding six verses of the book of Revelation accomplish four objectives:

- ✔ Authenticating the source of the message
- ✔ Inviting the reader or listener to respond to the message
- ✔ Warning against tampering with the message
- ✔ Wrapping up the entire book

Jesus himself validates John's message: "It is I, Jesus, who sent my angel to you with this testimony for the churches" (Rev. 22:16). The immediate audience is specified as "the churches." These churches were the seven churches of the Roman province of Asia and others in the same region (see Chapter 7). The early Christian church throughout the second and third centuries valued the book of Revelation and eventually, though not without a few dissenting voices, officially recognized its place in the canon of Scripture in the fourth century (see Chapter 1 for further discussion of this issue). Consequently, this book continues to proclaim "the testimony of Jesus" and summons believers in God to undivided loyalty.

In this section, we draw attention to John's finishing flourishes. He wraps up with a sweeping invitation and a severe warning. Fittingly, John allows Jesus to have the last word.

Signing the message

Saying, "I am the root and the descendant of David, the bright morning star" (22:16), Jesus signs off on the revelation given to John, using two titles that speak to the lineage and nature of Jesus.

Jesus, the Son of David

The title "root and descendent of David," firmly anchors Jesus's story in the larger story of Israel by reminding readers that he descends from one of the superstars of Hebrew history — David, the shepherd boy, slayer of giants, and son of Jesse. Both Matthew and Luke include a genealogy showing Jesus's lineage from the House of David (Matthew 1:1–18; Luke 3:23–38). Other Bible passages related to this title include the following:

✓ "When your [David's] days are fulfilled and you lie down with your ancestors, I will raise up your offspring after you, who shall come forth from your body, and I will establish his kingdom. He shall build a house for my name, and I will establish the throne of his kingdom forever. [. . .] Your house and your kingdom shall be made sure forever before me; your throne shall be established forever." (2 Samuel 7:12–13, 16)

✓ "For a child has been born for us, a son given to us; authority rests upon his shoulders; and he is named Wonderful Counselor, Mighty God, Everlasting Father, Prince of Peace. His authority shall grow continually, and there shall be endless peace for the throne of David and his kingdom. He will establish and uphold it with justice and with righteousness from this time onward and forevermore. The zeal of the Lord of hosts will do this." (Isaiah 9:6–7)

✓ "A shoot shall come out from the stump of Jesse, and a branch shall grow out of his roots. The spirit of the Lord shall rest on him, the spirit of wisdom and understanding, the spirit of counsel and might, the spirit of knowledge and the fear of the Lord. His delight shall be in the fear of the Lord. [. . .] On that day the root of Jesse shall stand as a signal to the peoples; the nations shall inquire of him, and his dwelling shall be glorious." (Isaiah 11:1–2, 10; see also Isaiah 55:3)

The prophets Jeremiah (Jeremiah 23:5–6, 30:9, 33:15, 33:21, 33:25–26), Ezekiel (Ezekiel 34:23–24, 37:24–25), Hosea (Hosea 3:5), and Zechariah (Zechariah 12:7–9) all add distinctive touches to an emerging portrait of a great descendant of David. Psalmists also join the prophetic chorus in heralding this descendant (Psalms 89:3–4, 89:19–37, 132:11–18).

The Apostle Paul clearly recognizes the portrait they painted. He announces the gospel of God as "promised beforehand through his prophets in the holy scriptures, the gospel concerning his Son, who was descended from David according to the flesh [. . .]" (Romans 1:1–3).

Jesus, the bright morning star

The derivation of the "bright morning star" in Revelation 22:16 is not as clear as that of the connection to David. Because of the brightness of the planet Venus seen in the morning skies, the Greeks identified Venus with Aphrodite (goddess of light, love, and beauty), and some commentators think John may have borrowed from this imagery.

Others, however, say it probably refers to an Old Testament prophecy. In Numbers 23–24, the prophet Balaam utters four oracles about the future of Israel and its relationship to the surrounding countries. The fourth oracle includes the following passage: "I see him, but not now; I behold him, but not near — a star shall come out of Jacob, and a scepter shall arise out of Israel..." (Numbers 24:17). In its context, the prophecy alludes to David who descends from Judah, one of the 12 sons of Jacob. The scepter speaks of his royal power as the founder of the Davidic dynasty. Several Jewish apocalyptic texts, predating the time of Jesus, interpret Numbers 24:17 as a reference to the Messiah.

Among the church fathers, Numbers 24:17 was interpreted as a reference to Jesus as the promised Messiah. They simply follow in John's footsteps. Already, Jesus's message to the church of Thyatira holds out this reward to those who keep the faith: "To the one who conquers I will also give the morning star" (Numbers 2:28). In short, the bright morning star is Jesus himself. The brightness of the morning star probably speaks of the glorified state that consists of brilliant light.

Invoking and inviting

Revelation 22:17 contains two invocations (calls) and two invitations. Both sets involve the climax of redemptive history. Jesus appears to be the one speaking: "The Spirit and the bride say, 'Come.'"

The Spirit is the Holy Spirit, and the bride is the church, or the Fellowship of the Lamb. The command *come* is singular, and it refers to Jesus the bridegroom. The Holy Spirit and the church — the reclamation project of the Holy Spirit — are both eager to bring biblical history to its grand consummation. The bridegroom himself encourages his bride to pray for his soon arrival. This striking metaphor conveys the spiritual union between Jesus and his church, mediated by the Holy Spirit.

Jesus urges those who read his prophecy to embrace its central message and join in the invocation: "And let everyone who hears say, 'Come.'" This is a genuinely universal offer of salvation.

The two invocations are followed by two invitations: "And let everyone who is thirsty come. Let anyone who wishes take the water of life as a gift" (22:17). These recall similar wording from the prophet Isaiah and from Jesus himself as recorded in John's Gospel:

- "Ho, everyone who thirsts, come to the waters; and you that have no money, come, buy and eat!" (Isaiah 55:1)
- "Let anyone who is thirsty come to me, and let the one who believes in me drink." (John 7:37; see John 4:13–14)

What does it mean to "come and drink"? This word picture conveys the notion of entering into a worshiping, obedient relationship with the Lord. It recalls the Lord's summons to Moses, Aaron, Nadab, Abihu, and 70 elders of Israel to climb Mount Sinai and commune with him (Exodus 24). It also recalls Jesus's invitation to his listeners during his earthly ministry: "Come to me, all you that are weary and are carrying heavy burdens, and I will give you rest. Take my yoke upon you and learn from me; for I am gentle and humble in heart, and you will find rest for your souls. For my yoke is easy, and my burden is light" (Matthew 11:28–30). By coming to Jesus — that is, accepting him as Savior and Lord — in the here-and-now, believers guarantee their eternal place in the there-and-forever.

Warning against tampering

One of the conventions of apocalyptic writings is a severe warning against alterations and deletions (see *1 Enoch* 108:6). John's apocalypse is no exception: "I warn everyone who hears the words of the prophecy of this book: if anyone adds to them, God will add to that person the plagues described in this book: if anyone takes away from the words of the book of this prophecy, God will take away that person's share in the tree of life and in the holy city, which are described in this book." (22:18–19)

John designates his entire book as a prophecy (see 1:3) even though it also incorporates a few features of first-century letters and, of course, not a few features of apocalyptic writings.

Covenant documents (such as testaments, marriage contracts, and national treaties) also carried weighty sanctions against tampering. In the Old Testament, the Lord warns against additions and subtractions to the Sinai covenant (Deuteronomy 4:2; 12:32; see also Proverbs 30:5–6). Covenant documents are of binding authority and are not amended or altered at the whim and fancy of those who are in possession of them and under its solemn obligations.

John simply makes it clear that any addition to the book or subtraction from it will bring on some nasty consequences. This is some serious copyright protection!

Getting a final word from the Lamb

For the third time in Revelation 22, the Lamb promises, "I am coming soon." (22:7, 22:12, 22:20). Only this time, there's one small but significant addition: the word *surely*. This translates the little Greek word *nai*, which, in this context, indicates a solemn declaration. This is no idle prediction: The Lamb says he really is coming again.

The Apostle John attaches his enthusiastic agreement: "Amen. Come, Lord Jesus!" This affirmative cry from the heart captures the very wording of the earliest Christians who voiced this prayer in Aramaic, almost certainly the primary language of Jesus and his Apostles. This little phrase also pops up (in Greek) in Paul's letter to the Corinthians (1 Corinthians 16:22). In Aramaic, it's two words that you may have seen or heard as one word: *marana tha* ("Our Lord, Come!").

P.S. Be blessed with grace!

Letters from the first century typically conclude with the equivalent of complimentary closings in business letters today. For example, you may append phrases like *Very truly yours, Sincerely yours, Cordially yours, Respectfully yours,* and so forth. On the other hand, a personal letter may end with a closing like *Affectionately yours, All my love,* or something similar, depending on the degree of familiarity between sender and reader.

John's closing is a grace benediction: "The grace of the Lord Jesus be with all the saints. Amen" (Rev. 22:21; see also see Romans 16:20; 1 Corinthians 16:23; 2 Corinthians 13:13; Galatians 6:18; Ephesians 6:23; Philippians 4:23; 1 Thessalonians 5:28; and 2 Thessalonians 3:18).

The word *grace* captures the heart of what the gospel is about: the free, undeserved intervention of God's saving power. It's easy to lose sight of the message of grace in the book of Revelation, with its horrific plagues and terrifying lake of fire. But the overarching message of the book is this: Grace and mercy triumph over sin and death. The devil and his demons do not have the last word; the last word belongs to Jesus, the Lamb.

Part IV
The Part of Tens

"Before I blow my trumpet and deliver a burning ball of fire down upon the earth, how about a few choruses of 'What a Friend We Have in Jesus?'"

In this part . . .

By now, you've probably discovered that the special number of Revelation is seven. *For Dummies* books have a special number as well — ten (though it doesn't exactly have prophetic significance). That's why this part devotes itself to two chapters based on the number ten. You begin by examining ten of the most common questions people ask about the end times. Finally, we round out the book with ten practical guidelines to consider when reading and interpreting Scripture.

Chapter 16

Ten Common Questions about the End Times

Although the last book in the Bible is officially titled Revelation, you may have other names that seem more appropriate (The Book of Confusion? John's Letter of Really Intriguing, Perplexing, and Confounding Stuff? Chronicles of a Bad Acid Trip?). However, as we explain, Revelation need not be a source of confusion if you get a handle on the symbolism and terminology.

In that light, this chapter is designed to provide you with answers to ten commonly asked questions people have about the End Times. Then, as you're ready, you can dive deeper into these questions at other locations in this book. (We mention much of the symbolism in terms of futurist, preterist, historicist, and idealist perspectives; for more on these interpretations, see Chapter 4.)

What Does Eschatology Mean?

The word *eschatology* originates from two Greek words — *eschatos*, meaning "last," and *logos*, meaning "subject-matter or teaching." *Eschatology* is the study of last things that are prophesied in the Bible. These final events, primarily those recorded in Revelation 4–22, include the Tribulation, the return of Christ, the Millennium, the Last Judgment, Armageddon, and heaven and hell.

What Do the Seals, Trumpets, and Bowls Symbolize?

Reference: Revelation 6–16

The seals, trumpets, and bowls symbolize the three stages of a series of events foretold in Revelation. As Jesus opens the seven seals of a heavenly scroll, an initial series of earth-rattling events begins to unfold (Rev. 6:1–8:1). A second series of more-severe events occurs when seven angels play trumpets (Rev. 8:7–11:15). Finally, seven bowls are poured out to symbolize the final, unrestrained set of disastrous events (Rev. 16:2–17).

Some commentators believe that the seals, trumpets, and bowls are successive and progressive events, with one set kicking off the next. Others believe that these symbols refer to a set of events that occur at the same time.

Here's how the different schools of interpretation view these symbols:

- ✓ Futurists teach that the seals, trumpets, and bowls are the key events that will transpire in the Tribulation period prior to Jesus's Second Coming.

- ✓ Preterists believe that these events were carried out at the destruction of Jerusalem in 70 CE.

- ✓ Historicists hold that these symbolic events are being carried out progressively throughout the church age, which is going on now.

- ✓ Idealists teach that the seals, trumpets, and bowls are allegories of the natural disasters and social evils that have existed throughout human history.

See Chapters 9, 10, and 12 for more on the seals, trumpets, and bowls.

What's the Great Tribulation?

References: Matthew 24:21; Revelation 7:14

The *Tribulation*, or *Great Tribulation*, is a short period of intense persecution of God's people living on the earth; it's the time in which the seal, trumpet, and bowl events of Revelation are carried out:

- ✓ Futurism teaches that the Tribulation is a seven-year period just before the return of Jesus. They usually divide it into two 3.5-year periods. The first half has restrained oppression and judgment, but the second half is typified by unrestrained disaster.

✔ Preterists believe that the Tribulation took place back in the first century at the destruction of Jerusalem in 70 CE.

✔ Some historicists think the Tribulation refers to the plight of the Jews since the first century, including events such as the Holocaust, and ending with the restored state of Israel in 1948.

✔ Idealists hold that the Tribulation period symbolizes the suffering that believers have had to endure throughout history.

See Chapter 13 for details.

What's the Rapture?

References: 1 Thessalonians 4:13–18; Matthew 24:29–31, 24:40–41; 1 Corinthians 15:52

The Bible never actually uses the word *rapture* in the sense people use it in respect to Revelation — that is, a sudden, instantaneous taking up of all living believers into heaven. But the idea isn't without precedent. In biblical history, two men experienced a similar phenomenon: Enoch (Genesis 5:24) and Elijah (2 Kings 2:11). Paul presents this idea in 1 Thessalonians 4:17, where he states, "Then we who are alive, who are left, will be caught up in the clouds together with them to meet the Lord in the air; and so we will be with the Lord forever."

The End Times *rapture* is the theory that believers living in the End Times will be physically removed from the earth and transported directly to heaven. Futurists and premillennialists hold this view, and they have various theories concerning the timing of the rapture:

✔ *Pretribulationists* (including dispensationalists, whom we discuss in Chapters 3, 4, and 13) hold that the rapture of the church will occur before the Tribulation period begins (at Rev. 4:1). By this approach, people who are believers prior to the rapture will be spared the terrible Tribulation period. This is the perspective of the *Left Behind* series.

✔ *Midtribulationists* hold that the rapture will occur midway through the Tribulation.

✔ *Postribulationists* argue that the rapture will occur at the end of the Tribulation, just prior to the Second Coming of Jesus. They hold that the church will be called upon to persevere through the Tribulation period and not escape it as pretribulationists believe.

✔ A final theory is that the rapture is already taking place, albeit in a more figurative manner.

Many within the universal Christian church (including Roman Catholic, Eastern Orthodox, and some Protestant churches) don't accept the idea of a literal rapture. This is true even among some who adhere to a literal interpretation of Revelation. These rapture dissenters say that the concept isn't based on explicit teaching of Scripture or historical teaching of the early church.

See Chapter 8 for the lowdown on the various views of the rapture.

Who Are the Four Horsemen of the Apocalypse?

Reference: Revelation 6:1–7

The four horsemen of the Apocalypse are one of the most familiar images of Revelation and the end of the world. The horsemen are the ultimate bearers of bad news and are implementers of nasty events; they're released when the Lamb, Jesus, opens the first four seals in Revelation 6. Here's the lineup:

- ✔ The first horseman rides on a white horse. He holds a bow, wears a crown, and rides out as a conqueror bent on conquest.

- ✔ The second horseman rides out on a fiery red horse. He carries a large sword and is given power to make war.

- ✔ The third horseman rides on a black horse. He carries a pair of scales, denoting scarcity of food and goods.

- ✔ The fourth horseman rides out on a pale horse. His rider is Death. The pale color of the horse represents sickly, deathly, greenish color.

Together, they're given power over 25 percent of the world to kill through war, famines, diseases, and other natural disasters. Though the text names only the fourth horseman, they're traditionally known as the Conqueror, War, Famine, and Death.

Opinions differ on whom the first horseman represents. Some suggest that he is Jesus riding in victory, others view him as a spirit of conquest, and a few believe that this rider is actually the Antichrist. Preterist idealists believe that all the horseman are symbolic of the ultimate power of God over evil. Some preterists argue that the first-century reader would've identified the first horseman as the Parthians, Roman enemies who traditionally rode white horses into battle.

See Chapter 9 for more on the four horsemen.

Who is the Antichrist?

References: 1 John 2:18, 22, 4:3; 2 John 7; Rev. 13:1–4; Daniel 7:7–8; 2 Thes. 2:3–4, 2:8–10

In connection with Revelation, the *Antichrist* (uppercase) is the archenemy of Jesus and the ultimate false prophet. The Antichrist emerges as a powerful leader who will deceive the world and defy God. He receives his power directly from Satan.

Although often associated with the Revelation's Tribulation period, the term *antichrist* (lowercase or uppercase) never appears in Revelation itself. Instead, it shows up only a handful of times in the epistles of John to label anyone who attempts to pervert the gospel (good news) of Jesus and lead God's people into false doctrines and beliefs. For example, in 1 John 1:7, John writes, "For many deceivers have gone out into the world, men who will not acknowledge the coming of Jesus Christ in the flesh; such a one is the deceiver and the antichrist."

Here are the four major interpretations of the Antichrist:

✔ Futurists believe that the beast from the sea, depicted in Revelation 13, represents the Antichrist. Others hold that the first horseman (see the preceding section) represents him.

✔ Preterists often understand Nero as the Antichrist, or beast.

✔ Historicists often understood the Antichrist as the Roman papacy, the office of the pope.

✔ Idealists don't identify the beast or Antichrist with a single individual; rather, he symbolizes the evil socio-political systems of the world.

People often believe numerous other Scriptures point to the Antichrist, including the fourth beast in Daniel 7, the false Christs that Jesus talks about in Matthew 24:5, 24:23–24, and the "man of lawlessness" that Paul discusses in 2 Thessalonians 2:3–4.

See Chapter 11 for the lowdown on the Antichrist.

What's the Mark of the Beast (666)?

Reference: Revelation 13:16–18

Literal interpretations understand the *mark of the beast* as a way in which the false prophet will control the economic system. The mark itself will be placed on a person's right hand or forehead and is required in order to buy and sell goods. John clearly states that believers must *not* receive the mark, because doing so identifies a person with the beast and defies God (Rev. 14:9–12).

John says in Revelation 13:18 that this mark is the number 666. This number has brought endless speculation. Some attempts to associate these numbers with letters of the alphabet have yielded several people as the Antichrist, including Nero, Hitler, Ronald Reagan, and even Homer Simpson. (Okay, we made that last one up, but the speculation can get pretty silly at times.)

John refers to 666 as "man's number." From a biblical standpoint, seven is often associated as the perfect number of God, and six is a human number — something less than perfect. So this implies that six is the number of imperfection, or even evil, and that 666 equates to a kind of trinity of evil. It's at least an interesting idea.

Here are some major interpretations of the mark:

- ✔ Futurists believe that the Antichrist will use the mark of the beast during the Tribulation as a way to control the economic system of the world. Theories about how technology could play a part in the beast's plans range from computer-chip implants to fingerprint-scanning devices.

- ✔ Preterists hold that the mark of the beast refers to the economic persecution that existed against Christians in the first century. Preterists often associate the beast with Nero.

- ✔ Historists traditionally believed that the mark of the beast was being Roman Catholic and worshipping in Latin.

- ✔ Idealists teach that the mark of the beast is a figurative symbol of false religion.

We believe that if we could definitively explain what 666 means and exactly pinpoint who the Antichrist is, this book would sell in the zillions! But we can't, and neither can anyone else.

If you'd like to know more, turn to Chapter 11.

What's the Significance of the Term Babylon?

References: Revelation 14:8, 16:19, 17:5, 18:2

In Revelation, *Babylon* symbolizes an organized entity that defies God. A first-century reader of John's Revelation would've clearly understood the evils of a symbolic Babylon. Ancient Babylon (a city located in contemporary Iraq) was a powerful empire in the Old Testament era, and it typified a powerful society that openly and aggressively defied the God of Israel.

Here are the futurist, preterist, historicist, and idealist takes on Babylon:

- ✔ Many futurists hold that Babylon symbolizes an actual city, country, or political system that will arise in the End Times; it emulates the idolatrous values of ancient Babylon. Others suggest that Babylon, at least in the first half of the Tribulation, refers to an apostate (God-defying) religious body, organized by the Antichrist.

- ✔ Preterists have mixed views about the symbol of Babylon. Some argue that it's a clear reference to Jerusalem; others believe it refers to Rome.

- ✔ Classic historicism holds that Babylon symbolizes the Roman Catholic Church.

- ✔ Idealism maintains that Babylon is a figurative description of human society organizing itself against God; society attempts to lure people away from Jesus.

See Chapter 12 for more on Babylon.

What's the Millennium?

Reference: Revelation 20:1–6

The *Millennium* is a 1,000-year period that John talks about in the first six verses of Revelation 20. He tells readers that at the start of this period, Jesus will bind Satan to prevent him from deceiving nations. After that, Jesus will reign with his people over the earth.

Three interpretations speculate on what the Millennium refers to:

- ✔ *Premillennialism* holds that John is referring to a literal 1,000 years after the return of Jesus.

- ✔ *Amillennialism* maintains the Millennium is a figurative term referring to the extended period between Jesus's birth and his return to earth. Instead of a literal reign of Jesus, this view teaches that he is reigning in heaven and, spiritually, on earth through his church.

- ✔ *Postmillennialism* teaches that the Millennium refers to the church age, the time between the birth and return of Jesus. This view maintains that the forces of Satan will eventually be stomped out as the Kingdom of God extends over the world. As soon as this has been accomplished, Jesus will return.

See Chapter 13 for more details on the Millennium.

What's the Lake of Fire?

References: Revelation 19:20, 20:10, 20:14–15

Talk about your hot-potato topic! Few people like the idea of being tossed into a literal lake of fire. However, according to the Bible, the *lake of fire* is the final destination for everything evil, including Satan, the beast (Antichrist), the lost prophet, and everyone except God's people. John refers to the lake of fire as the "second death."

Some believe the lake of fire is not a literal burning lake but that it represents never-ending physical torture of some kind; others hold it to mean the spiritual torture of being eternally separated from God. A final group believes the lake of fire will consume those who enter, and they'll cease to exist.

See Chapter 13 for more on this topic.

Chapter 17

Ten Tips for Interpreting Scripture and Prophecy

. . . .

In This Chapter

▶ Why a plain reading of a passage is often the best way to discover its meaning

▶ Why the context of a passage is so important

▶ How "fulfilled prophecy" can guide you as you explore Revelation

. . . .

*M*ost modern writing is pretty straightforward. For example, you don't have to consult outside references and read commentaries to make sense of a John Grisham novel. Or when you read the news online, you usually don't contact a friend so you can debate the true meaning of the reporter's sentences. The goal of most everyday writing is to communicate thoughts, ideas, stories, and information as clearly as possible.

However, as is true with many ancient texts, the meaning of the Bible isn't so easy to understand — even though it's now in your native language, just like your morning paper. You encounter a variety of obstacles:

✔ **Translation:** The original languages — Hebrew and Greek — are far different in structure, grammar, and idioms from modern English. Therefore, translating is both an art and science; it depends to some extent on the person doing the translation.

✔ **Culture:** The standards of conduct and presuppositions of the ancient Middle Eastern culture were radically different from the 21st-century Western mindset. The reason behind some actions performed or things left unsaid were obvious to the original readers, but modern readers may overlook or misinterpret these things.

✔ **Writing style:** The types of literary styles used throughout the Scriptures add a layer of complexity to the text. This is especially true with the apocalyptic writings, such as Revelation.

Whenever you read Scripture, you need to bridge these obstacles to gain a proper understanding of the text. Here are ten rules of thumb to help you out.

Don't Depend on English Words for Sorting Out Hidden Meanings

In most Scripture, you can take ordinary words and figures of speech at face value; you don't want to be looking for hidden meanings. A plain reading of the text usually gives you the best sense of the passage. However, according to some interpreters, the apocalyptic nature of Revelation often makes this book an exception to the rule.

Look at the words in the Bible in light of the meaning of the original language (Hebrew or Greek). A study Bible or commentary is a useful tool for diving into the original meanings of specific words. Online Bible studies and commentaries, such as StudyLight (www.studylight.org) and BibleGateway (www.biblegateway.com), may be good places to start.

Keep Verses in Context

In the Bible, words, when combined together, often form theological themes and concepts. Always try to understand these themes in their context so you can accurately interpret what the author is getting at. You should look at any theological concept within context of the particular verse it appears in, then the chapter, the book, and finally the entire Bible.

If you ignore context, then you can come up with some wacky theology. For example, in one epistle, the Apostle John says that "God is love" (1 John 4:16). When you examine that concept in context, you realize that John is saying that an integral part of God's nature and personality is his love. Yet if you just rip out that "God is love" idea and don't look to see how it fits into the overall picture of Scripture, you can conclude that God is nothing more than a benign, impersonal force behind the universe, which is not what John intended. In fact, he was stressing the motivating, driving force of a very personal God.

Look to Other Scripture as a Guide

Scripture always helps shed light on other portions of Scripture. So when you're investigating the meaning of a given passage, compare it to related portions of Scripture. For example, as Chapter 3 discusses, Revelation contains many symbolic references to the Old Testament. In order to fully understand a symbol's significance in Revelation, you should begin by looking at the original usage in Daniel, Ezekiel, or elsewhere.

Many Bibles have cross-reference systems located in the margins of the text. Use them!

Remember the Target Audience

Each portion of Scripture was written for a particular audience in the author's day. The more you understand about who these people were, what their culture was like, and the circumstances in which they lived, the more you can understand the author's intent. (For info on John's world, see Chapter 2; Chapter 7 discusses Revelation's intended audience.) A Bible commentary can provide background information to help you better understand the historical and cultural context of the day.

Look for the Original Meaning

The idea of *relativism* — what's true or right is in the mind of the individual — can creep into the way you interpret Scripture. In other words, instead of looking at the *intended* meaning, you can fall into the trap of focusing only on the *relevance* or significance of a passage to your life.

In order to look at the original meaning of the author, you need to view a given passage from multiple angles. Here are some steps you can take:

- ✔ **Look at what the text actually says.** Look at the original wording as best as you can. Online tools like StudyLight (www.studylight.org) or a Greek/Hebrew dictionary can enable you to look at the exact words used. So, too, modern study Bibles often provide an easy-to-understand version of this information integrated into the text.

- ✔ **Get a basic idea of the author's and book's historical backdrop.** Try to gain an understanding of what would've been in the author's mind during his lifetime. To get this info, you can use online Bible resources. Many study Bibles also provide this information at the start of each book.

Remember that Christians consider all Scripture to be inspired, written with an intended meaning from God. Therefore, when you read Scripture, your mission is to discover that meaning. The relevance of that message is always secondary.

Identify the Literary Style

The Bible contains a variety of literary styles, including historical, expository, worship, poetry, prophecy, and apocalyptic. As you read, be aware of the style of text you're reading because that can affect interpretation. For instance,

- ✔ You can understand expository/explanatory messages, as in Paul's epistles, quite literally.
- ✔ Poetry, as in Song of Solomon, may contain allusions, similes, and metaphors that you need to be look at in that context.
- ✔ Apocalyptic literature, such as in Revelation and Ezekiel, needs to be read with the understanding that the vivid imagery is highly symbolic in nature.
- ✔ You should read prophecy, as in Daniel, as important messages from God to his people.
- ✔ Read worship, as in Psalms, as prayers to God, some of which contain rich symbolism and poetic imagery.
- ✔ Historical text, as in Exodus, can be read as a chronicle or narrative of what happened in ancient history.

Therefore, as you consider the meaning of a particular passage, try to identify its literary style. A Bible commentary or study Bible is a great resource to turn to.

Remember that figurative language has always been a natural part of human communication. Symbolism, metaphors, and figures of speech are present across the Scriptures, regardless of literary style. However, these are usually clearly identifiable as such, so you can determine their meaning within the context.

View Fulfilled Prophecy as a Prototype

Many prophecies, particularly those in the Old Testament, have already been fulfilled. For example, Daniel or Isaiah foretells a coming judgment on Israel, and years later, that judgment actually occurs. In fact, probably around one-half of the prophecies were fulfilled within the timeframe of the Bible itself. Use these prophecies as signposts to help you better understand how prophecy in Revelation may be fulfilled. For example, over 400 years before crucifixion was invented as a means of capital punishment, Zechariah (12:10) describes the Messiah's death in language that reflects crucifixion.

Don't Try to Pin Down Timelines for Fulfillment

Although people are always trying to do so, you'll never be able to figure out the exact timing or duration of the fulfillment of a prophecy. In the Old Testament, some prophecy was fulfilled shortly after being given by the prophet; others took hundreds of years to transpire, and some still hasn't been fulfilled.

A plain reading of Old Testament prophecy usually makes it possible to determine whether the prophet is talking about things happening in the past, the present, or the future.

Note that Biblical Prophecy Can Have Stages of Fulfillment

Many people read prophetic messages and believe that their fulfillment will occur in one big swoop. Although that's true in many cases, some prophecies have multiple stages of fulfillment. Joel 2:28–32, is an example of a "swoop" prophecy that most commentators believe was fulfilled in Acts 2:17–21. In contrast, many see that Malachi 4:4–5, is fulfilled through the ministry of John the Baptist as well as through another prophet in the future (as discussed in Rev. 11:6).

Consider that Some Biblical Prophecy Is Conditional

As you read prophecy in the Bible, keep in mind two types of prophetic messages. Some prophecy is conditional, dependent upon how humans respond to God's calls for repentance and obedience; other prophecy is unconditional and inevitable. Context can usually help reveal what type of prophecy you're reading.

Appendix

Glossary

· ·

allegoricalism: *See* idealism.

amillennialism: A system of Christian eschatology (End-Times teaching) that holds that the Millennium depicted in Revelation 20 is not a literal 1,000-year reign of Jesus on earth. Instead, it symbolizes the current age of the church. Amillennialists believe the Second Coming of Jesus occurs at the end of the church age.

angel: A spiritual messenger of God used to carry out God's purposes.

Antichrist: During the Tribulation, the evil world leader who opposes Jesus (Rev. 13:1–10).

Apocalypse: A term that sometimes refers to the book of Revelation or to the end of the world. It's derived from the Greek word *apokalupsis,* which means "an unveiling."

apocalyptic literature: A genre of writing that's characteristic of Second Temple Judaism (around 300 BCE to 200 CE) and the early Christian church. The apocalyptic style makes heavy use of vivid imagery and symbolism.

apostasy: A desertion of or a departure from one's faith.

Ark of the Covenant: The sacred chest in which ancient Israel kept the tablets containing the Ten Commandments.

Armageddon: A geographic location at which the last battle between good and evil will take place (Rev. 16:16). The term comes from the Hebrew *Har Megiddo*, which refers to a hill near the town of Megiddo in modern-day Israel, a strategic military location that was the site of many ancient battles.

Asia Minor: A peninsula in southwestern Asia that forms the Asian part of Turkey.

Augustine: One of the great fathers of the early Christian church who lived in North Africa from 354–430 CE.

Babylon: Originally an ancient city located in what is now Iraq. In Revelation, John uses Babylon to refer to an organized entity that defies God.

bowl judgments: The final, unrestrained set of judgments that occurs when angels pour out seven bowls (Rev. 16:2–16:17).

beast of the earth: *See* false prophet.

beast of the sea: *See* Antichrist.

book of life: A registry of believers recorded in heaven.

bride of the Lamb: A symbol that refers to the church.

chiliasm: The belief in a literal 1,000-year reign of Jesus on earth (Rev. 20). It's derived from the Greek word *chilioi*, meaning 1,000.

Christ: *See* Messiah.

church age: The period of history that lasts from Jesus's ascent into heaven (following his resurrection) until his Second Coming.

covenant: A solemn agreement between God and his followers in which God promises to take care of them and his people promise certain behavior in return.

diadem: A crown signifying a sovereign ruler.

dispensationalism: A system of belief, introduced by J.N. Darby of the Plymouth Brethren Church in 1830, that held that human history is divided into seven "dispensations" (eras) that are represented by the seven churches of Revelation 2–3. Dispensationalists hold that humans today are living near the end of the sixth dispensation and that the seventh period will be immediately preceded by the rapture and the Tribulation.

Dionysius: A bishop and later the pope of the influential church of Alexandria during the third century. He was one of the first church leaders to contend that John the Apostle did not write Revelation, believing instead that an obscure early church leader name John the Presbyter was the author.

Domitian: A Roman emperor from 81 to 96 CE and a persecutor of Christians throughout the empire.

doxology: A hymn or Christian liturgy that focuses on giving glory to God.

epistle: A book of the New Testament that's written in the form of a letter from an Apostle.

eschatology: A term that refers to the study of the last days. It comes from the Greek word *eschatos*, which means "last" or "extreme."

Ezekiel: An Old Testament prophet who lived in the 500s BCE, during the Babylonian exile. Ezekiel authored the book of Ezekiel, one of the most vivid examples of apocalyptic literature in the Bible.

false prophet: An evil spiritual leader who teams up with the Antichrist to deceive people on earth (Rev. 13:11–17, 19:20).

final judgment: *See* Last Judgment.

First Temple: The Jewish Temple that King Solomon raised on Mount Moriah in Jerusalem in the tenth century BCE. It was destroyed in 586 BCE.

four horsemen of the Apocalypse: Executioners of judgment that are released when the Lamb (Jesus) opens the first four seals in Revelation 6.

futurism: The interpretation of Revelation that holds that, starting with Revelation 4:1, John's prophecy chronicles literal events that will take place on earth sometime in the future. Many futurists are also dispensationalists.

Gabriel (archangel): An angel who serves as a chief messenger from God in the Bible. He appears to the prophet Daniel and to Mary, the mother of Jesus. Some people believe him to be the unnamed angel who blows his horn in Revelation 10.

gentile: A person who is not Jewish.

gospel: Literally meaning "good news," the gospel refers to the good news of redemption (being saved from the punishment of sin) that Jesus proclaimed in his life and teachings.

Gospel: One of the first four books of the New Testament: Matthew, Mark, Luke, and John.

grace: God's unmerited favor made possible by the death and resurrection of Jesus.

Great Tribulation: *See* Tribulation.

great white throne judgment: *See* Last Judgment.

Hades: In the New Testament, a term that refers to the temporary location for dead unbelievers between earthly death and Last Judgment (Rev. 20:11–14). In the Old Testament, *Sheol* is the Hebrew term referring to the same place.

heaven: A place where God lives and rules.

hell: The permanent place of punishment for the wicked.

historicism: The interpretation of Revelation that maintains that John's prophecy reveals the entire course of history during the church age — starting in the early church and being continuously fulfilled. The historicist, therefore, sees Revelation as history in the making.

Holy of Holies: The inner sanctuary of the Tabernacle and the Jerusalem Temple in Jerusalem that only the High Priest could enter one time of the year — on Yom Kippur.

idealism: The interpretation of Revelation that holds that the book is a figurative description of the age-old battle between good and evil that exists throughout human history. The idealist, therefore, does not look for prophecy to be fulfilled in literal events. Also known as *spiritualism* or *allegoricalism*.

imperial cult: During the Roman Empire, the imperial cult was the worship of the Roman emperor as a god.

inspiration (of Scripture): The orthodox belief of the church that holds that God guided the writing of the Scripture in such a way that authors, through their own unique personalities and writing styles, wrote God's revelation exactly in the manner in which God wanted the text to be written.

Isaiah: An Old Testament prophet whose ministry took place between 740–687 BCE. He is best known for writing the book of Isaiah.

Jeremiah: A prophet who, from 628–586 BCE, warned Jews of coming disaster and urged his people to turn back to God. He's author of the book of Jeremiah.

Joel: A minor prophet in the Old Testament and author of the book of Joel.

Johannine: Relating to the Apostle John.

lake of fire: The eternal state of unbelievers and Satan separated from God because of their evil and their rejection of Jesus (Rev. 19:20). It's associated with the *second death* in Revelation 20:14 and Revelation 21:8.

Last Judgment: The judgment in which everyone whose name isn't written in the book of life is cast into the lake of fire (Rev 20:12–15). Also known as the *great white throne judgment.*

mark of the beast (666): Literal interpreters of Revelation believe the mark of the beast is a way in which the Antichrist will control the economic system of the world. The mark itself is placed a person's right hand or forehead, and it's required in order for someone to buy and sell goods (Rev. 13:16–18, 14:9–12).

Meggido: *See* Armageddon.

Messiah: A Hebrew title, literally meaning "the anointed one," that refers to the promised savior of ancient Israel. *Christ* is the Greek translation of Messiah.

Michael (archangel): An angel who is mentioned in Revelation 12:7 and is often considered to be the commander of the Army of God.

midtribulation rapture: The belief that the rapture will occur in the middle of the Tribulation (after 3.5 years).

Millennium: The period of time depicted in Revelation 20 in which Jesus reigns on earth for a 1,000 years. *Amillennialism* holds that this time period is symbolic, but *chiliasm* believes it to be a literal 1,000-year space-time event.

new Jerusalem: The new dwelling place for God's people after the Last Judgment.

Olivet Discourse: A sermon that Jesus gave on the Mount of Olives (found in the Matthew 24, Mark 13, and Luke 21); many scholars interpret it as prophecy concerning future events. It's also known as *Little Apocalypse*.

Parousia: *See* Second Coming.

Patmos: A small Greek island that John was exiled on when he scribed Revelation.

postmillennialism: The belief that the Second Coming of Jesus occurs after the Millennium.

posttribulation rapture: The belief that the rapture will occur at the end of the seven-year Tribulation period at or close to the Second Coming of Jesus.

premillennialism: The belief that all the events from Revelation 1–19 will occur before the Millennium begins.

preterism: The interpretation of Revelation that holds that John's prophecy refers not to future events but to events that already took place back in the first century. From this perspective, Revelation is largely fulfilled prophecy.

pretribulation rapture: The belief that the rapture will occur before the seven-year Tribulation begins.

prophecy: A special message from God, often concerning future events that God promises will happen on earth and in heaven. More generally, it can also refer to the act of speaking the mind and counsel of God.

rapture: An event in which all believers on earth are suddenly transported to heaven to be with Jesus. Futurists believe the rapture to be a literal space-time event in the future, occurring just before, in the middle, or at the end of the Tribulation. The term itself comes from the Latin translation of 1 Thessalonians 4:16–17.

seal judgments: An initial set of judgments that occurs on earth when the Lamb (Jesus) opens seven seals of a heavenly scroll (Rev. 6:1–8:1).

Second Coming: The time in history in which Jesus returns to the earth.

second death: Being physically and spiritually removed from the presence of God. Revelation refers to the second death in 2:11, 20:6, 20:14, and 21:8. *See also* lake of fire.

70th week of Daniel: This term refers to the Tribulation period, or the last seven-year period of the 70 weeks (490 years) that Daniel prophesies in Daniel 9:24–27. *See also* Tribulation.

666: *See* mark of the beast (666)

spiritualism: *See* idealism.

synoptic Gospels: A term referring to the first three books of the New Testament (Matthew, Mark, and Luke). These books are similar in sequence and structure, and they often use similar wording.

theophany: The appearance of God to a human.

Tribulation: The seven-year period of unprecedented evil that futurists believe will occur prior to the Second Coming of Jesus. During this period, Satan will show power of the earth through the Antichrist, and a series of judgments from God will occur on the earth (Rev. 6–19). Some people believe the period of great suffering that Jesus refers to in Matthew 24:21 is the last half of the Tribulation (sometimes known as the *Great Tribulation*). *See also* 70th week of Daniel.

trumpet judgments: A set of judgments more severe than the seal judgments that are carried out when seven angels play trumpets (Rev. 8:7–11:15).

Zechariah: A prophet from 520–518 BCE, during a time in which many Jews were returning from Babylonian exile to Jerusalem. He is author of the book of Zechariah.

Index

• E •

• S •